SEX AND
PUNISHMENT

SEX AND PUNISHMENT

FOUR THOUSAND YEARS OF JUDGING DESIRE

ERIC BERKOWITZ

COUNTERPOINT
BERKELEY

ISBN: 978-1-58243-796-5

Cover design by Charles Brock, Faceout Studios
Interior design by meganjonesdesign.com

Printed in the United States of America

COUNTERPOINT
1919 Fifth Street
Berkeley, CA 94710
www.counterpointpress.com

Distributed by Publishers Group West

10 9 8 7 6 5 4 3 2 1

FOR JENNIFER

INTRODUCTION

IN 1956, IN a village in Northern Rhodesia (now Zambia), a desperate woman sought help from a local tribunal made up of tribal elders in putting her marriage back on track. The relationship was in tatters. In recent months, both she and her husband had been diagnosed with a venereal disease. The husband insisted that it was she who had infected him, but she denied any infidelity and claimed he was at fault. He had threatened to stab her on one occasion and, worse, to use witchcraft against her. Yet none of that would have brought the couple to the tribunal had something more outrageous not happened, something so intolerable that the wife ran to court that very day: At dawn, she had awoken to find her husband with her breast in his mouth. She remembered his threat of witchcraft, and became terrified.

At the hearing, one of the elders demanded of the husband: "[W]hat were you thinking of when you were sucking your wife's breast? Are you a small child, like that one [pointing to a baby in the room]? . . . Why did you do it?"

The husband's reply only made his situation worse: "It was love," he said.

The elder was incredulous. "Love! You must be a strange person, practicing your love in that way while your wife was asleep." The elder and the husband went back and forth like this for a while, the husband protesting that he had merely been expressing tender affection for his wife while the elder became increasingly suspicious that the man was practicing sorcery. Finally, the elder said, "No, no . . . I am afraid that if you went with your wife, you might try to kill her." The woman was placed in the protective custody of the police for the night, with more court proceedings to follow.

It was not the only time in mid-twentieth-century Northern Rhodesia that such disputes required court intervention. Another man had been accused of causing his wife to become infertile by sucking her breasts, and wives often ran to the courts to stop their husbands from performing cunnilingus on them or having intercourse with them while they slept. On other occasions, wives accused their husbands of stealing their menstrual cloths and using them as charms to bring success in gambling. The tribal judges took these accusations seriously. To them, taking a sleeping woman sexually was like making love to a corpse, while sucking a woman's breasts at any time of day blurred the roles of adult and child. Cloths soaked with a woman's menstrual blood were, in that society, not simple rags; they contained the awesome power of reproduction, which could be used for good or ill. To use such cloths for luck in gambling dens was to waste the procreative powers of the cosmos. In this context, the tribunal's decision to post a guard to keep a breast-sucking husband away from his wife was a sensible response to an explosive situation.

The British colonial officials who reviewed the tribal decisions, however, shared none of these beliefs. They usually threw such cases out, reasoning that marital sex was the concern only of the husband and wife, for which court intervention was inappropriate. A man who enjoyed his wife's body while she slept was simply taking the erotic pleasure that was his due, and unless he used violent force the law had no role to play. All that talk about power and witchcraft and luck was quaint, but irrelevant. Local courts in the territory complained that the Europeans should be taking these cases seriously, but their protests went unheeded.[1]

These incidents exist at the flashpoint between conflicting views on how the law should deal with sexual issues. To the inhabitants of Northern Rhodesia, it was not a question of prudishness, liberation, or even morality as such. Rather, sex was one of the underlying forces moving heaven and earth. Improperly conducted sex summoned danger and caused everyone harm. By barring such sex, they were protecting the entire society from catastrophe.

Lest anyone snicker at the hapless couple, we should recognize that the differences between "modern" and "primitive" views on sex and law are not so clear—not clear enough, at any rate, to merit smugness. Sex and lawsuits have gone hand in hand everywhere, in every era, and few sexual transgressions have ever been too small to merit the meddling of one tribunal or another.

The wife in the Northern Rhodesia incident fell through a late-colonial justice gap. Her case did not fit the 1956 Western model of what a sex claim should look like. Yet had she and her husband lived in Europe a few centuries earlier, when courts regularly involved themselves in bedroom behavior, she would have found a more sympathetic hearing: European records are full of cases in which married couples were accused—and accused each other—of sexual sorcery. The judges who punished such transgressors often justified their decisions as necessary to save society from God's wrath. Indeed, dozens of sex acts in Renaissance Europe, both within and outside marriage, were believed to provoke divine vengeance. Sexual behavior was everyone's business because one person's sexual missteps, if bad enough, could cause war, famine, and hails of fire and brimstone.

Moreover, had the aforementioned African couple been students, married or not, at any number of present-day U.S. colleges, the wife's claim might well have been enthusiastically received. Many postsecondary institutions have adopted elaborate rules governing their students' sexual conduct, which they enforce with the zeal of the most devoted officers of the Inquisition. Gettysburg College's 2006 student handbook requires that all sex be "consensual," which it defines as "willingly and verbally agreeing (for example, by stating 'yes') to engage in specific sexual conduct." The handbook also prohibits the erotic touching of people's bodies while they slumber. Thus, a man wishing to "initiate sexual contact" with a sleeping woman would need to wake her up, make sure her judgment is clear, and then ask (for example), "May I suck your breast now?" If he does not do so, he stands to be expelled from school and reported to the police.[2]

The Antioch College Sexual Offense Prevention Policy of 2006 follows a similar line, although it is more detailed. "Grinding on the dance floor is not consent for further sexual activity," warned the policy; neither are body movements or "non-verbal responses such as moans." Sex is forbidden with any person who is asleep, intoxicated, or suffers from "mental health conditions."[3]

American university sex codes have been ridiculed as overly prudish, and college disciplinary boards mocked as kangaroo courts, but they are not going away. In fact, they recently became more accommodating forums for sexual misbehavior claims. In 2011, the U.S. government informed publicly funded universities that accusers in sex cases must win if it can be shown by a "preponderance of the evidence"—that is, a mere 51 percent likelihood—that misconduct took place, despite the fact that the question of sexual wrongdoing often turns on the murky task of defining the power relationships between the people involved. (In U.S. criminal courts, the standard of proof is "beyond a reasonable doubt.") Duke University's rules add to the ambiguity by stating that sexual misconduct may exist where there are "real or perceived power differentials between individuals" that "may create an unintentional atmosphere of coercion." How anything resembling justice can be dispensed under these standards is difficult to imagine.

REGARDLESS OF THE setting, no one questions the law's primary role in resolving sexual conflicts. A person violating the shifting rules of sexual conduct in modern Western societies will not be accused of witchcraft, but that is often just a matter of terminology. Anyone, no matter how highly placed, who engages in sexual contact that is out of sync with prevailing attitudes risks being demonized and steamrolled in public by the legal system. Consider the boorish men of influence who are caught taking what they see as the perquisites of their positions. The prominent French economist and politician Dominique Strauss-Kahn's allegedly violent sexual encounter with an African immigrant maid in a New York hotel suite quickly became an international incident in which the limits of class privilege were much discussed, especially in France. President Bill Clinton's dalliances with a White House intern, revealed in an unrelated sexual harassment case against him, resulted in his impeachment in 1998 by the U.S. House of Representatives (though he was acquitted by the Senate). Polish-French film director Roman Polanski, on the run since his well-publicized 1978 California conviction for having sex with a thirteen-year-old girl, again became a universal symbol of criminal sexual excess when he was arrested in 2009 by Swiss authorities at the request of U.S. authorities. (He was later released.) Even powerful corporations get tagged for inadvertent transgressions. The fleeting exposure of singer Janet Jackson's breast during the 2004 Super Bowl telecast resulted in more than $500,000 in government fines against the network that aired the game, CBS, and years of wrenching litigation over sexual "decency" on the American airwaves.

With sex law, context is everything and consistency should not be expected. Under slightly different circumstances, none of these events would have sparked a controversy. Many people still cannot accept that Strauss-Kahn was chased down and jailed for allegedly forcing sex on a maid; one of his defenders dismissed the entire affair as a mere *troussage de domestique* (roughly, "lifting a servant's skirt"), not worthy of too much attention. Taking the long view, this comment, while repulsive, has some logic. From the earliest times, female domestic servants have been viewed as snacks for the sexual appetites of their masters. Such women effectively had no rights to their bodies, much less to be taken seriously by police and the courts when they accused a powerful man of rape. Tellingly, the case against Strauss-Kahn was dropped after questions arose concerning his accuser's past history, but that did not resolve the question of whether he sexually assaulted her as she described. If he did force himself on the woman, both this writer and, it is safe to assume, the readers of this book would consider him to be a monster. However, it is instructive to remember that this perspective is the historical exception.

The strobe-quick exposure of Jackson's breast would have incurred no penalty had it been aired only on cable television or in a theatrical film, instead of during a major television broadcast. Jackson's "wardrobe malfunction" also occurred while an ultra-conservative government was in power. (Shortly before the Super Bowl, the country's chief law enforcement officer, Attorney General John Ashcroft, ordered that drapes be placed to hide a bare-breasted aluminum statue called Spirit of Justice, which had been standing undisturbed in the Great Hall of the Justice Department for decades.[4]) Bill Clinton, meanwhile, was hardly the first president to commit adultery, but he was the only one to be sued for sexual harassment, and the only one to suffer a vote of impeachment for lying about his infidelity.

Polanski's legal timing was arguably the most unfortunate. When he had sex with the girl, statutory rape was a felony in California, and a serious one at that. Had he done the deed a century or so earlier, when California's age of consent for sexual activity was twelve, England's thirteen, and Delaware's seven, he would have had no legal trouble. Even after the age of consent was raised, judges rarely imposed jail time on convicted men and the girls were often branded more as temptresses than victims. (It is true, however, that Polanski was not only accused of statutory rape: The girl testified that the director had drugged and intimidated her [an allegation he denied], but it is the statutory rape charge that has dogged him these past three decades.)

The existence of differing cultural mores usually has no effect on one's risk of punishment for sex crimes. A California man recently received a 152-year prison sentence for having sex with two twelve-year-old boys. Would his legal defense have been strengthened had evidence been introduced that certain New Guinea tribes believe boys need homosexual encounters in order to mature into manhood?[5] It is unlikely. In the stacks of court papers, legislation, and newspaper editorials on the subject of gay marriage, has anyone pointed to Sudanese Azande tribal traditions, which support the marriage of young boys to soldiers? Again, no. In the context of Western sex law, the customs of non-Judeo-Christian cultures are irrelevant. Far from appearing overly prudish, they appear to be not prudish enough. At the same time, Western observers express outrage whenever a Muslim wife faces being stoned to death for adultery, though the Old Testament itself (Deuteronomy 22:22) prescribes the death penalty for both adulterous women and their lovers. In early 2012, when this book went to press, gay marriage was allowed in eight American states and the District of Columbia, while the legality of mentioning homosexuality in Tennessee's public elementary and middle schools was being debated in that state's legislature.

SINCE THE EARLIEST periods of recorded history, lawmakers have tried to set boundaries on how people take their sexual pleasures, and they have doled out a range of controls and punishments to enforce them, from the slow impalement of unfaithful wives in Mesopotamia to the sterilization of masturbators in the United States. At any given point in time, some forms of sex and sexuality have been encouraged while others have been punished without mercy. Jump forward or backward a century or two, or cross a border, and the harmless fun of one society becomes the gravest crime of another. This book aims to tell that story.

I began my research on a much broader front, trying to trace the path of Western law generally by using colorful cases as examples. As I reviewed the first legal collections from the ancient Near East, I noticed that the earliest lawmakers were preoccupied with questions of sex. Everywhere I looked, there were specific rules on sexual relations with pigs and oxen, prostitutes, family members. Sex was evidently more micromanaged then than even now, with the surprising exception of same-sex relations—which

were ignored almost entirely by the law until the Hebrews labeled homosexuality a terrible crime on a par with murder. Additionally, sex was sometimes used as a punishment in itself, as when the wife of an Assyrian rapist
was ordered to be raped in turn as punishment for her husband's crime,
or when men who damaged Egyptian property markers were required to
deliver their wives and children to the rough affections of donkeys.

It soon became clear that sex law was as passionate and mercurial as
the sex drive itself, and could support a rather interesting book on its own.
Extraordinary flesh-and-blood cases—much flesh, more blood—jumped
out of the dustiest volumes, begging to be told. Building on the work
of modern historians such as Eva Cantarella (*Bisexuality in the Ancient
World*), Sarah B. Pomeroy (*Goddesses, Whores, Wives, and Slaves*), and
James A. Brundage (*Law, Sex, and Christian Society in Medieval Europe*),
as well as on translations of original sources, I have mapped out the story
of Western civilization from the perspective of law and libido.

The chapters organized themselves organically, according to time
period. The question was when to stop. As with any era of history, no
ceremony declared the end of one epoch and the beginning of another. I
decided, rather arbitrarily, to halt the inquiry in the last part of the nineteenth century, with the imprisonment of Oscar Wilde for "gross indecency" with one of his young lovers. If I traveled much further into the
present, I feared, the noise of our most recent century would drown out the
voices of our ancestors. Today's sex issues are touched on occasionally for
perspective, but a detailed treatment of the roiling twentieth and twenty-
first centuries will require another volume.

In any event, the experiences of the distant past cannot help but illumi-
nate the issues of the present, especially where sex and law are concerned.
For example, as the issue of gay marriage lurches through the courts and
legislatures of the United States and elsewhere, with all participants in the
debate claiming to have history on their side, it's helpful to know that
loving and committed unions between men were sanctioned by Christian

and secular law alike many centuries ago, when no one recognized homosexuality as what Michel Foucault called a "hermaphroditism of the soul." Similarly, before we rush to impose fines on television networks for broadcasting "indecent" images to the masses, it is useful to understand how obscenity fell under government control in the first place. Sexually explicit materials were never regulated until they became available to mass audiences through the advent of printing. Those who wrote and enforced the law always had access to all the smut they could digest. Finally, as we throw the likes of Strauss-Kahn and Polanski atop the trash heap of outdated boors, it helps to know how our legal and religious traditions made such sexual predators possible.

Of course, rape, adultery, incest, and all the other issues that unfold in the arena of sex law have been taking place since the beginning of human existence. All that changes are the methods people use to exercise control over one another's bodies, and the reasons they give for using them.

1
• • •

CHANNELING THE URGE:
THE FIRST SEX LAWS

F OR A FOUR-THOUSAND-YEAR-OLD Mesopotamian homicide case, the record is impressively intact. Decades of archaeological excavations have yielded multiple copies describing the case in detail, spelled out on broken clay tablets embossed with cuneiform writing. The duplication makes sense, given that the victim was Lu-Inanna, a high priest of Enlil— one of this civilization's most important gods—and that the murder took place in Nippur, a holy city. By the time the trial came up, Nippur had been continuously inhabited for thousands of years.

The charge was murder, although sex was all over the case. The accused were two freedmen, a male slave, and Lu-Inanna's widow, Nin-Dada. Given the severity of the crime and the high status of the victim, the case was taken first to the king in nearby Isin. He took a good look, and then assigned it to the nine-member Assembly of Nippur.

By the time the case reached the assembly, no one doubted that Lu-Inanna had been killed by the three male suspects, nor was there any question that they had told Nin-Dada what they had done. The key remaining issue was why Nin-Dada had not immediately given up the killers to the authorities. Rather, the record says, she "opened not her mouth, covered it up." Had she participated in the murder? If so, her execution—most likely by impalement—was a certainty. If she had not, then what crime had she committed by keeping her mouth shut?

First, a little law. It was forbidden in Mesopotamia not to report another person's misconduct, especially when sex was involved. (It was no different in nearby Assyria, where, for instance, prostitutes were not allowed to wear veils: If a man observed a prostitute wearing a veil and said nothing, he would be whipped, have a cord forcibly run through his ears like a horse's bridle, and then be led around town to be ridiculed.) Mesopotamian barmaids were required to eavesdrop on their criminal customers as they drank. If the barmaids heard something incriminating and failed to report it, they could be put to death. Adultery, at least when committed by women, was also punished harshly. A disloyal wife who had plotted against her husband was treated worst of all, by being stuck on a long pole and left to suffer a slow and very public death.

There was no proof that Nin-Dada had ever had sex with any of the killers, or that she had taken part in her husband's murder. Had she been well represented before the assembly, she might have squeaked through the trial with her life. Her supposed advocates could not have done a worse job, however. They presented a "weak female" defense, arguing that Nin-Dada was so helpless and easily intimidated that she had had no choice but to remain mute. As if that argument were not a sure enough loser, her defenders went even further, claiming that *even if* she had participated in the murder, she still would have been innocent because "as a woman . . . what could she do?"

Even after four millennia and translation from a long-dead language, the anger in the assembly's response rises from the tablets like heat:

A woman who values not her husband might know his enemy
. . . He might kill her husband. He might then inform her that
her husband has been killed. Is it she who [as good as] killed her

*husband. Her guilt exceeds even that of those who [actually] kill
a man.*

The Sumerian verb for "to know" meant the same as "to have sex,"
and Nin-Dada's silence after her husband's murder was enough for the
assembly to conclude that she was hungry for such knowledge. Far from
seeing her as a weakling, the assembly made clear that she should have
braved any intimidation to see that the murder was avenged. Nin-Dada
was sentenced to die.

So go the brief lives and unnatural deaths of a Mesopotamian husband
and wife, he murdered for unknown reasons and she for disrespecting her
husband's memory. They inhabited a world unknown to most of us, and
barely understood by specialists at that.[1]

WITH THE CASE of Nin-Dada, this chapter's inquiry into ancient sex law
begins at the time of the first known human writing. Although I shall touch
on earlier periods, the absence of documentation makes the journey hazardous. In 1991, for example, hikers found a frozen five-thousand-year-old
man in the Italian Alps. He had fifty-seven tattoos, still wore snowshoes,
and carried a copper axe that appeared to have been of little use to him
in his final moments. He was killed in some kind of violent confrontation.
The corpse, now known as Ötzi the Iceman, also appeared at first not to
have had a penis, which caused no end of questions (the penis was later
found, looking much the worse for wear). Was he ritually mutilated, or
castrated by a jealous husband? Or did his genitals, so cold and lifeless for
several millennia, just shrivel away? Without additional information—that
is, something we can read—it is impossible to tell whether he died at the
hands of the law or whether sex had anything to do with his fate. While
Ötzi is a relatively recent ancestor of ours, we do not know enough to
arrive at any conclusions about the sexual mores according to which he
and his tattoo-loving neighbors lived.

This chapter will draw on cases from as far west as Egypt, across Turkey and the Eurasian landmass, to what is now Iran. Its main focus will be Mesopotamia (modern Iraq), as well as the land that now comprises Israel and the Palestinian territories. This vast region has hosted urban civilizations as complex as those of Rome, Greece, and various caliphates down to the Ottoman Empire, and as elementary as tiny bands of nomadic hunters. Its peoples spoke a multitude of languages and dialects, most of them now lost. These Sumerians, Assyrians, Babylonians, Hittites, Hebrews, and Egyptians were slaves and freemen, priests and prisoners, whores and kings, gods and witches. They mixed, intermarried, and raped each other. Everyone had a role to play in their respective societies, and was subject to punishment for bad conduct—especially when it concerned sex. Sex for some was blessed, and for others, grounds for impalement.

All ancient civilizations were intent on controlling people's sex lives. The oldest extant written law, which hails from the early Sumerian kingdom of Ur-Nammu (circa 2100 BC), devoted quite a bit of attention to sexual matters. One of the earliest capital punishment laws on record anywhere concerned adultery. Ur-Nammu's Law No. 7 mandated that married women who seduced other men were to be killed; their lovers were to be let off scot-free. Death awaited virtually every other straying wife in the Near East, while the fates of their lovers were often left to the husbands to decide.

The first legal codes, such as that of Ur-Nammu, were founded on the customs of earlier precarious times. Even after small groups coalesced into identifiable societies, towns faced constant threat by bands of marauders looking to exploit any opportunity to invade and pillage. Adultery risked destabilizing the unity and bloodlines of a family, rendering an entire tribe or settlement that much more vulnerable. Ur-Nammu's death penalty for adulterous women was, in this light, no innovation; it was simply the first such punishment we know about that was written down.

Ancient societies influenced each other, and the laws of one group often were adopted by its enemies and then developed further. As centuries passed, for example, the elementary sexual prohibitions of Sumerian kingdoms like Ur-Nammu evolved into the obsessively detailed rules of the Hebrews, which in turn became the foundation for the sex laws of the church and every Christian state. Until recently, the Old Testament was believed to contain the world's first written laws. How could it be otherwise, when the Torah (the first five books of the Bible) was said to have been issued to Moses directly from God, on a mountain, amid thunder? As a product of divine revelation, the Bible could then have no predecessor, at least not one written by human beings. The 613 rules set out in the Torah were supposedly written by the same "hand" that molded the universe, and to say that the Bible drew from other societies in the Near East was to imply that God looked to pagan kings for advice.

The Hebrew claim of precedence was shattered in 1902, when French archaeologists found several large black stones in ancient Susa, Iran, which bore carved cuneiform text. When reassembled, the stones formed a single stele more than eight feet high. The writing, it was later proved, consisted of the Babylonian king Hammurabi's 282 laws, a highly sophisticated comprehensive legal code. The stele itself was carved around 1790 BC. Further investigation revealed that the Code of Hammurabi not only predated Moses and the Torah by at least five centuries, it also dominated Near Eastern law for at least fifteen hundred years. Like Moses, moreover, Hammurabi was merely the messenger: The stele bore the declaration that the king's laws also originated from heaven.

Several other legal codes have since been discovered (including that of Ur-Nammu), which were set down long before Hammurabi's own time. Many of the Bible's sex laws now look more like knockoffs of earlier regional laws than the original word of God. For example, one law, protecting men's testicles, from Deuteronomy 25:11–12, reads:

If two men . . . are struggling together, and the wife of one comes near to deliver her husband from the hand of the one who is striking him, and puts out her hand and seizes his genitals, then you shall cut off her hand; you shall not show pity.

Did that rule really come from on high? The Hebrews might have wished to believe that Deuteronomy was the revelation of Jehovah, but the truth is much more prosaic: It was likely borrowed from the neighboring Assyrians. The laws of Middle Assyria, which date from 1450 to 1250 BC, show similar concern for testicles and an equal readiness to punish women who hurt them:

If a woman in a quarrel injures the testicle of a man, one of her fingers they shall cut off. And if a physician bind it up and the other testicle which is beside it be infected thereby, or take harm; or in a quarrel she injure the other testicle, they shall destroy both of her eyes.

The similarity of these laws is evident, though the Assyrians were no friends of the Hebrews—they conquered the Kingdom of Israel in 722 BC and exiled its inhabitants. Assuming the Torah was in fact composed by men and not dictated to Moses by the Creator of the universe, it appears that this Hebrew law was a reflection of a regional testicle fixation. There are multiple other instances of Hebrew laws overlapping with the laws of their enemies. For example, section 117 of Hammurabi's Code holds that a man can put his family members into service as slaves in order to pay a debt, but only for three years. A nearly identical Hebrew law permits such enslavement for up to six years.

Western sex law, whether via Assyrian testicles or Hebrew whorehouses, was thus created by ancient peoples who legitimized their rules by claiming that they originated in heaven. It is easiest to work with written records such as the cuneiform tablets in Nin-Dada's trial, but doing so can prove deceptive as well. If it could be shown that other trials had taken place in the Assembly of Nippur on similar grounds, in which the widows were let off without punishment, we would not then be able to draw the same conclusions about Babylonian society. It stands to reason that there were many, perhaps thousands, of sex trials, the records of which have been lost to history. We are forced to work only with what we have discovered, and what we are able to decipher.

There is little to be learned by separating documented ancient history from *prehistory*. No ceremony, solar eclipse, visit from angels, or resetting of calendars marked the "start" of history. No one, presumably, knew or cared whether the stories of their lives were being preserved for people who would remain unborn for another four millennia. Nor was there a sudden change in morality; when people first wrote down their laws, the prehistoric mind-set was still in place. The written laws of Ur-Nammu, Hammurabi, and Moses reflected the crosscurrents of long-established, illiterate societies.[2]

BLOOD RELATIONS AND BLOODY RELATIONS: THE FIRST SEX CRIMES

Early law thus emerged from prehistoric traditions. There is a lot of guesswork involved in determining exactly what these traditions comprised, but we can be certain that sexual impulses themselves would have been as urgently experienced then as they are today, driving people to do things with their bodies for which they were punished. For Saint Augustine, the insistent demands of the genitals were God's curse on humanity for the sins of Adam and Eve; every sex act and thought was a new penalty for the wrongs of the first man and woman. Coming at the same subject from a different perspective, Plato also recognized humanity's intense craving for sex, saying in his last dialogue, *The Laws*, that it "influences the souls of men with the most raging frenzy—the lust for the sowing of offspring that burns with the utmost violence." For Plato, the sex drive was a mad subconscious effort to reunify humanity's fractured nature.

Early peoples did not characterize the sex urge in those words, but they certainly felt it. They surely recognized that something had to be done to corral the "frenzy" if people were to live together in large groups. Until the sexual impulse was tamed and subordinated to common needs, civilized life would be impossible. For men, that meant trying to reconcile themselves to the mystery of the female. In primitive societies, men presumably regarded women with the same awe and terror they felt toward the natural world. Early humankind was at perennial war with nature, the forces of which were lethal as well as incomprehensible. The core of the natural world was the female womb, from which newborn human life tumbled out in a gush of blood and screams.

It was not until about 9000 BC (roughly one hundred and eighty-five thousand years after the advent of *Homo sapiens sapiens*, or modern humans) that the link between sexual intercourse and pregnancy was confirmed. Until then, sex and childbirth were likely too far separated in time for people to make the connection, and in any event, women spent much of their short adult lives either pregnant or lactating. Children seemed to just appear in the womb. Even more incomprehensible, and perhaps horrifying, was the blood that periodically flowed from women's bodies. Blood was life itself, magical and dangerous to lose, yet women bled freely for days at a time with no injury, and no one knew why. The one clear fact was that menstrual blood came from women only, and from the same place where human life began.

The first sexual prohibitions could well have taken the form of Paleolithic taboos against intercourse with women during their periods. (Such rules still exist in many cultures, grounded on the supposed "unclean" nature of menstruation.) These proscriptions would have had much deeper foundations than mere hygiene, however—perhaps the sudden appearance of menstrual blood reminded men that, despite their superior physical strength, they could not generate human life on their own. Perhaps menstrual blood was considered a sign of female shame or even infertility, as women only bled when they were not pregnant or lactating. Most likely, the rejection of women while their blood flowed was a precautionary move, a way to appease the threatening divine presence men felt when confronted with the unknown.

By barring sex during specific times of the month, primitive societies could impose order onto the chaos of sex and reproduction. As time passed, men's fear of women often evolved into outright hostility, to the effect that menstruating women were regarded as equal parts dangerous and filthy. The belief was amplified in later centuries, in various cultures. To ancient Hindus, menstruation was a zero-sum game: Sex with women during their periods was thought to sap the "strength, the might and the vitality" of men, while avoiding sexual relations with menstruating women was believed to add to men's wisdom and vitality. In Babylon, everything a woman touched during her period, from furniture to people, was considered contaminated, and to the later Assyrians the very word "menstruation" was synonymous with "unapproachable."[3]

No one took menstrual fear further into the realm of obsession than the Hebrews. The Torah, which decrees that women and everything they touch are unclean during their periods, also pronounces that this contamination extends to things touched by people who are themselves touched by menstruating women. For example, if a man "lies" with a woman during her period and later sleeps on another bed, that bed becomes unclean. The Bible also requires that at the conclusion of a woman's period, she is to bring two turtledoves or pigeons to a priest for sacrifice. Until the birds were slaughtered, she would be separated from everyone in her community, including her husband. In any event, women were not to be touched for seven days following the beginning of their periods, regardless of when the bleeding stopped. Later versions of Jewish law pronounced women "unclean" for about half the month, requiring them to take ritual baths before returning to their husbands' beds and mandating that wives test themselves for blood with rags before having sex. Violations of these laws subjected the man and the woman to arrest and, at least in theory, the death penalty.

Over the centuries, menstrual blood found its way into recipes for sex potions as a key ingredient. In several European cultures during the Middle Ages, mothers collected their daughters' first menstrual flows, saving them and later mixing them into aphrodisiacs to spark desire in their sons-in-law. In fifteenth-century Venice, a lower-class girl used a mixture of her own menstrual blood, a rooster heart, wine, and flour to make a young aristocratic man "insane" with love for her. She was put to death; the young man was viewed by the court as an unwitting victim. As late as 1878, *The British Medical Journal* ran extensive correspondence on the question of whether or not a ham could turn rancid at the touch of a menstruating woman.[4]

ANOTHER PREHISTORIC SEXUAL taboo, which probably led to the first formal law of any kind, banned incest. While few would disagree that sex within families is repulsive, the rule against it is not so simple. For most of human existence until relatively recently, there were no cities or towns, and very few people. Life was lived in tiny groups, and while interbreeding between tribes did occur, bands of several dozen people might live for extended periods without ever seeing any other human beings. Reproduction between close relatives must have occurred all the time. Nevertheless, without prohibitions against close inbreeding, human DNA would never have acquired the strength to adapt to the climatic and other challenges faced by our ancestors. The formation of cross-tribal societies about fifty thousand years ago allowed people to "outbreed," diversifying their genetic makeup and making possible the most recent stages of human evolution.

Anthropologist Claude Lévi-Strauss regarded the incest taboo as a critical element of "culture itself," and much of ancient history backs him up. The Babylonians treated incest as a source of contagion and punished it with banishment, drowning, or burning. Once the deed was done, the pollution had to be cleansed regardless of whether or not either of the participants was at fault. A mother raped by her son, for instance, would burn to death right alongside him. The fact that she was taken by force meant nothing; for the sake of everyone and to appease the gods, she had to die. The Hittites and Assyrians also considered incest an abomination punishable by death, as did their neighbors the Hebrews and most every other society since then. Even monkeys avoid it.

Thus incest appears to be not only the first, but also the one universal, "natural" sexual taboo. If that were the case, though, no one told the peoples of ancient Hawaii, Peru, Mexico, and especially Egypt and Persia. For the ancient Egyptians, incest was not only a natural aspect of human life, it was also the key event in one of their most sacred and enduring creation myths: that of Isis, the mother-whore-goddess who divided earth from heaven and assigned languages to nations. Isis married her brother, the sun god Osiris, whom she adored even when they were still in their mother's womb. Their perfect union was shattered when Osiris was murdered by his brother Set, god of darkness. Set cut Osiris into pieces, which he flung all over Egypt. Bereft, Isis searched for her beloved everywhere. She managed to retrieve every part of him except the most important one, the engine of their sacred union—his penis. Nevertheless, she resuscitated him and, with the help of a replica of his genitals, the reunited lovers produced a child, Horus. This tale, told in countless versions throughout the Mediterranean, made Isis a holy and deeply resonant symbol of renewal and immortality. During celebrations, Osiris was represented as a giant phallus.

Egyptian pharaohs often married their sisters, half sisters, and daughters, especially during the Eighteenth Dynasty (1570–1397 BC). The idea was to exclude outsiders from the bloodline, and ensure that the bounty of conquest would not be shared with in-laws. Sometimes, as in the families of the pharaohs Seqenenre Tao II and Ahhotep I, royal daughters were only allowed to marry their fathers. However, the same restrictions never bound the pharaohs themselves: They kept a supply of secondary queens at hand with whom to have children. New kings were usually mothered by nonroyal women, which sometimes made family lines quite complicated.

Egyptian incest was not restricted to the society's upper crust; the practice was adopted by the lower orders, and became common among people of all ranks. At the time of the Roman conquest of Egypt in 30 BC, sisters typically married their full or half brothers or their fathers. In the cities, one-third of all young men with marriageable sisters married them, doing away with any need to find a bride from outside the family. (In Arsinoe, virtually *every* man with a living younger sister married her.) The Romans shared none of the Egyptians' incestuous customs, and worked hard to suppress them—after about three centuries, they succeeded.

In ancient Persia, marriage within immediate families was seen as a blessed thing. Under Zoroastrianism, which came into being sometime between the second millennium and sixth century BC, royal, priestly, and common families all practiced incest. Such unions were praised in legal and religious texts as "perfect" acts that brought great rewards in heaven and wiped away nearly all sins. Said one ancient source:

> [B]lessed is he who has a child of his child . . . pleasure, sweetness and joy are owing to a son that begets from a daughter of his own, who is also a brother of that same mother, and he who is born of a son and a mother is also a brother of that same father; this is a much greater pleasure, which is a blessing of the joy . . . the family is more perfect; its nature is without vexation and gathering affection.

For the Persians, a sexual union within a family was so sanctified that the fluids produced by an incestuous couple were thought to have curative powers. A passage from the Vendidad, a collection of Zoroastrian holy texts, advises corpse-bearers that they may purify themselves with the mingled urine of a closely related married couple. Conversely, any reluctance on a man's part to marry his sister or mother was considered a grave sin deserving of "damnation in the highest degree," even if he troubled to find his intended bride another husband. Women who refused to marry their relatives fared even worse: In one Zoroastrian text, a visitor to hell finds a woman condemned to suffer the pain of having a snake crawl in and out of her mouth for eternity. The visitor is told: "This is the soul of that wicked woman who violated next-of-kin marriage."

Like the Egyptians, the Persians used intrafamily marriages to hoard property, but that only partly explains why such unions—so rare in the ancient and modern worlds alike—were venerated. A full understanding requires a greater degree of probing into the religious practices of these societies than this book permits, but the key point is that there are in fact no "eternal" or "natural" sex laws. What is contrary to nature for one group can be a blessing for others. The Egyptians and Persians were not nomads or cave dwellers who had no choice but to reproduce within close family groups. Theirs were two of humanity's longest-lasting civilizations. Lévi-Strauss was surely wrong, then, to claim that the ban against incest is culture itself. Like homosexuality, fellatio, and dozens of other sex acts that have been condemned as both unnatural and against God's will, intrafamily sex was a matter of choice.

Taboos against incest and sex during menstruation have evolved in nearly opposite directions. Bans against sexual contact with women during their periods persist in some religious contexts, but have been ignored by secular law. The Talmud requires flogging for such things, but no modern Western government has given the subject any attention. Incest, however, remains a "universal taboo" and is a crime almost everywhere. It is a felony in nearly every American state, punishable by prison terms of up to twenty years. In Utah, a five-year prison sentence awaits anyone having sex even with a "half" first cousin. Many states also mandate punishments even when the incestuous sex is forced, or when, as with sexual relations between step- and adoptive relations, there is no risk of genetic harm. It is enough that such relations resemble sex within the same blood family for the offenders to be removed from society.[5]

VIRGIN TERRITORY

Female virginity was a commodity in the ancient world, with a price, a market, and laws to protect its male owners. Ancient Egyptians had little concern with a woman's virginity at marriage, but that was atypical. Virtually everywhere else, "a maiden who has never stripped off her clothes in her husband's lap" or, somewhat less graphically, a woman who "has not known a man" was precious indeed—or at least her maidenhead was. The right to deflower a girl belonged to her husband and no one else, and anyone interfering with it was severely punished.

During Ur-Nammu's reign, a man who raped a betrothed virgin was put to death. The punishment did not address the violence committed against the girl, but rather the theft of the intended bridegroom's opportunity to be the first to have her. By the time of the Assyrians, more than a thousand years later, the laws were more intricate and, in keeping with Assyrian tradition, more vicious. Rapists of betrothed girls were killed as they always had been, but the law now also turned its attention to the rape of females who had not yet been promised in marriage. In such cases, compensation was due to a father for his lost chance at marrying his daughter off at the high price virgins commanded. He could sue the rapist and collect three times his virgin daughter's marriage value, and then either force the rapist to marry the girl or keep her to sell off to someone else. A sullied girl would fetch a smaller bride-price on the open market, but the father still came out ahead. To add a dollop of sweet revenge to the deal, Assyrian fathers in such cases also had the option of taking a rapist's wife as a slave to rape and abuse as often as he wished. Thus two innocent women might suffer when a man raped a virgin girl: the victim herself, who might be forced by her father to spend the rest of her life with the man who attacked her, and the rapist's wife, who might be delivered into the vicious embrace of the victim's family.

An Assyrian father could cash in on his daughter's lost virginity even when she gave it away willingly. In that case, the girl's lover would still owe the father three times her marriage value, but he would not be required to serve up his own wife for abuse. Rather, the father was encouraged to take out his anger on his daughter: "The father shall treat his daughter in whatever manner he chooses." This sentence was perhaps legal overkill, as there were no restraints on what a father could do to his children. In any event, women were no better treated after they were married. The law was clear that a husband could punish his wife by whipping and hitting her, pulling her hair, and mutilating her ears.

The Torah tracks the Assyrian system of compensating fathers for their daughters' lost virginity. As everywhere else in the Near East, respectable Hebrew girls had no right to choose their sex partners. Only prostitutes could do that. If a virgin girl decided to have sex with a man anyway, that choice was made permanent: Any man who slept with such a maiden was required to pay the girl's bride-price (that is, her price as a virgin) to her father, then marry her. As with the Assyrians, the father was also allowed to take the money and marry his daughter off to someone else, presumably for a lower price. The thinking changed somewhat if the maiden had been taken by force. In that case, the man was bound to pay the father a larger sum of money and then marry the girl without the possibility of ever divorcing her. Again, the happiness of the girl was immaterial. The pain of having been raped would be compounded by having to spend the rest of her life with the assailant, subject to his will as his wife.

The laws of the Bible are less violent than those of Assyria—for example, there is no recourse to raping another man's wife as retribution—but biblical mythology is just as savage. The book of Genesis tells the story of Dinah, daughter of the patriarch Jacob, who "went out" from her house and then was "taken" by a neighboring prince named Shechem. The text is not clear as to whether the "taking" was the result of rape, persuasion, or something in between, but there is no doubt that Shechem fell in love with Dinah and, after installing her in his house, decided to marry her. Yet he had made a terrible mistake by not going to Dinah's family for permission before bedding her. The disgrace he brought to Jacob's house would need to be wiped away before anything else could take place.

Shechem and his father Hamor tried to make amends by offering Jacob any bride-price he demanded, no matter how much. This offer of money would normally have been enough to assuage a family's hurt pride and lost investment in the girl's virginity. It seemed to have been acceptable to Jacob, but not to Dinah's brothers, whose rage could only be assuaged with violence. They told Shechem and Hamor they would accept the offer of money, and then, after their enemies were lulled into a state of vulnerability, they made their attack:

> Simeon and Levi, Dinah's brothers, took their swords and attacked the unsuspecting city, killing every male. They put Hamor and his son Shechem to the sword and took Dinah from Shechem's house and left. The sons of Jacob came upon the dead bodies and looted the city where their sister had been defiled. They seized their flocks and herds and donkeys and everything else of theirs in the city and out in the fields. They carried off all their wealth and all their women and children, taking as plunder everything in the houses. Jacob was angry when he heard what his sons had done, and also scared of reprisals, but Simon and Levi had one concern on their minds: "Should he [Shechem] have treated our sister like a prostitute?"

To Dinah's brothers, the destruction of Shechem's city and the murder and enslavement of its inhabitants constituted appropriate payback for their sister's lost virginity. Dinah's fate was not spelled out because it did not matter. She was merely a prop in the story. The main issue at stake was the lost honor of her male family members, and what they did to regain it. Dinah's intentions would only have entered the picture had she sneaked off with Shechem and willingly had sex with him. Luckily for her, that did not happen.

Any Hebrew man who formally accused his bride of being impure at the time of the wedding set off a high-stakes legal process. The bride's father would have been required to prove his daughter's virtue, which he normally did by giving the soiled wedding bedclothes to the town elders to inspect. If the bloodstains on the fabric were deemed insufficient, the bride was stoned to death in front of her father's house. Just as Shechem did wrong by taking what was not his, so did the sexually experienced bride commit a grave crime by deciding when, and with whom, she would have sex. (It is easy to imagine savvy fathers splattering animal blood on the bedclothes to make sure their daughters were exonerated.) If, on the other hand, the bedclothes passed inspection, then the accusing groom would be beaten by the elders, forced to pay the bride's father one hundred silver shekels, and barred from ever seeking a divorce. Again, the bride's well-being was of least concern. She would be condemned to living out her days with a husband who most likely hated her—a small price to pay for her family's honor.

Given the differences in marriage value between virgins and non-virgins, it was illegal everywhere even to spread rumors that a bride was something less than intact on her wedding day. The laws of Lipit-Ishtar, another Sumerian ruler (circa 1900 BC) who predated Hammurabi, required a man making such an accusation to pay a fine if proven wrong. The question is how such proof was made. The Hebrews and others used bloody bedclothes, but that was not a universal test. Neighboring cultures were not nearly as convinced that blood always resulted from a female's first intercourse. The only way to prove conclusively that a girl had had sex was either to catch her in the act or to observe her belly swollen with child.

Why was it so critical for men to marry untouched women? It makes sense that adultery should have been forbidden, as husbands wanted to be assured that their children were actually their own, but there is no corresponding concern with marrying sexually experienced brides. If a wife gave birth less than eight or nine months after the wedding, it would have been simple enough to allow the husband to disown the child. But ancient law did not go in that direction; rather, it barricaded women and girls from sexual opportunities and punished them if they transgressed. Explanations for the virginity obsession seem to be limited to men's desire for a "tight fit," as well as the assurance that the human property they purchased was truly brand new. Most likely, though, the fixation on virginity—which never existed where men were concerned and has persisted to this day in many cultures—was simply one more avenue for men to control and dominate females. Having a virgin for a bride was power incarnate for a husband, and keeping her untouched before marriage was a test of control for her fathers and brothers.[6]

THE JOYS OF MARRIAGE

The sexual restrictions ancient societies placed on girls and women did not loosen with their marriages. The restraint fathers expected of their daughters was merely training for their duty of fidelity as wives. Everywhere, married women were kept on short leashes and disciplined. The Assyrian law mentioned above that allowed husbands to beat, whip, and mutilate their wives for misbehaving extended to anything short of killing them. Presumably, qualifying offenses included going about town unveiled. If only sexually available women, such as prostitutes and slaves, uncovered their heads in public, a respectable wife who did so would therefore be signaling her availability and, even worse, that her husband had lost control over her. For that, wives would suffer violence.

Married Assyrian women who kept their veils on but associated with other men were also running big risks, as were the men. Any man who "traveled" with an unrelated woman had to pay money to her husband and prove—sometimes by jumping into a swiftly flowing river and surviving—that he had not taken the woman as a sexual partner. Palace females were completely off-limits. It was a capital offense for a woman of the royal court and a man to stand together with no one else present. If another palace woman were to witness such an encounter without reporting it at once, she would be thrown into an oven.

The Code of Hammurabi made wives' lives no less hazardous. Married women who were "not circumspect" or who shamed their husbands by disparaging them or leaving their houses without permission risked death by drowning. This penalty accomplished two purposes: It got rid of a troublesome wife and it washed away the husband's dishonor. If a wife was so impudent as to steal her husband's property or denigrate him in public, then he had the choice of either casting her out of his house or—in a delicious gesture of revenge—keeping her around as a slave while he remarried.

The overriding goal of these laws was to prevent even the *appearance* that a wife was committing adultery. Virtually nothing consumed ancient lawmakers more than female infidelity, and few crimes were so severely punished. With the exception of the Hebrews, men who had sex outside of marriage were never at risk of punishment, but even Jewish law skewed hard against women. Married Jewish men were technically discouraged from having sex with other women, but were never punished to the same degree as their wives, and prostitution flourished in ancient Hebrew society. The men were also permitted to take multiple wives and concubines.

As a rule, women in the ancient Near East who had extramarital affairs and were caught suffered, died, or suffered and then died. That this should be the case was never questioned. The main legal issues concerned just when the punishments would be inflicted, and by whom. Could a husband go on a killing spree when he learned his wife had been unfaithful, or was the state to perform the executions? Was he allowed to forgive his wife or (less likely) her paramour? Was his decision final? As far back as the Sumerian kingdom of Eshnunna, in about 1770 BC, no forgiveness was permitted. "The day [a wife] is seized in the lap of another man, she shall die, she will not live." Later Mesopotamian cultures allowed husbands to pardon their wayward wives and not kill them, so long as they also gave a pass to the wives' lovers. In other cases, kings had the power to trump the husband's decision, either by pardoning the sinning couple despite the husband's desire to kill them or vice versa.

Assuming that punishments for adultery went forward, as they must have in most cases, they were nasty indeed—at least for the women. We have already seen how the unfortunate Nin-Dada was condemned and most likely impaled on the mere suspicion that she had committed adultery with her husband's killers. In another case from the same period, a man named Irra-malik came home to find his wife, Ishtar-ummi, making love with another man. Rather than commit violence on the spot, Irra-malik kept his head: He tied Ishtar-ummi and her lover to the bed with rope and dragged them to the assembly for trial.

Although the case record is short on detail, it appears that the assembly took the evidence in front of them—the two lovers tied and wriggling on the bed—as proof that adultery had taken place. This would have been sufficient to seal Ishtar-ummi's fate. Irra-malik, however, decided to pile more charges upon her. He accused her of stealing from his grain storehouse (perhaps to give a gift to her lover) and opening his jar of sesame seed oil, covering it again with a cloth to hide her theft. While these additional charges seem piddling next to adultery, they were framed as part and parcel of female wrongdoing: Bad wives not only took lovers, they also wasted their husbands' resources.

Ishtar-ummi's life was headed for a cruel end, but death appeared to be too much for her to hope for. The assembly first ruled that her pubic hair be shaven—whether this was merely to humiliate her or to prepare her for a lifetime of slavery, we do not know. It is probable that she was to be downgraded from wife to slave in Irra-malik's house, to be abused daily by him and his new wives. Before that happened, however, the assembly also ruled that she was to have her nose bored through with an arrow before being led around the city in disgrace, like a mule. The fate of her lover is not recorded, although it is likely that if she was not killed, neither was he.[7]

Wives never had any right to complain when their husbands took lovers, except when they were refused sex altogether or belittled in public. In that case, at least in Babylon, they could attempt to divorce their husbands—but that was a risky step, for the trials inevitably covered the wives' sexual behavior as well, and if they were found to have been promiscuous themselves they were thrown into a river to die. Given the risks involved, it was a far safer, if more bitter, decision for wives simply to put up with their husband's misbehavior.

Rivers were also involved when wives were accused of adultery without solid proof. Under what has become known as the "river ordeal," a woman could clear herself of suspicion by having herself thrown into the water. If she survived, she was declared innocent; if she sank, she was guilty. In either instance, the matter was decided. In one case that unfolded in the Sumerian kingdom of Mari, an unnamed woman made a detailed public statement just before the start of her river ordeal. She declared that she had indeed had sex with a father and his son before marrying the father. After her wedding, while her husband was away, the son came back to her to demand sex once again. "He kissed me on my lips," she reported. "He touched my vagina." She insisted, however, that they never went past the heavy petting stage: "His penis did not enter my vagina." Moreover, she scolded her aggressive stepson for coming after her, telling him that she would never do her husband "unforgivable harm" by letting him possess her again. Her declaration reads as if she doubted that she would survive the river, but the gods apparently believed her story. She floated.

A married Assyrian woman who invited a man to have sex with her could be punished by her husband in any way he chose. The lover usually walked away, but not always: If a man knew the woman in his bed was married, both were put to death. The problem for the courts was figuring out who knew what and when they knew it, especially when everyone's stories were plausible. To decide the undecidable, the Assyrians also used the river ordeal. A man who insisted he did not know his companion was married, or who claimed that there had been no sex, could prove his case by being thrown into a river. If he lived, he was exonerated, though he still had to pay the husband for the trouble. If the accused man sank, then the matter was over for him anyway. The errant wife's fate at that point was her husband's decision.

One knotty Assyrian sex case began when a wife left her husband and went to another man's house, where she stayed in the company of the host's wife for a few nights. The runaway wife's husband tracked her down, at which point he had the right to take her home and mutilate her to his heart's content. The woman who had taken care of her was presumed to know she'd harbored a disloyal woman, and was subject to having her ears cut off. The male host was at risk of paying a big fine if it could be shown that he'd known his guest was married. If no one believed him, he would have to undergo a river ordeal.

Thousands of years later, the spicy details of this dispute are left to the imagination. Why did the woman leave her husband? What brought her to the new home? Was she seeking sex with the host or refuge with the host's wife? As critical as each of these questions might seem to us, they were irrelevant to Assyrian justice. By law, husbands *owned* their wives, and were free to treat them as they wished. The sole issue was whether or not there was any way to assuage the fragile pride of the runaway's husband.

THE FREEDOM OF husbands to do violence to their adulterous wives seems to have diminished slightly by the Neo- and Late Babylonian periods (roughly the seventh to sixth centuries BC). By then, punishments against wives for taking lovers were often spelled out in advance, in marriage contracts. Several of the contracts that have survived contain an interesting clause, loosely translated as "Should [the wife] be discovered with another man, she will die by the iron dagger." Why this kind of language was put into marriage contracts at all, when the law had long allowed husbands to kill their adulterous wives, is the main question here. Were the contracts simply reminding young brides what awaited them should they stray? Perhaps, but a better interpretation is that the expression "she will die by the iron dagger" meant that the unfaithful wife would no longer be punished by the angry husband, but by *state authorities*, and in a public, example-setting way. As awful as dying "by the iron dagger" was, the clause was probably inserted into these contracts at the insistence of the brides' families to limit the husbands' options if their women were caught with other men. Rather than grant license to kill the lovers on the spot, the contracts most likely forced the husbands to bring them before the authorities. There was nothing a father could do to save his daughter's life once she had been unfaithful, but at least he could negotiate a fair shot at justice for her.

According to the Greek historian Herodotus, it was not easy to find a faithful wife in Egypt. He told of a king named Pheros, who had gone blind after showing disrespect to the Nile. Pheros's journey into darkness lasted for ten years, after which an oracle told him he would recover his sight when he washed his eyes with the urine of a faithful wife. Pheros went first to his own spouse, but her urine was tainted with adultery and could not heal him. He then tried the urine of "a great many" married women, one after another, until at last he found one who had been faithful—and his sight was restored. He gathered all the adulteresses he had tested (including, presumably, his own wife), sequestered them in a town known as Red Clod, and burned them to death. For good measure, he burned down the town, too. Afterward, he married the woman whose urine had retained the healing powers of fidelity.

Herodotus, of course, was all too often ready to sacrifice accuracy for a good tale, but he makes a fair point: Ancient Egyptian culture was deeply intolerant of women having extramarital sexual relations, and Egyptian law was ready to punish adulterous wives. The punishments were usually carried out by the husbands. In one account, dating to the New Kingdom (sixteenth–eleventh centuries BC), a man who had learned of his wife's attempted seduction of his younger brother chopped her to bits and fed her to the dogs. Other records tell of a man named Webaoner, whose wife regularly met with a townsman for adulterous trysts. Webaoner hired a magic crocodile to snatch the townsman and drag him to the bottom of the river. On orders from the king, the adulterous wife was then burned alive. (Burning and dismemberment were punishments calculated not only to cause pain but also to do eternal damage, as failure to preserve the intact body of a corpse was believed to ruin a spirit's chances to pass peacefully from this world into the afterlife.)

Not every adulterous woman in Egypt was treated with such savagery. The hocus-pocus in the stories of Pheros and Webaoner only illustrates the most extreme cases. Unless an Egyptian wife was caught in the act—in which case her husband would be forgiven for killing her in a fit of rage— she was most likely punished by having her nose slit or cut off; her lover could be given a thousand lashes. Not pleasant, to be sure—but hardly as bad as being dragged to the deep by a magic crocodile.[8]

GOOD GOATS, BAD SHEEP, AND LONG-SUFFERING SLAVES

Female adultery was one of the worst sex crimes in the ancient world, but there were many others. The first written laws covered the full gamut of sexual behavior from intercourse with cows and horses to affairs with another's slave. Sex itself was also used as a form of punishment. In Assyria, a married man who raped a virgin was considered a criminal, but it was his wife who paid the worse penalty: The law required that she be given up to be raped by the victim's father. In Egypt around 1000 BC, bestiality was both punishment and blessing, depending on the animal and the circumstances. Men who damaged stone property markers were forced to give up their wives and children to be raped by donkeys, but sex with goats was regarded as a form of divine devotion. Herodotus later tells us that goats were often seen as incarnations of the procreative god Pan. In countless instances, woman worshipped the goat god by copulating with specially trained bucks in temples.

Hittite punishments for sex with animals also depended on the particular beast involved. Cows, dogs, and sheep were strictly off-limits. Any man taking one of them for his pleasure was subject to the death penalty. The king was permitted to spare the animal lover's life, but the man would be treated as unclean and would never be allowed in the king's company "lest he defile the royal person." Sexual relations with horses and mules were permitted, but reluctantly. Men who enjoyed the intimate company of these animals would not risk execution, but they were barred from approaching the king and from becoming priests. Oxen and pigs were treated as potential sexual predators: Any ox that turned from its labor and "leaped" on a man "in sexual excitement" was to be killed. The man would escape execution, but a sheep was killed in his place. As for pigs, the law was clear that it was "not an offense" when a pig raped a man—but if the man was the sexual initiator, he was put to death.

Rape between human beings was also dealt with according to who was doing the raping and who was suffering it. We have already considered the penalties for raping betrothed virgins. Husbands, of course, could never be charged with raping their own wives; the idea would have been regarded as incomprehensible, if not insane. Men owned their wives, and were at liberty to use them at their pleasure. Men also owned their slaves, though slaves were not technically people and thus had far fewer rights. Giving oneself to one's master sexually was part of the job description. The question in terms of the law was what to do when a freeman had sex with another freeman's slave without first obtaining permission. On that subject, ancient lawmakers had *much* to say.

As far back as the days of Ur-Nammu, in the third millennium BC, the penalty for raping a slave girl was as trivial as a speeding ticket is today. A fine of five silver shekels was levied, but that was it. It was not much different in Babylon, where the fine for taking another man's virgin slave girl rose to twenty silver shekels, and so on into the era of Hammurabi. In one famous Babylonian case, again before the Assembly of Nippur, a man named Lugalmelam was accused by the slave owner Kuguzana of "seizing" his slave girl, dragging her into a building, and then "deflowering" her. Lugalmelam denied everything, but Kuguzana found witnesses to back up his charges. The assembly decided that Lugalmelam had indeed taken the girl "without her owner's knowledge," and charged him a substantial fine.

It need hardly be pointed out that no one asked Kuguzana's slave whether or not she had consented to having sex with Lugalmelam. The only consent that mattered was that of her owner. Slaves were bought and sold like animals, given as gifts, offered in payment of debts, and shipped abroad as merchandise. At any moment in their perilous lives, their owners could use them as they wished. Even the rules against sex within families were loosened when slaves were involved, as no one recognized that slaves themselves could have families as such. Under the laws of the Hittites, for example, if a freeman had sex with sisters and their mother, "it [was] an abomination," but if he slept with slave sisters and their mother, "it [was] not an offense."

The cruelty of slavery was nevertheless sometimes softened, especially when slaves produced children for their masters. Under the Code of Hammurabi, a slave concubine who bore her master's children was automatically freed after he died. If a slave owner was forced to hand over a female slave to pay a debt, moreover, he was allowed to buy her back later if she had already given him children. This situation must have come up with some regularity, as female slaves were often used as surrogate mothers. When a freeman's wife was unable to have children, she was permitted to find a slave woman to do the job. The slave was then given certain additional rights, though not enough to challenge the wife's position in the household. The laws of Lipit-Ishtar required that the slave mother not live in the house of her masters. The Babylonians went one step further, explicitly allowing the wife to continue treating the slave-mother as a piece of property.

The rape of a married woman incurred the death penalty only when it took place on the open road, and only if the woman had vigorously fought back. The fact that the sex occurred outdoors, and that she did her best to stop it, helped show that she was taken by surprise and was not looking to have an affair. If she was at home when the sex occurred, the suspicion of bad intentions on her part was almost impossible to shake. The Hittites, in fact, resolved cases of home rape against the wife even before it occurred:

> *If a man seizes a woman in the mountains (and rapes her), it is the man's offense, but if he seizes her in her house, it is the woman's offense: the woman shall die. If the woman's husband discovers them in the act, he may kill them without committing a crime.*[9]

PROSTITUTION, SACRED AND PROFANE

The rules changed when sex was for sale. Prostitution was a legal transaction like any other, so long as it was carried out according to custom and respectable women were not involved. An Assyrian man who had sex with a married woman in a tavern or brothel (which were often one and the same) could be put to death for taking another man's wife, but his knowledge of the fact that she was married would first have to be proven—which could be difficult, given the circumstances. If he could show that he had believed he was paying a single woman for her company, then no one could lay a hand on him, even if she had been married to an aristocrat.

In Egypt, religion and prostitution were closely associated. The Egyptian goddess Isis was, among her many other incarnations, a whore. At first, prostitution was barred from religious precincts. However, by the time the geographer Strabo traveled in Egypt in 25 BC, customs had changed. In the temple of Zeus, prepubescent girls were being served up for men's pleasure:

> To Zeus they consecrate one of the most beautiful girls of the most illustrious family . . . She becomes a prostitute and has intercourse with whomever she wishes, until the . . . purification of her body [by menstruation] takes place. After her purification, she is given in marriage to a man, but before the marriage and after her time as a prostitute, a . . . ceremony of mourning is celebrated in her honor.

Herodotus wrote of another girl who had got into the trade: the daughter of the pharaoh Khufu (or Cheops, 2589–2566 BC). Her life was decidedly unglamorous, however. She was put to work on her back to pay for her father's death monument:

> When [Khufu] was short of money, he sent his daughter to a bawdy house with instructions to charge a certain sum—they did not tell me how much. This she actually did, adding to it a further transaction of her own; for with the intention of leaving something to be remembered by after her death, she asked each of her customers to give her a block of stone, and of these stones (the story goes) was built the middle pyramid of the three which stand in front of the great pyramid. It is a hundred and fifty feet square.

That's a lot of stones, and a lot of clients.

Another story from Herodotus told of the Thracian prostitute Rhodipus, a beauty whose hard work in Egypt brought her great fame and wealth, some of which she used to dedicate temples at Delphi. Rhodipus worked with the opportunities she had: Selling sex, sacred or otherwise, was one of the few ways unmarried women could get ahead. In Egypt, women were nearly equal to men under the law—but only in theory. Only money could buy true independence, and there were few ways in Egypt for women to earn their own living. Unless they were supported by men, their options were limited to prostitution, the performing arts, or, as was often the case, a little of each at the same time. The droves of prostitutes who did not reach the heights of Rhodipus trailed construction crews to building sites and followed pilgrims to religious destinations. It was tough going and made for short, bitter lives.

No Mesopotamian civilization attached any stigma or restriction to prostitution. By 1750 BC, during Hammurabi's reign, the city of Babylon was busy with trade (both male and female) in the temples and on the streets. Temple prostitutes were the most desirable, and the most expensive. Their precise religious function is unclear, but it seems they worked both as skilled pleasure-givers and as intermediaries between customers/worshippers and temple deities. Whether the path to godliness truly ran through the body of a woman selling sex is anyone's guess, but this was doubtless a profitable form of worship. The earnings of sacred prostitutes comprised a substantial part of the temples' revenues.

The Babylonians forced *all* women to put in time as temple prostitutes. According to Herodotus: "[E]very woman who is a native of the country must once in her life go to the temple of Aphrodite and there give herself to a strange man." Only after they had performed this duty were they permitted to leave. The scene at the temple was chaotic, with women and customers constantly coming and going. Women from the wealthy classes arrived to do their service in covered carriages with dozens of servants milling about, while others showed up on foot. Special gangways were installed to permit the men to stroll through the assembled females and make their selections. "Once a woman has taken her seat she is not allowed to go home until a man has thrown a silver coin in her lap and taken her outside to lie with her," Herodotus continues. The attractive ones were plucked up right away, while the homely ones were sometimes forced to remain on display at the temple for years. Once their service was done, the women were off-limits once again.

Attractive Babylonian women also assisted their less beguiling neighbors in finding a mate. Once a year, all girls of marriageable age were collected from their villages to be auctioned off to prospective husbands. The pretty ones from good families were taken first, often after furious bidding, while "the humbler [men], who had no use for good looks in a wife, were actually paid to take the ugly ones." When all the attractive women had been sold, the auctioneer "would call upon the plainest one to stand up, and then ask who was willing to take the least money to marry her—and she was knocked down to whoever accepted the smallest sum." The money came from the sales of the beauties, "who in this way provided dowries for their ugly or misshapen sisters."

Men lacking the means to purchase temple whores could frequent downscale taverns and wine shops. Both the prostitutes and the (mostly) female proprietors of these dives were seen as a sluttish, thieving lot. Drinking houses were often hideouts for fugitive bandits, which is why Hammurabi took pains to control them, while imposing no restrictions on the tavern-based prostitution within. A barkeep marketing prostitutes in her back room was liable for nothing more than taxes, but faced capital punishment if she overheard customers talking about a crime and failed to turn them in.

Strict dress codes had the dual effect of putting prostitutes on perpetual display as well as making clear which women were unavailable for rent. From the earliest Sumerian times, married women went veiled. By the Middle Assyrian period, this tradition had evolved into a harsh law that made veiling a privilege of the better classes. Prostitutes and slaves were not permitted to go about veiled. Conversely, all daughters, wives, widows, and other women of status were to be covered in public. Prostitutes caught wearing veils had hot pitch poured on their heads and were beaten with fifty blows. Such punishment left them disfigured and, undoubtedly, less salable. Slaves who hid their faces in public, meanwhile, stood to lose their ears and their clothes.[10]

HOMOSEXUALITY BEFORE MORALITY

Before the biblical period, sex law had nothing to do with morality as we know it, nor was forbidden sex laden with the psychology of guilt. The main question concerned the protection of property. The founding principle of sex regulation was that women were possessions to be cultivated for marriage and childbirth, or used for sex and then discarded. A husband was free to fornicate to his heart's content, because it had no effect on his property. His wife, of course, could be put to death for doing the same thing.

The question then turns to whether or not men had the option of fornicating with other *men*, and the short answer is that they usually did. Before the Hebrews labeled male-male sex an abomination of the worst kind, there were almost no restrictions against it. As detailed as the early legal codes were on the subject of sex, same-gender relations were mostly ignored—not because homosexual sex did not take place (it certainly did), but because there was no reason to actively restrict it: Anal sex generally was subject to no taboos, and sexual escapades among men constituted no more of an interruption to their marriages than their dalliances with female prostitutes or slaves. Male prostitutes even worked in the Babylonian temple of the mother-goddess Ishtar at Erach, where they were known as men "whose manhood Ishtar has changed into womanhood."

The Assyrians shared the Babylonians' indulgent attitudes, but only up to a point. A man who spread false rumors that another man allowed himself to be regularly penetrated was subject to being whipped, fined, and having his hair cut off. Such punishments were mild by Assyrian standards, and they did not mean gay sex was illegal; but they do indicate that being considered as available for the pleasure of other men was bad for a man's reputation. Far worse was the rape of a man by another of his own class. For that, the aggressor was punished by rape, followed by castration. Yet we still cannot say with certainty that these laws signaled a general retreat from thousands of years of legal indifference to homosexual relations. The law, after all, only prohibited rape between men of the same class. A master's forced penetration of his male slave was perfectly legal, as were relations with male prostitutes and consenting male acquaintances. Taken together, however, they probably contributed to a mind-set that viewed same-gender sex as being somewhat inferior to heterosexual relations. The Hebrews would carry this idea to extreme lengths, as they did with their rules forbidding every form of sex that wasn't intended to produce legitimate children.[11]

SIN: THE GIFT OF THE HEBREWS

From about 1047 to 597 BC, a collection of contentious Hebrew tribes had held unsteady control over coastal land in Palestine, where they lived by their own religious law. The early Jews developed their legal system with a view to surviving in a region filled with other ethnic tribes, with whom they were at war; but the true accomplishment of their laws was to differentiate the Hebrews by imposing the stamp of "Jewishness" on just about everything they did. Integral to that sensibility was an intense preoccupation with restricting sexual activity. The Jews meant to make their entire lives holy, whether in their business dealings, their food customs, or their methods for having sex. To achieve this, they developed a sprawling range of rules and regulations. The Hebrew kingdoms were short-lived, and, compared to the colossal ancient empires of Persia and the Mediterranean, insignificant. Had Judaism not spawned Christianity and then Islam, Hebrew law would have remained a marginal development in Western history. Like the laws of the Babylonians and the ancient Egyptians, the Hebrew Bible would have been chiefly of interest to later academics. Instead, the moral strictures of the ancient Jews, held together with the molasses of shame and the terror of God's punishment, have been more influential on Western sexual attitudes than any other collection of ideas.

The body of Jewish law is immense, so broad that it is virtually unknowable to any individual. I shall concentrate here mostly on the rules that were supposedly dictated, word for word, to Moses by God—in particular the book of Leviticus, where most of Judaism's most significant rules concerning sex are to be found. Maddening in its repetitious hodgepodge of demands, threats, and curses, Leviticus is one of the foundations of Hebrew life, and, along with the rest of the Torah, is meant to be an indispensable guidebook to a godly existence. Nothing before or since has so effectively equated the body, the state, and the collective moral soul.

Jewish law places no distance between flesh and spirit. The body, considered an extension of God, was to be harnessed in building a holy nation. "You shall sanctify yourself and be holy, for I am holy," commands God, and in Leviticus he instructs the children of Israel how to do this. To follow God's commandments was to live, to "be fruitful and multiply" (Genesis 1:28); to ignore them was, in extreme cases, to anger God to the point where he would "vomit out" the Jews from the land they held so tenuously. Every passing thought had powerful social and religious significance, and everything a Hebrew did with his or her body, more so. Sex and reproduction were thus at the core of Hebrew lives and law.

The scriptures spell out in detail what may go in and out of the body, particularly via the mouth and genitals. Many foods are forbidden, as God's decree holds that they cause contamination. A multitude of bodily fluids such as menstrual blood and semen are also regarded as polluting, and must be carefully channeled lest they infect the community. Sexual intercourse was necessary to fulfill the commandment to multiply, but it took very little to transform the sex act from one of blessed procreation into a sin that put the entire nation at risk. While sex was essential to marriage, it was also a political act: Having sex (or rejecting it) according to Mosaic law was both a declaration of faith and a repudiation of the Hebrews' hostile neighbors.

Before God spelled out the multiple sexual prohibitions in Leviticus, he issued a commandment *not* to "do [have sex] as they do in Egypt, where you used to live," and also "not [to] do as they do in the land of Canaan, where I am bringing you. Do not follow their practices." There were many such "practices" to reject, including incest and bestiality (both were prevalent in Egypt), which became death-penalty crimes, and the temple prostitution common in Canaan and Babylon. To further distinguish the Hebrews from the cultures around them, Leviticus also forbade adultery by men as well as women. Violating any of these prohibitions thus not only made one immoral in the eyes of God, but also subverted everyone else's safety.[12]

CIRCUMCISION AND FLUID CONTROL

One practice the Jews *did* adopt from their neighbors was male circumcision; the Egyptians had already been snipping off the foreskins of their boys and male adolescents since the third millennium BC, long before the Hebrews began to do so. The ritual, performed by Egyptian "circumcision priests," was done on as many as 120 males at a time. Although, in Genesis 17:9–11, Abraham receives a divine revelation that male circumcision is to mark a "covenant" between God and his followers, the practice is said to have become institutionalized only when the Hebrews fled Egypt—presumably reinforced by the Egyptian convention. For good measure, the Hebrews also circumcised their slaves, as well as all slaves bought with their money. To be uncircumcised was to be unclean. The practice of circumcision later spread throughout the Near East and became common among Muslims (although it is not required by Islamic law).

The surgical modification of a boy's reproductive equipment is a strong statement of faith, but there remains the question of whether or not it was also meant to affect his later erotic experiences. The medieval Jewish scholar Moses Maimonides argued that circumcision decreases sexual desire, which he thought was a good thing. He was not alone: In the nineteenth century, circumcision was one of the "cures" used to reduce the urge to masturbate. Some modern researchers agree that the procedure diminishes sensation, which they refer to as "erotic harm." In many countries where circumcision is common, notes one authority, "women must often become accustomed to performing fellatio (the so-called 'Berber wake-up call') on men to spur their sexual response."

The thirteenth-century Jewish sage Isaac Ben Yedaya argued, by contrast, that circumcision *increases* male erotic sensation to the point of sparking premature ejaculation:

> *He will find himself performing his task quickly, emitting his seed as soon as he inserts the crown. If he lies with her once, he sleeps satisfied, and will not know her again for another seven days . . . As soon as he begins intercourse with her, he immediately comes to a climax. She has no pleasure from him when she lies down or when she arises . . . [S]he remains in a state of desire for her husband, ashamed and confounded.*

To Ben Yedaya, this was preferable, as uncircumcised men give women too much pleasure, which in turn invites a host of different problems:

> *She too will court the man who is uncircumcised in the flesh and lie against his breast with great passion, for he thrusts inside her a long time because of his foreskin, which is a barrier against ejaculation in intercourse. Thus she feels pleasure and reaches an*

orgasm first. When an uncircumcised man sleeps with her and then resolves to return to his home, she brazenly grasps him, holding on to his genitals, and says, "Come back, make love to me." This is because of the pleasure that she finds in intercourse with him, from the sinews of his testicles—sinews of iron—and from his ejaculation—that of a horse—which he shoots like an arrow into her womb.

Whatever its long-term erotic effects, circumcision was rejected by the Greeks and Romans, who found the practice repulsive and barbaric. The Greeks viewed penile foreskins as emblems of virtue and strength; altering nature's design was nothing more than the odd fetish of oddball religious cults. The Greek king Antiochus IV Epiphanes (175–164 BC) outlawed circumcision altogether, as did later Roman edicts punishing circumcision with death. Some Jews, wishing to escape punishment and integrate themselves into pagan cultures, mutilated themselves trying to restore their foreskins—but such measures are rare in the record.[13]

Being a Jewish male has always meant, first and foremost, being circumcised. Unless their foreskins were removed, Jewish males were considered impure. Circumcision was only the first step in a sanctified life, however; *staying* pure before God took constant effort, as impurity hovered around all sexual activity. When a husband and wife had sex, for example, the transmission of semen made them both unsuitable for contact with anyone else. Until they were cleansed, everything they touched was contaminated. Even an involuntary discharge of semen, such as sometimes accompanies a man's erotic dreams, was an unhygienic catastrophe. The bed in which the dream took place was now defiled, the bedclothes unusable until scrubbed, and any clay pots touched by the man were considered so unclean they had to be smashed to bits. This process would continue for a week, after which the hapless wet dreamer was compelled to seek out a priest to help him make a sacrifice of doves or pigeons and beseech God's forgiveness. Menstrual blood was no less radioactive: Any contact with it required intense cleansing efforts and strict separation of the offending woman from the community until the taint was washed away.

When the body's fluids were misused through forbidden sex, the risk was multiplied drastically. An individual's defilement, if bad enough, tempted God to destroy the Jewish nation in its entirety. God makes his position quite clear:

> *Do not defile yourselves [sexually], because this is how the nations that I am going to drive out before you became defiled. Even the land was defiled; so I punished it for its sin, and the land vomited out its inhabitants. But you must keep my decrees and my laws. The native-born and the aliens living among you must not do any of these detestable things, for all these things were done by the people who lived in the land before you, and the land became defiled. And if you defile the land, it will vomit you out as it vomited out the nations that were before you.*

In other words, "Follow my commandments and you will live. Ignore them and I will throw you off the land and will kill all of you."

If sex between a man and a menstruating woman polluted them both, the mixture of fluids between humans and animals was far worse: Both the human offender and the animal were to be killed.[14] Incest was no different, as it represented an intermingling among family that would then infect everyone. In its most intimate forms, such as copulation between a mother and son, the law demanded that both parties be killed.

Given the above, one Bible story is particularly ironic, telling of a man who paid a terrible price for refusing to engage in intrafamily sex. According to Genesis, following the death of a man named Er, God commanded Er's brother Onan to impregnate the deceased's wife. Onan obeyed to the point of going to bed with the widow several times, but each time he "spilled his semen on the ground" rather than ejaculate inside her. God was not amused, and struck Onan dead. In the context of ancient life, God's demand was not unusual. When a husband died without issue, it was common in many societies for his brother to take the widow as a wife and try his best to give her children. Onan's sin was rebellion against this custom (called levirate marriage) via coitus interruptus.

As the practice of levirate marriage diminished over the years, the story of Onan should have faded from interest as well. But it found new life when Christian theologians seized it to emphasize that any form of semen wastage was forbidden, whether accomplished by masturbation, unfinished copulation, or otherwise. The masturbation angle resonated more than the others, to the point where "Onanism" came to denote self-abuse. In the eighteenth century, the Swiss doctor Samuel-Auguste Tissot named his hugely popular antimasturbation diatribe *L'Onanisme*, after the man who refused to complete the sex act with his sister-in-law.

The Jews also tightened regional prohibitions against adultery, throwing it in the gallery of crimes so abominable they put all Hebrews at risk of destruction. Other Near Eastern laws let the cuckolded husband punish his wife and her paramour—which was logical, given that it was the husband who was "injured" by the wife's infidelity. Jewish law saw the crime differently. A wife's straying from her husband was condemned as treason against the entire community, which demanded public involvement and communal retribution. For everyone's benefit, *both* male and female adulterers were supposed to be publicly strangled. The law was no less strict when sex took place between a man and a girl who was engaged to be married. The pair would be stripped and placed on public ground to suffer large stones dropped on their bodies until they died.[15]

The Hebrews expanded the reach of adultery law, but not at the expense of their men's sexual freedom. Married men were not allowed to have affairs as such, but they were permitted to take as many wives as they pleased—King Solomon reputedly had seven hundred official wives—and also to keep concubines and visit prostitutes. A Jewish man was forbidden from marrying a prostitute, but even on that point the law was rather weak. Unlike other ancient societies, in which a woman was marked as a whore for her entire life once she took up the trade, a prostitute in ancient Palestine could marry a Jewish man if she reformed herself for at least three months.

As for other girls who sought premarital sexual experiences, Jewish law was relatively lenient. A lost maidenhead was gone forever, to the permanent detriment of the girl's marriage value, but the Bible dictated a simple solution: Unmarried males and females (other than prostitutes) who had sex had to get married. The boy's family had to pay the girl's top bride-price (as though she were still a virgin), and the girl's father had no choice but to accept both the money and the union. The premarital sex would force the father's hand in granting his consent, but it also required the lovers to live with their decision for the rest of their lives: Divorce between the new husband and wife was forbidden.

Adultery was as much of a challenge to prove for the Hebrews as anywhere else, so they enlisted God's help. As we have seen, the men of Babylon and Assyria already used the "river ordeal" to determine whether or not their wives had been faithful. Generally, if the women survived a toss in the river, they were considered innocent—the river god had spoken. If they were guilty, the case was closed anyway. The Jews, in turn, focused on the fluids flowing *inside* the bodies of the accused wives. In the only ordeal known to Hebrew law, the Bible requires that a woman accused of infidelity drink "bitter waters." Her reaction to the beverage would determine her guilt or innocence. This trial of the *sotah* (straying woman) commenced when "feelings of jealousy" washed over a husband "and he suspect[ed] his wife." The husband would take the woman before a priest, who would then give her a mixture of holy water, dust from the floor of the tabernacle, and the charred remains of a grain offering. "If no other man has slept with you and you have not gone astray and become impure," the priest would tell the wife, "may this bitter water that brings a curse not harm you." But if she had been less than pure, the priest had this to say: "May the Lord cause your people to curse and denounce you when he causes your thigh to waste away and your abdomen to swell." In other words, if you have been messing around, may God show it by tearing your uterus out of your body. The woman would drink the potion, and then . . .

We don't know what happened next. The Bible tells us that if she was innocent, she would become pregnant, but if she was guilty she would lose her uterus. Presumably she would then be publicly executed like other adulteresses. What is not explained is when and how God would work his justice. As we do not know the chemical makeup of "bitter waters," we cannot say whether or not any such liquid could have caused a woman's thigh to "waste away" or her "abdomen to swell." It seems unlikely.

Moreover, if the woman's innocence was proven by a later pregnancy, did that mean that her jealous husband was supposed to have sex with her even if she was suspected of being "defiled" by adultery? The text is silent on these critical points as well. However, it says much about protecting husbands when their adultery accusations were proven wrong. Most people in the Near East were punished if they forced others to suffer ordeals needlessly. Hebrew husbands, on the other hand, faced no such risks. Even if their adultery accusations were proven wrong, the men were considered innocent of any wrongdoing. Thus they were permitted to have their wives poisoned time and again on nothing more than a jealous hunch.[16]

TREMBLING BEFORE GOD: HOMOSEXUALITY AMONG THE HEBREWS

With the exception of requiring husbands to be faithful to their wives—at least in theory—the Hebrews treated adultery much as their neighbors did. They struck out on their own, however, in designating a new sexual "abomination" where there had been no precedent: The Bible made anal sex between men a crime of the worst order, for which death by stoning became the only option. "Do not lie with a man as one lies with a woman; that is detestable," commands Leviticus. "Their blood will be on their own heads." Men had been "lying together" since the beginning of civilization, of course. This was the first time they risked their lives by doing so.

The Code of Hammurabi, which ordered society in most of the Tigris-Euphrates Valley for more than a thousand years, has nothing to say about homosexuality. The laws of Eshunna and Egypt are also silent on the subject. The Hittites forbade father-son relations, but that was part of a general rule against incest. The Assyrians thought it shameful for a man to repeatedly offer himself to other men, and also prohibited men from raping males of the same social class, but all other male-male sexual relations were ignored. The Hebrews, by contrast, made no distinctions and left no exceptions. Sexual intercourse between men was out, regardless of who was doing it and how it was done. The Jewish God hated it so much he wrecked the cities of Sodom and Gomorrah to prove it.

But before that story (and here's the punchline: It's not true), it is worth looking briefly at why the Hebrews would have adopted such a position. As we saw earlier, the ancient Jews were consumed with a sense of physical vulnerability, which they translated into spiritual terms. By drawing rigid sexual boundaries, the Jews were trying to bulk up the body politic. Men having sex with men blurred the lines by putting males in the "receptive" role of females in sex acts that, like bestiality, produced no children. Sexual pleasure was never forbidden among the Hebrews so long as it occurred while husbands and wives were producing *more* Hebrews. When they sought erotic pleasure for its own sake, or when they had sex that resulted in illegitimate children (as in cases of adultery or incest), the nation of Israel as a whole was weakened.[17] God threatened to destroy the Jews: If they enfeebled themselves from within, they would be destroyed from without.

In this context, biblical antihomosexual laws were also instruments of foreign policy. Male-male sex was forbidden (the scriptures ignore lesbian relations) precisely because the Jews' neighbors permitted it. Just as sex with animals was common in the region, so was a benign attitude toward same-gender sex. As it was the mission of the Jews, based on the commandment of their God, to "not do as they do" in other, non-Jewish societies, homosexual sex was just one of a litany of "filthy foreign" practices the Jews defined themselves by rejecting.[18] If the Hebrews' enemies permitted homosexuality, it was inevitable that Jewish law would forbid it.

The book of Leviticus was supposed to come to Moses directly from the mouth of God, so its threats of destruction for homosexual sex were taken, so to speak, as gospel. But a simple law is rarely enough in itself to change people's behavior. The point needed to be driven home with a gruesome example of God making good on his threat. Oddly, the Bible provides no such illustrations. In a book crammed with anecdotes, allegories, and repetitions, the subject of homosexuality is addressed just twice, and in the comparatively dry language cited above. To fill the gap, some later scholars decided to recast the old Genesis story about the destruction of Sodom and Gomorrah. The effort was forced, to say the least—there is no evidence that either of those cities was a hotbed of homosexual sex—but it was very successful in the end. The tale of these two accursed cities became history's single most influential myth to transmit antihomosexual prejudice.

Abraham's nephew Lot was a resident of Sodom, a locale known, along with Gomorrah, as one of the evil "Cities of the Plain." News of the cities' wickedness reached God, who sent two angels in the guise of foreign travelers to investigate. Lot offered them lodging for the night, but their presence in his house agitated the townspeople. Before the angels retired for the night, a mob of men gathered outside Lot's house. They demanded to see the travelers "that we may know them." Lot refused, which enraged the mob even more. The key to this part of the story is the meaning of the word "know" (*ve'nida'ah* in the original Hebrew text). Did the word mean simply "to become acquainted with," as many scholars argue? Or did it directly imply sex? Were the townspeople demanding only to look the visitors over, or did they want to rape them? It is impossible to say, especially given Lot's response: "I have two daughters who have never slept with a man. Let me bring them out to you, and you can do what you like with them. But don't do anything to these men, for they have come under the protection of my roof." The crowd was not interested in deflowering Lot's daughters; they wanted to "know" his guests. As they surged forward to break down Lot's door, the angels struck them all with blindness. The next morning, Lot fled with his family, and God rained down fire and brimstone on Sodom and Gomorrah, destroying these cities forever.

There is general agreement today that the Sodom mob's crime was to ignore the custom of providing hospitality to strangers. By housing and protecting the two angels, Lot was doing what any decent Bronze Age Near Eastern host would do. The mob's unruly demands to "know" the disguised angels were worse than rude, even if they had no intention of "knowing" the strangers carnally. But truth has never gotten in the way of a good story, and it did not take people long to turn this passage into a cautionary tale against homosexuality. The Jews themselves seem to have been the first to do so when, in the first century AD, they were horrified at all the homosexual sex going on among the Greeks and Romans. The reinterpreted story was soon swallowed whole by the Christian church, and thereafter became the basis of history's most virulent antihomosexual laws. As early as the sixth century AD, the (Christian) Byzantine emperor Justinian pointed to Sodom and Gomorrah as the reason for his persecution of homosexuals. "Because of such offenses," went one of Justinian's laws, "famine, earthquakes, and pestilence occur."

BY THE MIDDLE Ages, the word "sodomy" had come to encompass not only male-male sex, but also an ever-shifting list of forbidden sexual

LOT AND HIS DAUGHTERS

. . .

The biblical story of Lot, who tried to protect two angels from the bad people of Sodom, has been invoked time and again to support antihomosexual laws. Yet gay sex had nothing to do with the story. Lost in all the talk of fire and brimstone was Lot's invitation to his townsmen to rape his virgin daughters. Later, when Lot and the girls were hiding in a cave, they got their father drunk and had sex with him. ©TOPFOTO practices. Occasionally, lesbian sex was included in the definition, and when it was, lawmakers made sure to tie it back to the supposed debauchery of Sodom and Gomorrah: The "mothers of lust," as the women of those cities were called, could not be satisfied with men, so they turned to other women. While sodomy was defined differently everywhere, the example of God's wrath against the two cities was viewed as justifying the cruelest possible treatment of sodomites. "[I]t is well known how much the sin of sodomy is detested by Our God," said Venice's ruling Council of Ten in 1407, "since it was the reason that he destroyed and ruined by his last judgment cities and peoples in which they [sodomites] lived."

The myth of Sodom and Gomorrah was picked up by England's most important legal authority, William Blackstone, who commented, in the eighteenth century, that "the infamous crime against nature" was a "disgrace" so revolting that it should "not . . . be named among Christians," and should be punished by death, as God had shown his disfavor by working "the destruction of two cities by fire from heaven." Modern American courts have been no less ready to embrace the story as truth. One Alabama court dealing with a 1966 sodomy case wrote: "We cannot think upon the sordid facts contained in this record without being reminded of the savage horror practiced by the dwellers of ancient Sodom from which this crime was nominally derived." In 1968, the North Carolina Supreme Court, when passing on charges against a man for homosexual sex, referred to the "famous Biblical lore in the story of the destruction by fire and brimstone of the cities of Sodom and Gomorrah where the practice was prevalent." By this time there was, of course, doubt as to how the two cities were destroyed, but there was still total certainty that "the practice" of sodomy was the cause of God's anger.[19]

As the "good man" in one of sex law's most powerful fables, Lot was still a rather dodgy character. His readiness to offer up his virgin daughters for rape showed badly misplaced priorities, even by ancient standards. But all of that is now beside the point. For at least two thousand years, the story of Sodom and Gomorrah has been enough for lawmakers to justify the monstrous treatment of same-gender sex. Had Jewish law not become the cornerstone of Christian morality, the myth of the Cities of the Plain would have remained confined to a small, gay-bashing Near Eastern religion. But that was not how matters turned out. The ancient Hebrews' antihomosexuality mania became the foundation for generations of intolerance.

But before that would take place, another set of cultural traditions would take hold in the Mediterranean, going on to shape Western culture no less than early Judaism. Just across the water from Palestine, the Greeks were organizing themselves under a set of assumptions that had nothing to do with God or Hebrew law. No one disagrees that Greek arts and culture reached the limits of the sublime, but few Greeks thought much about such things. Most were simply trying to get through the day, and many were involved in a lesser-known Greek obsession: litigation. Greek law was played out in public, in trials that involved thousands of people—and the Greeks loved nothing more than a good sex trial.

2

· · ·

HONOR AMONG (MOSTLY) MEN:
CASES FROM ANCIENT GREECE

NEITHER THE SEX slave nor the wife ever had a chance. On every
Athens street corner, every statue of the god Hermes, his penis erect,
pointed to female powerlessness. The slave could not hope for loyalty from
her owner, Philoneos—not when he could sell or torture her on a whim.
Nor did the wife of Philoneos's friend have any right to demand fidelity
from her husband. The dust of the city's streets was stamped everywhere
with the prints of prostitutes' studded sandals, beckoning with messages like
"Follow Me," and nothing prevented men from pursuing these trails directly
to the city's houses of pleasure. So when Philoneos decided to sell his slave
to a brothel, and when his friend began to lose interest in his wife, the two
women were left with few options to keep their men. They were desperate.

One evening, when the two men were drinking together at the husband's house, the wife called the slave over. In whispers, she told the girl
that she had obtained a potion that would turn their men's attention back to
them. The only question was how the women would slip it to them. The men
dined habitually with concubines and prostitutes, not their slave or wife.
Nevertheless, the wife suggested that the slave do it, and this was agreed.

The opportunity came when Philoneos and the husband were together
in Piraeus, the port of Athens. Philoneos was there to offer a sacrifice to
Zeus; the husband was preparing to embark on a sea journey. The two

friends set about eating a good meal and getting drunk. Afterward, they burned frankincense and poured libations "to secure the favor of heaven." While they offered up their prayers, the slave poured the philter the wife had given her into their wine, pouring the lion's share of the potion in her master's cup.

The concoction was not the "happy inspiration" the women had hoped for: It killed Philoneos that night. The husband died from the poison a few weeks later.

These were some of the accusations made by the husband's son at the murder trial of the wife, his stepmother—hence the case was referred to as *Against the Stepmother*. The young man had not been present during any of the critical events; his evidence came from the sex slave's agonized confession as she was being broken on a wheel. The stepson accused his stepmother of tricking the slave into poisoning his father to death, but the slave couldn't confirm this. Nevertheless, all trials are about stories more than realities, and the stepson's tale was compelling. The jury, which numbered up to 2,501 men, was unlikely to give the wife a break in any event. The mere fact that she would *try* to mold her husband's emotions, even with a substance she might have believed harmless, was bad enough.

A well-known orator named Lysias had been hired by the stepson to write his trial speech. Lysias well knew the whoring habits and misogyny of Athenian men. He himself was a loyal client of a well-known Corinthian brothel, and likely of others in Athens itself. He crafted the stepson's speech to push all the right emotional buttons and bring the jury to a state of maximum anger.

The slave was killed without trial, despite everyone's agreement that she hadn't meant to harm anyone. "She got what she deserved," Lysias said. The specifics of the wife's fate are not recorded, but it is clear that the rest of her life was going to be short and unpleasant. If the jury agreed that her aim had been to kill her husband rather than merely pump him up with aphrodisiacs, she probably would have faced strangulation. Avoiding execution would have been little better for her, as she would have been returned to the control of a male family member who would be certain to mete out his own home-based punishment.[1]

The accusation of murder that the son leveled against his stepmother is understandable, but the question of why she would intentionally kill her husband remains: Doing away with him, after all, meant eliminating the one person able to protect her from oblivion. Her actions only make sense if she had been trying to bring her husband closer to her. She was reaching the end of her useful life, knew little of the world, and had few to zero prospects without him. Marriage in Greece was meant to generate heirs for fathers, but her husband had already had a son when she married him. Minus his desire, she was more vulnerable than ever to being replaced with a newer model.

A respectable woman in Athens was viewed as merely a sperm receptacle, what Sophocles called a "field to plow." Semen was held to do the real work in conception; the womb merely cooked it up. Aeschylus (in his *Eumenides*) put it bluntly:

> *She who is called the mother is not her offspring's*
> *Parent, but nurse to the newly*
> *sown embryo.*
> *The male—who mounts—begets.*

The key function of women was physical in Greek culture. It was thus pointless to educate them or to allow them to participate in public life. Instead, they spent their days in the airless inner rooms of walled-in houses, interacting only with slaves and family. Wives never attended their husbands' whore-greased dinner parties, called symposia, nor did they interact much with their husbands in daily life. The differences between husband and wife in age and cultivation, along with the availability to men of sex from other quarters, virtually guaranteed that spouses would remain strangers to each other. Recognizing this, the early Athenian lawgiver Solon required men to mount their wives three times per month: Sex between husbands and wives was thus a legal duty.

Men could divorce their wives by simply returning the dowries to their fathers-in-law. Women, on the other hand, needed first to get the approval of a male relative, then go to court—the single opportunity in their lives to do so—and take their chances. After spending so much of their existence indoors, encouraged to say little and think less, choosing such a course must have been like emerging from a dark cave into blinding sunlight.

Only three women are known to have attempted divorce, most notably Hipparete, wife of the volatile and sexually unquenchable general Alcibiades. Her disastrous experience was a cautionary tale for other wives, especially as she had a good case: She came from a wealthy family, had a clear reputation, and had been repeatedly humiliated by her husband.

The union between Hipparete and Alcibiades had gotten off to a bad start. On a humorous bet with friends, Alcibiades had punched Hipparete's father Hipponicus III in the face. When the rest of town didn't get the joke and Alcibiades's reputation began to suffer, he went to Hipponicus, ripped off his own clothes, and begged the old man to flog and chastise him any way he saw fit. Hipponicus demurred, but was impressed by the young aristocrat's bravado and offered up Hipparete for marriage. Alcibiades took her in exchange for a dowry of ten talents. (He later bullied the family into giving him ten more.)

Hipparete was a dutiful wife, but she could not suffer Alcibiades's constant debaucheries, especially his habit of bringing home foreign prostitutes. Thinking she could influence him by making a dramatic move, she went to live with her brother. Alcibiades barely noticed. Finally, Hipparete went to court to plead for a divorce. She must have known that her chances were long, but at least this way Alcibiades risked being forced to return the twenty talents to her family. *That* got his attention.

The law courts were located in the agora, the city's tumultuous nerve center, where food vendors crowded with streetwalkers and magistrates and the shouts of Phoenician merchants competed with bell-clanging fish-mongers. Alcibiades was known as a powerful, brilliant, and temperamental figure, and was admired as a public speaker—which, in Athens, was saying quite a lot. This time, however, he was in no mood to talk: He had been disrespected by his wife and stood to lose control of a fortune. He marched through the agora, seized her, and carried her home.

As the unhappy couple passed the statues of Hermes that marked the agora's boundary, the crowd must have been entertained by the unusual (but not illegal) sight of one of the most admired men in Athens dragging his wife around like a barbarian. Far from trying to stop Alcibiades, they probably nodded their approval for taking the problem in hand. Plutarch, considering the case around 450 years later in his *Life of Alcibiades*, believed the Athenian was doing the right thing under the law:

> *I should explain that this violence of his was not regarded as being either inhuman or contrary to the law. Indeed, it would appear that the law, in laying it down that the wife who wishes to separate from her husband must attend the court in person, is actually designed to give the husband the opportunity to meet her and recover her.*

So much for an Athenian woman's right to complain of her husband's infidelity. Hipparete died in Alcibiades's house not long afterward. Years later, Alcibiades himself was killed in Turkey—by some accounts at the hands of the family of a wellborn girl he had seduced.[2]

WHERE THE WIFE in *Against the Stepmother* had probably tried to save her marriage by having her husband's slave spike his wine, the slave herself was attempting to preserve an intimacy she had no right to expect. By law, slaves weren't sentient beings worthy of protection; they were thus prey to all who owned or rented them. Not all slaves were prostitutes, and not all prostitutes slaves—but the two roles overlapped often enough. The slave in *Stepmother* was likely a hetaera, an upper-end courtesan of the type hired to spice up symposia with conversation, music, and dance. Their performance and sex fees were regulated and taxed, though price limits were ignored in bidding wars for the most desirable ones.

Despite the mercantile basis of their affections, many hetaerae grew close to their clients, and sometimes had children by them. But slave prostitutes were still slaves, and therefore vulnerable. Their owners had every right to sell them, syndicate their sexual services to multiple investors, or, as the slave in *Against the Stepmother* feared, consign them to brothels and forget about them.

A special legal council resolved investor disputes over prostitutes, which sometimes became complicated. One knotty court case, referred to as *On a Wound by Premeditation*, involved two men who had come to blows over an unnamed slave concubine. The problem arose following an agreement to settle a business dispute by exchanging property. The slave was transferred along with oxen and other goods, but the two men disagreed as to whether she would be available to both of them on a shared basis—as the defendant argued—or whether she would become the plaintiff's sole sexual property.

Fortified by an evening of drinking with "boys and flute-girls," the defendant broke into the plaintiff's house with some friends, grabbed a shard of broken pottery, and hit the plaintiff with it, blackening his eye. The plaintiff sued, claiming the defendant had tried to kill him. The latter testified that he had been too drunk to intend much of anything and was, in any event, justified in his attack, as the girl was his to share. He also argued that the slave was the one best equipped to resolve the issue, as she was a witness to nearly everything that had transpired. As the law held that a slave's testimony was only allowable if obtained by torture, the best thing to do, he added, was to inflict pain upon her and hear what she had to say. (The defendant may have cared for her, but not enough to think twice before putting her through agony.)

As with many Athenian court cases, the record is not complete. The defendant was facing exile, and the plaintiff risked losing control over the woman. If the case looked as though it was going to favor the defendant, the plaintiff probably would have agreed to serve up the slave for torture. However, unlike the slave in *Stepmother*, her life was probably safe—at least two men still desired her.[3]

THE THRUST OF ATHENIAN SEX LAW

In both *Stepmother* and *Wound*, sex was the *cause* of the offense, not the crime itself. There was little direct regulation of sexual behavior in Athens, or anywhere in ancient Greece for that matter. What laws there were advanced two main goals: safeguarding the honorable participation of male citizens in public life, and ensuring that fathers could leave property to their legitimate sons without complications. Unless one of these concerns was affected by sexual behavior, it is likely that a given carnal conduct was permitted.

A man's honor was a fragile bloom to be pampered and kept on display. Courts in the contemporary United States and United Kingdom often reject what is called "character evidence" on the grounds that a person's reputation does not indicate how he or she will act. The opposite was true in small, gossipy Athens, where a man's reputation was always up for review. In many cases, verdicts were based on a jury's opinion of a man's whole life, not just on the facts of the case at hand. Given that juries could number in the thousands, a good slice of the citizenry made these calls.

Athens was not a place for rugged individualists. A man of standing lived his life in public, away from his wife. "This is a peculiarity of ours," said Pericles. "[W]e do not say that a man who takes no interest in politics minds his private business. We say that he has no business at all."

Women could be sued and put to death, but were not allowed to testify in court. Instead, they testified out of court or their men testified for them.

Moreover, too much female company was potentially toxic to a man's reputation. A man "under the influence of a woman" was classified along with the old, insane, and sick as incompetent to testify in court.

Though men married unschooled ciphers and kept them in seclusion, they could never be too sure about their wives' loyalty. Women were thought to possess a molten sexuality that required constant vigilance. Rakes and roués lurked everywhere, ready to jump between the legs of hungry wives and wreck a good man's reputation. Moreover, female fidelity ensured that a man's children were indeed his own. His honor, in turn, depended on his ability to enforce that purity.

In early Greece, the head of an *oikos*, or extended household, guarded his family's reputation with his fists. But as the *oikos* became absorbed into larger communities, it was no longer practical for angry patriarchs and their clans to be storming around the countryside attacking every man they suspected of dishonoring them. The rules of urban society prevented blood feuds, but also raised the stakes of some sexual transgressions. No longer was sexual infidelity a private matter of concern; it became everyone's problem.[4]

CAUGHT IN THE ACT

Adultery was never far from the minds of Athenian husbands. By the time the city's earliest legislator, Draco, laid down its first written constitution, in about 620 BC, efforts were being made to reconcile honorable revenge with the prevention of inter-*oikos* warfare. Men could cheat on their wives, but could not take another man's woman. Doing so brought penalties, depending on where the taking took place. If the sex happened in the street, whether by force or not, the ravisher only paid a fine. If he crossed into the husband's house, and if the couple was caught in flagrante, he could be killed immediately. Sounds simple enough, but—as shown in the trial of one Euphiletus for the killing of his wife's lover, Eratosthenes—application of the rule could prove a challenge.

Eratosthenes was a practiced seducer of women. Rather than pluck his quarries from the safe ranks of foreigners, slaves, and prostitutes, he liked risk. That meant hanging around the few places where married women appeared, such as funerals and religious festivals. Indeed, Eratosthenes spotted Euphiletus's wife at a funeral, and later sent her messages via her maid, expressing his desire for her. She was interested, and the affair began.

Liaisons were made easier by the layout of the married couple's house. Men and women in Athens typically occupied different floors, which were connected only by a ladder. Euphiletus slept upstairs to allow his wife to care for their baby below. He later told the jury that he had slept peacefully, confident that his wife was "the chastest woman in all the city" and ignorant of the fact that she and Eratosthenes were going at it downstairs. "This went on for a long time," he said, "and I had not the slightest suspicion."

The lovers had one close call when Euphiletus returned early from a trip out of town. Eratosthenes hid while the wife gave Euphiletus a warm welcome, a good meal, and a taste of her love. All was peaceful until the baby started to cry downstairs; Euphiletus told his wife to go calm the child. She resisted, saying she was worried he would take the opportunity to violate the upstairs maid. "Once before, too, when you were drunk, you pulled her about," the wife joked. Euphiletus laughed too, nevertheless insisting that she go downstairs. She followed his instructions, but first "playfully" locked his bedroom door and put away the ladder. The following morning, she returned to him, wearing makeup. He asked what all the nighttime creaking had been about, and was told that she had had to go to a neighbor's house to rekindle the lamp in the child's room.

With Euphiletus missing such obvious signs of his wife's infidelity, the affair could have gone on indefinitely had not one of Eratosthenes's rejected lovers decided to retaliate against him. She sent her "old hag" of a maid to tell Euphiletus the truth: "[Eratosthenes] has debauched not only your wife," the maid said, "but many others besides; he makes an art of it." Euphiletus went to his own maid and told her to tell him the truth or "be whipped and thrown into a mill." She took the first option.

To the jury, Euphiletus described the ambush he staged a few evenings later:

> *Eratosthenes made his entry; and the maid wakened me and told me that he was in the house.*
>
> *I told her to watch the door; and going downstairs, I slipped out noiselessly.*
>
> *I went to the houses of one man after another. Some I found at home; others, I was told, were out of town. So collecting as many as I could of those who were there, I went back. We procured torches from the shop near by, and entered my house. The door had been left open by arrangement with the maid.*
>
> *We forced the bedroom door. The first of us to enter saw him still lying beside my wife. Those who followed saw him standing naked on the bed. I knocked him down, members of the jury, with one blow. I then twisted his hands behind his back and tied them. And then I asked him why he was committing this crime against me, of breaking into my house.*
>
> *He answered that he admitted his guilt; but he begged and besought me not to kill him, to accept a money payment instead. But I replied: "It is not I who shall be killing you, but the law of the state, which you, in transgressing, have valued less highly than your own pleasure. You have preferred to commit this great crime against my wife and my children, rather than to obey the law and be of decent behaviour."*
>
> *Thus, members of the jury, this man met the fate which the laws prescribe to wrongdoers of his kind.*

Eratosthenes's fate was death on the spot at the hands of Euphiletus. A murder prosecution by the dead man's family followed.

At trial, the jury would judge Eratosthenes as either a guilty murderer or an innocent wronged husband, nothing in between. Draco's laws could allow Euphiletus to beat a murder rap *if* he could prove he caught his rival *while* having sex with his wife. If Euphiletus had only found them lying in bed relaxing after making love, it would have been too late. Euphiletus's recruitment of his neighbors to accompany him as he burst in on the couple and his statement that Eratosthenes was "still lying next to" his wife and that others saw him "standing naked on the bed" were meant to fit the case into the law. Whether it was true is impossible to say, and we do not know the jury's decision, but Euphiletus had done a good job of maximizing his chances of walking free.

Draco's laws only limited punishments against men who killed their rivals. Other laws set out the consequences for unauthorized sex by females. Unmarried virgins would see their marriage value diminish in the event of illicit sex, and to recover the loss their fathers were allowed to sell them into slavery—even if the sex had in fact been rape. Married women who committed adultery put their husbands in the position of being required to divorce them or lose their own civic rights. This stipulation was intended to prevent couples from trapping men and extorting payoffs. Women caught in the act were barred from wearing ornaments and participating in religious life: Any citizen had the right to slap around adulteresses who later showed up to sacred ceremonies. Such sanctions were harsh, but far less severe than the death and mutilations faced by adulterous wives under Babylonian, biblical, and Roman law.[5]

FISH, VEGETABLES, AND HOT PITCH

Euphiletus took a big chance by killing Eratosthenes. All trials are gambles, and in the rowdy Athenian courts the judgment could well have gone against him. He had other options in considering revenge against

Eratosthenes while retaining his honor, such as imprisoning the seducer in his house and ransoming him to his family. He could also have taken Eratosthenes to the authorities for prosecution. Had Eratosthenes denied the charge and been found guilty, he would not have faced execution. Instead, Euphiletus would have been allowed to beat him up in public and ram foreign objects such as spiky scorpion fish and large radishes into his anus. Euphiletus also could have removed Eratosthenes's pubic hair with hot pitch, or even plucked it out. (One comic poet asked how men "ever manage to fuck married women when, while making their move, they remember the laws of Draco.")

Severe though the pain might be, the emphasis would have been on degrading Eratosthenes and others like him by making them take on "womanly" characteristics. Depilation was a female practice, so forcing it on a man was to feminize him. It was acceptable for women to submit to anal penetration, but deplorable in the case of freeborn men. These punishments not only bruised the adulterer's reputation, but also gave the aggrieved husband the pleasure of reciprocating a vicarious sexual attack to settle the matter.

Sparta had no such preoccupations with adultery. Because men there spent so much time with their military units, it was impossible to expect women to remain faithful and still guarantee a steady supply of babies. Marriage was an institution meant to deliver warriors to the state, not heirs to the father. The Spartan government couldn't care less where a woman's child came from, so long as the father was a citizen. With that objective in mind, an elderly man was free to ask a young one to deposit "good seed" in his wife, and a healthy man in a barren marriage could impregnate another man's spouse if the woman's husband agreed. (Nevertheless, Spartan law encouraged passionate marriages. Husbands and wives were kept apart for long periods to increase desire and make children as energetic as their parents' lovemaking.)[6]

AN INSTRUMENT OF PUNISHMENT

• • •

In ancient Greece and Rome, the husbands of adulterous women had several options for revenge. Most of the punishments allowed a husband to shame his rival by inserting foreign objects, such as spiky fish and radishes, into his anus. ©WELLCOME LIBRARY, LONDON

HOMOSEXUAL LOVE—AND BERRIES

Sex was more of a contest for Athenians than an expression of affection. The partner in the active role prevailed to his masculine glory, while the penetrated one played the woman and was thereby defeated. Somewhere in this harsh exchange was what Plato saw as the highest form of love.

Much of the Greek world was dazzlingly permissive in its attitudes toward homoeroticism and sex between men. From a modern perspective, Greece was an Eden of homosexuality, where male-male affection was prized. Athens's venerated lawgiver Solon wrote erotic poetry to boys, and the city's great men openly sought the company of male youths. Taking this view one step further, the United States would only match the tolerance of Athens about three thousand years later, in 2003, when the Supreme Court nullified most American antisodomy laws.

Can we say, then, that the United States has finally begun to follow the ancient Greek example, allowing its millions of gay citizens to take their rightful place as social equals to heterosexuals? Not at all. Even now, a man caught engaging in the type of homosexual sex admired in ancient Greece (i.e., older men taking adolescent boys) will do extensive jail time. If he manages to serve his sentence without being killed by other prisoners, he faces a lifetime of ankle bracelets, residence restrictions, and inclusion on public lists of sex offenders. No one but the most strident of civil libertarians would defend him, much less talk to him. He would be known forever as a pedophile, the worst sort of social deviant.

By contrast, the same-gender conduct decriminalized in the twentieth century by Western courts, that of two adults engaging in "sexual practices common to a homosexual lifestyle," would have been revolting to most ancient Greeks. "Homosexual lifestyles" as such did not exist, nor did the concept.

Again, the key distinction for the Greeks (as well as for other ancient societies) was in the taking and giving. To be the active partner was to embody *male* qualities—powerful, principled, in charge. The partner in the passive role was simply *female*, even if he had a penis. Thus there were no explicit prohibitions against same-sex relations, but, depending on one's age, class, and position in bed, homosexual sex could be risky indeed. To make the wrong male into a female was a potentially life-threatening gamble, made even more treacherous by the city's confusing web of laws and customs.

Greek attitudes toward homosexuality resulted in part from a cultural belief in the origins of the sex drive. Plato traced it back to humanity's initial division into three genders: male, female, and both at once. Originally, humans had two faces, two sets of genitalia, four legs, and four arms each. The original body design of these proto-people worked so well that they grew uppity in the face of the gods, which prompted Zeus to chop them all in two. The result was human beings as we know them: creatures condemned to a lifelong search for their missing halves. Those who came from androgynes craved the opposite sex. Women hewn from double-females sought women, and those cut from double-men were attracted to males. The relief people feel when they conjoin with others in the same lonely condition is a key aspect of what Plato called love.

Plato himself made no secret of his preferences. Those cut from double-males "are the best of their generation," he said, "bold, brave, and masculine." Naturally, they had no interest in marrying women, "although they are forced to do this by convention."

These ideas carried some weight as late as the turn of the twentieth century, when Oscar Wilde referenced *The Symposium* to the jury presiding at his first trial for sodomy. In a packed London courtroom, he intoned Plato in defending the "love that dare not speak its name," describing it as "the noblest form of affection" and stating that "there is nothing unnatural about it."[7] (See Chapter Eight.)

Not all of Greece agreed with Plato's ideas, of course, but many Greek communities incorporated male-male sex into their educational systems. In Crete, men symbolically kidnapped boys and took them to the countryside for manly outdoor training. After a few months, the boys were given military kits and welcomed as adults. The process was conducted along strict guidelines, and the boys had a duty to report whether or not their teachers pleased them sexually; if they did not, the boys were permitted to get rid of them.

Spartan boys were entrusted to the care of respected men at the age of twelve. Penalties awaited men who refused to provide such tutelage, or who did so poorly. The relationships were definitely sexual, as attested by the twenty-six-hundred-year-old carved inscriptions still visible on a seaside rock wall in the former Spartan colony of Thera. There, a few dozen meters from the old temple of Apollo, Spartan men brought in expert stone carvers to record their accomplishments: "Here Krimon had anal intercourse with his *pais* [boy], the brother of Bathycles," reads one inscription.

Cultures that permitted homosexual sex established regulations as to how and when it could occur, especially in Athens, where young males were protected from unauthorized advances. Slaves suffered fifty lashes for courting free boys or even following them around, and death awaited any man who walked into a school without permission. Those allowed to teach boys were required to be older than forty, when their ardor was believed to have diminished. Athletic coaches were trusted least. According to one source:

> A wrestling master, taking advantage of the occasion when he was giving a lesson to a smooth boy, forced him to kneel down, and set about working on his middle, stroking the berries with one hand. But by chance the master of the house came, wanting the boy. The teacher threw him quickly on his back, getting astride of him and grasping him by the throat. But the master of the house, who was not unversed in wrestling, said to him, Stop, you are smuggering the boy.

None of this seems to have stopped the likes of Socrates and the orator-statesman Aeschines from passing days at the gymnasium, where they spent much of their time ogling pretty boys. The temptation was evidently too great.[8]

ONCE A HUSTLER . . .

If the idealized union of Greek males was an exchange of sex for learning and social connections, such arrangements were rare. Far more frequent were men and boys selling their bodies for money. These male *pornai* (prostitutes) hustled the brothels and streets and took all comers, even slaves. Higher-end gigolos were kept by one man or shared among a group. Athenian men, married or not, suffered no penalty or shame for using male prostitutes so long as they were not adults or wellborn. The idea of sex between adult men was especially distasteful, and bachelorhood was avoided.

Prostitutes carried on their trade legally and paid taxes, but were forever barred from participating in public life, including court cases. Many former male *pornai* presumably kept themselves far enough below the radar to avoid trouble, but not everyone could. In one well-known case, a man rose from a youthful career as a prostitute to the cream of Athenian society, only to have his past return in court decades later and swallow him up. The main issues in *Against Timarchus*, as the case was known, had nothing to do with whoring. Timarchus's accuser, the aforementioned Aeschines, happily admitted to being a "nuisance" in the gymnasia and getting into fights over boys. He also had no quarrel with male prostitution per se. He did, however, vehemently object to Timarchus's right to appear in court against him. In one of legal history's great "gotcha" moments, Aeschines defeated Timarchus in a major case by exploiting his past as a dockside hustler.

The original question was whether or not Aeschines had sold out Athens in negotiating a peace treaty with an aggressive foreign power.

In 347 BC, Athens had sent Aeschines and two other prominent citizens to discuss peace with Macedonia's King Philip II. The irascible king, best remembered as the father of Alexander the Great, had the better strategic position, and forced Athens into a deal that put it at a disadvantage. The agreement was received badly back home, and resulted in finger-pointing between the diplomats.

The result was a series of court clashes between some of Athens's most outsized personalities. The orator Demosthenes rounded on Aeschines, but his charges against the latter were grave enough to prompt him to seek the prestigious support of Timarchus, who had already authored one hundred pieces of legislation. Timarchus and Demosthenes accused Aeschines of treason, i.e., taking payoffs from Philip. Everyone on the jury knew the players by reputation, so it must have been quite a shock when Aeschines managed to change the subject from his own alleged corruption to Timarchus's prior sex life.

Aeschines accomplished this by filing his own suit against Timarchus. He had only a few hours to speak, so he delivered his twenty-thousand-word speech at warp speed, steamrolling the jury with details about how Timarchus had, in his youth, bounced from house to house, giving his "well-developed, young" body to hungry men and even to a slave. "This foul wretch here was not disturbed by the fact that he was going to defile himself," boomed Aeschines, "but thought of one thing only, of getting [the slave] to be paymaster for his own disgusting lusts; to the question of virtue or of shame he never gave a thought." A man so weak, so willing to turn himself into a "creature with the body of a man defiled with the sins of a woman," he said, could neither accuse him of treason nor show his face in court.

Undoubtedly it was the seriousness of the treason charge that made Aeschines strike back so hard. He must also have been concerned that because Timarchus's wrongdoing had occurred so many years earlier, the jury might be prone to making light of the issue. Whatever the reason, he smeared his opponent as one who had not only done wrong but was, in light of his past, incapable of ever doing right.

The strategy worked. Aeschines won by a narrow margin, and Timarchus later hanged himself. In the fray, the critical question of whether Athens had indeed been sold out to a dangerous enemy was subordinated, at least for a while, to the popular fascination with dirty sex. This was not the last time a public figure's sex life would be hauled out of obscurity to wreck him politically, but in its scope and effect *Against Timarchus* remains a milestone. Prominent men like Timarchus, who lived in the public eye, were probably subject to stricter behavioral standards than the average citizens sitting on the jury. Still, the law forbade all men who "feminized" themselves for money, or who seemed to enjoy it too much, from public life. The defeat of Timarchus was a lesson in caution for all Athenians.[9]

FINDING A BALANCE

Given this minefield of punishment and shame, how were male-male relationships to be managed? Could anyone ever have passive sex and still have a civic profile? Not likely, if he was an adult. For a boy it was still risky, as *Against Timarchus* shows, but possible, if rigid courtship rules were followed.

"A love affair in itself is neither right nor wrong, but right when it is conducted rightly and wrong when it is conducted wrongly," said Plato. A good male lover was supposed to be "constant" in his feelings, and love the boy's character as well as his body. When this noble purpose was matched by the boy's interest in acquiring wisdom, the union was "heavenly." "[T]hen and then alone is it right for a boyfriend to gratify his lover."

Homoerotic love was almost a zero-sum equation in which a man's honor in winning a boy was equaled, potentially, by the boy's dishonor in being taken. If the boy submitted too readily, he risked being viewed as woman-like or even bestial. If he resisted too much, he stood to lose the sponsorship of an elder who could help him get ahead in the world. His ambition was, in a sense, achieved at the potential cost of his status.

That said, adolescent boys were the main objects of desire for Athenian men, and they did submit. Greek boys (at least those belonging to the elite) were taught to accept sexual intercourse in the same way that respectable Victorian ladies were taught to put up with it: not as a pleasure, but as a duty. It was wrong to be caught quickly, and boys were supposed to maximize their advantages by playing suitors off one another. The cat-and-mouse process bestowed honor on the successful pursuer, and protected the boy.

In almost all other cases, it was ruinous to play the passive role. One vase painting shows a happy Greek soldier, erection in hand, about to sodomize his Persian counterpart—this was not an erotic image; rather, it expressed Persia's humiliating defeat by the Greeks in easy-to-understand terms. On the home front, comic poets and playwrights had a large reserve of humorous epithets for men who took it from behind. Aristophanes was the peerless leader of those who enjoyed baiting passive homosexuals, repeatedly calling attention to the supposed elasticity of their sphincter muscles and effeminate mannerisms.

Those men who took the laboring oar in anal sex suffered no opprobrium and saw no need to hide their desires. Indeed, the anuses ridiculed with such glee by Aristophanes were also celebrated in poetry as delectable "buds" and "figs." In a poem by Rhianus, a sweetly oiled "backside" is asked by an anxious lover whom it loves best. The answer—"Menecrates, darling"—is not what the lover wants to hear.[10]

DO ASK, DO TELL

One type of homoerotic relationship, praised by Aeschines in *Against Timarchus*, was the love between soldiers. He celebrated the intense bond between the Trojan War hero Achilles and the younger warrior Patroclus. Theirs was a love that "had its source in passion," Aeschines argued, and represented everything admirable. Honoring Achilles in a public speech was an easy shot, like extolling the virtues of motherhood today or the valor of a nation's own troops in battle. It surely came off well, despite its irrelevance to the case. Aeschines was a pompous blowhard, but his references to Achilles and Patroclus underlined the general belief that love and sex among soldiers was something to be emulated, not punished.

Far from barring homosexuality in the military, as the United States famously did in 1942, or embracing a "Don't Ask, Don't Tell" policy as it did fifty-one years later, Greek societies saw no incompatibility between male-male love and military discipline. As we have seen, pederastic coming-of-age rituals in Crete and Sparta served mainly as preparation for military service. In Thebes, however, the ideal of homosexual warriors reached its apotheosis.

In 378 BC, the Theban army organized an elite unit of 150 pairs of "young men attached to each other by personal affection," which formed the core of its famed military machine. The group became known as the Sacred Band of Thebes, the descriptor "sacred" most likely deriving from Plato's *Symposium*, in which he refers to a male lover as a divine friend; but Plutarch makes it clear that the Sacred Band was organized for tactical reasons:

> For *men of the same tribe or family little value one another when dangers press; but a band cemented by friendship grounded upon love is never to be broken, and invincible; since the lovers, ashamed to be base in sight of their beloved, and the beloved before their lovers, willingly rush into danger for the relief of one another.*

The pairs of lover-soldiers were, at first, distributed throughout the Theban infantry, but later consolidated into a single fearsome unit. They were undefeated until they and their Athenian allies met up with Philip II and his son Alexander at the Battle of Chaeronea in 338 BC. The Athenians were routed, which left the Thebans alone, surrounded, and overwhelmed. Despite certain death, they refused to surrender, and kept fighting until they were annihilated. Rather than cheer his victory by taunting the vanquished soldiers or abusing their bodies, Philip had only respect for them:

> [W]hen Philip, after the fight, took a view of the slain, and came to the place where the three hundred that fought his phalanx lay dead together, he wondered, and understanding that it was the band of lovers, he shed tears and said, "Perish any man who suspects that these men either did or suffered anything that was base."

Thirty-eight years after that battle, the Thebans erected a giant stone lion on a pedestal at the burial site of the Sacred Band. The restored statue still stands as a monument to some of the bravest—and gayest—soldiers ever to fight on the field of honor.[11]

DARK PLEASURES, BRIGHT CONVERSATION

However beguiling fifteen-year-old hairless boys might have been to aristocratic men, it doesn't take long to consume a fig. Callow adolescents could not have been interesting company for men so far beyond them in education and experience. Here women return to the picture, in the form of the hetaerae, that sophisticated class of prostitutes who passed long evenings with the city's prominent men. (Demosthenes observed that Athenian men kept wives for "the production of legitimate children," concubines for the "care of the body," and companions for "pleasure.") Many of these women stimulated the mind as well as the body—Greek courtesans were known throughout the ancient world for their refinement and ability to match wits with the best minds in Athens. Top-tier courtesans often enjoyed better lives than their clients' wives.

That many of them survived childhood, much less became beloved companions to the likes of Pericles, spoke to their scrappy ingenuity.

Many hetaerae either were the children of prostitutes or were acquired by brothel-keepers after being left to die as babies. If they later showed an aptitude on their backs, they could try to persuade their clients to buy them out and invest in their liberty. Under these conditions, and without the benefit of formal instruction, some managed to learn music, philosophy, and rhetoric.

Hetaerae didn't have long to make their mark. In a culture even more worshipful of youth than ours today, time was their main enemy. Their prime earning years were often spent laboring as slave prostitutes. By the time they scraped together enough money to purchase their freedom, many had, in the words of the comic poet Philetairos, "rotted away fucking" and were no longer able to command top fees. Facing a decline in earning power, the more enterprising of them became brothel-keepers themselves, buying babies and girls and living off their earnings. This kind of work generated more than its share of litigation.

IN THE EARLY fourth century BC, one married man's love for an elderly prostitute in his employ caused an inheritance battle. This fellow, Euktmon, was advanced in years himself, and had money, a family, and a number of profitable whorehouses. One of his prostitutes, the well-known Alce, worked at his brothel in Piraeus until she became too old to generate much money. She remained at the house where she serviced a few clients, had a couple of babies, and plotted a way to survive in her old age. First, she convinced Euktemon to let her manage his brothel in the potters' district of Athens. Then she set out to manage Euktemon himself. Despite his ninety-six years, the records show that he began to spend far more time at the brothel than was necessary to collect the receipts:

> Sometimes [Euktemon] took his meals with [Alce], leaving his wife and children and his own home. In spite of the protests of his wife and sons, not only did he not cease to go there but eventually

lived there entirely, and was reduced to such a condition by drugs or disease or some other cause, that he was persuaded by the woman to introduce the elder of the two boys to the members of his ward under his name.

When Euktemon's son resisted his father's attempt to legitimize Alce's son, the old man threatened to marry her and recognize her offspring as his heirs. His son decided to cut his losses by agreeing to the legitimization, so long as the boy's inheritance was limited to a single farm.[12]

Another lawsuit involved a man who had bought a slave boy from a courtesan named Antigone, but claimed that he was so aroused when he made the deal that he didn't realize he was being tricked. The purchaser, Epicrates, told the jury that Antigone and her partner in the sale, Athenogenes, convinced him to buy the boy's brother and father as well, and take on their debts in the perfume business. "It is a trifling amount," Athenogenes reportedly told him, "counterbalanced by the stocks in the shop, sweet oil, scent-boxes, myrrh . . . which will easily cover all the debts." Epicrates testified that he did not pay much attention to the contract when it was read to him. He could think only of the moment when he would have the slave boy to himself. The sale went through, and Antigone used her portion of the money to buy another child prostitute.

Not long afterward, Epicrates regained his senses and realized that he had taken on more debt than he could pay. He gathered some friends and went to confront Athenogenes. A crowd gathered, a fight erupted, and a lawsuit resulted. At the trial, Epicrates tried to persuade the jury to let him out of the contract. There is no record as to whether or not he was successful, but it does not seem likely that a jury would agree that sexual excitement should excuse a buyer from reading what he signed.

ANTIGONE'S AND ATHENOGENES'S legal problems were nothing compared to the tumultuous existence of the Corinthian hetaera Neaera. The lawsuit *Against Neaera* describes her fight against accusations that she, a foreigner, had illegally married an Athenian man and fraudulently passed her daughter off as an Athenian citizen. The case, which was at least the third one filed in Athens against Neaera and her husband, threw her entire life open for inspection, covering decades in the sex trade. According to Neaera's accuser, Apollodorus, she was sold as a little girl to Nikarete, a Corinthian madam with a "good eye" for the earning potential of children. There, in the prostitution vortex that was Corinth (the city lent its name to the Greek verb *korinthiazein*, meaning "to fornicate"), Neaera was put to work before being physically able to have intercourse, and spent her early years learning how to please men and succeed in the business. To command a higher price, Nikarete marketed Neaera as one of her daughters.

It was tough work, but at least Neaera got to travel. One of the business's best customers was the famous Athenian orator Lysias (the same as hired by the stepson in *Against the Stepmother*), who was smitten with Neaera's "sister" Metaneira. As a gift, he brought Metaneira, Nikarete, and Neaera to the religious festival at Eleusis, where he paid for their initiation into the sacred mysteries of the goddess Demeter.

After about twenty years in Nikarete's employ, Neaera was sold to two customers as their shared sex slave. The three-thousand-drachma sale price was equivalent to five years' worth of a laborer's wages, but the buyers must have figured it was less than paying retail every time they wanted her company. The arrangement worked fine for about a year until the men each decided to get married and lighten their financial burdens. They offered Neaera her freedom at a substantial discount of two thousand drachmae if she left Corinth forever.

This was the chance for which Neaera had been waiting many years. Nothing was going to stand in the way of her freedom, not even the boorish perversions of the man who gave her the money, Phrynion. He brought her to Athens, where he "had intercourse with her openly and whenever and wherever he wished"—outrageous conduct even by local standards. At one banquet, Phrynion allowed everyone present, including slaves, to have their way with her while she slept in a drunken stupor.

Neaera was used to humiliation, but this last act went too far. She waited until the time was right and packed up her clothes, along with some of Phrynion's household possessions and slaves, and left for Megara to start up her own brothel. The business foundered, but Neaera's personal life improved when she met the Athenian Stephanos, who agreed to take her and her children back to Athens. Stephanos was kinder to Neaera than Phrynion—their thirty-year relationship implies devotion on his part—but he had a long list of enemies. Once back in town, Neaera began to lure wealthy men to their home for sex, where Stephanos waited to "discover" them in the act and shake down the unsuspecting mark for money.

Their racket continued until Phrynion showed up. He sued Stephanos for receiving both Neaera (whom he deemed a runaway slave) and the property she had nicked from his house. Rather than risk everything at trial, Stephanos agreed to have Neaera return most of the stolen belongings, and further allowed Phrynion to take her home for sex on a set schedule.

Disposing of Phrynion turned out to be the simplest of Neaera and Stephanos's legal worries. Some years later, Stephanos gave Neaera's wild-child daughter Phano away in marriage to the sober Phrastor, assuring him that the girl was Athenian. The marriage was a disaster. Phano refused to assume the reserved manner of a good Athenian wife, and was thrown out of Phrastor's house. He filed a lawsuit claiming he had been defrauded into believing Phano was a citizen, and not the daughter of a Corinthian whore. Stephanos countersued for the return of Phano's large dowry, but must have realized that he was going to lose the case, and settled. Phrastor kept the money.

Phano moved back home, joined the family extortion business, and sparked more litigation. This time, Stephanos "caught" her in bed with Epainetos, a former client of Neaera's, and held him in the house until he extracted a promise to pay three thousand drachmae. However, as soon as

Epainetos was released he filed suit against Stephanos, claiming that there had been no cause to hold him. Phano was, he charged, no ordinary daughter living in a common Athenian home. Rather, she was a prostitute, and the household a brothel. Again, Stephanos saw that he would be defeated in court, and gave up his claim.

By the time Apollodorus sued Neaera, he had already faced off in court against Stephanos on other matters, and hated him. His lawsuit, which was based on Neaera having passed herself off as a respectable Athenian wife and mother, was admittedly brought out of spite against Stephanos. The fact that Apollodorus was not directly affected by Neaera's actions didn't matter; anyone could sue for violations of the citizenship laws. As Apollodorus harangued the jury for three hours, giving all of the details of Neaera's "service in every kind of pleasure," the former hetaera must have felt that her luck was running out. If she lost the case, she faced a return to slavery. (Stephanos, moreover, stood to lose his civil rights as an Athenian citizen.) We have no record of the speeches for the defense, nor do we know the jury's verdict, but it seems well within likelihood that her lifelong jig was up.[13]

NEXT TO NEAERA, Athens's best-known courtesan was Aspasia, the brilliant mistress of Pericles. The great statesman-general's love for her was open and passionate, to the point that some historians believe he got rid of his wife to live with her. Most marital relations in Athens were arid affairs, but Pericles felt tender affection for Aspasia. "Every day, when he went out to the marketplace and returned, he greeted her with a kiss," wrote Plutarch. Far from the model of respectable Athenian wives who were supposed to be ashamed even to be seen, Aspasia's life was lived in public. Even Socrates took his disciples to learn rhetoric from her.

Aspasia had traveled a long way up to breathe the rarefied air of Athenian high society. A native of Miletus, she had most likely come to the city under the usual grim circumstances of foreign-born prostitutes—enslaved and exploited. Eventually she obtained her freedom, setting up a high-end bawdy house that functioned as both a philosophy salon and an urban resort for wellborn men seeking good food and sexual adventure.

Aspasia's attachment to Pericles was both a benefit and a risk to him. As the case of Timarchus demonstrates, sexual misadventure was a trap for politicians in Athens. Pericles's many enemies spared no effort in using Aspasia as a way to get to him. She was reviled as the product of sodomy and as a skin trader who filled "all of Greece . . . with her little harlots." Despite her acclaimed political wisdom, she was also accused of influencing Pericles to act against the city's best interests. (It was said that she had goaded Pericles into a war with Samos, a rival of her native Miletus.) Aristophanes took these accusations one step further, in satire, supposing that Aspasia had even convinced Pericles to start the catastrophic Peloponnesian War after two of her prostitutes had been stolen by residents of Sparta's ally, Megara.

Finally, Aspasia was sued on a charge of "impiety," allegations of which included procuring freeborn girls to satisfy Pericles's perversions and defiling temples. In a monumentally dramatic scene, Pericles—preeminent man of the city, military and political leader, orator, builder of the Parthenon—went to court personally on her behalf. According to Plutarch, he "burst into floods of tears" before the jury, begging them to acquit Aspasia. The jury complied.[14]

It is virtually impossible to imagine a present-day political leader pleading with a jury to show mercy to his mistress, much less tearfully acknowledging his love for her. Think of Bill Clinton's conduct when sued for exposing himself and demanding sex from Paula Jones, an Arkansas state employee. He denied everything, hired top Washington legal talent, and eventually won the case on a procedural technicality. Before that happened, however, he lied under oath about his encounters with another young woman, Monica Lewinsky—a denial that was easily disproved and gave his enemies in Congress a pretext on which to impeach him. That

Clinton beat the impeachment and served out his presidency with much popular support only highlights the paradox: Would any of his loyalists, including his wife, have stayed with him had he acknowledged his sexual relationship with Lewinsky or, worse, that he cared for her? Probably not. (The president's affectionate gift to her of a copy of Walt Whitman's *Leaves of Grass* was never explained—with good reason.)

Pericles took a chance by defending Aspasia, but that was not the end of their legal struggles. Their next obstacle arose from a law Pericles had championed years earlier, which denied citizenship to children whose parents were not both native Athenians. Some time after the impiety trial, illness killed Pericles's sister and his two sons by his first wife. With no living heirs, he asked his countrymen to accept his son by Aspasia as legitimate. The Athenians understood that his misfortunes "represented a kind of penalty which he had paid for his pride and presumption," and granted his request.

Let's Make a Deal

As the Classical period in Greece gave way to the more cosmopolitan Hellenistic Age, women with money began to demand more equality from their husbands. For example, a marriage contract between two Greeks in Egypt, dated 311 bc, included the requirement that the husband remain sexually loyal to his wife—at least at home. The bride, Demetria, had some bargaining power: She brought one thousand drachmae worth of clothing and ornaments to the union, which was evidently enough to get her husband, Heraclides, to agree to refrain from doing what Greek husbands had done for centuries:

> It shall not be lawful for Heraclides to bring home another woman
> for himself in such a way as to inflict contumely on Demetria, nor
> to have children by another woman, nor to indulge in fraudulent
> machinations against Demetria on any pretext.

The contract had sharp teeth. Had Heraclides broken the deal, he would have been forced to return the dowry and also forfeit one thousand drachmae worth of his own property. He was still allowed to visit all the prostitutes he wanted—he just could not bring them by the house or sap the family's finances in taking care of his stray children.

Of course, the curb on Heraclides's freedom with other women did not imply matching liberties for Demetria. Any infidelities on her part were still strictly forbidden under the marriage contract—although it is interesting that the husband felt the need to reaffirm this in writing rather than just rely on the law. However, changes were coming, at least with regard to the number of people who were allowed to control her life. Local law still permitted a father to step in and dissolve his daughter's marriage at will, but as Egypt came under Roman control, married women would be allowed to defy their fathers' demands and remain with their husbands.[15]

Rome, of course, was then transforming itself from a backwater city-state on the Italian peninsula into a territory-gobbling war machine. By the mid-second century BC, it had rolled over Greece and was rapidly Hellenizing itself. The Athenian Greek "phallocracy," as the historian Eva Keuls so nicely puts it, would mix with Rome's pagan—and, later, Christian—values to create a long-lasting model for modern sexual regulation.

3

. . .

IMPERIAL BEDROOMS:
SEX AND THE STATE IN ANCIENT ROME

O N THE BANKS of the Tiber River stood a sacred grove of trees where the worship of the wine god Bacchus by his cult had got way out of hand. It was in the shadows of those trees that an episode began—one of many in ancient Rome—in which power politics fed on sexual scandal. The bacchanals might have been morally and sexually corrupt, but they were never a serious threat to Rome. Nevertheless, their orgies and especially the liberties they took with wellborn young men became pretexts for years of jolting government repressions. In 186 BC, the sounds of bacchanalian ecstasies ringing out of the woods were suddenly replaced by the cries of thousands of people being killed.

The worship of Bacchus (Greek: Dionysus) was nothing new in urban Rome or elsewhere in the Mediterranean, nor was the cult's association with sexual abandon. Dionysian festivals in Athens were famously drunken and lewd. In Egypt the god was honored with parades featuring 180-foot golden phalluses. However, the sect had never been officially integrated into Roman religion, and it was now growing in numbers and in disorderliness. The cult in Italy was previously all-female, but men and women were now worshipping together, greasing themselves up with wine and crossing all sexual boundaries. "Every person found at hand that sort of enjoyment to which he was disposed by the passion predominant in his nature," wrote the Roman historian Livy, including "frequent pollutions of men with each other."

The celebrants drifted from sexual vice to sorcery and other crimes. "From this storehouse of villainy," Livy wrote, they plotted frauds and forgeries, committed murders, and cast dark spells. The men predicted the future as their bodies contorted on the ground. The women, their hair disheveled, ran down to the river, where they plunged blazing torches into the water and then pulled them out still burning. The bacchanals couldn't hide their revels—bacchanalia—in the crowded city, so they beat drums and crashed symbols to make sure that "none of the cries uttered by the persons suffering violence or murder could be heard." Those percussive noises had become common of late: The cult's celebrations had increased to five times per month from three days per year.

Like everyone else, Rome's senators heard the racket, but they were still shocked when they learned what the cult had got up to, especially with regard to the bacchanals' initiation of Rome's favorite sons. Well-born young men were being hazed into the group with sodomy, and killed if they resisted. The whole matter came to light when the consul Spurius Postumius Albinus, one of Rome's two top officials, learned that an aristocratic young man named Publius Aebutius was about to be served up to the cult by his parents.

Aebutius's mother and stepfather had been stealing from him for some time, and wanted him neutralized before he found out. Killing Aebutius was too risky, so they planned to ruin him with bacchanalian sexual disgrace. Ignorant of what awaited him, he told his favorite prostitute, Hispala, that he would have to refuse her affections because bacchanalian rules required him to abstain from sex before his initiation. Horrified, Hispala cried out that he was being set up for a bad fall. She told Aebutius that she knew from personal experience that young men were raped by the cult's priests and then went on to do "everything that was abominable" themselves. She begged Aebutius with copious tears to promise her that he would steer clear of the bacchanals. He listened to her, and went to his parents to tell them of his refusal to join the cult. They took the news poorly, accusing him of disrespecting them and the gods, and even worse, of being too weak to resist the sexual lure of the "serpent" Hispala even for a few days. Aebutius was literally thrown out of the house.

In gossipy Rome, it wasn't long before the young man's problems came to Postumius's attention. He summoned Hispala to tell him what she knew. Shaking with terror in his presence, she told him that the bacchanals had begun to admit males after a priestess brought her own sons into the rites. Young men all over Italy were now joining. In fact, initiates were restricted to people no more than twenty years old. At such an age, she explained, they were "more liable to suffer deception and personal abuse" and accept the priestesses' command to "think nothing unlawful." Postumius checked out the story and realized that he had a whale of a good—and exploitable—scandal on his hands. He got to work organizing the repression of the cult.

This story of Aebutius and Hispala, told by Livy about two hundred years after the events took place, is too dramatic to be entirely credible. An aristocratic boy—the hope of Rome—is rescued from his thieving parents at the last minute by a whore with a heart of gold; a heroic consul takes action to save the boy, and Rome, from perdition. It's too much. Yet whether or not Livy gilded the narrative lily is beside the point. However the subject of bacchanalian excesses got to Postumius, the cult was made to order as an excuse for a decisive exercise of state police authority. Young male Roman citizens were now involved: That changed everything.

Rome was still reeling from the memory of almost losing a war with Carthage. The city had been thrown into turmoil after losing more than fifty thousand men to the general Hannibal in the Battle of Cannae in 216 BC. Roman control of Italy was still tentative. Nothing was more important than Rome's military, and nothing would be allowed to weaken it. The army's ranks were open only to upper-class Roman citizens; Postumius could accuse the bacchanals of enfeebling the men Rome relied on most by taking in youngsters such as Aebutius. In a rousing speech, the consul demanded to know whether Rome's weapons should be entrusted to "wretches brought out of that temple of obscenity," and whether those "contaminated with their own foul debaucheries and those of others [should] be champions for the chastity of [Rome's] wives and children."

The answer: no. The cult was infecting Rome like a disease, Postumius warned, and had to be put down. The Senate gave him and Rome's other consul unprecedented powers to root out suspects, and to execute them without the possibility of appeal. Almost immediately, the consuls unleashed a massive wave of terror that lasted two years and claimed about seven thousand lives throughout Italy. The crackdown, which included political enemies as well as fornicators, caused panic and mass suicides. Suspects trying to flee Rome were arrested by guards posted outside the city and thrown in prison. The majority were quickly sentenced to death. The men were executed by the state; the women were delivered to their homes for punishment.

No Roman religious repression had ever reached this scale. Given its scope and the severity of the violence, one would think that the bacchanals actually threatened to "crush the commonwealth," as Postumius had claimed. However, that was not the case. By the time of the crackdown, the cult had long been tolerated in Rome. A state that had defeated Carthage and Hannibal had little to fear from sex-crazed soothsayers and cymbal-crashers. Had the bacchanals remained a rural, female-only cult, they probably could have continued their celebrations as they had been doing throughout the peninsula for centuries.

The government's propaganda exploited the cult's sexual deviance, especially its "feminizing" of wellborn young men. Male-male sex was widespread, but Romans, like the Greeks, still condemned passive homosexuality. Any accusation that sodomy was being forced on noble boys was a sure way to stir up indignation. When the news broke that young men such as Aebutius were getting involved, especially at the age of army service, the conditions became ripe for a power play. The repression was staged to give Postumius and the Senate the chance to flex their muscles and consolidate control over the entire Italian peninsula.

As noted, it is unlikely that the bacchanals were actually orchestrating the mass rape of Rome's better class of young men. If they had been, the news would have gotten out long before Postumius had his sit-down with Hispala. The cult probably did get to a few youngsters, though, and people were willing to believe the worst—especially if the perpetrators were women. That a cult priestess could deliver up her own sons for such outrages, or that Aebutius's mother would try to get rid of him this way, was shocking but conceivable: This was a period in which many thought Rome's women were overstepping their bounds and weakening the state as a result. Rome was in the ascent, but there was the nagging feeling that something was slipping.[1]

GROWING PAINS: UPPITY WOMEN

Rome was still a republic in the second century BC, but it was already trying on the jeweled crown of empire. Its conquests, especially in the east, had brought in a flood of luxuries, which were engorging the city with wealth. For the fortunate, the hard edges of domestic life were softening. People redecorated their houses with bronze couches and ornate Asian rugs and tapestries. Dinner parties became more elaborate and expensive. No host who truly cared would think of hosting guests without live entertainment from pricey dancers and harpists. Even cooks, traditionally regarded as among the lowest of menial slaves, were now sought after as artists.

Not bad, then, but all that fine living made many Romans concerned that Rome was squandering its essential virtues for luxury and going soft on a diet of misplaced priorities. They feared that their fellow citizens were losing their mastery over their passions, as well as the singleness of purpose that had long defined the Roman ideal character. The conquering Roman armies in the east were already seen as corrupted; their discipline was "completely destroyed" even before they came home, to the point where their general was almost prosecuted. Back home, the newly rich or richer Romans appeared soft, cruel, and sexually unhinged. Though no one could know then how far things would later degenerate under the "bad" emperors, there was a sense that a growing moral rot was setting in, which required energetic countermeasures. The repression of the bacchanals was just one of many such efforts.

Just as Postumius's witch hunt was dying down, the censor Cato the Elder imposed heavy taxes on boy slaves, expensive women's jewelry, and fancy carriages. He also expelled seven men from the Senate in one year for immoral behavior. One of them was Lucius Quinctius Flamininus, an admiral from an old family who had successfully commanded a fleet against the Macedonians. For his victories he was elected consul and given authority over Roman Gaul. However, on account of his later lusts and dissipation, he lost everything: Lucius had developed a weakness for a young Carthaginian hustler named Philip and paid the boy extravagantly to accompany him on a trip to Gaul. Philip went along, but complained bitterly that the journey prevented him from attending a gladiator contest in Rome.

The young man's grousing was most likely a play to drive up his escort fees, but Lucius still felt obliged to give him something extra. One drunken night in the tent they shared, a local nobleman appeared as a refugee with his children to beg the consul's protection. While the man made his plea through an interpreter, Lucius turned to Philip and asked: "Since you left the show of gladiators, have you a mind to see this Gaul dying?" Phillip said he did, and Lucius grabbed a sword and hit the Gaul across the head. As the nobleman turned to flee, Lucius ran him through with the blade. Another version of the story has Lucius pandering to a female harlot in Rome. During an elaborate meal, while she reclined her head on his chest, she told him that she had never witnessed an execution and would dearly love to see one. Lucius then called a prisoner into the banquet hall and sliced his head off on the spot. In both these accounts, the message is the same: Luxury wasted a good Roman's reason.

Cato dressed Lucius down hard in the Senate. It was "a disgrace," the censor hissed, for him to intoxicate himself with "wine and lust" and then kill for the sport of it, especially when the purpose of the murder was to entertain "an acknowledged wanton." Nothing could be less Roman.

Roman men such as Cato believed women were already hardwired for weakness and immorality, and were getting worse. Tens of thousands of husbands had failed to return home from war, leaving their wives wealthier for their grief. In the absence of men, women were busy managing family fortunes and developing habits of conspicuous consumption. Many also took advantage of opportunities for sexual liaisons. By law, all women were supposed to be controlled by one man or another throughout their lives. When no male family members were around to do the job, the state appointed guardians for them. The problem was that the guardians were often unwilling to make the efforts necessary to keep their wards in line. With their new resources and increased autonomy, women were riding around the city in carriages, wearing ostentatious clothing, and not even troubling to hide their sexual adventures.

That made them targets. Women's sexual habits probably hadn't changed much over the years, but they were now harder to ignore. As Rome adjusted to its preeminent position in the world, much of the blame for the state's moral growing pains was placed on its females and especially its newly empowered matrons. Women (and men who had sex like women) were pinned as the real source of the problem in the bacchanalian scandal, for example. The strength of Rome would depend on keeping women in line and preventing the corrupting influence of femininity in men.[2]

Delusional nostalgia played a big role in shaping moral attitudes toward women. Romans had a persistent fear that wealth and comfort had made them go bad. "Since the day when Roman poverty perished, no deed of crime or lust has been wanting to us," wrote the first-century satirist Juvenal. "Filthy lucre first brought in amongst us foreign ways; wealth enervated and corrupted the ages with foul indulgences." The women of the new Rome were compared, almost always unfavorably, to an idealized past of rural virtue when people lived in "chilly caves." Back then, according to Juvenal, "acorn-belching" husbands had iron control over their families, and simple "hill-bred" wives lined their beds not with imported silk but with leaves, straw, and hides.

Before men became weak and women loose, a husband could beat his wife to death for something as minimal as drinking wine. What's more, the virtuous women of the past preferred to die rather than let themselves be taken by the wrong men.[3] Legends of female honor usually involved well-born women undergoing extraordinary pains in defense of their virtue. Their sacrifices usually benefited their families, but the extreme sufferings of the saintly Lucretia enriched Rome itself: Her violent modesty sparked both the overthrow of Rome's corrupt early kings and the founding of the cherished Republic.

Lucretia had unwittingly participated in a contest among a group of princes as to whose wife was the most virtuous. The men went around to each of their houses at night to catch their wives by surprise. Most of the women were banqueting the night away, but only Lucretia was doing what a good wife should be doing when alone: spinning wool. Satisfied with his victory, Lucretia's husband, the consul Lucius Tarquinius Collatinus, invited his royal mates to stay at his house and dine. During the visit, one of the guest princes soon had something besides food on his mind: The sight of the virtuous Lucretia made her irresistible to Sextus Tarquinius, son of the murderous Roman king Lucius Tarquinius Superbus ("Tarquin the Arrogant"). Sextus decided then and there that he loved her, and that she must be his—though he had an odd way of showing his affection.

A few days later, Sextus went to Lucretia's bed while she slept. "Burning with love," he rousted her. "Be still, Lucretia!" he whispered. "I am Sextus Tarquinius. My sword is in my hand. Utter a sound and you die!" He confessed his love for her and begged her to make love to him. She refused. Finally, when he threatened to kill her and then place a dead slave next to her body to make it appear as though she had committed adultery, she allowed Sextus to take her. After he left the house she called her husband and father to tell them what happened. She made them promise to take proper revenge. Then she pulled out a knife, proclaiming, "I am innocent of fault, but I will take my punishment. Never shall Lucretia provide a precedent for unchaste women to escape what they deserve!" With these words, she fell onto the blade.

Lucretia's family's grief quickly turned to rage. They took their revenge and then some, parading her bloody corpse around the forum and inciting a violent revolt that brought down Tarquinius Superbus and ended Rome's monarchy. Lucretia's unshakeable virtue became the crucible in which the Republic—the essence of Roman freedom from tyranny—was forged.

No less archetypal was the legend of Verginia, the irresistible young virgin who refused to submit to the lust of the powerful Appius Claudius Crassus. Appius took his revenge by having her arrested on her way to school and falsely accused of being from slave stock. (As a slave's descendant, she would be available for ravishment.) The outcome of the subsequent trial over her status was never in doubt: Appius was the judge. Even the histrionics of Verginia's father, who arrived at the trial from out of town at the last minute and accused Appius of "rushing into random fornication" like a wild animal, could not change the outcome. All he could get from the judge was a few minutes alone with his daughter before she was to be punished.

Once granted their moment aside, Verginia's father took a large knife from his cloak and pointed it toward her. "This is the only way, my daughter, in which I can deliver you to freedom," he said, and stabbed her through the heart. Removing the wet knife from Verginia's chest, he turned to Appius and called out: "By this blood, Appius, I bring down vengeance on your head." The arrogant Appius would indeed be brought down in the aftermath of this affair.

THESE WERE TOUGH acts to follow. Next to Lucretia, Verginia, and the hide-clad cavewomen of old, any female looked morally shaky—but that was the standard by which they were judged. In 195 BC, the issue of women's looks and behavior came to a head. Debate broke out over a set of rules collectively called the Oppian Law, which curbed women's flashy habits and taxed their wealth. However, the issue was really about female sexual license. The Oppian Law had been passed in 215 BC, in the turmoil following Rome's loss to Hannibal at the Battle of Cannae. Female ownership of gold was limited to half an ounce; the rest of it went to the treasury. Women were also barred from wearing expensive clothing or traveling in carriages, except to religious festivals. Twenty years later, well after the war against Carthage had been won and with Rome at relative peace, women were pushing for the repeal of these rules.

As senators gathered to decide whether or not to keep the law, crowds of angry women jeered them. To the lawmakers' horror, the mob had been growing for two days, swollen by women pouring in from nearby towns. Inside the Senate, Cato scolded his brethren for letting matters get so far out of hand. Because they had given their women a taste of independence, he said, men's liberties were now in danger of being "crushed and trampled on." The Oppian Law, Cato continued, was minor next to traditional Roman rules curbing women's excessive behavior. If the Senate allowed the rules to be repealed, it would be a slippery slope to equality of the sexes, or worse. "Give loose rein to their uncontrollable nature and to this untamed creature and expect that they will themselves set bounds to their license . . . it is complete liberty, or rather if you want to speak the truth, complete license they desire . . . From the moment they become your equals, they will become your masters."

Cato's appeal was passionate, but the Oppian Law was nevertheless repealed. Mark one small victory for women's rights in Rome. The Senate voted away curbs on women's spending, but the senators did so knowing that women were still subject to the authority of men. Moreover, if women were now allowed to wear gold or trim their clothing in expensive purple dyes, Roman men did not let up on their efforts to quell females' "uncontrollable nature," particularly through religion. Soon after the repeal of the Oppian Law came the witch hunt against the cult of Bacchus. Other, less violent religious measures were taken as well.

Construction of the temple of Venus the Compliant, for example, was funded by fines against women for adultery, and meant to stand as a warning to unfaithful wives. There was also the shrine to Plebeian Chastity, built for the same purpose but geared toward lower-class women. Still another pro-fidelity cult was instituted in honor of Venus Verticordia (the "Changer of Hearts"). The woman responsible for consecrating the statue in Venus's honor, Sulpicia, was credited as being the most faithful wife in the city. It is impossible to know how successful these efforts were at influencing married women to remain loyal to their husbands. Most likely, women made their vows and then did what they were already disposed toward doing. In any event, it seems clear that many men remained dissatisfied. According to Juvenal, who should be taken with several big grains of salt for exaggerating to make a point:

> *Did you even wonder why some women make crude remarks and lewd gestures as they pass the Temple of Chastity? That's where they stop every night to relieve themselves—and piss on the goddess. Then they strap a phallus on the statue and take turns riding it. Next morning, some husband on his way to work slips in the puddle . . . [In the temple of Bona Dea, they] drive themselves crazy; they shriek and writhe—worshipers of Phallus. And sex. They moan, they quiver with lust; there's a steady stream running*

down their legs. The aristocratic matrons challenge the profes-
sional whores—and win . . . If they can't find any men, they raid
the stables and rape the donkeys.

Juvenal enjoyed making satiric attacks on Roman women, highborn and otherwise. They were all hussies to him. But he took no shots at the Vestal Virgins, the priestesses whose sexual restraint was indispensable to the safety of Rome. The Vestals were too important, and the consequences of their broken chastity vows too terrible, to ever be humorous.[4]

VIRGINITY'S PRICE:
THE VESTAL VIRGINS AND THE FATE OF ROME

The primary goal of Roman sex law was to channel female sexual behavior, not forbid it outright. Women were expected to marry and produce legitimate children. Total abstinence was never part of the plan, with the exception of six priestesses whose untouched bodies symbolized Rome's unbroken walls, and whose holy virginity ensured the safety of the city. It took just a single sexual detour by one of them to transform stability into chaos. When that happened, there were meticulous rituals in place to purge the curse and restore hope: Failed Vestals were buried alive in an underground chamber, and it was left to Vesta, the goddess they served, to decide whether they lived or died.

For minor offenses, a Vestal risked being whipped in private by Rome's highest priest, the pontifex maximus. But a Vestal's violation of her vow of chastity was a public curse. All participated in the expiation. Immediately after her conviction, the guilty priestess was flogged and then bound in thick cloth to muffle her cries. Churning like a larva, she was put on a litter bed and carried through the forum. Thousands watched in tearful silence as she passed. "No other spectacle is more appalling," wrote Plutarch of such sights, "nor does any other day bring more gloom to the city than this." The crowd's somber mood came not from the woman's imminent death—gory public executions were common enough—but from terror at what might result from the Vestal's loss of virginity.

The procession ended near the Colline Gate, just inside one of the city's walls, where the burial chamber awaited. The room was supplied with furniture, a lamp, and bits of food, milk, and oil. The Vestal was unfastened from her coverings except for a veil over her face. As her soiled body stood in the wind, an object of grief and scorn, the pontifex maximus stretched his hands toward heaven, muttered some prayers, and then sent her down into the hole. As soon as she was underground, attendants sealed the room with stones and spread earth around it so that no traces of it, or her, remained.

Technically, this was not an execution. No one shouldered the responsibility of killing a Vestal, even a guilty one. The few provisions supplied to the accused priestess absolved the priests for her death and gave Vesta the opportunity to hand down the ultimate ruling. If the Vestal was, in fact, found by the goddess to have broken her chastity vow, Vesta rebalanced the celestial scales by letting her starve and suffocate. If she was innocent, Vesta could lift her up and restore her. Of the ten or so Vestal Virgins who endured this process over the centuries, none was resurrected. Their guilt was confirmed beyond doubt and Rome was saved, at least until the next Vestal misbehaved.

ONLY GIRLS BETWEEN six and ten years old who were deemed perfect in all respects were eligible for service in Vesta's temple. No marks, lisps, or other defects were allowed. Both parents had to be alive and married, with no divorce, scandal, or slave blood clouding their lineage. Selected girls underwent an elaborate initiation process that put them in service to Vesta and Rome and no one else. All Roman women belonged to one man or another, but not the Vestals. They alone were free from male control, because they were the sisters, daughters, and wives of the city itself.

They were taken from their homes to Vesta's temple in the forum, where they lived for at least thirty years. Vesta was the goddess of the hearth, and of the earth itself. The perpetual flame that burned in the *Atrium Vestae*, or the "House of the Vestals," was the fulcrum of Roman life. Just as early Rome's daughters tended the flames of their families' homes, the Vestals kept Rome's fire alive. They also maintained a storehouse of holy substances and took care of dozens of other ritual duties. For that, the priestesses received extraordinary privileges. They were allotted prime seats at the theater and games, and rode in ornate carriages with bodyguards to move people out of their way. Even consuls had to step aside. If, during their travels around town, they encountered a criminal about to be executed, the man's life was spared. However, anyone with the nerve to pass under a Vestal's carriage would be killed. When Vestals died, they were among the very few inhabitants of Rome whose burial was permitted within the city's sacred precincts.

Most Vestals kept their bodies and reputations intact. There were precautions in place to prevent temptation (their temple was closed to all men at night, even doctors), but it was inevitable that some would fail. When a Vestal had sex, the crime was *incestum*—an offense that incorporated incest (all Roman men were their family) and sexual defilement. Because that loss of virginity was a direct assault on the state, general calamities were often blamed on Vestal *incestum*. In what seemed like an instant, they transformed from high priestesses to monstrous scapegoats.

The very fact of Rome's troubles was taken as proof of Vestal unchastity. In 483 BC, the city was at war with the Volsci and the Veii. Rome's superior resources should have permitted it to make short work of these enemies, but Rome was wasting its advantages on internal struggles. To make matters worse, there were daily heavenly prodigies showing the gods' anger and portending disaster. The city was in a panic. Its priests could not figure out what was causing the problems, even after consulting animal entrails and bird flight patterns. They then concluded that a Vestal must have been misbehaving. "These terrors finally resulted in the Vestal Virgin Oppia being condemned for *incestum* and executed," wrote Livy.

In 215 BC, in the alarm over Rome's defeat at the Battle of Cannae, the Vestals Opimia and Floronia were found guilty of *incestum*. One of them was buried alive; the other was allowed to commit suicide. A century later, after the destruction of the army of Marcus Porcius Cato in Thrace, three Vestals were put on trial for conduct more fitting to prostitutes than to professional virgins. "Three had known men at the same time," wrote Cassius Dio. "Of these, Marcia had acted by herself, granting favours to one single knight . . . Aemilia and Licina, on the other hand, had a multitude of lovers and carried on their wanton behaviour with each other's help."

If that was not bad enough, the fire in Vesta's temple began to sputter out on its own—a sure sign of Vestal misconduct—and a bolt of lightning killed a noble girl on her horse, leaving her singed dress hiked up above her waist. At first, only the Vestal Marcia was found guilty, but the public's thirst for a sufficient remedy for all this trouble was too strong for a single verdict to stand. A second trial was convened, and the other two Vestals convicted. All three were buried alive.

Vestals were sometimes prosecuted in the absence of a calamity. Emperor Domitian's moral reforms were punctuated by trials against Vestals for *incestum*. The chief Vestal, Cornelia, was buried alive in 83 AD, but she did not go down quietly: "Is it possible?" she demanded of Domitian as he watched her being led to the hole. "Does Caesar think that I have been unchaste, when he has conquered and triumphed while I have been performing the rites?" In other words, how dare Domitian accuse her when he has enjoyed good fortune? The execution went forward.

Some Vestals were able to acquit themselves at trial with impressive feats of magic. The priestess Tuccia was charged, in 230 BC, with giving away her virginity based on one man's accusation. Calling Vesta to her aid, she led a crowd to the Tiber River, where she pulled up a quantity of water with a sieve. To everyone's amazement, the water did not drain out of the holes. She took it back to the forum, where she dumped the river water onto the feet of her judges. Her life was spared, and her accuser was never heard from again. Another time, after the sacred fire went out on the Vestal Aemilia's watch, the priests inquired as to whether she had been entertaining men. In the presence of everyone, she cried out:

> O Vesta, guardian of the Romans' city, if, during the space of nearly thirty years, I have performed the sacred offices in a holy and proper manner, keeping a pure mind and a chaste body, manifest yourself in my defence and assist me and do not suffer your priestess to die the most miserable of all deaths; but if I have been guilty of any impious deed, let my punishment expiate the guilt of the city.

She then threw a piece of her clothing on the cold altar where the fire had burned. Instantly, a flame burst through the linen. With that, the city was safe again, and Aemilia cleared.

The Vestal college lasted for about a millennium, until the fire was put out forever and the order disbanded in the fourth century AD by the Christian emperor Theodosius. Judging by Rome's long run, the priestesses mostly protected the people well by keeping the sacred fire lit and men out of their beds. In a sex-soaked culture in which aristocratic women tried to register as prostitutes, the Vestals' untouched genitals were a guarantee of Rome's longevity.[5]

BODIES FOR SALE:
SLUMMING IT WITH PROSTITUTES AND PERFORMERS

Until the Christian era, Rome welcomed its droves of prostitutes without moral qualm, taxing their earnings and never interfering with men's enjoyment of them. They were everywhere—in taverns, brothels both luxurious and squalid, on the streets, and in the marketplaces. It was disgraceful to be a prostitute, but the sex trade was legal. Rather than stop the activities of prostitutes, Rome's laws were designed to prevent respectable wives and daughters from acting like whores. That turned out to be quite a challenge. Many Roman women with healthy sexual appetites were not ready to live out their lives in domestic rectitude. This resulted in often-futile legal mesures by Roman men to prevent Roman women from engaging in unsanctioned sex.

Prostitutes lived on the margins, and had almost no legal protection. There are no examples of Roman prostitutes agitating for more rights than they had. Many were slaves, and would have been killed had they tried to do so. But, like slaves and sewers, prostitutes were indispensable. Sex workers were excluded from most temples and almost every other aspect of public life, but they still enjoyed a small measure of integration into society and religion.

Every year, on the first of April—the same day on which matrons renewed their fidelity vows in the cult of Venus Verticordia—other celebrations went on in men's bathhouses. There, the shamed women who serviced men for money burned incense to Fortuna Virilis, the aspect of the goddess Fortuna that represented women's sexual fortune. These simultaneous celebrations expressed Rome's paradoxical beliefs about the sexuality of women. Fortuna Virilis was concerned with the fortunes of women who sold sex, while Venus Verticordia was supposed to steer married women in the opposite direction. Wives were tolerated at best, but as the mothers of Roman citizens they were capable of gaining public respect—if they kept themselves out of trouble. Prostitutes were savored even as they were degraded.

The popular springtime Floralia festival was also the domain of prostitutes. Flora was a successful courtesan who had left a pot of money on her death to finance games and celebrations in her honor. The Senate, uncomfortable with an event built around a prostitute, tried to dress up the celebrations with respectability by recasting Flora as a fertility goddess associated with flowers and crops, and the festival as a ritual meant to guarantee a good harvest. However, dignity seems to have been the last thing on anyone else's mind. The five-day festival was a combination of a sexual be-in and prostitution trade fair, "celebrated with all wantonness as is suitable to the memory of a harlot," according to Lactantius, writing in the early fourth century AD. Prostitutes fought as gladiators in the arenas and performed lewd farces and mimes in the theaters. They walked onstage wearing clothes, but never for long, as the audience would soon demand that they remove their garments and display themselves. When the priggish Cato stormed out of one performance—one wonders what he expected to see there—the audience was relieved that he'd left, rather than remained and inhibited the show. When the Senate could take the lewdness no longer, it discontinued the festival—but subsequently reinstated it after a hailstorm damaged the springtime blossoms.

Prostitutes were, then, good for something else besides sex: flowers and seeds, at least. The Floralia did nothing to make the trade respectable, but it was sanctioned by the government. The memory of Flora did not tempt respectable women to cross the line.[6] Not all whore-goddesses kept themselves at such a safe distance, however.

The Egyptian deity Isis, loving and merciful mother, wife, and harlot, was beloved of Romans of all classes and especially by women. Unlike Roman-grown cults, with their precise rituals and rigid membership rolls, the worship of Isis was flexible and inclusive. Her temples were often found near brothels, and were natural gathering places for prostitutes, but the cult's easy, sensual mix of social groups sparked repeated government repression, especially when it influenced matrons to forget themselves.

In 19 AD, Emperor Tiberius found the perfect opportunity to shut the operation down. He was told of a virtuous if rather stupid wife named Paulina, who had given herself in the temple of Isis to a Roman knight impersonating a god. The knight had been trying unsuccessfully to bed Paulina for some time. Knowing of her devotion to Isis, he paid temple priests to tell her that Anubis, a divine associate of Isis, had fallen in love with her, and that the god wanted to meet her at the temple. She happily agreed, and spent the night in sacred intercourse with her disguised seducer. Despite their friends' smirks, Paulina and her husband were convinced they had been blessed. Finally, the self-satisfied knight could hold the secret no longer, and told her that she had been had. The news got to Tiberius, who crucified the priests, demolished the temple, and had the statue of Isis thrown into the river. The cult would pop up again, but official Rome was never comfortable with any organization that mixed wives and prostitutes.

ROME PUT ITS prostitutes on the same level as actors, animal fighters, and gladiators. All were marked with *infamia*, because they made their living with their bodies. As people who were used and leered at, they were living affronts to the *dignitas* of Roman citizens and were open to physical abuse. Protection from corporal punishment marked citizens from noncitizens, particularly slaves. If a prostitute was beaten or raped by a customer, she had no cause to complain. Actors were also subject to beating for anything that "violated the public order." Gladiators, whose business was violence, were reduced to the vulnerability of slaves when they took an oath to suffer branding, beating, and death. Living at such a reduced level, these *infames* were barred from doing anything other than plying their trades. They were not allowed to join the army, hold public office, or marry freeborn Romans. As people without a shred of honor, they also could not be trusted to tell the truth in court.

A prostitute was condemned to a life of being the Other. The word "prostitute" itself comes from the Latin *prostare*, "to stand out," and Roman prostitutes were indeed marked apart. Under a law passed during the reign of Augustus during the first century AD, they were forced to wear a toga distinct from the *stola* worn by matrons. The rule permitted no subtle distinctions among women: They were either prostitutes or not.

Prostitutes were also registered by the state—not out of health concerns, but to prevent downward migration by upper-class women through licentious behavior. Membership on the list lasted a lifetime.

At the same time, life outside the boundaries of respectability had its advantages. Prostitutes and other *infames* had almost complete sexual freedom, greater than many of the men they serviced. The lives of prostitutes (or at least an idealized vision of them) made more than a few respectable women envious. "Slumming it" by the upper classes has always been glamorous in its way, and this was especially true in Rome. Good women were not supposed to degrade themselves, but did so often enough. More common than stories of virtuous Roman women dying for their honor were cautionary tales of upright wives and daughters gone wrong.

Perhaps the most lurid example was that of the "imperial whore" Messalina, young wife of the emperor Claudius. As Juvenal and the consul-historian Cassius Dio tell it, she stole away from the palace late one night disguised in a blonde wig and cloak. Attended by only one maid, she slipped through the city's darkened streets to a brothel, where she installed herself in a cell "reeking with long-used coverlets." There, assuming the name Lycisca ("Wolf-girl"), she transformed herself into a champion whore. She took on dozens of men in a sexual contest with the other women of the house, beating them handily and "asking from each [customer] his fee."

When closing time came and the brothel-keeper dismissed the girls, Messalina was "still hot from the stretching of her stiffened vulva, worn out from her sexual partners without being satisfied by them," and was not ready to leave. Reluctantly, she returned home, stained by the grime of her night's work. Nor was that her only venture into prostitution: She also did business in the palace, where she set up a brothel with a staff of women drawn from the "highest ranks."

Emperor Augustus's daughter (and later Tiberius's wife) Julia the Elder was no better. She sold herself on the very spot in the forum where her father had proposed a set of restrictive marriage and adultery laws.

That she was married and living one of the highest possible profiles mattered nothing to Julia. "Whatever she desired she claimed as her right," wrote Seneca. Her embarrassed father had no choice but to exile her.

LICENTIOUSNESS FOR ITS own sake is understandable, but what was the attraction for wellborn women of doing it for pay? For all that has been written on the subject, there is no ready answer. Messalina and Julia didn't need the money. Neither did the notorious noblewoman Vistilia, but for her becoming a prostitute was a practical solution to an urgent legal problem: While prostitutes were exempt from prosecution for adultery, women from aristocratic families like Vistilia's were not. She did not sell herself for money, but she was an adulteress. Facing charges in 19 AD for conducting extramarital affairs, she decided to register herself on the official list of prostitutes. As an adulterous wife, she would have faced a series of penalties, only one of which was being downgraded to the status of a prostitute; yet if she was already a registered prostitute at the time of trial, she would avoid a conviction altogether. The shame of being on the list was supposed to be enough to discourage women from the respectable classes from ever considering prostitution, but by Vistilia's time that was no longer always the case. Other women of rank were trying to do likewise, not because they were selling their bodies but because they faced big penalties for sleeping around.

Vistilia blew it for everyone: Her ploy in court failed, and she was exiled to an island and most likely stripped of her citizenship. Her husband, the latest of six, was also called into court to explain why he had let her cheat on him without divorcing and prosecuting her. He barely escaped a pimping charge. The Senate also decreed that all women whose fathers, grandfathers, or husbands were knights were barred from trying to register as prostitutes. If the shame of being a prostitute were not enough to keep women from downgrading themselves, the law would have to do it for them.[7]

While women were trying to expand their sexual opportunities by becoming prostitutes, wellborn men were taking up acting and gladiator fighting. Regulations were in place as early as 38 BC to keep them off the stage and out of the arena, but the laws were unevenly enforced. In 11 AD, the restriction was lifted for a short time, at least with regard to the equestrian class:

> *The knights—a fact which may cause surprise—were allowed to fight as gladiators. The reason for this was that some were making light of the disfranchisement imposed as the penalty for such conduct. For inasmuch as there proved to be no use in forbidding it, and the guilty seemed to require a greater punishment, or else because it seemed possible that they might even be turned aside from this course, they were granted permission to take part in such contests. In this way they incurred death instead of disfranchisement; for they fought just as much as ever, especially since their contests were eagerly witnessed, so that even Augustus used to watch them.*

When they weren't granted special exemptions, some nobles tried to avoid restrictions on participating by downgrading themselves through morality convictions. In 19 AD—the same year the temple of Isis was destroyed and Vistilia exiled—this practice was also banned.

The degradation of the upper ranks wasn't always voluntary. Messalina forced matrons to work in her bawdy house, and the emperor Nero made compulsory prostitution for elite women and children into feature attractions for public amusement. He also forced one thousand senators and knights of "unblemished reputation" to fight in the arena. The emperor Caligula famously opened a brothel in his palace, in which he required the wives and daughters of Rome's foremost families to work. The attraction of such spectacles for the public was the sight of high-ranking people brought low. It was a turn-on for some aristocrats; for the rest, it was the worst kind of humiliation.

Caligula did not set up the brothel just to amuse people. He also used the entire prostitution trade to bulk up tax revenues. Under his rule, a novel prostitution tax was imposed (in 40 AD). The tariff was based on what an average prostitute would charge for sex, probably on a per-day basis. All prostitutes were charged the tax regardless of how many clients they saw. For those working constantly or at high rates, the tax was just another cost of doing business. A little more work or a price boost could meet the government's demands. For part-time prostitutes, on the other hand, or for those at the tail end of their earning power, the tariff was crushing. Even those who had left the business were charged. At first, professional tax farmers made collections, but soon too much money was being lost along the way from the bed to the treasury. The military picked up the effort with brutal efficiency: Soldiers could be depended upon to know where all the prostitutes near their posts were located, even the part-timers, and to keep the money safe.

Rome's early Christian emperors also depended on the prostitution tax, even as they were embarrassed by it. The levy was collected until 498 AD. Prostitution was a direct violation of the Christian ban on fornication, among other things, but the emperors chose to make small tweaks rather than frontal assaults on the trade. Male prostitution was supposed to be forbidden in the third century AD after the emperor Marcus Julius Philippus saw a hustler who resembled his son, but the practice continued, and was taxed for a long time afterward. In the fourth century, Constantine ruled it illegal for nuns to be put in brothels. He also denied honors to upper-class men who produced children with prostitutes. At the same time, he treated prostitution mostly as an urban zoning issue, creating a special red-light district in Constantinople and forcing all harlots to stay within its confines.

It was not until the deeply religious sixth-century Byzantine emperor Justinian that prostitution was forbidden, when brothels were banned in Constantinople and brothel-keepers fined. The money was used to help prostitutes start new lives. Pimps were flogged and expelled from the city, slave prostitutes were freed, and freeborn women were released from brothels. Justinian took a special interest in the subject at the insistence of his wife Theodora, a reformed prostitute herself. She urged him to give Christian mercy to fallen women—whether they wanted it or not. Justinian and Theodora converted a palace high on the bluffs above the Sea of Marmara into the Convent of Repentance (*Metanoia*), where about five hundred former marketplace prostitutes were forced to live chaste Christian lives. Many of them were so unnerved by this mandatory conversion into nuns that they threw themselves off the cliffs and into the water below.[8]

FAMILY VALUES, ROMAN-STYLE

Before Christianity arrived with its odd notions of penance and salvation, there was no need for the law to "reform" anyone for his or her sexual misdeeds. People did what their social positions allowed. If they went too far, they stood to be punished, not changed. Slaves, actors, and prostitutes were there to be used. Male citizens could take whoever was available to them, and married women were to be protected from themselves. Messalina, Julia, and Vistilia notwithstanding, most freeborn women saw themselves as the opposite of prostitutes. If they did not always stick close to their husbands, they at least reached a sexual accommodation with them.

There was no abundance of love between husbands and wives. Marriage and family didn't exactly fall out of fashion as the Republic gave way to the empire in the last century BC, but neither were they always seen as necessary. When people did marry, sensual affection often had nothing to do with it. Married men and women shared the same bed only when required to get the business of procreation done. Divorce was easy, families were small, and spouses pursued sexual affairs with little hesitation. Much of what we would now call adultery happened in the household, with men taking advantage of slaves of both genders and generating a confusing muddle of offspring. The man of the house might take his pleasure with his servant woman, her daughter, and her son at the same time—all of whom might technically be his children. Such complications didn't matter, legally or morally, because slaves and the children produced with them were beneath concern: That was what they were there for.

As in ancient Greece, with all of this sex available to Rome's men, wives were just one choice among many. By the time Augustus put forth his landmark "family values" legislation, the population of Rome's upper classes was on a troubling downward trajectory. No one could stop high infant mortality rates or short life spans, but Augustus believed the state could at least influence the production of more freeborn children.

In a collection of laws first enacted in 18 BC, Augustus encouraged the "right" kind of reproduction between the "right" sorts of people. First, he provided a powerful incentive for freeborn men to find and keep acceptable wives: Men older than twenty-five who did not stay married until they were sixty, or married too far beneath them, lost their inheritances and were heavily taxed. Those who married and did not have children only received a fraction of their legacies. Couples with children who survived infancy were rewarded. The laws also freed up the ranks of ex-slaves as acceptable mates for most upper-class people, which made it much easier to find a husband or wife.

Augustus's plans received a cool reaction from senators, who had no interest in being told whom or when to marry or in losing any part of their inheritances. Augustus's marriage to his second wife, Livia, with whom he had no children, was itself a violation of the laws he was advocating, and no example of righteous living, for when Livia wasn't procuring girls for Augustus he took them himself, even if they were married and from the upper orders. (Mark Antony accused him of taking a woman from her husband at a banquet and returning her, some time later, with "red ears" and her hair in "great disorder.") The difference between Augustus's personal habits and the ones he imposed on the upper classes earned him a lot of gibes. He took them in his stride, letting senators say their piece and then appealing to their practical natures:

> If we could survive without a wife, all of us would do without that nuisance; but since nature has so decreed that we cannot manage comfortably with them, nor live in any way without them, we must plan for our lasting preservation rather than for our temporary pleasure.

The laws went further than encouraging marriage and children. They also laid out a fearsome set of punishments for upper-class Romans who had sex outside prescribed channels. Traditionally, that was governed by custom and enforced by the (male) head of a household. Lucretia's father, for example, consulted no law books before he killed his unchaste daughter. It was his right to do it. The women arrested in the bacchanalia scandal were sent to their families for punishment. Now, adultery and transclass sex were made public crimes, punished by the state in special courts.

Men were still allowed to sate themselves with prostitutes, actresses, and long-term concubines, but the new laws explicitly barred them from having sex with other men's wives or daughters. If they did so, they risked being brought to court on adultery charges, losing much of their property, and being banished to an island.

As always, men who seduced protected women risked violence by the women's men, but the new laws limited the scope of revenge. If the woman's father caught the adulterous couple in the act, he could still kill the lover on the spot, but the father also had to kill his daughter. The seducer had a better chance of keeping his life if the husband caught him. Unless the woman's lover was an actor, prostitute, or pimp, the husband

was not allowed to kill him. However, the husband could still do the man
harm by raping him, serving him up to his slaves for rape, or shoving a
foreign object in his anus. The husband could also castrate the seducer if
he wished, and send him out of his house a bloody eunuch with no trace
of manliness left.

Most Roman men were not as cruel as this, and many seem to have
made their peace with their wives' affairs, but the new laws brooked no tolerance. Husbands were forced to renounce and prosecute their wives when
they discovered adultery, or face charges themselves. A man who overlooked his wife's dalliances was worse than a cuckold; he would now be
considered a pimp. One senator who did bring adultery charges against his
wife was still charged with procuring, because he did not formally divorce
her. The laws left men who traveled for a living at an obvious disadvantage, which is why the Senate later rejected a proposal barring wives from
accompanying their husbands on provincial assignments. Women were
distractions on the road, but because "it is the husband's fault if the wife
transgresses propriety," argued the consul Valerius Messalinus, a husband
should at least have the opportunity to keep his wife close by and prevent
trouble.

The Augustinian adultery restrictions were marketed as an effort to
rebuild the strict morality of Rome's rustic early days. Augustus drew a
bright line between good and bad behavior, especially for married women.
Once a wife was branded as an adulteress, she would be forever downgraded to the rank of prostitute, regardless of whether or not she had
ever charged money for sex. From that point forward, she was forced to
wear the prostitute's toga and was barred from remarrying within her former social class. Like the actors and other *infames*—who were now her
equals—she would henceforth be sexually available to all, and subject to
physical abuse. That may have been a kick for Vistilia and her ilk, but it
was not for the majority of wellborn Roman women, who did not want to
be robbed of their money or their inheritances. There is evidence that some

adulteresses were forced to work as prostitutes until as late as 394 AD, but even if they were not compelled to earn their living selling sex, they had few other practical choices.

MORAL REFORMS ALWAYS generate victims, but they rarely change the public's day-to-day behavior. The Augustinian rules, like other sexual dictates from above, merely highlighted the differences between what people do and what they are *supposed* to do. The laws generated thousands of adultery lawsuits, but they neither raised birthrates nor renewed a sense of sexual honor among the upper classes. Augustus set no lasting example by banishing his daughter and granddaughter for engaging in "every form of vice." Indeed, the excesses of Messalina, Caligula, Nero, and the rest occurred in the decades after Augustus's laws were passed. Tiberius banished Vistilia and crucified the priests of Isis, but his own habits during his retirement on the island of Capri were probably more influential. Not only did he pay to have boys nibble his thighs while he swam, he also developed a fetish for debasing highborn women—even driving one to kill herself rather than submit to his adulterous demands.

It took the adoption of Christianity in Rome, centuries after Augustus, for men to feel tangible restrictions on their sexual freedoms. Saint Augustine's injunction to married women against allowing their husbands to fornicate would have been laughed at in pre-Christian Rome, but starting with Constantine, who converted the empire to Christianity, such sentiments resonated. The emperor tried (with limited success) to forbid married men from taking concubines, and tightened rules on male adultery. By the following century, a husband's adultery would become grounds for a woman to divorce him and take back her dowry.

The slow tightening of male sexual freedoms reflected Christian discomfort with all sexual pleasure, even within marriage. Godliness and sex were thought mutually exclusive. "Nothing is filthier than to have sex with your wife as you might with another woman," wrote Saint Jerome. To early

Christian thinkers, all sexual passions were obscene. Constantine repealed Augustus's laws penalizing men for not marrying, in part to accommodate devout Christians who remained single. Avoiding marriage in service to God was one thing; however, a man who devoted his sexual energies to other men was quite something else. The late Roman Empire would witness a series of convulsive measures against homosexual behavior, with long-lasting effects.[9]

CHARIOTS AND SALVATION:
HOMOSEXUALITY IN THE LATE ROMAN EMPIRE

About a half-century after Constantine, in 390 AD, a celebrated chariot racer's penchant for other men would weaken the Roman Empire, humiliate the emperor, and strengthen the political power of the Catholic Church. The charioteer never meant to do anything other than win races, and his sexual tastes were not unusual. But the violent popular response to his imprisonment under one of Rome's first antihomosexuality laws triggered a bloody chain reaction that ripped across the empire and resonated for centuries.

Male-male sex, long common in the ancient world, was repugnant to the Goth garrison policing the Greek city of Thessalonica, and especially to its commander, Butheric. The Christian-inspired law gave the soldiers the authority they needed to strike out against local practices. The exact charges made against the (supposedly) effeminate chariot racer are unclear. He might have been thrown in jail for something as mild as making a pass at Butheric's slave, or as grave as homosexual rape. Regardless, his absence left one hundred thousand spectators at the city's hippodrome without their favorite competitor. The crowd appealed to Butheric to let the charioteer participate in the games, but they were refused. Deprived of their hero, and nursing a deep hatred against the outnumbered Goth barbarians, the Thessalonicans then rampaged violently in the streets.

The mob mutilated Butheric and dragged his remains around the city. When news of the riot reached Emperor Theodosius in Italy, who then further learned that one of his favorite generals had been lynched, he flew into a rage and ordered savage retaliation. Just before the start of the next Thessalonican games, the reinforced garrison locked the hippodrome's gates and moved in to exact the emperor's revenge. The soldiers did not bother to distinguish who had been responsible for the riot from who had merely been there for a day's entertainment. As one Roman historian described it: "All together were cut down in the manner of corn in harvest time."

In one harrowing recorded vignette from the massacre, a merchant who had brought his two sons to the games begged the soldiers to kill him but spare his children. The Goths agreed to save one of the boys, but the merchant was told to choose between them. "The father, weeping and wailing, beheld both of the two sons and committed to choose neither, but rather continued being bewildered until the time when they were killed, succumbing equally to a love of both."

At least seven thousand killings later, the soldiers' work was done. The slashed and beaten bodies of men, women, and children were left strewn around the stadium to rot in the Greek sun. The news of this horrible murder of Roman subjects sent widespread, intense shock waves throughout the empire, in no small part because Theodosius was known for his Christian mercy. The emperor was wracked with remorse, but the deed was done.

Enter Ambrose, the bishop of Milan (and later saint), who was familiar with the emperor's mood swings as well as the intensity of his present grief. The bishop refused to receive Theodosius personally. Instead, he confronted him with a letter threatening to withhold the Eucharist—and thus the emperor's salvation—unless he excommunicated himself or did penance. "I dare not offer the sacrifice if you intend to be present," he wrote. "Is that which is not allowed after shedding the blood of one innocent person, allowed after shedding the blood of many? I do not think so."

Never before had a church official had the cheek to demand public penance from a Roman emperor. Yet Theodosius had no choice but to submit: His soul was at risk. In an unequalled display of self-abasement, the "Ever-Victorious, Sacred Eternal Augustus, Lord of the World" put down his regalia and could be seen weeping and groaning on the cold stone floor of Milan's cathedral. After eight months, Theodosius was allowed to take communion, but his soul had been saved at a colossal price: The empire had lost a critical contest of prestige with the church.

Ambrose soon pressed his advantage, pushing Theodosius to step up the repression of paganism and ending any pretense of Roman toleration of pre-Christian religions. In little more than a century, all male homosexual behavior would be officially classified as an offense against the Christian God, and forbidden on pain of death. What had begun as the arrest of a provincial chariot racer resulted, in just a few months, in a turning point in Roman and Christian history. The fate of the nameless charioteer is unknown, but it is a safe bet that his glory days were numbered, as were those of the ancient pagan religions. By enforcing an unpopular sex law, Theodosius subordinated the empire to the church. The crowd that tore Butheric to pieces was of indeterminate religion, but the rioters had been evidently far less troubled by homosexuality than their emperor was—at least when it concerned something as important as the games.[10]

Male-male sex had been mostly legal in the Roman world, although powerful cultural norms in Rome (as Greece before it) had long demanded that men of standing take only the active sexual role. Slaves, noncitizens, and other *infames* such as prostitutes were meant to occupy the passive, "womanly" part. Seneca wrote that losing one's virtue through sexual passivity is "a crime for the free-born" and "a necessity in a slave." The Latin expression for a male being penetrated was *muliebria patitur*, i.e., "having a woman's experience." The word for "man," *vir*, was not defined merely by physical characteristics. Rather, it meant a Roman male citizen who would never suffer the sexual outrages that were the lot of women and slaves.

*In 390 AD, the popular outcry against the arrest of a beloved gay chari-
oteer set off a violent chain of events that weakened the Roman Empire,
humiliated the emperor, and strengthened the power of the Catholic
Church. Here, Ambrose refuses to admit Theodosius into the cathedral
of Milan because the emperor has enforced Rome's first antihomosexual
laws too vigorously.* ©TOPFOTO

Whereas in certain elite strata of Greek society an adolescent boy could maintain a delicate relationship with an older man in which he gave sex in exchange for tutoring and social connections, in Rome it was otherwise: Young male citizens were *never* supposed to be put in a passive position. One of the few scattered homosexuality laws before Theodosius was a ban on pederasty, but only when it involved upper-class boys. Young male citizens wore amulets in the shape of erections to warn everyone that they were off-limits. It was illegal even to follow freeborn boys around in the street.

A Roman citizen could be excused for breaking the law to protect his manliness. As early as 326 BC, the practice of enslavement as settlement of debt was abolished after a magistrate's son, Titus Ventruius, went broke and was sold to a man who tried to have sex with him. The purchaser had every right to violate Titus, now a slave, but the young man resisted and denounced him to the consuls. The purchaser was then jailed.[11]

Two hundred years later, an army officer and nephew of the famous general and consul Gaius Marius was killed by a soldier he had repeatedly tried to seduce. Under most circumstances, the soldier would have been executed, but Marius honored him instead. To condone his nephew's intention to use the soldier for pleasure would have transformed the latter's body from an instrument of conquest into something weak—and that Marius could not allow.

HOMOSEXUALITY IN ROME (at least the passive variety) was always shameful, but until the Christian era it was not *illegal*; still, it was practiced often enough. Accusations of passive homosexuality were common but usually harmless insults. Unless the target of the gibe was caught taking a freeborn male against his will, he was probably safe from harsh penalty. Julius Caesar, that paragon of Roman virility and conqueror of Gaul, was popularly believed to have admitted Nicomedes, king of Bithynia, into his backside. His soldiers even chanted in his presence that "Caesar got on top of the Gauls, but Nicomedes got on top of Caesar." He survived the insult. Caesar's nephew Octavian (later called Augustus) was accused of submitting to the homosexual desires of his famous uncle—a terrible slur, to be sure, but Octavian's career was also undimmed. With the exception of Claudius, all of Rome's first fifteen emperors enjoyed sex with other men. Presumably, some of them were not too fussy about how they did it.

Despite the potential for ridicule, men in the ruling classes followed suit, having sex either discreetly among themselves, openly with prostitutes, or with their slaves. "The poor chap who has to plough his master's field is less of a slave than the chap who must plough the master himself," mused Juvenal. It is less clear how many male citizens below the upper ranks shared such views. A humble man is imagined by Quintilian as saying in court: "You rich don't marry, you only have those toys of yours, those boy slaves that play woman for you."

With the growing dominance of Christianity in the fourth and fifth centuries, however, homosexuality would become illegal as well as shameful. Male-male sex came to be associated with paganism and suffered intense official harassment. Constantine destroyed pagan temples in Phoenicia after the priests there were accused of succumbing to the "foul demon known by the name of Venus . . . where men unworthy of the name forgot the dignity of their sex." In Egypt, the emperor went further, exterminating a group of river priests on the same charge. Constantine's sons, Constans and Constantius II, came under the influence of a Christian senator who was passionately opposed to homosexuality. The brother emperors issued a historic decree in 342:

> When a man couples as though he were a woman, what can a
> woman desire who offers herself to men? When sex loses its func-
> tion, when the crime which is better not to know is committed,
> when Venus changes her nature, when love is sought and not
> found, then we command that the laws should rise up, and that

the laws should be armed with an avenging sword, so that the
shameless ones today and tomorrow may suffer the prescribed
penalties.

The wording is obscure, but most historians agree that the "shameless ones" targeted by the law were passive homosexuals. Those inflicting the shame were still in the clear from the state's avenging sword—at least for a while.

Forty-eight years later, in 390, Theodosius issued the law that ensnared the Thessalonican charioteer. It stated that Rome's "revenging flames" would consume all those who condemn "their manly body . . . to bear practices reserved for the other sex." Again, the statute was long on rhetoric and short on specifics, but it is clear that Theodosius was focused mainly on male brothel workers, the only group the law clearly mentioned. Did the emperor mean that active homosexuals should be burned alive as well? Probably not, given that the law still stressed the unnaturalness of a man's body being used as a woman's, but it was nevertheless enough for Butheric to arrest the charioteer (who seems to have enjoyed both types of homosexual sex) and unwittingly spark the power plays of Saint Ambrose.

Even with all this Christian fervor, an explicit law against active homosexuality would not come about until 533, when Justinian ruled that those who "perform actions contrary to nature herself" without repentance were to be killed. Homosexuality in all forms was now officially an offense against God. Rome's punishments were merely the tools of divine will. By this time, Justinian was already executing homosexuals, especially those in the clergy. More than a decade earlier, he had gone on a rampage against rural homosexual bishops. Several were captured and brought to Constantinople, where they were tortured. At least one was castrated and carried around the streets as he bled to death. Death through castration became one of the official penalties against homosexuals of all stripes.

Justinian accepted as true the story that Sodom was destroyed as punishment for the homosexuality supposedly practiced there. He also blamed male-male sex for the earthquakes that shook Constantinople during his reign. But however genuine his belief that he served God by being the "enemy of unmanly lust," his antihomosexual efforts were plainly vicious and corrupt. Wrote the eighteenth-century historian Edward Gibbon:

> *The cruelty of his persecutions can scarcely be excused by the purity of his motives. In defiance of every principle of justice . . . a painful death was inflicted by the amputation of the sinful instrument, or the insertion of sharp reeds into the pores and tubes of most exquisite sensibility . . . A sentence of death and infamy was often founded on the slight and suspicious evidence of a child or servant: the guilt of the green faction of the rich [which opposed the emperor], and the enemies of [Empress] Theodora, was presumed by the judges, and pederasty became the crime of those to whom no crime could be imputed.*

As we have seen, the ancient Greek and Roman worlds based their sexual categorizations not on differences in gender but on the active-passive dichotomy. The fact that a man had sex with other men was usually incidental. The key question was what exactly he did with them. The Bible made no such distinctions, and neither did Western sex law after Justinian. For about fifteen hundred years, *all* homosexuals would be associated with heresy and pathology, and would suffer dearly under the law.

As late as 1986, the U.S. Supreme Court relied in part on the Roman law used against the Thessalonican charioteer when it upheld the state of Georgia's ban on "homosexual sodomy."[12] Rather than condemning the statute as hateful and unjust, Chief Justice Warren Burger cited the law as an example of "millennia of moral teaching." Burger omitted the fact that the Roman law probably left half of all homoerotic sex partners—the active ones—in the clear. He also failed to mention that the Roman law had sparked a popular revolt and thousands of deaths, and caused a permanent reduction of imperial power.

In the centuries after Justinian, life would get a lot worse for homosexuals and, indeed, all people who enjoyed sex.

4

...

THE MIDDLE AGES:
A CROWD CONDEMNED

U NTIL THE FOURTH century AD, the followers of Jesus Christ made up one of many outlaw religious cults in the Roman Empire. As the early Christians fled from persecution, their souls yearned for the world to come, a deliverance they were convinced was just around the corner. The men who built Christianity into an organized religion lived, at least for a time, as ascetic monks or hermits, and treated their devotion to God as part of the physical ordeal. Their outlook hardened further as they sought to distinguish themselves from the licentious pagan world around them. It was from this hothouse of deprivation that Christian doctrine announced that the body was an object of horror, and that the soul could be saved only through rejection of the flesh.

Had Christians not gained real political power, they would be remembered as an austere sect. Their insistence on the conflict between the body (which craves sex) and the spirit (which sex destroys) would be a point of historical interest, nothing more. There were a number of religious sects that did battle with the body, some of which had more adherents than Christianity in its early days. That was not the way things turned out, of course. From the reign of Emperor Constantine to the present, the Christian notion that sexual love brings spiritual death has been the cornerstone of Western sex law.

In fairly short order, Christianity transformed itself from a collection
of infighting provincial fanatics into a critically important branch of the
Roman government. The first step was Constantine's Edict of Milan in
313, which took the heat off Christianity by giving official toleration to
all religious beliefs. By the end of the century, Christianity had become
Rome's official religion, and the oppressed had become the oppressors.
Under the influence of bishops, the empire furiously suppressed paganism.
At the same time, Christianity's various factions cohered into a sophisticated organization. As Rome's hold over Europe, Africa, and the Occident
peeled away in the coming centuries, the church was the only institutional
power capable of filling the vacuum. The long-term consequences for sex
law could not have been greater.[1]

Jesus Christ said much about love, but precious little about sex.
Although his own life was relatively chaste by local standards, the fine
points of sexual behavior were not his main concerns. He made no state-
ments on carnal relations between the unmarried or homosexuals, he was
tolerant of prostitutes, and he was less harsh toward adulterers than the
Jews had been. But Jesus the man did not last long in this world, and
soon his word was taken up by others. His most influential followers were
consumed with sex in all of its permutations and devoted much of their
attention to questions of sexual morality. Jesus's relative indifference never
prevented the Christian fathers from devising a violent array of restrictions
in the Savior's name.

THE DOMINANT FIGURE in the first generation of Christian sages was
the Apostle Paul, who taught that sexual behavior could be nearly as bad
as murder: Homosexuals, masturbators, adulterers, anyone who sought
sexual satisfaction for its own sake were, he said, to be barred from the
kingdom of God. Intercourse between husband and wife for the purpose
of procreation was the only way for people to join as "one flesh" with
each other, though Paul was no great proponent of matrimony either. For

Paul, marriage was a crutch for those too weak in their faith to give up sex entirely. "It is better to marry than to burn," he said—but not much better.

Like his contemporaries, Paul was convinced that the Second Coming of Christ was imminent. The world as they knew it was about to end. Such earthly trivialities as marriage and children were distractions from the urgent spiritual business at hand. In the meantime, he taught his followers to follow a carnal holding pattern. Those who were virgins should remain so if they could stand it; those who were already married should stay with their husbands and wives. No more divorce, remarriage, prostitutes, or concubines were permitted. To keep a lid on adulterous desires, Paul instructed husbands and wives to submit to each other's sexual demands. Celibacy was the preferred means of preparing for salvation in the next world, but Paul recognized that only spiritual giants (like himself) could carry it off: "I wish all men were as I am," he mused, but he knew they were not. For the common Christian, sex was acceptable in limited quantities, at least until Judgment Day.[2]

That day never came, either in Paul's lifetime or afterward, but rather than adjust religious doctrine to the ongoing realities of human desire, succeeding Christian fathers amped up the campaign against the libido. Sex and salvation became mutually exclusive. After Paul came Saint Jerome (circa 347–420), who taught that *all* sexual relations were unclean—even in marriage. "Everything [is] poison which bears within it the seeds of sensual pleasure," he preached. No less strident in his disapproval of all sexuality was Jerome's contemporary, Augustine of Hippo (354–430), bishop and later saint. A late convert to Christianity, Saint Augustine perfected the idea of original sin, the doctrine that pits the needs of the sex organs directly against the purity of the spirit.

Before the Fall, Augustine wrote, sex was an arid affair. Reproduction was accomplished by something akin to copulation, but it was a function of "will," not lust. Human genitalia were obedient tools, like hands or feet. Everything changed after Adam and Eve were expelled from paradise.

Then they looked down at their crotches and saw monsters, fleshy tyrants demanding to be touched and rubbed. Adam and Eve became incapable of refusing their bodies' demands and hated themselves for it, so they made aprons of leaves to cover their shame. However, the first human genitals remained ruthless and insistent, as has every sex organ since. In paradise, reproduction was morally neutral. Outside of Eden, it became simply fucking. Wrote Augustine: "The insubordination of [genitalia], and their defiance of the will, is clear testimony of the punishment of man's first sin."

The only weapon against genital demands was moral will, then, but the smart money was always on the gonads. A good Christian might resist the urge for a while, but Augustine knew the world well enough to see that a lifetime of abstinence was too much to hope for. As he was composing one of his tracts, he was told that "a man of eighty-four, who had lived a life of continence under religious observance with a pious wife for twenty-five years, [had] just bought himself a music girl for his pleasure." As Augustine saw it, the sins of Adam and Eve and the lasting damnation of humanity were to blame for this old man's fall from grace. Every stirring of desire, every child born from lust, was proof positive of original sin. We are all, and always will be, a *massa damnata*: a crowd condemned.

Augustine was no stranger to sexual urges, as he readily confessed. A veteran of many affairs, including a fifteen-year relationship (and a son) with a concubine, Augustine had had more than his share of sexual experience for much of his early life. "I poured myself out," he wrote, "frothed and floundered in the tumultuous sea of my fornications." He loved his concubine, and only left her for a marriage his mother had arranged with an eleven-year-old. While he waited for his wife to come of age, he was still "a slave of lust . . . so I got myself another woman, in no sense a wife." Meanwhile, he prayed, although with something less than full faith: "Grant me chastity and continence," he begged of God, "but not yet." It was only after Augustine had lived a rich sex life that he converted to Christianity and went on to become one of the most powerful advocates of celibacy the world has ever known.[3]

IF SEX WAS by nature impure and disgusting, it was only a short step to conclude that Jesus must have come from something better. The Christian apologist Arnobius was typical in his claim that it was blasphemous to believe the Savior was born "as the result of the spewing forth of senseless semen." Christ's mother was recast as the virginal opposite of Eve, a feminine ideal molded from the dry bricks of abstinence. One extreme early Christian sect held that Jesus had come into the world as an adult, and barred the sacraments to anyone who had actually had sex, even if they were married.

If Christian life was, in the words of the second-century theologian Tatian, "unthinkable outside the bounds of virginity," what was a Christian to do with his libido? Augustine faced down his desires with faith and willpower. Others went to war with their bodies. Saint Benedict could not get the image of a woman he had seen out of his mind, so he tore off his clothes and rolled on beds of thorns until his entire body was cut up. "Thus," the story goes, "he forced out the sickness of his soul through the wounds of his body, and conquered sin." Others, like the renowned third-century scholar Origen, cut their genitals off entirely.

The church outlawed castration in 325, but still pressed the message that spiritual purity required chastity. Christians didn't invent the ideal of sexual continence, but they took it to remarkable lengths. The lives of the early saints and monks, told time and again by priests to their flocks, often included episodes of intense sexual temptation successfully resisted. Augustine was inspired by the example of Saint Anthony, who spent thirteen years in the desert battling the nasty thoughts Satan sent his way: "At night the devil would turn himself into the attractive form of a beautiful woman, omitting no detail that might provoke lascivious thoughts." Saint Abraham was of a lesser order than Anthony, but he still got high marks for running away from his wife on their wedding night.

Nor was there any shortage of female saints going to extreme lengths to remain chaste. Saint Alexandra walled herself up in a tomb in Egypt for ten years in order not to tempt men. Saint Radegund was captured and forced into a marriage with a Frankish king circa 540, but refused his advances and spent her nights praying on the cold ground near the privy. The king gave up after a while and let her escape to a nunnery. The greatest admiration was accorded to female saints who chose torture and death over sexual impurity. Rather than submit to the desires of a Roman consul, the third-century Saint Agatha of Sicily cheerfully let herself be stretched on a rack and torn apart with iron hooks.

Although these are impossible examples to follow, lay Christians were somehow supposed to do so. No major Western religion had ever demanded that its rank and file fight so hard against their reproductive urges. Restrictions on sexuality had always been in place, but the goal was to *direct* sex, not stop it. The difference between Christian and pagan sex policy could not have been starker. Under Roman law, men and women (at least those of rank) were supposed to marry, and were punished if they did not have children. Men were free to keep concubines and use as many prostitutes as they could afford. However, as Rome was Christianized, the ideal of celibacy became government policy. The older laws were thrown away.

When lawmakers view sex as bad, they write bad sex laws. No one found a way to regenerate without coitus, so sex had to be tolerated at least some of the time, but the church quickly started to restrict the options. Under earlier Roman law, marriages existed so long as there was "consent," and men were free to abduct women as wives so long as they or their families later "agreed" to the union. That began to change during the reign of Constantine. Marriages started to become formalized, concubinage outlawed, and divorce made much harder to accomplish. Sex was still permitted among husbands and wives, but barely. Building on Augustine, Pope Gregory the Great (circa 540–604) declared that marital intercourse was blameless only when there was no pleasure involved. By the end of the sixth century, new rules were coming into place to make sure that was the case.[4]

The Penitentials and the Price of Sex

The masses of early European peasantry never studied Saint Augustine. Nearly all could not read. Rather, they relied on their local clerics to translate the word of God into comprehensible terms. Abstruse questions about the divinity of Christ or the nature of the Trinity were irrelevant in the villages and farms. What did concern people, and what priests spent much of their time addressing, was sex. Clerics were the moral police of the early Middle Ages. They taught that deliverance from hell depended on avoiding sex whenever possible and having it, when necessary, in limited ways.

The broad outlines of Christian sex policy were crafted by the likes of Augustine and Jerome, but for more than five hundred years the real business was accomplished in church confessionals. Many of the priests and penitents must have known each other well, but in the dark of the confessional booth their relations were anything but neighborly. When priests took on the role of confessors, they were no longer old friends or spiritual guides: They were judges who sized up the penitents' misdeeds and meted out the consequences. The sacrament of confession required penitents to divulge every detail of their sex lives—their dreams, emissions, positions, infidelities. As nearly everything people did sexually was forbidden, the process must have been terrifying. Upon hearing the confessions, the priests consulted handbooks called penitentials, which assigned specific penances for every sin. The penitentials were the church's field guides for ranking good and bad sexual behavior.

The handbooks were not written by the top officials of the church but compiled locally, and varied considerably from parish to parish. Despite their differences, they all delivered the same basic message: All sex was dirty and polluting, but some kinds of sex were worse than others. Some penitentials listed hundreds of different sex acts and thoughts, each carrying its own penance. The purpose of doing penance, which usually consisted of fasting along with additional restrictions on sexual conduct, was to earn God's forgiveness, but some sins required more forgiveness than others. "Just as it is more abominable to mix [a man] with a mule than with a male," one penitential held, "so it is a more irrational crime [to mix] with a male than with a female." Similarly, a wet dream was not as sinful as masturbating while awake.

The first penitentials came out of the grim wastes of sixth-century Ireland, where abstinence among Christians had become a fetish. One well-admired hermit named Scothian tested his virtue by living in the same room with two "pointy-breasted" women who tried to arouse him every day. When he could bear no more temptation, he jumped into a tub of cold water. In this environment the Celtic missionary Saint Columbanus wrote his guidebook, which he brought from Ireland to England and the Continent. The utility of a catalogue of sins and corresponding penances was quickly understood, and soon penitentials were being compiled throughout Europe, each adapting itself to local priorities. The process went on until at least the twelfth century, when they were in use everywhere confession was taken.

Some penitentials suggested lines of questioning for priests to smoke out sinful behavior. One eleventh-century guidebook required that men be asked: "Have you coupled with your wife or another woman from behind, like dogs?" The same book required that women be asked about aphrodisiacs, lesbianism, bestiality, masturbation, abortions, oral consumption of semen, and the use of their menstrual blood as a love charm. Saint Albertus Magnus said such detail was required because of the "monstrous things heard these days in confession," but others worried that too much hot talk in the confessional was counterproductive. In 821, Theodulf of Orléans warned confessors not to put ideas into people's heads with such detailed questions:

> There are many vices recorded in the penitential which it is not proper for a person to know. Therefore, the priest ought not to question him about everything, lest, perhaps, when he goes away

he be persuaded by the devil to fall into one of the crimes of which
he had been previously ignorant.

For the same reasons, Pope Nicholas I told Bulgarian churchmen a few years later not even to *show* penitential handbooks to laymen.

The penitentials prohibited sex between husbands and wives during the first three days of marriage as well as Sundays, Wednesdays, Fridays, and Saturdays, the three Lents, the weeks following Easter, the days preceding the Pentecost, the two months around Christmas, and hundreds of other holy days, not to mention during a woman's pregnancy, lactation, or menstruation. At best, that left about four days per month. Even then, there were strict rules. Sex was never to take place during the daytime, and there was to be no fondling or lewd kisses ever. One handbook forbade husbands from seeing their wives naked. No sexual positions other than the missionary, male-on-top variety were allowed, because they were animal-like and too stimulating. Oral and anal sex were punishable by up to twenty-five years of fasting and abstinence. After sex took place, moreover, people were expected to vigorously wash themselves and avoid going to church.

With such a battery of restrictions, sex was always risky. Many married couples presumably avoided making embarrassing revelations to their priests, but their silence could not have erased their fear of divine punishment. Priests told their congregations harrowing stories of children born with defects or leprosy because they were conceived during forbidden periods. As hard as it was to do penance, it seems that many married people were still forthcoming in confession. How else could the writer of one penitential even know about a wife mixing an aphrodisiac using her husband's semen, or a couple compulsively engaging in fellatio, or another couple practicing rear-entry sex in a standing position to accommodate the husband's obesity? All of these were forbidden, and assigned penances.

If married couples were supposed to act like monks most of the time, priests and nuns were under even tighter sexual restrictions. Marriage among the clergy was common until finally forbidden in the eleventh century, but the church exhorted coupled priests to have "chaste marriages," meaning that they were to abstain from having sex with their wives. Church authorities were not fooled by priests who kept servant women in their houses or monasteries, either. As early as 325 AD, all females were barred from cohabitating with priests except their mothers and women who were "above suspicion."

Sex with an unmarried woman brought one year of penance for a layman, but a cleric could expect to incur three to seven years of fasting, and a bishop twelve. If a priest took another man's wife to bed, one penitential demanded that he live on bread and water for up to twelve years, depending on his rank. A further range of penalties applied when a church official used enchantment to spark his partner's desire: "If anyone has used magic to excite love . . . let him do penance on bread and water for a whole year, if a cleric . . . if a deacon, for two; if a priest, three." A lonely monk who took a cow as his lover would be punished twice as severely as the lay owner of the beast would be for committing the same sin.

Every penitential forbade masturbation, but priests gave each other light penances for it. The ninth-century *Paenitentiale Bigotianum* gave a three-week penance to self-abusing priests while forcing lay offenders to repent for up to a full year. Clerics also seemed to expect that their religious meditations would be interrupted by sexual thoughts. The *Canons of Theodore* gave a priest only a week of penance if he ejaculated with "thoughts alone"—but the book radically increased the punishment if he erupted in the company of a woman. For laymen, the punishment for masturbation depended on who did it and how it was accomplished. Women, for example, were punished more harshly than men for using artificial aids. Men who used mechanical help were required to undergo only forty days of penance, while a woman's use of a dildo carried a penance of one year if she used it alone and three years if she shared it with another woman.

Masturbation came in for much harsher treatment in later centuries. In 1388, the French theologian Jean Gerson deemed it an abomination that led to sodomy. He wrote an entire treatise for priests to use on hearing the confessions of masturbators. Gerson recognized that few boys or men were ready to confess to the act, so he counseled priests to take a blunt approach: "Friend, didn't you touch or rub your member the way boys usually do?" If the penitents still refused to disclose their offenses, priests were to remind them how serious it was to lie in confession. He also recommended a series of cooling-off exercises for masturbators such as frequent prayer, flagellation, dousing of cold water, and spitting on the ground while renouncing the devil.

The writers of the penitentials also universally condemned homosexual activity, but, as with masturbation, the penances varied depending on what one did and how often. According to one Irish penitential, boys experimenting with anal sex were to do penance for two years, men were given three years for the same commission, and habitual offenders, seven. Some confessors imposed lifelong sentences for fellatio (whether performed by men or women). Lesbianism was also treated harshly, especially when compared with other sexual crimes. One German penitential mandated three years of fasting for it—the same penance given to a man who raped a widow or virgin.

People's close proximity to livestock is reflected in the benign treatment the early penitentials accorded for bestiality. At first it was treated merely as a form of masturbation, but eventually the penances became more severe—especially if the offender was a cleric. One penitential seemed to understand that boys were prone to experiment with animals, but that was expected to end with the coming of adulthood. Boys confessing to bestiality were given only forty days' penance, while adults were ordered to do one year's worth. The animals were treated with much less compassion:

Theodore's penitential demanded that "animals polluted by coitus with men are to be killed and their flesh thrown to dogs."

Perhaps one reason animals received so little mercy was that they had no money to pay anyone off. Many penitentials allowed sinners to buy their way out of atonement. This kept church coffers full and allowed people of means to avoid the fuss and embarrassment of doing penance. Newlyweds who wanted to consummate their marriage on their wedding night, when sex was normally forbidden, could usually get the divine go-ahead by giving the church some money. In England, the one-year penance for having sex during Lent could be ignored upon payment of a substantial sum. Another penitential allowed a rich man to avoid a seven-year fast by paying 840 men to fast with him for three days.

Despite inevitable corruption in the atonement process, penitentials provided Christians with clear guidance as to what they could do with their bodies, and at what cost. A man who had sex with a pig knew that he was being less offensive to God than he would be if he had anal intercourse with his wife, and women in some regions knew they could draw a longer period of penance for performing fellatio on a man than for killing him outright. We can't know the extent to which the penitentials were actually followed, but it is safe to assume that many offenders tried to fall in line: Fear of damnation is a hard burden for a believer to bear, even if it means having sex only a few days per month. The population of Europe declined from the year 500 to 1050 (approximately)—the period when the penitentials held their greatest influence. As later Christian law allowed married couples to engage in sex more often, the population began to grow. There are, of course, dozens of good reasons for such broad demographic changes, but every explanation must accept the simple truth: Population growth depends on plentiful intercourse.

The penitentials were gradually replaced after the new millennium by general laws enforced by formal courts, but the former's influence would be felt for centuries. Sex in all its forms retained its immoral stench, and we can still smell it. As recently as 1980, Pope John Paul II declared that married men were morally guilty of adultery if they felt passionate sexual desire for their wives—an attitude we can trace directly back to the early medieval period and the gloomy moral universe of the penitentials.[5]

SEX ON DEMAND: RAPE, THE MARITAL DEBT, AND THE *DROIT DE SEIGNEUR*

Rape was not condoned in the Middle Ages, but neither was there much concern about it. Only in the rarest of cases was it taken seriously as an act of violence. Rape was seen by late medieval/early Renaissance courts as a kind of mating ritual, after which the attackers and victims were required to marry each other. Even where rape was explicitly condemned, the courts looked for ways to go easy on the accused attackers, either by ruling that the females had consented to the sex or that they should have submitted to the man under the circumstances.

Rape disputes traditionally focused less on sex than on money. Roman law viewed rape as a species of theft: the abduction of female property from her guardians. Women were little different than horses or furniture. As Christianity took hold in Rome, rape was patchily redefined as a sexual crime in itself, but the law still remained very hard on the victims. Wellborn girls could be executed along with their abductors if they were found to be willing. In many cases, females were punished even if they did not consent, on the theory that they could have put up more effective resistance. Furthermore, if their maids or chaperones were found to have helped the rapist come into the house, molten lead was poured down the servants' gullets.

In the sixth century, the Roman emperor Justinian made the abduction or rape of females a capital crime, applicable to all classes. The families of the victims were allowed to kill the culprit if they caught him in the act. To prevent payoffs, females were barred from marrying their ravishers.

These changes were significant in that they defined rape as a crime not only against property, but also against women. However, the concept did not endure, and did little in the end to protect females from forced sex or marriage by capture.

The penitentials punished most violence and all illicit sex, but rarely put the two together. Those that did so were more concerned with preventing unarranged marriages than with protecting women. Significantly, the penitentials gave no breaks to female victims for being unchaste, regardless of whether or not they had been forced into sex. Even abused boys were punished: "A small boy misused by an elder older one, if he is ten years of age, shall fast for a week," according to one penitential. "If he consents, for twenty days." Later medieval church law punished *raptus* with excommunication, but also allowed rapists to escape punishment entirely if they could convince their victims to marry them.

IF CHURCH DOCTRINE was often vague on sexual violence, secular law contained no subtleties. Rape was translated into money: The higher the victim's rank, the more the rapist paid. In Ireland, for example, local chieftains were worth seven *cumals*—and each *cumal* was worth seven female slaves or twenty-one milk-producing cows. As a wife's honor was worth half of her husband's, a man who raped a chieftain's wife would have to pay 3.5 *cumals*, an amount equal to the value of twenty-four and a half slaves. In England, a man could expect to pay five shillings for fondling a free woman's breasts without permission. The fine doubled if he were to throw her on the ground, and the fine jumped to sixty shillings if he forced intercourse on her. Continental Frankish tribes followed the same pattern. If the girl was freeborn and the sex was consensual, the man paid her family forty *soldi*, but if the sex was forced and the man wanted to keep her as his wife, the price jumped tenfold. It was much cheaper to rape servants.

Rape victims always risked the accusation that they had invited the sex, or not fought off the violation hard enough. Irish law gave no legal protection to women who were slow to accuse men who had forced themselves on them. In Lombardy, girls who had voluntarily had sex with their ravishers could expect to be killed or sold off by their families. Unsurprisingly, many of them went to great lengths to avoid compromising situations. The eighth-century monk Paul the Deacon sang the praises of several Lombard princesses who had been turned over to invading Avar troops to be gang-raped. The girls were prepared:

> They put the flesh of raw chickens under the band between their breasts, and this, when putrified by the heat, gave out an evil smell. And the Avars, when they wanted to touch them, could not endure the stench that they thought was natural to them, but moved far away from them with cursing, saying that all the Lombard women had a bad smell.

The sisters had had good sense. Absent extreme measures, there was no way they were going to make it through the experience in one piece, even if they had survived the rapes. As it was, they were able to keep their honor and, when matters calmed down, secure marriages to princes and kings.

Even when there was no doubt that sex had occurred by force, the suspicion still lingered that the victim must *somehow* have been at fault. In one medieval French exemplum used by preachers in composing sermons, a young woman convinced a court that a man had taken her virginity with violence. The rapist was told to pay her a sum of money immediately, which he did. After she left the courtroom, the judge instructed the man to find the girl on the road and get his money back by any means necessary. The rapist did as he was told, and attacked the woman a second time. She resisted him so tenaciously that he was unable to take the money from her, and he returned to court empty-handed. The judge then called the woman back to court and ordered her to return the awarded sum. Had she fought to preserve her virginity as forcefully as she did to keep the money, the judge said, the rape would never have taken place.

If a rape resulted in pregnancy, the woman who carried the child had almost no chance of winning in court. The "two-seed" theory of conception, which was prevalent at the time, held that both men and women needed to "ejaculate" to conceive a child. As ejaculation was always accompanied by pleasure, the pregnancy would be considered proof that the woman had enjoyed herself. (Anyone tempted to laugh at this as premodern foolishness should review the 1995 comments of North Carolina legislator Henry Aldridge: Arguing against a bill to aid pregnant rape victims, he claimed, "The facts show that people who are raped, who are truly raped, the juices don't flow, the body functions don't work, and they don't get pregnant.")[6]

The picture was more nuanced when it came to forcible sex within marriage. First, the simple part: It was legally impossible for a husband to rape his wife. Once the two consummated their union, the husband then owned his wife's body. Under law, she had consented to a lifetime of sexual submission. Of course, we have no way of knowing how frequently men used force on their wives, but if husbands were patient and willing to spend some money on litigation, there was another route to compel their wives to submit: the church court.

ECCLESIASTICAL COURTS HANDLED the majority of cases involving marriage throughout the Middle Ages, including disputes where one spouse refused to have sex with the other. A husband whose wife was no longer interested in him could obtain a court order forcing her back into bed. As far as the judge was concerned, the wife owed her husband a sexual debt that she was obliged to pay. It was no different than ordering payment for a wagonload of animal feed. This "marital" or "conjugal" debt was enforceable even when conditions changed during the marriage. No less an authority than Pope Alexander III (1159–81) ruled that a wife still owed the marital debt even when her husband contracted leprosy.

Yet the marital debt doctrine ran both ways: Wives also had the right to ask ecclesiastical judges to order their husbands to service them properly, even if they became less attractive over the years. Thus a leprous wife was able to demand that her husband go with her to a leper colony and continue to have sex with her, and a woman who lived apart from her husband could get a church court to force him to pay her sexual visits. The ruling declared: "We hold the [husband] bound to pay the conjugal debt to the [wife] in her father's house one night each week and to keep up this obligation faithfully, until we shall order otherwise."

The idea of the church forcing people to have sex with each other is one of the many paradoxes of Christian sex law. If sex was sinful in marriage, what was the church doing requiring spouses to have it? The answer comes from bedrock Christian belief reaching back to Saint Augustine— that the sex urge was uncontrollable. No matter what one did, the original sin of Adam and Eve ensured that the genitalia would continue to demand satisfaction. The goal of the church was to corral the sex urge into marriage to prevent it from seeking other outlets. Without their spouses, men and women risked doing things that put their souls at even greater risk.

The marital debt was so fundamental that it trumped almost anything else. One authority ruled that a wife who demanded sex during her menstrual period (when it was otherwise forbidden) should not be refused if it appeared that she would go outside the marriage for satisfaction. The same was true when a serf's wife demanded sex while he was supposed to be working in the fields. If it looked like the wife could not wait and would commit adultery, the serf was allowed to take time off work and take care of her needs. Men were even forced to ask their wives' permission to go to the Holy Land on the Crusades, as the women could be tempted to seek the company of others during their absence.

The consequences for not meeting a spouse's sexual demands were severe. If refusal caused the other to masturbate or commit adultery, then the refusing spouse shared the guilt for the transgression. The spouse who denied sex could also face substantial physical dangers, as discovered by a Serbian priest, his wife, and a cow on the night before Easter:

> On Holy Saturday evening [when sex was forbidden], a priest was tormented by a demon of lust. Remembering the requirement of abstinence, his wife refused to satisfy his urges. As a result, the priest went out to a barn and sought release with a cow. The next day, during the Easter mass, flocks of birds attacked the church. The priest ordered that the doors and windows be barred against the onslaught, and tearfully confessed his sin before the congregation. The priest and the congregants then opened the door and were allowed to leave unharmed. When the priest's wife went out, however, the birds descended on her and tore her to pieces.

The message was clear: The priest would not have sinned had his wife gratified his lust. She was the responsible party, and paid the price.[7]

ANOTHER TYPE OF sex on demand was a noble landowner's prerogative to take his female serfs, generally on their wedding night—although the existence of *droit de seigneur* ("lord's right") or *jus primae noctis* ("right of the first night") is disputed among scholars.

Most likely, no formal law was ever written allowing nobles to deflower female serfs before their husbands did, but at the same time many lords did take advantage of females under their power without the slightest fear of punishment. The higher one was on the social scale, the broader was the privilege to take liberties with one's inferiors. That was a fact of feudal life, regardless of what any statute said. Only divine authority could intervene.

The ninth-century count (and future saint) Gerald of Aurillac saw an attractive serf girl and, as was his birthright, resolved to take her as his own. According to one version of the encounter, God stepped in at the last moment, not to save the girl but to safeguard Gerald's holiness:

> [Gerald] was tortured, therefore, allured, and consumed by blind fire. Overcome at length, he sent word to the mother of the girl that he would come by night. [Although still praying to be delivered from temptation] . . . Gerald came to the agreed place, and the girl entered the room; because he was cold he stood at the hearth facing her; divine grace looked on him just then, and this girl appeared to him so deformed that he could not believe it was she whom he saw, until her father asserted that it was so.

Gerald turned tail and rode away, thankful that the girl's miraculous ugliness had allowed him to remained celibate. The truth of the matter must have been more prosaic. The girl's parents had probably disfigured their daughter in a last-ditch effort to save her from rape. Again, we cannot know how often ruses like this were used or how many noble rapists were as gullible as Gerald. Like the weak everywhere, girls of the lower orders in medieval Europe were taken in countless unrecorded sexual assaults.[8]

By the thirteenth century, English law had severe penalties for rape on the books, but the process was still weighted heavily in favor of the accused men. If the alleged rapist was a member of the clergy (as most English rape defendants were), he stood a good chance of getting the case heard in a church court, where milder punishments were the rule. If the accused was an aristocrat, he could demand that the case be heard in a court of his own peers, where he was likely to be treated well. However, if the defendant could be roped into a general civil court, and if the victim was persistent and savvy enough to muscle the case all the way through, there was, at least, a chance that the death penalty could be imposed.

The legal process in such cases was grueling and hazardous for females. Immediately after the assault, the victim (who was often a child) was required to raise a "hue and cry" and display her bloody garments to the nearest group of respectable people. Then she was to have run to various public authorities to report the crime, making sure to describe it precisely the same way each time. Within forty days, she was to file a lawsuit. Other papers were also required. Any variance in the papers or other procedural missteps destroyed the lawsuit and exposed the woman to imprisonment for filing false charges. This was no mere threat. About half the number of women who dared to accuse a man of rape ended up in jail themselves.

On a March evening in 1320, Joan Seler, the eleven-year-old daughter of a London saddler, stood outside her house on a crowded London street. Suddenly a French merchant named Reymond Limoges grabbed her arm and dragged her across town to his room. According to court records, Limoges threw her onto the floor:

> *[Limoges] Raised the clothes of the same Joan . . . to her navel, she being clothed in a blue coat and a shift of light cloth and feloni-ously . . . with both his hands separated the legs and thighs of this same Joan, and with his right hand took his male organ of such and such a length and size and put it into the secret parts of the same Joan, and bruised her watershed and laid her open so that she was bleeding, and ravished her maidenhead, against the peace of our lord the King.*

Limoges fled as soon as he was done. Joan went immediately to local officials and to her father to report the assault, after which Limoges was apprehended. Eight months of legal skirmishing later, the case was thrown out because one of Joan's filings said the attack had taken place on a Sunday while another said it had happened on a Tuesday. Joan had also filed the rape suit after the forty-day time limit. Flush with his win, Limoges sued Joan for filing a false case. He also went after her father and others for "conspiracy" in helping Joan pursue the suit. The record ends with Joan's father being arrested.

Limoges walked free not because he was innocent, but because of the Selers' technical errors in moving the case through the system. In 1287, a girl even younger than Joan and even more cruelly molested lost her case because she was found to be too young to have been legally raped. A man named Hugo had attacked seven-year-old Agnes, "causing blood to come from her mid-section and her nostrils" as he struggled to have intercourse with her. Agnes's small size prevented Hugo from completing the act of coitus and rendered his assault, in the words of the court, a "worthless act." To constitute rape, at least in this court, the sex had to be pursued to its grim completion. Hugo was acquitted.

Legal authorities in Venice treated rape as a kind of seduction. In 1455, a man named Blasio took ten-year-old Maria by force, after which he made a promise of marriage to the girl's family. The family accepted the offer, and the problem appeared to be solved. Only after Blasio disappeared did legal proceedings begin. He was found and brought to court, then sentenced to a beating and jail. He was also to give Maria's family money for her dowry. The court then told Blasio he could avoid punishment if he made good on his promise to marry Maria. He accepted the deal immediately.

In cases where marriage between rapist and victim was not an option (as when they came from incompatible social classes), Venetian authorities punished the crime severely. In 1320, a cloth merchant's son made the grave mistake of raping a nobleman's daughter. He fled the city. In his absence, the authorities banned him perpetually, and also ruled that if he ever did return he would be dragged around the city, have his hands cut off, and then be hanged in Piazza San Marco. Presumably, he did not return.[9]

No Can Do: Impotence and Frigidity

Rape cases involved men who were capable of having sex, albeit with unwilling partners, but even when both parties were amenable, it didn't always go as planned. Sometimes it didn't go at all. Medieval law treated impotence in the same contradictory way it dealt with all carnal relations. Sex was inherently wrong, but husbands and wives still owed each other sexual submission, at least enough to prevent adultery and generate children. A person's inability to perform sexually—that is, to pay the "marital debt"—was one of very few allowable grounds for divorce. The trick for the courts was separating cases of true incapacity from ruses.

The issue of impotence was tied to the thorny question of when marriages began and ended. It was not until 1563 that a formal ceremony with a priest was required for a marriage to be valid. Before then, marriages began when the couple consented to wed each other and sealed the union with sex. The medieval marriage chapel could thus be a bed or a patch of soft ground. Most people never bothered to have formal weddings, and when they did their offspring were often in attendance. The key event that made the marriage was the initial sexual encounter, which both ensured that the marriage could be fruitful and activated the marital debt.

Couples usually conducted sexual "test drives" with each other before letting the world know they were married; but not everyone did so, and if impotence ended the sexual relations (or prevented them from ever beginning) the marriage could end too. The hard part was determining why sex had stopped, and how long the couple should keep trying. In 1206, Pope Innocent III weighed in on a case in which the wife's vagina was apparently unable to accommodate her husband's member. The pope ruled that the marriage should be declared null, and that both parties were free to find more fitting partners. However, if the woman's capacity was later increased through surgery or natural maturation, the pope said, she was to return to her former husband. In the event the woman remarried and was made more capacious through successful intercourse with her second husband, the pope also held that she should end that marriage and resume the first. Had the good pontiff known anything of the realities of married life, he might have realized that his solution would cause more problems than it would solve.

In cases of male impotence, the main issue was to determine whether the problem was permanent or temporary, and whether or not the husband or wife was fabricating the claim in order to obtain a divorce. In one English case, the court turned a team of prostitutes loose on the husband to test his capacity for arousal. He failed to rise. One of the women later testified that she had "exposed her naked breasts, and with her hands warmed at the said fire, she held and rubbed the penis and testicles of the said John . . . the whole time aforesaid the said penis was scarcely three inches long . . . remaining without any increase or decrease." The poor man was cursed by the prostitutes for "presuming to marry a young woman, defrauding her as he could not serve and please her better than that." In another case, the court-appointed prostitute testified that the husband was "large enough for any woman living in this world." Presumably, no divorce was granted.

In fifteenth-century Venice, a man named Nicolò disputed his wife's accusation of impotence and arranged a public inspection by prostitutes to prove his virility. He took a scribe, his boss, and a priest to a brothel, where he hired two women. Soon after he started in with one of the women, he called the priest over. The priest testified that Nicolò had placed the clergyman's hand on his erect penis, bragging: "Look here, I am a man, even though some say I cannot get it up." Nicolò then had intercourse with the prostitute on a bench while the witnesses watched, after which he smeared his ejaculate on the hands of the scribe. Nicolò's successful sexual performance continued into the night.

Not all men had Nicolò's ardor, however, and many blamed their sexual shortcomings on the sorcery of women. Dark magic was often suspected when a man was impotent with one woman but functional with another. Usually it was pinned on the husband's next sexual partner, as reflected in the penitentials. One penitential made women go through seven years of repentance for using "magic art [to take] away the ability to have intercourse from men." Another required priests to grill women about whether or not they had been casting spells:

> Have you done what some adulterous women are accustomed to do? When first they learn that their lovers want to take legitimate wives, they extinguish the men's desire by some magic art, so that they cannot be of use to their legitimate wives, or have intercourse with them. If you have done this or taught others, you should do penance for forty days on bread and water.

Magically caused impotence was a common ground for men trying to divorce their wives, even at the highest levels of society. France's King Philip II Augustus (1180–1223) claimed that his wife, Ingeborg of Denmark, had bewitched him to the point where he could not consummate the union. People speculated that he discovered on the wedding night that she was not a virgin or had some kind of hidden deformity—or that she simply had bad breath. Regardless, Ingeborg herself claimed that the union had in fact been sealed with sex. The divorce was not granted. Philip then locked Ingeborg up in grimy quarters and married his true love, Agnes of Merania, with whom he fathered several children. Only after Agnes's death and Pope Innocent III's relentless work on behalf of Ingeborg did Philip take her back.

Judging by some of the potions in circulation used to quell men's sexual energy, it is a wonder that more impotence cases did not end up as homicides. One medieval Arab *grimoire*, translated into Spanish as the *Picatrix*, suggested that women try the following process to calm men down:

> Take half a drachm each of the brain of a black cat and mandrake seed. Mix these two together and blend them very well.

Afterwards make an image of wax, and make a hole in the top of the head, through which you force the abovementioned mixture. Then make an iron needle and push that needle into the image, in the place where he enjoys a woman. Then take four drachms of pig's blood, two drachms of hare's rennet and swallow's brain, and a pound each of sheep's milk and myrtle sap. Mix all of the above together and give it as a drink to him whose desire for a woman you wish to take away, and fumigate the image with two drachms each of incense and galbanum mixed together. And what you wish will happen.

Assuming that the man only became impotent and did not die from this poison, the *Picatrix* advised a less invasive method of undoing the spell. The sorceress should make new wax images of herself and the stricken man, wait for the right moment, and then join the dolls together in an embrace, also bathing them together in rosewater.[10]

PROSTITUTION: A MOSTLY UNHOLY INSTITUTION

Medieval sex law reached its irrational zenith when it came to sex for sale. The prostitute was everything Christian society despised: She had prodigious sex outside marriage, practiced contraception, aborted her children, lured husbands from their wives, and left men poisoned before God. Yet this paragon of sin was not only tolerated much of the time, she was often pimped by both religious and secular authorities for healthy profits. There were periodic measures to stamp out prostitution, to be sure, but the utility of prostitutes as money machines was too great for any of these efforts to last.

Christian ambivalence about prostitution reaches back to Saint Augustine himself, who, we will remember, condemned all sexual desire as unclean and wicked. At the same time, he recognized that men were going to follow the call of their gonads. There was nothing worse than a prostitute, but Augustine also saw that if they were pulled from circulation, men's lust would seep everywhere and pollute the world. Prostitutes were damned, but their souls were to be sacrificed for the betterment of good society. Nearly one thousand years later, the influential theologian Saint Thomas Aquinas had the same outlook: "Prostitution in the towns is like the cesspool in the palace: take away the cesspool and the palace will become an unclean and evil-smelling place." Taking this thinking one step further, church and city authorities concluded that so long as there was a need to clean out human muck, they should make some money in the process.

Thus was born the licensed brothel, a factory of evil serving the common good. By 1358, the Grand Council of Venice would declare that prostitution was "absolutely indispensable to the world." Besides filling the coffers of the ruling classes, official whorehouses were thought to allow good maidens to guard their virginity. Once married, women also could keep their marriages pure by letting their husbands satisfy their unusual sexual demands outside the home. Indeed, the more institutionalized prostitution became, the more it was lauded as a bastion of family values. In 1403, the city of Florence set up an "Office of Honesty," which established a municipal brothel. It was believed that the birthrate was falling because too many men were experimenting with homosexuality before they reached marriageable age. If men accustomed themselves to sex with attractive women, it was hoped, they would avoid "the filthiness of the horrible crime which is the vice of sodomy" and choose nice girls to marry.

The specialized skills of prostitutes were always in high demand. We have already seen how they were used as experts in courtroom impotency disputes, but that was far from all. Successful prostitutes had a deep understanding of local townsmen's sexual skills. Some recognized the value of such information, and made money off it. One London tart built a business as a consultant to girls contemplating marriage, telling them of their potential husbands' sexual strengths and weaknesses. Her bad review of one man caused a wealthy widow to back out of a marriage, and the man sued the prostitute for the loss of the money he would have made in the union.

Brothels owned by local businesspeople were heavily taxed. Municipalities also supported their own brothels, which must have generated much better profit margins. In the fifteenth century, the city of Dijon and its surrounding area had a population of less than ten thousand, yet the city supported a public bordello and eighteen private establishments. In Strasbourg, there were fifty-seven brothels in six streets alone. Prostitutes worked in the city cathedral's bell tower, where they were called "swallows," and in an establishment owned by the city's bishop. The church's involvement in prostitution was never hidden. In 1457, the archbishop of Mainz granted the brothel franchise to an aristocratic family, which raises the question of how an archbishop had the right to run brothels in the first place. The law establishing the Avignon city brothel gave the local abbess the key and charged her with keeping order there and making sure revenues were collected. In 1608, the Dominicans of Perpignan even collected alms from their congregants for the refurbishment of the order's bordello.

In Paris, prostitution was confined to certain neighborhoods close to the city center, often near institutes of higher learning. While masters of rhetoric and theology delivered lectures in the upper rooms, working women delivered their own brand of knowledge downstairs. The university in Toulouse split the proceeds of the town's brothel with the city. Oxford and Cambridge universities, however, were not so liberally inclined; in 1461, the chancellor of Oxford was authorized to "banish from a circumference of ten miles around the said university all bawds, whores and incontinent women," which he seems to have done with relish.

THE TOLERANCE OF prostitution during the Middle Ages was neither consistent nor universal. There was no shortage of efforts to stamp it out.

The saintly Louis IX of France, for example, closed the brothels before he set off on a Crusade—only to find that the prostitutes he had banished had followed his army all the way to the Holy Land. Cities also expelled their prostitutes periodically, but never for very long. Venice banished prostitution in 1266 and again in 1314, but by the early sixteenth century an interested customer could make use of an official directory of prostitutes, which set out prices, specialties, and contact information.

City and church authorities were often more interested in protecting their own brothels from competition—especially from freelancers—than in eradicating the practice entirely. They also restricted whom the women could take on as customers. Jewish men, for example, were often barred from patronizing Christian prostitutes, which was in line with general prohibitions against sex between Jewish men and Christian women. Avignon threatened Jewish men with the loss of a foot for walking into a public brothel. In Venice, prostitutes were also at risk of punishment if they knowingly took Jews on as customers, as one record reflects:

> *One day in contempt of Catholic faith [a Jewish man] entered a whore's room near the Rialto and began to have intercourse with her, putting his member in her. But the other prostitutes outside, knowing that he was a Jew when he entered, called out saying this whore has a Jew in her room. The said whore then pulled away rapidly, not allowing the Jew to expel or project his semen.*

Prostitutes in most cities were compelled to distinguish themselves from respectable women. In Paris and Avignon, they were required to put red shoulder knots on their dresses. Leipzig demanded that its prostitutes wear yellow cloaks trimmed in blue, while other cities prescribed cloaks and caps of other colors. In Milan, anyone meeting an illegally clad strumpet had the right to strip her on the spot. In some French cities, prostitutes had their improper clothing confiscated along with their jewelry and sold by local constables, who kept part of the proceeds. The same was true in

London, where prostitutes were forbidden from dressing like "good and noble dames and damsels," and laws specifically barred "common lewd women" from wearing fur or "noble lining." The sheriff was charged with confiscating all such colored hoods or fur.

Prostitutes working in official brothels lived better than streetwalkers, but had few legal rights. In Mantua, a man turned down by his regular prostitute tried to force himself on her. Could she sue him for attempted rape? No, the jurists held. By putting up her body for sale, she was incapable of ever being raped. In another case, a customer broke down a prostitute's front door to get to her. Behind him came a band of thieves, who stole her furniture. Was the door-breaker responsible for the theft? No, again. His lust justified the break-in, the judges said, and he could not be held responsible for what others did afterward. Still, a prostitute had the right to demand and keep a reasonable wage for her services—but only if she was honest about what she was selling. If she made herself up to appear younger or more beautiful than she actually was, she was only allowed to charge what she was really worth; the customer kept the difference. If the customer was crafty enough to get the prostitute to service him and then leave without paying, she was out of luck: The courts would not listen to her claim.[11]

Money was never the key component of harlotry under the law. Rather, a prostitute was usually defined merely as a promiscuous woman available for the pleasures of many men. The question was: How many men? Some authorities said five lovers sufficed, others as few as two or as many as twenty thousand. Whatever the variations in local law or custom, there was no distinction between a woman whose virtue was for sale and one who was merely easy to get. Both of them had the same vulnerable legal and social status.

IT IS NO surprise that a great many nuns, especially those who had been forced into the convent, never made good on their vows of chastity. Saint

Throughout the Middle Ages and the Renaissance, the Jew was considered an agent of Satan, a sexual deviant and a confederate of the goat, an animal associated with sexual incontinence. Sex with Jews was almost always tightly restricted and sometimes punishable with death. ©TOPFOTO

Boniface complained as early as the seventh century that nuns making pilgrimages to Rome often ended up working in roadside brothels. The question arose as to what to do with the nun-prostitute's earnings. In the mid-fifteenth century, Franciscus de Platea instituted a kind of shop rule, holding that nun-prostitutes should remit their fees to their convents, but also that convents could not keep the money for themselves. Rather, they were told to use it to support pious causes. Far more numerous were nuns who had sex for the fun of it. Like other unmarried, sexually active women, they were technically prostitutes. When the French theologian Jean Gerson complained that "cloisters of nuns have become as it were brothels of harlots," he meant to say that the nuns were entertaining great numbers of visitors, not that they were making money. The Swiss preacher Johann Geiler von Kaisersberg proclaimed in the Strasbourg Cathedral that "he would rather his sister should become a prostitute than that she should be thrust into a nunnery of lax life." By this he was asserting that a brothel was in fact a better choice than a convent.

Venetian convents served as holding pens for upper-class girls who had either got themselves into trouble or whose families couldn't yet bankroll their dowries. Therefore, many educated, sexually mature young women donned nun's habits that they planned to remove as soon as the opportunity for sex arose. The result was a collection of convents that must have been rather stimulating places. No fewer than thirty-three Venetian convents faced criminal prosecution in the fourteenth and fifteenth centuries for illegal sexual activity. Most notorious was the convent of Sant'Angelo di Contorta, which was populated by girls from the city's best families and which was prosecuted fifty-two times. One of the sisters there, the infamous Liseta de Boura, was repeatedly charged, including once for serving up a young virgin to one of her lovers, until she was finally barred from the convent. Without missing a beat, she went to live with a famous courtesan and continued her affairs. Pope Sixtus IV tried to close the place down in 1474, but it stayed open without authorization and generated even more trouble. Finally, it was converted into a storehouse for gunpowder and, in 1589, blew up. No trace of the place exists.

Were Sister Liseta and her ilk prostitutes? Yes, but as nuns they still required special treatment. They were subject to the jurisdiction of church courts only. The records of Venice's ecclesiastical tribunals from this period are lost, but it seems the sisters were not treated harshly. By contrast, the nuns' lovers were tried by the city's secular tribunals, which were prone to handing out extreme punishments. The accusations against the men often included the charge of adultery, in which the aggrieved husband was Jesus Christ himself. In 1395, Antonio Vianaro was prosecuted for entering the convent of Santa Croce several times to sleep with Sister Ursia Tressa in her cell. He was formally accused of "not considering how much injury he caused the Highest Creator by violating the bride of Jesus Christ" and also of "committing wicked incest, fornication, adultery, and sacrilege, [and] not keeping God before his eyes." In this case, Christ was put in the same position as any other cuckolded husband. The court took on the responsibility of defending his honor, and Vianaro was put in jail for two years.

With divine manhood on the line, there was little room for mercy in punishing men who slept with nuns. Still, the courts were sometimes ready to waive the punishments. In one case, a young nun named Polisena Cavatorta was wooed in the convent by the noble Giovanni Valier. After several moonlit walks in the garden and proposals of marriage, they finally made love. The affair continued, and soon their baby boy was born at the convent. All would have proceeded without incident had Valier not convinced the nun to run away with him; he was sentenced to two years in jail and a fine, but the court said the sentence would be ignored if he gave her a thousand-ducat dowry and made her his wife. The record ends there, but it seems reasonable to assume that love won the day, and that the honor of God was disregarded.[12]

SODOMY, JEWS, AND SHARED BREAD: SEXUAL DEVIANCE AND GAY UNIONS

Medieval laws governing sodomy were as irrational as sexual desire itself. Depending on where they took place, the same sex acts could bring death at the stake or be overlooked entirely. At the same time homosexuals were being hunted down and killed, same-gender couples were living together under one roof after publicly pledging their lifelong commitment to each other. The fates of people who preferred their own gender (or animals, with which homosexuals were often equated) were often ill-defined, but they were also never easy.

The harsh measures against homosexual behavior prescribed by Emperor Justinian were neither effective nor uniformly applied, and with the collapse of the Western Empire, Roman law lost much of its force anyway. What remained were patchworks of local laws and religious doctrines that, taken together, reflected a malignant toleration of same-gender sex: Nowhere approved and everywhere considered sinful, it was nonetheless only sporadically punished.

The pivotal questions regarding sodomy concerned who was hurt by it and whether or not the damage could be repaired. Was the urge toward "unnatural" sex a purely individual failing and therefore a threat only to the souls of the sodomites themselves? If so, could the sin be forgiven if they repented? Or was sodomy an offense against God so bad that hellfire would fall upon everyone unless sodomites were wiped out? Both beliefs existed simultaneously, although people were more ready to forgive sodomy before the turn of the millennium than afterward, when same-gender sex and bestiality came to be viewed as major crimes deserving of cruel punishments.

THE BELIEF THAT homosexuality could provoke famine, pestilence, and earthquakes remained strong wherever people used the Bible for moral guidance. The book of Leviticus, we will recall, declared that men who lie with men "as women" pollute the land and must be put to death lest they provoke God to vomit everyone out. Justinian had that belief clear in his mind when he suppressed homosexual activity, but even he believed that homosexuals could be forgiven if they would "submit themselves to God" and "report their disease" to a priest. The penitential handbooks framed homosexual sex as a terrible mistake, but one that could be fixed with prayer and fasting. A man might incur a fifteen-year punitive diet of bread and water for having sex with another man (more than that if fellatio was involved), but once the price was paid the offender's moral slate was wiped clean. Nothing in the penitentials demanded that homosexuals be punished to save the community.

That changed drastically from approximately the twelfth century. As Crusade after failed Crusade highlighted the threatening military power of the Arab Muslims, and as plague after plague beat down the European population, the terrified people of Christendom looked for scapegoats and found them in Muslims, Jews, and witches. An array of new laws marked these groups for brutal treatment. Each was routinely accused of denying God, working to harm Christian society, and having homosexual sex.

The battles against the Muslims in the Holy Land and in Iberia generated a demonology that linked Islam with sexual excess and especially homosexuality. Muhammad was said to have introduced sodomy to the Arabs back in the seventh century and got them hooked on it. Four hundred years later, the First Crusade began after a letter purportedly appeared from the Byzantine emperor Alexios I Komnenos urging the Christian kingdoms of Europe to save the Holy Land from the perverted rule of the Muslims. The appeal, which has since been identified as a fake, emphasized that Muslims were sodomizing "men of every age and rank" and had even killed a bishop in the course of raping him. This kind of libel continued throughout the Middle Ages, when Islam became synonymous in the West with deviant sexual practices.

Even Christians who fought Muslims were accused of acquiring "effeminate" ways, as the Knights Templar bitterly discovered. The order was founded in Jerusalem in 1120 to defend the parts of the Holy Land that the crusaders had conquered. In short order, the riches taken by the Templars in battle, and the interest they earned in the moneylending business, made them quite wealthy. They owned a network of castles throughout the Levant and established a large base of operations in Paris called the Temple, where they resided as a quasi-sovereign power. As envy inevitably follows money, in the fourteenth century King Philip IV of France (known as Philippe le Bel, or "Philip the Fair") turned his avaricious eye on the Templars. In 1307, after the order's leader, Jacques de Molay, bragged of the riches buried beneath the Temple, Philip had the Templars under his control arrested and declared their property forfeited.

The charges Philip brought against the Knights Templar were calculated to spark indignation. The knights were accused of worshipping Muhammad, performing human sacrifice, stomping on the cross, and serving the devil. They were also charged with every variant of homosexual sex. "We shudder with violent horror," said Philip in his order of arrest, "in thinking of the gravity of [the accusations]." Before crowds of eager spectators, inquisitors wrung confessions out of many accused knights, although very few confessed to sodomy. In one gruesome spectacle, more than one hundred Templars were burned at the stake simultaneously. Pope Clement V formally dissolved the order in 1312, and two years later de Molay himself was put to death. As the flames rose around him, he cursed both the king and the complicit pope, predicting that neither man would live out the year. (Both of them, in fact, died soon afterward.)

In an atmosphere in which Christians felt acutely threatened both from abroad and within their communities, the call was made everywhere to punish homosexuality. God had destroyed the wicked people of Sodom and Gomorrah, according to one new law, because "they engaged in that sin which is against nature." Now, "every man should be on guard against this failing" or risk "famine, plague, catastrophe, and countless other calamities." To the late medieval mind, sickness and defeat were the natural result of heresy, and heresy was almost always accompanied by deviant sexual practices. In earlier years, sodomites could be forgiven; now people felt that they should be cast out or killed.[13]

During the late twelfth century, the church issued a canon requiring harsh sanctions against all heretics, Jews, moneylenders, Muslims, and homosexuals. Those who had sex with their own gender "on account of which the wrath of God came" were to be excommunicated and driven out of society. Many secular laws followed up by imposing laws requiring cruel executions. A Castilian law from the thirteenth century was typical:

Although we are reluctant to speak of something which is reckless to consider and reckless to perform, terrible sins are nevertheless sometimes committed, and it happens that one man desires to sin against nature with another. We therefore command that if any commit this sin, once it is proven, both be castrated before the whole populace and on the third day be hung up by the legs until dead, and that their bodies never be taken down.

Elsewhere, homosexual offenses brought burning at the stake and hanging by the "virile member." By 1300, there were laws in place punishing homosexual behavior harshly in virtually every jurisdiction. One city required that homosexuals not only be burned, but that their families be forced to watch the execution and to remain until the fire was out.

Many of the same laws that punished homosexuals were also directed against Jews, who were particularly despised. Jews were suspected, among other things, of drinking the blood of Christians and sometimes feasting on semen as they collaborated with the devil. Mob violence against Jews exploded with the First Crusade in the 1090s, and soon they were being massacred for allegedly working with Muslims to poison well water. When the Black Death broke out in 1348 and killed over one-third of the

European population, anti-Semitic passions reached a frenzy as Jews were widely blamed for causing the contagion with poisons and evil spells. Some thought the Jews had brought about the plague in anger over laws barring Jewish-Christian intermarriage; others were convinced that they were doing the bidding of Satan. Regardless, a broad swath of Christian society was convinced that Jews were the worst kind of heretics.

Sex with Jews was barred almost everywhere. It was commonly believed that they stank of the devil and gave birth to goats and pigs. Any contact with them was thought to transmit filth. In 1215, to prevent any accidental sexual assignations between Jews and Christians, the church ordered Jews to wear distinctive badges and clothing (the notorious yellow stars of Nazi Germany were a later revival of this tradition). Vienna required them to wear a hat shaped like devil or goat horns. When local bans on Jewish-Christian sex were ignored, the penalties were harsh. One Jew named Pandonus was publically castrated in front of the papal palace in Avignon for sleeping with a Christian woman. In 1222, an Oxford deacon was burned to death on a charge of bestiality for marrying a Jew. At about the same time, a Parisian man who had fathered children with a Jewish woman was also burned. The charge was sodomy, but the rationale was the same: "Coition with a Jewess is precisely the same as if a man should copulate with a dog."[14]

MEDIEVAL LAW VIEWED bestiality and homosexuality as no less heretical than Judaism and Islam. The German word *Ketzer*, meaning heretic, was also used to mean sodomite; "to commit heresy with one another" was a euphemism for male-male intercourse. In this heated atmosphere, "sodomy" became a catch-all term for forbidden sex in its most extreme forms. By the close of the thirteenth century, a new legal text appeared in England prescribing live burial for anyone having sex with Jews, animals, persons of their own gender. The details of the sex were unimportant to the law. They were all insults to God, and deserving of the worst punishments.

Even in cosmopolitan Venice, which had a well-deserved reputation as a destination sex resort, sodomy was prosecuted as a "diabolical" crime against God. Death at the stake was the normal penalty, although there was some passing concern for the suffering such punishments caused. In 1445, authorities considered how to make sodomy executions less painful. It was suggested that the condemned be tied to wooden boards with their neck tightly chained, so that as the wood burned away they would be quickly strangled. The proposal was rejected.

With the Black Death and subsequent plagues, Venice's ruling class feared that homosexuality on the city's trading ships would provoke God to destroy the fleets. The city's antisodomy rules had traditionally been ignored on the high seas, making thousands of merchant vessels informal safe zones for male-male sex. "It is surprising," said a high criminal tribunal, "that divine justice has not sunk them."[15] The loophole was closed in 1420 with a new law barring "the vice of sodomy" on Venetian ships wherever they might be, and offering rewards to anyone reporting seaborne sodomites to the authorities. As with all sexual legislation, it is impossible to tell how effective this rule was in stopping sexual activity among merchant sailors. What it did do was make such sex much riskier.

Despite regular roundups and the torture of sodomy suspects, the Venetian authorities were convinced that the "abhorrent vice" was on the rise.[16] Rumors swirled that men were meeting for sex in apothecaries and bakeries, as well as in churches and on street corners. To understand the scope of the problem, authorities commissioned what historian Guido Ruggiero has called a "sodomy census." Two nobles from each of the city's parishes spent a year scouring neighborhoods for signs that sodomy was taking place. The city also required doctors and barbers to report all cases in which their young or female patients' hindquarters showed excessive wear and tear:

To eliminate the vice of sodomy from this city is worth every concern and as there are many women who consent to this vice and are broken in the rear parts and also many boys are so broken and all those treated, yet still none are accused and their deeds go unpunished; therefore, because it is wise to honor God . . . those who are broken in these parts be they boys or women are to be denounced.

Given the risks, few people must have sought treatment for "breaks" in their "rear parts," although the law seemed to go a bit lighter on young passive homosexuals. In a 1474 prosecution against a homosexual "ring," the men who did the penetrating were decapitated and then burned. A ten-year-old boy who had been the recipient of sex was only whipped. However, an eighteen-year-old passive boy in the same group was found to be old enough to know better: He received twenty-five lashes and had his nose cut off.

The Venetian authorities were also ready to show some lenience for bestial sodomy, but only when there was a solid excuse. An artisan named Simon, facing the death penalty for taking his pleasure with a goat, claimed that an accident had left him useless with women and unable to masturbate. Animals, he claimed, were his only sexual option. He was examined by surgeons, who found that while he had a "normal member" he was still unable to feel normal sensation or emit sperm. Simon was then set upon by two prostitutes, who used their skills "to see if the said Simon could be in any way corrupted." He was able to achieve an erection but not much else. In the end, Simon lost his right hand and was branded and beaten—savage treatment, to be sure, but still preferable to being burned alive.

The city of Florence used a carrot-and-stick approach to fight sodomy. As discussed, a municipal brothel was chartered to reinforce heterosexual tastes in the city's young men. The city also established an "Office of the Night," which put boxes on the streets in which people could leave anonymous sodomy charges against others. Anyone so accused would be interrogated and pressured to name others. The penalties were dropped if the men denounced themselves and identified their partners; about forty men per year did so.

While all sodomy was condemned in Florence, as in Venice it was considered particularly outrageous and embarrassing for grown men to take the "womanly" role. A sixty-three-year-old man condemned to death for passive homosexuality had his sentence reduced to a fine and a lifetime diet of bread and water, but not because anyone forgave him: The authorities were concerned about the bad publicity. To execute a man for acting like a woman sexually would be to admit that such things happened within city limits.

THE SPANISH INQUISITION got into the sodomite-killing business in 1524, when it received permission to go after Don Sancho de la Caballeria, the prominent descendant of a converted Jew. Don Sancho had been one of the Inquisition's most outspoken critics, and inquisitors had been trying to get him for years. They were unsuccessful until they found a witness willing to denounce him for sodomy. The problem was that the Inquisition had not yet been given authority over sodomy cases in Aragon, where Don Sancho lived. Secular authorities were already terrorizing sodomites, often hanging them upside down with their genitals tied around their necks, but the Inquisition wanted to punish Don Sancho itself. The fight over who would deal with him went all the way to Pope Clement VII, who sided, predictably enough, with the Inquisition, and gave it jurisdiction over sodomy cases in Aragon.

Don Sancho lost his case but died naturally before his appeals were over. However, the Inquisition was just getting started. Hundreds of executions followed in the coming decades, both for homosexual relations and bestiality. In one case, twelve men were publicly burned to death at once.

Nine of them were Aragonese peasants charged with raping mules and donkeys; the other three were foreigners convicted of homosexual practices. It must have been a long day, as the executioners had problems collecting enough wood to burn everyone at once.

The Spanish Inquisition also received authority to go after married couples for sex crimes. Several men were burned for having anal intercourse with their wives, while one field hand, accused by his estranged wife of having forced her to perform both oral and anal sex with him, was sentenced to ten years as a slave on a galleon. Whether this miserable life was better than death remains in question, but the inquisitors believed they were being merciful. They had concluded that the man had not been wholly responsible for the crimes, because he had been underage when he had last sodomized his wife.

For many married couples, anal sex was a common form of birth control, but for many men it was also a titillating, if not cruel, pleasure. Records show that girls as young as seven were being stocked in brothels for the purpose, and female prostitutes who dressed as men to attract male clients (and then presumably supplied them with anal sex) were singled out for harsh condemnation. One cannot blame the prostitutes for doing what they could to fulfill marketplace demands, which were skewing toward homosexuality: By 1511, after more than a century of intense repression, Venice's patriarch announced that sodomy among men was so prevalent that female prostitutes were going out of business.[17]

WHILE LESS IS known about female-female sex during the medieval period, it seems clear that it was repressed, although not widely. As we have seen, lesbianism was strongly condemned in the penitential handbooks, but later church pronouncements paid little attention to the subject. The first known antilesbian law, from France in 1270, raised more questions than it answered:

He who has been proven to be a sodomite must lose his testicles. And if he does it a second time, he must lose his member. And if he does it a third time, he must be burned. A woman who does this shall lose her member each time, and on the third must be burned.

The drafters of this law had clearly meant to impose the same castration-based penalties on women as on men, but what female "member" were they referring to? If the first offense called for the inflicting of some kind of genital mutilation such as a clitoridectomy, what "member" was the woman to lose the second time? We cannot say. Later antilesbian laws were more specific, and, if possible, even more brutal. A statute from the Italian town of Treviso required that any females older than twelve caught having sexual relations with each other, even for the first time, "be tied naked for a full day to a stake in the Street of Locusts and then burned at the stake."

For lawmakers, the most immoral aspect of lesbianism occurred when women simulated heterosexual sex. The Inquisition, for example, was not permitted to go after women for having sex with each other unless "artificial instruments" were involved. Women who did not use such objects, inquisitors were told, were not committing sodomy. The same was true elsewhere in Europe, where it was an open question whether or not female-female sex without penetration, or at least without a woman taking on the male role, was sex at all. All legal ambiguities evaporated when a dildo appeared in the bed.

In 1477, Katharina Hetzeldorfer was put to death in Speyer on accusations that she had her "manly will" with other females and "behaved exactly like a man with women." Hetzeldorfer confessed, presumably after torture, that she had used a "piece of wood that she held between her legs" to simulate a penis, and also that she had "made an instrument with a red piece of leather, at the front filled with cotton, and a wooden stick stuck into it." It was the contraption and her use of it to pose as a man in the sexual sense that infuriated the judges. In the same way, two amorous nuns in sixteenth-century Spain would likely have survived their legal problems had they not "polluted" themselves by penetrating each other with objects and impersonating men. As it was, they were burned to death.

The French essayist Michel de Montaigne wrote of several girls from the French town of Chaumont-en-Bassigny who had secretly agreed to "dress themselves up as males and thus continue their life in the world." One of them became a weaver and assumed the identity of "a well-disposed young man who made friends with everybody." She eventually married a young woman from the town of Vitry-le-François. The two lived together for several months, "to [the wife's] satisfaction," until the weaver was denounced. She was charged "for using illicit devices to supply her defect in sex," and was hanged—a fate she said she would rather endure than return to living as a female. It is simple enough to recognize the dynamic at work in such cases: Male judges recoiled at what they saw as the theft of male sexual prerogatives.

The situation became more complex when men dressed as women, professionally, in order to attract other men. The customers could not be blamed; they believed they were paying for a female. Yet did a cross-dressing prostitute commit any crimes? We have few records about male transvestite prostitutes during this period, but that does not mean they were rare; nor does it show that they were at peace with the law. There can be little doubt that many paid for forsaking their male identity.

Such was probably the case with John Rykener, a transvestite hustler arrested in London in December 1395. Rykener, whose *nom de rue* was "Eleanor," was caught dressed in women's clothing while performing "libidinous" acts on his customer, John Britby. Evidently Britby had believed Rykener to be a woman when the two crossed paths on Cheap Street, and still thought so when he and Rykener went to a nearby stall to commit what records called the "unmentionable, and ignominious vice." Rykener told police that he had been trained in the finer points of cross-dressing by Elizabeth Brouderer, a pimp. A prostitute named Anna had given him further instruction on how, in the words of the London authorities, to "practice this detestable vice in the manner of a woman." He was a quick study and soon had his own customers, all of whom had believed that "Eleanor" was female. Not long before the arrest, Rykener had worked in Oxford as an embroiderer and a female prostitute, counting at least three university scholars as his customers. He added that he preferred to service clerics because they paid well.

Rykener was certainly unusual, but did he do anything illegal? We do not know what he was charged with. Most likely he was not accused of illegal prostitution, as that was an offense only women could commit. There are no known English cases from this period in which a man was charged with prostitution. Assuming that Rykener was too male to be a prostitute, was he too female to be a male sodomite? It is unclear. The records consistently refer to Rykener as "Eleanor," as though the police who recorded the confession also accepted him as a woman. If they did, and if he was taken for female, his sex with Britby, the priests, and the other men might not have been characterized as sodomy.

Another case against a male transvestite prostitute, this time in Venice, involved even blurrier gender lines. Rolandino Ronchaia was, at least to some extent, a hermaphrodite. He was born with male genitalia and was raised male, though he also had an unusually feminine face and enlarged breasts. Ronchaia tried marriage as a young man, but the union collapsed on account of his inability to achieve an erection. After his wife died from the plague, he assumed a female identity, took the name "Rolandina," and went to work on the Rialto as a female prostitute. Rolandina's "many and infinite" customers believed they were having sex with a woman. "He deceived them," declared the court, with the following ruse: "When they were on his body he hid as much as possible his member . . . and took the member [of the other] and put it in his rear parts and stayed with this until they emitted sperm giving them every delight as do true prostitutes." The authorities were intrigued by his physical peculiarities but had no trouble sentencing him, in 1354, to a fiery death between the Columns of Justice in Piazza San Marco.[18]

ONCE WE GRASP the level of savagery meted out to sodomites during the late Middle Ages, we must ask whether or not it deterred anyone from having forbidden sex. Did the horror of watching people consumed by fire in city squares scare anyone away from their own gender? How many Christians saved their souls by swearing off the "unnatural vices?" Did the association of sodomy with plagues and heresy prompt people to live by the rules of Leviticus? Other than an informal "sodomy census" in fifteenth-century Venice (which showed an increase in the vice), there were no studies of homosexual behavior during this period. Yet even without hard data, we can make some cautious assumptions.

Homosexual sex very likely continued apace even as sodomites were being executed. Neither the law nor religion ever seems to have lasting changes on what people do in bed. The increasing frequency of sodomy prosecutions is itself evidence that the message was not getting through; add to that the steady flow of poetry, letters, and other writings being generated that can only be understood as homoerotic. The twelfth-century monk-poet Bernard of Cluny was exaggerating when he said that homosexual sodomites were as "numerous as grains of barley, as many as the shells of the sea or the sands of the shore," but he still made a point. There is no reason to believe that any threats from the law or the pulpit ever had a lasting effect on people's sexual decisions.

Is this because those who engaged in homosexual sex were hardwired for it, in effect homosexual by nature? Probably not. Until the nineteenth century, no concept existed of heterosexuality or homosexuality as full-time orientations. The term "homosexual" was not coined until about 1870. As in ancient societies, people in the Middle Ages did not identify themselves or others as exclusively interested in one gender or another.

Rather, sodomy was a broad category of forbidden conduct, something one did in violation of the laws of God and man. Most people likely had sexual relations with the opposite gender most of the time, but some form of sodomy was likely a reality for many people. Sodomy, in any of its forms, was a crime anyone could commit.

However, there are numerous examples of people who did lean heavily toward their own gender, such as the much-reviled king of England, Edward II (1307–27). Although he managed to father at least four children, his intemperate affection for young men became his undoing. Edward's lavishing of gifts and privileges on his lovers brought him into constant conflict with his wife and the nobility, and eventually resulted in him being forcibly deposed. In 1326, his lover Hugh le Despenser was castrated, and his genitals were burned publicly before he was beheaded. Edward himself was later murdered, according to many accounts, by an assassin's insertion of a red-hot poker in his anus. The significance of this kind of punishment could not be clearer.

Edward's ineptitude as a monarch (both Scotland and much of Ireland were lost on his watch) destined him for an unhappy end, but he was far from the only medieval man of high position to openly pursue loving relationships with other men. One of Edward's predecessors, the crusading king Richard I (the "Lionhearted"), had a lasting affair as a young man with Philip II Augustus, the king of France, with whom he spent much of his time and shared a bed. Richard's piety led him to resolve more than once to give up his relations with men. When he fell gravely ill, he promised on his sickbed to lead a "holier" life if he survived. The king lived on, but it is unclear whether or not he kept his promise. He died without legitimate offspring, leaving a wife with whom, most agree, he had "no marriage."[19]

Despite the risks, devotional relationships between men were common, at least among the literate, and many of these affairs must have included sex at some point. Knights, aristocrats, and especially clerics left expansive evidence of their intense passions for male lovers, relationships that often ended in side-by-side burials. A letter from a respected monk-scholar in Charlemagne's court named Alcuin (circa 735–804) to a beloved bishop shows how thick those relations sometimes became:

I think of your love and friendship with such sweet memories, reverend bishop, that I long for that lovely time when I may be able to clutch the neck of your sweetness with the fingers of my desires. Alas, if only it were granted to me, as it was to Habakkuk, to be transported to you, how would I sink into your embraces . . . how I would cover, with tightly pressed lips, not only your eyes, ears, and mouth but also your every finger and your toes, not once but many a time.

While this epistle is unusually erotic, it reflects the intimacies that existed among men everywhere. Assuming, as we must, that at least some of these men's sexual longings were fulfilled, the next question is the extent to which intimate homosexual relationships were tolerated. Love was one thing, sodomy another. If male hustlers on the Rialto were burned to death and other European sodomites were being cut to ribbons, could long-term, loving relationships among men ever be permitted?

The answer, paradoxically, is yes. In the period up to roughly the thirteenth century, male bonding ceremonies were performed in churches all over the Mediterranean. These unions were sanctified by priests with many of the same prayers and rituals used to join men and women in marriage. The ceremonies stressed love and personal commitment over procreation, but surely not everyone was fooled. Couples who joined themselves in such rituals most likely had sex as much (or as little) as their heterosexual counterparts. In any event, the close association of male-marriage ceremonies with forbidden sex eventually became too much to overlook as ever more severe sodomy laws were put into place.

Such same-sex unions—sometimes called "spiritual brotherhoods"— forged irrevocable bonds between the men involved. Often they involved missionaries about to set off on foreign voyages, but lay male couples also entered into them. Other than the gender of the participants, it was difficult to distinguish the ceremonies from typical marriages. Twelfth-century liturgies for same-sex unions, for example, involved the pair joining their right hands at the altar, the recital of marriage prayers, and a ceremonial kiss.

Same-sex unions were denied to monks to the same extent that men in monastic orders were forbidden to marry women, but other clerics who were allowed to marry took part. One thirteenth-century Ukrainian story tells of the deacon Evagrius and the priest Tit, whose "great and sincere" love for each other led them to a same-sex union. Unfortunately, that love found its limits and the men had a bitter falling-out. When Tit later fell ill, some monks brought Evagrius to his sickbed to help the couple reconcile before the end. Evagrius refused and was struck dead, and Tit recovered.

Even had Tit and Evagrius made up and lived happily ever after, they would never have produced natural offspring, which was the main difference between same-sex unions and traditional marriages. Yet the couple's barrenness did not impede sanctification of their relationship by the church. One version of the liturgy had the priest recite:

> O Almighty Lord, you have given to man to be made from the first in Your Image and Likeness by the gift of immortal life. You have willed to bind as brothers not only by nature but by bonds of the spirit . . . Bless Your Servants united also that, not bound by nature, [they be] joined with bonds of love.

It is difficult to believe that these rituals did not contemplate erotic contact. In fact, it was the sex between the men involved that later caused same-sex unions to be banned.

With the widespread criminalization of homosexual relations starting in the thirteenth century, the marriages of men in churches could not last.

The Byzantine emperor Andronicus II decreed in 1306 that, along with incest and sorcery, sex between men was prohibited. He added: "If some wish to enter into ceremonies of same-sex union, we should prohibit them, for they are not recognized by the church." No Latin versions of the ceremonies survive—presumably they were destroyed—and several of the surviving Greek texts appear to have been defaced over time by disapproving churchmen. By the sixteenth century, Montaigne would write of a "strange brotherhood" in which Portuguese men in Rome "married one another, male to male, at Mass, with the same ceremonies with which we perform our marriages, read the same marriage gospel service and then went to bed and lived together." They were burned to death.

GIVEN THAT MEN could no longer marry in a church without risking punishment, and that long-term love between men was not going away, something less inflammatory had to take the place of matrimony. In England and many Mediterranean societies (especially southern France), the new institution for same-sex unions was the *affrèrement* ("brotherment") contract. *Affrèrement* was not designed specifically to accommodate same-sex love relationships; it was adapted to permit such couples to live together in peace. An *affrèrement* was a written agreement between two people to form one household and share *un pain, un vin, et une bourse* ("one bread, one wine, and one purse"). In Italy, the contracts used a similar phrase: *une pane e uno vino*. The reference to sharing the same bread and wine was meant to signify that the people would share all their property in the years to come.

Affrèrement agreements were used when brothers (*frères*) jointly inherited a farm and wished to continue living there together with their families, or when cousins joined forces and merged their properties. They were formal and public, usually sworn before notaries and signed by witnesses. In 1606, the brothers Pierre and Jean Alary, living in southwestern France, agreed that *[i]n consideration of the great love and fraternal affection which they bear and have borne to each other in the past, having lived and worked in common all their life, have been brothered together. All that they have and that they will acquire henceforth shall be common amongst them. They and their family will live together for eating and drinking, making one table, one house, one fire.*

From that point forward, Pierre and Jean were tied to each other by much more than the same parents. They and their families were bound to a common future. Typically, the brothers' agreement also specified that they would both contribute the dowry of their daughters. Pierre was already married, but the contract added that if Jean married, his wife's dowry would become part of their common fund.

Not all parties to *affrèrement* contracts were related. Many people from different families formed *affrèrements*, especially after the plague had depopulated the land and made an abundance of cheap land available. As the survivors plucked up abandoned property and formed large personal holdings, *affrèrements* were the most convenient legal instruments for them to work collectively. In Provence, the Black Death left vast stretches of land ready for the taking. The foreigners who came in to settle the terrain frequently formed *affrèrements*. However, no one entered into these contracts purely for business reasons; they were deeply personal commitments. *Affrèrements* were opportunities for people, in effect, to create families on the basis of love and mutual interest rather than reproductive chance.

Loving male couples were in the minority of *affrères*, but they were there. When, for example, Jean Rey's wife ("a bad woman") left him around 1446, Rey turned to his friend Colrat with whom he shared an intense "affection, affinity, and love . . . from the heart." Rey and Colrat contracted an *affrèrement* under which they agreed to live and work together for life. Their relationship was probably sexual at least some of the time, but that is not entirely the point. The fact is that the two men were able to fashion a life in which they were joined emotionally and economically

under one roof. Contracts similar to *affrèrements* had been around for
centuries in one form or another, but surged during the period roughly
corresponding to the repression of same-sex marriage unions. *Affrèrements*
had just the right amount of ambiguity within which homosexual behavior
could be overlooked. The community accepted that two men who loved
each other could live together. More than that, no one wanted to know.

In a sense, *affrèrements* were an early application of a "Don't Ask,
Don't Tell" policy for homosexual relationships. At least until the sixteenth century, when the custom finally died out, same-sex couples were
often permitted to join society as full participants so long as they did not
mimic religious heterosexual marriage institutions too closely. The resem-
blance to present-day controversies over gay marriage is unmistakable. The
most vocal opponents of marriage among homosexuals routinely cite the
imaginary "history" of marriage as a sacrament only between a man and a
woman, with its prime purpose being the production of children. This argument won a key victory in the United States in 1996, when President Bill
Clinton signed the Defense of Marriage Act, which states that "the word
'marriage' means only a legal union between one man and one woman as
husband and wife." But church-sponsored same-sex unions and *affrèrements* reveal a much more textured historical picture. Just as the law of the
Middle Ages forbade "unnatural" sexual acts, so did it also accommodate
the reality that some people of the same gender genuinely loved each other
and wished to live together.[20]

The abolishment of *affrèrements* left a void for gay couples that would
not be filled until civil unions—marriages in most legal aspects, without
being called marriages—were sporadically recognized in the late twentieth
century. In the intervening four hundred or so years, and especially during
the religiously charged sixteenth and seventeenth centuries, the nature of
household relationships would become much more of a public business.
Newly empowered state governments took on the responsibility of searching out sexual deviance wherever it occurred.

5

...

GROPING TOWARD MODERNITY:
THE EARLY MODERN PERIOD, 1500–1700

D URING HIS TWENTY-FIVE years on the throne of England beginning in 1660, Charles II missed few opportunities for sexual pleasure. He fondled women's breasts in the theater, reached under ladies'
skirts in chapel, and took so many mistresses to his bed that he is credited
with siring at least twelve illegitimate children. His court was a fireworks
display of licentiousness. Behind every door, dukes, duchesses, ladies, and
servants went at it with the vigor of caged beasts released into the wild.
Even the argot of the court reflected this new burst of sexual freedom. The
formerly shameful crime of adultery, for example, was now referred to
using a French-based term of honor: "gallantry." Engaging in dalliances
became virtually prerequisite to attaining higher standing within the court.
One hidebound lord who remained loyal to his wife was counseled to find
a mistress immediately, lest he be "ill looked upon" and lose "all his interest at court."

As Charles happily "rolled from whore to whore" with the "proud-
est peremptory Prick alive," and the goings-on at court became source
material for some of England's first waves of popular pornography, all
of English society reveled in a rediscovery of sexual gratification. After
decades of Puritan austerity, the coronation of the rakish Charles marked
the start of a more balanced approach to the regulation of pleasure. Under

the Puritan influence that had held sway until then, serial adultery had been a crime punishable by death; cockfighting and horse racing had also been banned, theaters and brothels shut down, and alehouses harassed. By the end of the century, however, clerics were complaining that their parishioners were drinking, fornicating, and attending cockfights rather than honoring the Sabbath. The magazine *Town and Country* featured the landed elite's sexual adventures, and English theater regained form with bawdy Restoration comedies. The court system run by the church, in which few sexual misconduct charges had ever been turned away, now waned in influence.[1]

BACKLASH: THE PROTESTANT REFORMATION

Prior to the rise of Charles II, sexual restrictions could scarcely have been any tighter, in England or anywhere else on the Continent. The tumultuous sixteenth century and the first half of the seventeenth had witnessed a prolonged and violent face-off between Catholics and the upstart Protestants, in which both sides scrabbled for Christian souls. Increasingly religious states vied for bragging rights in piety, and tried, therefore, to micromanage sexual behavior as never before. The Protestant Reformation, ignited by the German priest Martin Luther in 1517 when he nailed his Ninety-five Theses to the door of a church in Wittenberg, had challenged every aspect of Catholicism, including its position on sex. To Luther, the Catholic Church was a moral sinkhole, and the pope a "shameless whore." Catholics threw back ridicule at their Protestant rivals with equal zeal.

As states aligned themselves with one or the other side of the schism, Catholic and Protestant armies set forth to kill each other in vast numbers, along with civilian populations. As mutual hatred grew more intense, the kingdoms of Europe lurched into war during the early seventeenth century. Armed conflict and the elevated religious temperature made people

increasingly suspicious and intolerant of each other. They expected their
rulers take an active hand in regulating morality, which most were only
too happy to do. The French theologian John Calvin spoke for nearly all
Protestants when he declared that the purpose of government was to create
"a public form of religion." Individual sexual conduct thus became mainstream state business.

Protestants attacked Catholic morals as being too rigid in theory and
too loose in practice. Luther derided the notion of priestly celibacy, just
as he attacked the Catholic ideal of sexual abstinence as a whole. He was,
indeed, correct in observing that few Catholic priests kept themselves away
from sex: At least 95 percent of them in Bavaria had concubines, for example. But ridiculing clerical hypocrisy was just the beginning. Luther and
other Protestant leaders turned the whole Catholic conception of sex and
marriage on its head. To them, matrimony was not a concession to mankind's innate sexual evil. Rather, sex was godly, and marriage a requirement for a good life. To forbid it to anyone, whether priests or farmhands,
was to ensure earthly corruption.

Protestants accepted that sex was as essential to life as sleeping, eating, and drinking. If indulged in with "appropriate modesty" and in the
marriage bed, it was "a sign of [God's] goodness and infinite sweetness."
But while sex between husbands and wives was good, all other carnal relations were damned. On this there was no compromise. All adulterers, fornicators, and whores deserved nothing less than the gallows. In Puritan
England and parts of Protestant Germany, adultery was a capital offense.
As for prostitution, gone was the idea that brothels washed away filth
from good society. Instead, prostitutes were seen (in Luther's inimitable
phrasing) as "scabby, scratching, stinking" and syphilitic monsters who
deserved to be "broken on the wheel and flayed" or branded with hot
irons. The men who patronized them were little better. City-run whorehouses, so common in the centuries before the Reformation, were now

During the Reformation, Catholics and Protestants commonly hurled sexual slanders at each other. The Catholic priesthood often got the worst of it, as Protestants attacked what they viewed as the myth of priestly celibacy. Here, a monk is depicted as taking unholy liberties with a woman in a cornfield. ©THE TRUSTEES OF THE BRITISH MUSEUM marked as particularly loathsome. Wherever Protestantism was adopted, official brothels were closed.

In response to the Protestant challenge, the Catholic Church characteristically dug in its heels. In 1563, after a twenty-year conference known as the Council of Trent, the Catholic Church rejected every criticism Luther, Calvin, and the other reformers had thrown at it. Rather than concede the failure of requiring priestly celibacy, the Catholic Church strengthened its commitment to it. Far from abandoning the idea that abstinence was superior to sex, moreover, it now affirmed that virginity was in fact more blessed than marriage.

For the Vatican, sex stank as badly as ever, and with Protestants constantly accusing the Catholic Church of loose morals, it was time for it to prove its prudish mettle. Now, even masturbation drew intense Catholic condemnation. Some canonical writers cast it as a form of sodomy, worse than fornication or even adultery. One Catholic teacher focused his attention on "spontaneous" orgasms, i.e., those that occurred with no external stimulation. (Anyone who felt one coming on was told to lie still, make the sign of the Cross, and beg God to prevent the pleasure from reaching its peak.) Municipal brothels were closed as well, lest Catholic governments be accused of profiting from vice. Paris shuttered its brothels in 1556. Ten years later, the pope ordered Rome's prostitutes to leave town—although that decree was annulled when authorities saw that twenty-five thousand people were preparing to vacate the city.

The repression of prostitution was part of a general lockdown on sex. European history had seen bursts of official prudishness before, but they were rarely so in line with popular sentiment. With all the screaming and Bible-thumping, the strict morality being preached everywhere was sinking in. We can never know exactly what people got up to behind closed doors or in the fields, but to judge by the decline in the number of illegitimate births and pregnant brides in France and England, for instance, it appears that there was less sex going on outside of marriage.[2]

HEDGE WHORES AND BAWDY COURTS

The antipleasure principle in England also showed in people's readiness to denounce each other to the courts for immorality. Many of these court cases were brought to secure advantages in other, unrelated quarrels, but that did not stop the courts from imposing humiliating punishments on the parties found guilty. Between 1595 and 1635, the number of immorality cases in the church courts more than doubled, sometimes comprising half their caseloads. With jurisdiction over "adultery, whoredom, incest," and "any other uncleanness and wickedness of life," there were no details of people's lives into which the "bawdy courts," as they came to be known, could not pry. In Essex County alone, adults had a one-in-four chance of being accused in a church court of sexual misconduct. Add to that the flood of sexual slander suits citizens brought against each other, and bucolic preindustrial Albion begins to look like a very unpleasant place. Quarrels and lawsuits were part of the firmament of village life, and nothing focused people's attention more than a sex suit.

In 1628, Isaac Chiverton was socializing with some young men when they jokingly asked him how he had lived as a bachelor for so long without ever being accused of fornication. He replied that "when he was a young man as they were it might be that he played with some wenches." For that remark, he was hauled before an ecclesiastical court to explain whether or not he had ever committed fornication or adultery. Another man was accused of sexual misconduct after neighbors complained that he and his wife shared a bed with a maidservant. Even married couples could be sued if they were suspected of having deviant sex—or of simply enjoying it too much. Each suit was expensive, time-consuming, and risky. Sometimes casual contact was enough to sustain an immorality action, as when a shepherd ducked into a woman's house for an hour, seeking shelter from a storm. Other, seemingly closer encounters were treated lightly. In 1623, Richard Tench was let off with a caution after he admitted to kissing and fondling the breasts of another man's wife.

Many cases came from people's genuine outrage at their neighbors' conduct, but just as many were brought out of sheer malice. Immorality suits were filed in retaliation for such minor harms as the killing of a dog or pig, or as strategic gambits in long-running quarrels. No one ever filed such lawsuits to get rich, however. The church courts did not award money to successful plaintiffs; rather, defendants found guilty were forced into humiliation through public repentance. Sexual deviants were often forced to wear white sheets, sometimes with a paper attached to their head spelling out their wrongdoing and confessing their crimes. Sometimes the guilty parties would be required to get down on their knees in public and beg forgiveness of their accusers. Moral offenders could also be ostracized from the community and—worst of all—thus rendered unable to sue others in court.

Religious justice was supposed to emphasize reform rather than retribution, but that was not how cases actually played out. In the backbiting environment of the English village, genuine expressions of remorse were likely to backfire. Consider Edward Peinton, who, after months of secretly visiting a married woman, experienced a genuine bout of conscience. He told a friend about the affair, and the other man promptly snitched to the local minister. The minister persuaded the adulterous couple to confess by promising he would keep it quiet, but was no truer to his word than Peinton's friend. When he publicly refused Peinton communion, local suspicions were confirmed, and an adultery case was filed in the court of the bishop of Salisbury.[3]

The subject of illegitimacy in particular consumed English justice. Despite the decline in the rate of children born out of wedlock, bastardy remained a big problem and was treated with severity, if not cruelty. Once convicted, both mothers and fathers were often stripped to the waist and whipped through the streets. Mothers of bastard children were, of course, easier to identify than the fathers. If they proved too afraid of naming their seducers, the midwives who attended them would be instructed to browbeat them during labor, refusing all assistance until they gave in. When this stratagem failed, parish ministers would sometimes refuse to baptize the children.

Illegitimacy proceedings were wrapped in biblical cant, but the court's concern was economic. ("We are already overpressed with too many poor bastard children," read one suit.) Women who bore illegitimate children, such as a mother sued in Castle Combe in 1606, were considered worse than fornicators: They were infectious drains on public finances. To conceive a child with no husband was, in the words of a minister, a

> *filthy act of whoredom . . . by which licentious life of hers not only God's wrath may be poured down upon us inhabitants of the town, but also her evil example may so greatly corrupt others that great and extraordinary charge for the maintenance of baseborn children may be imposed upon us.*

An unmarried woman's swollen belly was proof that something very wrong had gone on, and that someone expensive was coming into being. To avoid the burden of feeding an unwanted child, authorities often drove expectant mothers from town, forcing them to give birth in the fields, where babies had a higher chance of dying. Failing that, their goal was to get someone else to pay the child's expenses. For this reason, illegitimacy cases almost always got the attention of the courts. Many desperate women also resorted to abortion-inducing concoctions, physical abuse of their wombs, and even infanticide.

Most of the women who bore children illegitimately were already well acquainted with their seducers. Many must have intended to marry the men, as the 20 percent rate of pregnant English brides suggests. But confusion as to who intended or said what leading up to or during the act of love was as common then as ever. Many unwed mothers testified to their belief that their lovers would soon be their husbands. If the men involved were already married, or if there had been no real courtship, then the excuse was rejected and lenient treatment refused. A woman's claim that she believed the marriage promises of a traveling merchant, for example, was likely to be met with scowls.

A large number of the women charged with producing bastard children were domestic servants taken by their masters. Even though the sex should more properly have been characterized as rape, maidservants knew that pregnancy meant the loss of their jobs in any case—so they had little to lose by telling the truth. In 1592, one servant girl claimed that she had long tried to resist her master's advances, "but in the end her said master did beat her and so by foul means . . . obtained his desire." The master of another maid had an easier time getting her to succumb: She admitted that that she gave herself to him in exchange for a pair of gloves. Such cases likely resulted in the master being ordered to pay child support for at least a short period, and in the girl being whipped in public.

The problem of unwanted children was at its worst in overcrowded London. Between 1500 and 1700, the city's metropolitan population increased almost tenfold, to five hundred and fifty thousand souls, as waves of people straggled in from the countryside. The city had few facilities to care for the poor, and whatever did exist for this purpose was strained from overuse and underfunding. The governors of two hospitals, Bridewell and St. Thomas's, set up their own courts to decide who deserved help, who should be punished, and whose problems should be passed off for others to deal with. The courts doled out moral punishment and charitable aid in equal parts. A "whore" such as Mary Lee, who was brought to Bridewell after having a child with the married Anthony Shippe, was ordered whipped before she could receive aid. The baby had died, so there was no need to deal with the child's upkeep; had it lived, the hospital would have stuck Shippe with the bill.

In identifying the men who fathered bastard children, the London hospital courts were not fussy about reaching the correct results so long as *someone* with money was ordered to pay for the child. Thus benefit of the doubt was often accorded to the women. In a 1569 Bridewell case, Alice Bruster claimed that her master, William Saywell, "got her with child and . . . promised her marriage and abused her half a dozen times in the shop and other places." Saywell was immediately brought to the court at Bridewell, where he denied everything. Bruster was allowed to call up witnesses at a later date; they corroborated that Saywell had offered her money not to sue. Confronted with this testimony, Saywell confirmed her story and the hospital was off the financial hook.

Masters who kept their hands off their servants were still often told to pay for the care of their maids' babies on the theory that they should have kept better order in their houses and shops. Moreover, when the hospital courts learned of situations that might result in the production of illegitimate children, they took preventive action: In one instance, a tailor was punished when it was discovered that his servants were cavorting in his bed while he was out.

For poor village girls and women, unwanted pregnancies presaged lives spent on the run. In large towns they stood a chance of remaking themselves as something other than "whores." The penalty for skipping out on a church court case was excommunication, but that was no worse than staying around to face the charges. With no money or standing, the lives of these unwed mothers consisted of unmitigated horror until they found some safe haven. It was worse for the babies, many of whom were killed or abandoned by their desperate mothers along the way.

English law forbade anyone to harbor a fugitive pregnant woman. Some people gave shelter out of compassion or family ties, but many did it for money or in the hope of return favors. One 1592 case told of a man who gave refuge to a gentlewoman he believed was "kin to the Marquess of Winchester and . . . was [also] towards Her Majesty" Elizabeth I. Another man with less grandiose designs merely hoped that the baby's father would "do him a good turn in exchange." Taking in a fugitive single pregnant woman was a transgression malicious neighbors were often all too willing to report, though there was nothing to be gained from doing so other than the cruel joy of watching a neighbor dressed down in public. By the time these cases got to court, the girls had usually fled again, either to the city or to another Good Samaritan's barn or woodshed.[4]

CHURCH COURTS ALSO specialized in slander suits. Insults and malicious gossip were, if possible, more common in the sixteenth and seventeenth centuries than today—with the difference that they were taken much more seriously. If left unanswered, offhand accusations that one was a whore, whoreson, or cuckold (to choose just three of hundreds of epithets) could truly harm one's sexual "credit" in the community. The most common slander, "whore," connoted a promiscuous woman, regardless of whether or not she took money for sex. Women who had adulterous sex or illegitimate children were whores. Even women who had the "wrong" kind of sex with their husbands could be whores.

In 1513, the gossip Agnes Aspenhalghe accused Emmota Whittaker of acting the "whore with her husband," adding that she saw Whittaker in a pig house "upon [her husband's] bely and her bely nakyd." Whittaker had no choice but to go before a court and try to prove her accuser wrong. If she won her case, she would have the satisfaction of forcing Aspenhalghe to get on her knees in public and beg her forgiveness. If she lost, then she stood a good chance of being charged for immorality herself.

Accusations such as "hedge whore," "barn whore," "hollow tree whore," and "bitchery whore" were frequent and harmful enough to make sexual slander cases the most common type of suit heard in church courts. Often the suits were the result of private, face-to-face insult exchanges. When, in John Streme's London house, a man accused Streme's wife of having "hadd a childe by a priest," it was only a matter of time before Mrs. Streme ran to the churchwarden and initiated a suit. The man later tried to apologize, but her mind was made up: "Thou art never abyll to make me amendys," Mrs. Streme said. She had not actually mothered a priest's child, so the insult could not have been believed by anyone, but that was not the point. It had been uttered.

Similarly, when Hugh Pare passed by the house of John Call, he heard the nasty Elizabeth Hertford accusing Call of being a "horeson," "cocold," and—inevitably—"horeson cocold." Did anyone actually believe Call's mother was a whore, or that his wife had committed adultery? Probably not. Nevertheless, Pare testified that Hertford had lowered Call's reputation among his neighbors, whom he heard say "those words come not of noght."

The remarks that sparked English slander cases seem no more worthy of being taken seriously than the modern epithets "skank," "asshole," and "son of a bitch"—insulting, to be sure, but not the stuff of lawsuits. But in the thin-skinned society inhabited by Call, Streme, and Hertford, slander suits were necessary follow-ups to brawls and catcall exchanges. To let an insult pass unchallenged was to lose face. In 1618, to take another case, the ferocious Mary Crooke stood in front of Anne Moxam's house and screamed that Moxam was a "bobtail whore and whore bitch" who had "showed her arse before the king." Again, no one could possibly have believed that Moxam had displayed herself to royalty, but even a ridiculous insult could not be ignored. Moxam's decision to turn the other cheek was criticized as cowardly by her neighbors. To defend her honor, she should have confronted Crooke in the street or sued her for slander, or both, as was commonly done.

Slander actions were often sideshows to meatier disputes. When Elizabeth White heard Rachel Townsend encourage her husband not to pay his debts to White's husband, the dispute quickly went from financial to sexual. Elizabeth confronted Rachel, telling her she was a "scurvy woman." Rachel shot back: "I am not so scurvy a woman as you for I never sould my daughters maidenhead for money." For good measure, Rachel further accused Elizabeth of taking five pounds for her daughter's virginity. In short order, a mundane money problem between husbands had spawned a fight about sexual honor between the wives.

When sexual slander caused people to lose money, as it sometimes did, the church courts were useless. Religious justice was intended to cure the health of the soul, not the purse. Beginning in about 1500, then, the secular common-law courts allowed people to sue for money damages in slander suits. From that point on, for example, a girl who lost out on a profitable marriage by being called a whore had the option of saving her reputation in church court or suing the slanderer for money in common-law court. As one would expect, the volume of slander cases in the secular courts rose dramatically.

Looking back, the courts' open-door policy toward sexual slander lawsuits seems excessive. Too many of them were transparently malicious attacks between people who already hated each other. When Maud Spender sued Alice Francklin for calling her a "fine whore, a burnt tailed whore, and a pocky whore," evidence showed that the two women already had a long history of legal disputes; allowing Spender's slander action to go forward could only worsen their quarrel. The better course for the court would have been to throw the case out. The incessant conflicts were bad enough; why exacerbate them with grudge-match lawsuits?

There were several reasons. The courts evidently believed that sexual reputation was worth guarding even at the price of encouraging feuds. Furthermore, both civil judges and church deacons recognized that these suits placed them in charge of the minutiae of people's day-to-day lives, which reinforced the courts' authority. Perhaps, too, there was just too much money to be collected in fees and payoffs to turn these suits down. (It was common for people to pay off church courts rather than suffering penances.) Whatever motivated the courts to keep hearing these kinds of cases, one thing is certain: Hatred between the litigating parties was real, as was the potential for violence. Deadly force was a common response to even the pettiest insults, so allowing people to play out their interpersonal dramas in court rather than on the street with fists or weapons served a valuable social function. However nasty, the litigation process was an alternative to leaving people to solve their problems among themselves.

VIGILANTISM OR MOB justice in sex-related cases was common. When the courts did not act quickly or decisively enough, neighbors disciplined one another. People suspected of adultery, whoredom, or the like could expect to be awakened in their beds by their peers, outside making "rough music" by clanging pots and pans. Such treatment wrecked the targets' reputations, no matter what courts later said. Before a cuckolded husband could sue his wife's paramour for adultery, he might find himself publicly humiliated by being forced onto a donkey, facing backward, and led around town. And a wife who believed another woman had seduced her husband was bound to think little of slitting her rival's nose, branding her forever with a "whore's mark."

Almost as odious as sexual deviants were "scolds," or sharp-tongued women who spread scandalous lies about others. Once convicted of slander, either in court or by popular opinion, scolds were dunked in ponds or forced to wear iron and wood "scold's bridles." If they were acquitted but the mob nevertheless disagreed with the verdict, they were punished anyway. When Agnes Davis got into a nasty, insult-laden fight with Margaret Davis (no relation, evidently), both women were tried for being scolds. Agnes won her case, but Margaret was dunked in a pond. In revenge, Margaret's allies broke into Agnes's house, urinated in her porridge, and plunged Agnes in the river seven times.

England, and especially the English village, was already an ill-tempered, contentious place when the Reformation began. Puritan rule and the steady narrowing of sexual options only made matters worse. In many ways, the sex lives of the English were more regulated in the period before Charles II took power than at any time before or since. If it wasn't a church tribunal, secular judge, or justice of the peace nosing into one's life, it was neighbors peeking through the window: busybodies who might well fetch the local constable, to whom full power was given to break into any home and drag the alleged moral offenders away. It was not until the late seventeenth century that the break with Puritanism was decisive, and the English libido began to rediscover itself.[5]

GERMANY: BIG BROTHER IN THE BEDROOM

Lest England take the rap on its own for intolerance, it should be emphasized that sex was no less controlled on the Continent. Nowhere did the Reformation have a greater impact on sexual mores, in fact, than in the German-speaking lands where Protestantism began. As religion became radicalized, the German states stepped up efforts to require people to lead Christian (i.e., morally restricted) lives. State authority came to depend, to an extensive degree, on sexual repression.

As in England, the assumption of state power over sex in Germany was assisted by an increasingly narrow-minded populace. Shame, punishment, and casual violence awaited those who stepped outside the lines. In German towns of all sizes, adulterers, unwed mothers, and the like were subject to beatings by their neighbors. State and city governments were just as ready to humiliate moral offenders, adopting, for example, the practice of forcing adulterers and fornicators to stand in public clad in white smocks. Other deviants were pilloried, tied to stones, and fitted with headdresses with bells on them. These measures were meant to be less severe than imprisonment or corporal punishment, but people put on display for sex crimes could find themselves pelted with stones and otherwise abused.

Powerful trade guilds, which traditionally controlled much of the economic and social life in the towns, also demonstrated a readiness to exclude anyone for dishonorable behavior. They became a model for Reformation-era sex laws. Guild rules were strict: A master who had worked his entire life to attain his position could lose it all if his wife gave birth too soon after their marriage, for example. Guild members whose wives committed adultery were required to divorce and sever ties with them—forgiveness was not an option. The threat of banishment was used by the guilds to keep their ranks thin and their prices high, but it also reflected a moral consensus. When a guild ruled that the children of adulterous masters were to be forever excluded, it did so because people believed an adulterer's entire family line was stained. It was better for a family to be cut off and fall into poverty than for the guild to be dishonored.

The penalty of banishment for adultery also found its way into state laws. In 1635, Bavaria's sprawling morals ordinance required that double-adulterers (lovers who were each married to others when they had sex) be banished for five years. If they were caught indulging their carnal appetites with each other again, they were supposed to be put to death. The rationale for such harsh punishment was made clear in the law itself:

> [I]f these grave sins are not prevented or punished with all possible energy and seriousness, almighty God will be greatly offended and angered and will be moved to send and inflict all manner of serious, immediate war, unrest and other country-wide punishments.

Both Catholic and Protestant German states saw no limit to their authority to regulate their subjects' behavior. Multiple and detailed sex laws popped up everywhere. Sometimes they overlapped so that the judges themselves could not figure them out. But the explosion of new morality regulations caused a much deeper problem as well: The more the states tried to govern sex, the weaker they felt their power to be, as there was simply no way to control individual behavior on such a minute scale. Ordinances could be passed, such as the one in Baden barring males and females from bathing together, but who really knew whether or not the law was being followed? How were lawmakers to be sure their subjects were *not* romping together in the water? They could not. There are no witnesses to what does not happen.

By making more sex acts illegal, the states also multiplied the possibilities for lawbreaking. A shared bath, a tryst, a visit to a prostitute—everything outlawed by the welter of new laws became an act of civil disobedience simply because it was illegal. The more people ignored the laws, the more enfeebled lawmakers felt themselves to be. In 1624, Friedrich V, Margrave of Baden, complained that despite all the restrictions against fornication and adultery already in place, criminal sexual behavior had not ceased: "We have, alas, variously discovered, with extreme displeasure and consternation . . . damnable fornication and adultery have so increased and proliferated that they are scarcely held to be sins any more."

This pervasive feeling of vulnerability drove German states ever deeper into people's sex lives. Every new measure was, in effect, an admission that the prior ones were being ignored. In 1629, Maximilian I, Elector of Bavaria, became fixated on the idea that his subjects were having illegal sex with each other and with priests. He set up a top-level commission to conduct an "energetic" hunt for such lawbreakers. The commission hired spies who did their best, but they were unable to satisfy him. At one point, they apologized for the lack of results: "The said spies excuse themselves," they wrote to Maximilian, "as no such clerical concubines or secret trysting spots have come to their attention." Maximilian badgered the commission to keep at it—for eight more years.

German governments also set up a network of marriage courts to regulate most aspects of sexual behavior, whether marriage-related or not. These held sway in the Old Swiss Confederacy as well: Court officers in Zurich warned women not to receive men who were not their husbands, and also began punishing prostitutes. In Bern, women were barred from riding in sleighs unless accompanied by their fathers or husbands. At the same time, "discipline masters" were deployed to make sure that "each and every scandal, sin and act which is against God" was dealt with. To meet these ambitious goals the masters relied on informants, denouncers, and spies.

Morals violators in Germany were also subject to a bewildering array of punishments, often applied in combination. Fines were usually levied, either by themselves or as add-ons to other measures. In Bavaria, fornication fines brought in more money to the lower courts than any other source of income. Many of the fines were deliberately steep; a maid or cook found guilty of fornication might be obliged to forfeit a year's salary. In actual practice, however, judges adjusted the penalties to fit people's circumstances.

The increased state involvement in the sex lives of the Germans came at the expense of traditional church-based morality controls. The same process took place in England, and by 1660 the English church courts were sneered at as corrupt and ineffective, especially as about half of the people sued in court chose to be excommunicated rather than show up to face the charges. By the end of the seventeenth century, church courts still controlled marriage disputes, but their primacy in other morality cases was seriously slipping.[6]

The turf battle between church and state over which would govern sexual misconduct was less of an issue in Protestant states than in Catholic realms. Protestants saw no difference between civil and religious discipline. In their view, the state was there to enforce religious doctrine. But the Catholic Church didn't want to give up any of its powers, and fought hard to keep the upper hand—especially, as we shall see, when its own secrets were at issue.

TASTY MORSELS AND FUCKING FAUCETS: THE BIRTH OF OBSCENITY

The laws of sex often change, but the acts themselves remain constant. Adultery, incest, bestiality, same-gender sex—all of it has gone on every day since the beginning of human civilization, if not earlier. With the Early Modern period, however, came an entirely new form of forbidden sex—one that inhabited the handiwork of printing machines rather than being embodied in flesh and blood. On the virgin battlefield of obscenity, the law fought against materials depicting people having sex, rather than sex itself. For this fight there was no ancient rulebook. New laws had to be created.

"Where there is no law, there can be no transgression," said a flummoxed English judge about a dirty book. "I owe that [the book] is a great offense; but I know of no law by which we can punish it." In England, laws against obscenity had not yet come together. But on the Continent, ecclesiastical and state authorities alike had long been haggling over who would write and enforce the rules against sexy words and pictures. For some time, it was anyone's guess as to who would eventually be in charge.

Blatantly sexual depictions are as old as the "Venus" figurine found in Germany by archaeologists in 2009, which dates back an estimated thirty-five thousand years. Its oversized breasts, ample hips, and clearly defined vagina, researchers said, confirmed that "ancient humans had sex on their minds"—which is, of course, no surprise. Such totems were most likely symbols of fertility rather than strictly erotic in purpose, but the line between the two was just as likely unimportant.

Sexual images were not forbidden in the ancient world. The word "pornography" comes from the Greek *pornographe*, or "writing about whores"—of which there was much at the time. (Athens was also blanketed with statues of Hermes, featuring splendid erections.) The word "obscene" probably derives from the Latin *caenum*, which means "filth and excrement" but also meant "penis" and, in its plural form, could refer to either genitals or buttocks. The word may also derive from *scaena*, or "stage." Joined to *ob*, it could thus have meant "offstage," i.e., inappropriate for public exhibition. Whatever the etymology, sexually explicit writing and pictures were everywhere in Rome, much of it intended to arouse consumers. For the most part, it was tolerated. (Tellingly, the French *obscénité*, a long-disused word, was revived in France in the

1660s, just as the printing of frankly sexual material became a crime under French law.)

When the educated classes of Renaissance Europe rediscovered the Greek and Roman classics, many took special interest in the eroticism of Ovid and the filthy verses of Martial and Juvenal. Renaissance men and boys also delighted in antiquity's profusion of explicit images and descriptions of sex. But while there were plenty of educated people "masturbating to the classics," sexual material was sparse in circulation. Until the advent of mass printing, any one piece of pornography was certain to remain just that: a singular object for private consumption.

When modern printing and reproduction techniques came into use at the end of the fifteenth century, private pleasures became public phenomena. A pornography mass market materialized across all social classes almost overnight. Had such materials remained in manuscript form, circulated only among the elite, censorship of sexual depictions would have been far less likely to have arisen, but the creation of a consumer audience for pornography sparked a rush by secular and religious authorities to control and punish it.

Early editions of printed porn were, like their manuscript predecessors, literate and geared to upper-class tastes. A set of erotic verses attributed to Virgil, *Carmina Priapeia*, went to twenty-two editions by 1517. Another printed collection of dirty jokes appeared in 1450, in Latin, authored by the scholar Poggio Bracciolini. The volume's sexual and scatological double entendres were clever, but were intended only for the educated classes. They did not reach anyone who did not understand Latin or care about clever wordplay. The growing mass market demanded much earthier fare. As a prostitute urges in the *Dialoghi* (*Dialogues*) of Pietro Aretino, one of Italy's most infamous sixteenth-century pornographic works:

> *Speak plainly and say "fuck," "prick," "cunt," and "ass" if you*
> *want anyone except the scholars at the University of Rome to*

*understand you. You with your "rope in the ring," your "obelisk
in the Coliseum," your "leek in the garden," your "key in the
lock," your "bolt in the door," your "pestle in the mortar," your
"nightingale in the nest," your "tree in the ditch," your "syringe
in the valve," your "sword in the scabbard," not to mention your
"stake," your "crozier," your "parsnip," your "little monkey,"
your "this," your "that," your "him," your "her," your "apples"
. . . "carrot," "root," and all the shit there is—why don't you say
yes when you mean yes and no when you mean no, or else keep
it to yourself.*

The new crop of budding pornographers took this as sound marketing
advice, and set about supplying Europe with cheap, explicit works.

When dirty books left the academy and spread to a broad base of
readers, authorities decided something had to be done. At first, the men-
ace of the printing press was more about religion and power than sex.
By the mid-sixteenth century, when sexual censorship began in earnest,
the Catholic Church was already in a very touchy mood. It had been
bad enough when that malcontent Luther hammered his Ninety-five
Theses to a church door; much worse was the spread of the theses, in
print, throughout Christendom. Luther was the world's first best-selling
author. By 1520, his assault on the church had sold more than three
hundred thousand printed copies virtually everywhere in Europe—and
this was *before* he published his German translation of the Bible, which
allowed millions of people to bypass the Catholic Church altogether
when they prayed. (Luther was excommunicated in 1521, but the sales
of his books continued to rise.) The Protestant Reformation could never
have been as effective without the printing press to disseminate its key
texts.

Meanwhile, the Vatican's sex secrets were seeping out. The painter
Giulio Romano had drawn sixteen hard-core pictures, each depicting

various forms of copulation, which found their way to the walls of the Sala di Constantino in the Vatican. Given that the audience was limited to churchmen and their invitees, the pictures caused no controversy and were, no doubt, well appreciated. But when the prominent engraver Marcantonio Raimondi reproduced them for mass circulation in 1524, he was thrown into a Vatican jail cell. Raimondi languished there for more than a year, freed only after the irrepressible writer and satirist Pietro Aretino interceded on his behalf with Pope Clement VII. Had all of Raimondi's prints and plates been destroyed as the Vatican insisted, the matter might have ended there—but Aretino's interest had been piqued. Curious to see what all the fuss was about, he had a look, and then set about writing scandalous verses for each one, declaring:

> *I desired to see those pictures which had caused the [Vatican] to cry out that the worthy artist ought to be crucified. As soon as I gazed at them, I was touched by the spirit that had moved Giulio Romano to draw them. And since poets and sculptors, in order to amuse themselves, have often written or carved lascivious objects such as the marble satyr in Chigi Palace attempting to rape a boy, I tossed out the sonnets at the foot [of each of the drawings]. With all due respect to hypocrites, I dedicate these lustful pieces to you, heedless of the scurvy strictures and asinine laws which forbid the eyes to see the very things that delight them most . . . What wrong is there in seeing a man mount a woman?*

Aretino published his sixteen lusty sonnets in 1537, along with the Romano/Raimondi engravings, in a volume called *Sonetti lussuriosi* (though the work soon came to be known as *Aretino's Postures*). As soon as they were released, the pope himself ordered all copies of the work destroyed, but some survived. Aretino still managed to put out another edition, which was also suppressed. By that time, however, the work was being reprinted all over Europe in multiple pirated editions.

Ever the self-promoter, Aretino touted his sonnets as a groundbreaking effort to portray sex not as high art, but as body parts doing what they do best. His opening lines declare his intentions:

This is not a book of sonnets . . .
But here there are indescribable pricks
And the cunt and the ass that place them
Just like a candy in a box.
Here there are people who fuck and are fucked.
And anatomies of cunts and pricks
And asses filled with many lost souls.
Here one fucks in more lovely ways,
Than were ever seen
Within any whorish hierarchies.
In the end only fools
Are disgusted at such tasty morsels
And God forgive anyone who does not fuck in the ass.

In the same way the breakout success of *Deep Throat* defined the pornographic film explosion of the 1970s, *Aretino's Postures* represented the apogee of sixteenth-century mass-produced obscenity. To be sure, there were other successful works in circulation that were no less vulgar, but none had Aretino's reach or influence. The Sienese aristocrat Antonio Vignali, for example, produced *La Cazzaria* (*The Book of the Prick*), in which he depicted Siena's political scene as a struggle between patrician Pricks (Big and Little) and Cunts (Ugly and Pretty), aristocratic Balls, and plebeian Assholes. But for all Vignali's charming profanity, *La Cazzaria* was intended primarily as a political read, not a sexually stimulating one. Only a tiny group of cognoscenti could understand the jokes. Aretino's readers, by contrast, needed no prep course to get it. His sonnets were satiric, but also stood on their own as purely titillating works. One sonnet, accompanying an image of an aroused man standing over a woman while holding her legs, made its point clearly:

Open your thighs so I can look straight
At your beautiful ass and cunt in my face,
An ass equal to paradise in its enjoyment,
A cunt that melts hearts through the kidneys.

Aretino's works spawned legions of imitators, some of whom published under his name, but none of them reached the Italian's iconic status. By the end of the century, an Italian phrasebook for English tourists included a dialogue in which an Englishman asks a Roman book dealer for "the works of A[retino]," only to be told: "You may seek them from one end of the row to the other, and not find them . . . [b]ecause they are forbidden." Other booksellers were not so discreet. A Venetian in Paris claimed to have sold more than fifty copies of Aretino's works in less than a year. In England, two professors at Oxford's All Souls College were caught in 1675 using the school's press to print off copies of *Aretino's Postures*, presumably to profit from strong local demand. Sex always sells, but forbidden sex sells better: The banning of Aretino's works increased their allure. The more the authorities tried to suppress them, the more sought after they became.

Aretino's Postures joined the select company of the works of Martin Luther, Giovanni Boccaccio, Johannes Kepler, and Niccolò Machiavelli, among others, in the Vatican's first *Index librorum prohibitorum* ("List of Forbidden Books") in 1559. The *Index* emerged from the Council of Trent, a landmark Catholic council held over twenty-five sessions from 1545 to 1563. It was primarily intended to suppress heretical works and the writings of Protestants, but also banned books concerning "things lascivious or obscene." As stated in the council's canons and decrees:

[N]ot only the matter of faith but also that of morals, which are
usually corrupted through the reading of such books, must be
taken into consideration, and those who possess them are to be

FOUR POSTER BED

• • •

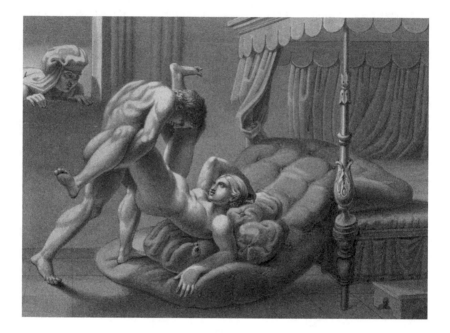

One of Europe's most enduring works of popular pornography, which was immortalized
when it was placed on the Vatican's first "List of Forbidden Books," was a collection of smutty
sonnets written by Pietro Aretino accompanied by a series of explicit engravings. The book,
commonly known as Aretino's Postures, was widely copied, reprinted, and censored.
This image corresponds to Aretino's Sonnet No. 11. "Open your thighs," commands the
man to his recumbent prey, "so I can look straight at your beautiful ass and cunt in my face."

severely punished by the bishops. Ancient books written by hea-
thens may by reason of their elegance and quality of style be per-
mitted, but by no means read to children.

The church had gone prudish, right down to covering up the exposed genitals of the figures in Michelangelo's famous Sistine Chapel fresco, *The Last Judgment*, with painted wisps of fabric and fig leaves. However, a maturing pornographic consumer culture was already in place, and nothing could eliminate it. If printing Aretino's works in Italy was dicey, less regulated English and Dutch printers were only too happy to do the job. Getting hold of pornography was as easy as buying liquor in the United States during Prohibition. By the end of the sixteenth century, erotic images were sold openly in Venice's Piazza San Marco along with sexy depictions of famous courtesans.[7]

With its *Index* and attacks on *Aretino's Postures*, the church was first out of the gate in the race to halt the spread of pornography, but its influence would not last. In France, Sorbonne University theologians ran the censorship business until 1618, when civil authorities began to take control of sex on the printed page. The disappointed professors were left only with the right to condemn unsanctioned religious books. A key stage in this power struggle was the state prosecution of a trashy little collection of verse put out by a Paris printer in 1622. The book, *Le Parnasse des poètes satyriques*, featured a sonnet by Théophile de Viau:

Phyllis, tout est f . . . , je meurs de la vérole,
Elle exerce sur moi sa dernière rigueur:
Mon v . . . baisse la tête et n'a point de vigueur,
Un ulcère puant a gâté ma parole.

J'ai sué trente jours, j'ai vomi de la colle;
Jamais de si grands maux n'eurent tant de longueur:

L'esprit le plus constant fût mort à ma langueur,
Et mon affliction n'a rien qui la console.

Mes amis plus secrets ne m'osent approcher;
Moi-même, en cet état, je ne m'ose toucher.
Phyllis, le mal me vient de vous avoir f . . . !
Mon Dieu! je me repens d'avoir si mal vécu,

Et si votre courroux à ce coup ne me tue,
Je fais vœu désormais de ne f . . . qu'en cul!

(Phyllis, everything is all f . . . up; I'm dying of syphilis,
It's attacking me with all its might;
My c . . . lowers its head and has no strength
A stinking ulcer has spoiled my speech.

I sweated for thirty days, I vomited paste;
Never did such great pains last for so long;
The most steadfast spirit would have died from such languor,
And my affliction has nothing to console it.

My most intimate friends do not care to come near me;
Even I dare not touch myself in this state.
Phyllis, I caught the disease from f . . . you!
My God, I repent of having so badly lived,

And if your anger does not kill me this time,
I swear from now on to f . . . only in the ass!)

At the time, replacing words with ellipses or single letters was usually sufficient to avoid trouble with the law. The one body part spelled out in the poem—*cul* ("ass")—sparked legal proceedings that eventually brought de Viau down. Not long after the book's publication, the Parlement de

Paris issued an order for his arrest, which he avoided by leaving town. He was then burned in effigy.

It would have likely ended there, the matter forgotten, had not a Jesuit fanatic called Father François Garasse become fixated on de Viau and *Le Parnasse*—especially the passage about "f . . . [ing] only in the ass." Garasse published a lengthy book soon after the trial in which he attacked de Viau as a drunkard and sexual degenerate. The "ass f . . . er" in the poem was de Viau himself, Garasse argued, a lowlife "freethinker" who "has contracted an infamous disease from a prostitute, and swears to God to remain a SODOMITE all the rest of his days" (capital letters original). Sodomy carried a death penalty, which is exactly what Garasse sought. A month after de Viau's effigy was set aflame, police arrested the poet himself and put him in a miserable Paris dungeon. He remained there for two years while defending himself.

The evidence against de Viau consisted of his poems as well as rumors of his own promiscuous behavior. The hearsay about his debauchery was easily disproved, but the "sodomite sonnet," as Garasse called it, was there in black and white. De Viau had also written another sonnet containing a line—"And you will jack off my lance"—that prosecutors argued was an invitation by the author to another man to masturbate him. De Viau argued that the speakers in his poems were products of his imagination, not records of his own experiences: "To write a verse about sodomy doesn't make a man guilty of the deed; poet and pederast are two different occupations." His defense was taken more seriously than might have been expected, and as there was no direct proof that he had actually committed sodomy, he was banished and not executed. Nevertheless, his years in the underground dungeon had ruined his health. He died the following year.

Other than weakening de Viau to the point of death, the *Le Parnasse* trials accomplished several ends. First, they affirmed the role of the French civil (as opposed to religious) authorities to punish people for pornography.

Garasse was responsible for instigating de Viau's retrial, but his role was limited to whining, not judging or sentencing. The trials also made the explicit naming of body parts illegal. The publisher's replacement of the word "prick" with a single letter highlighted the fact that the penis was dirty enough not to be named, but by leaving the word for "ass" intact, and implying that it was there to be penetrated, *Le Parnasse* had gone too far. The trials also put authors squarely at risk for obscenity prosecutions. De Viau had had no idea his sonnet would be published in *Le Parnasse*, and in fact he had lodged a complaint against the bookseller who printed it. Nevertheless, it was de Viau himself who paid the price. Indeed, while he was incarcerated, the publisher capitalized on a good marketing opportunity and put out another edition.

THE NEXT MILESTONE in obscenity suppression, in 1655, involved a work that did much more than simply recite dirty words. *L'École des filles* (literally "the school for girls" but translated into English in the eighteenth century as *The School of Venus*) made the act of reading a sexual (i.e., masturbatory) experience. *L'École* was one of the first of what Jean-Jacques Rousseau called, in his *Confessions*, "those dangerous books . . . that can only be read with one hand." Its tremendous international success reflected the public's craving for longer, more detailed, and more purely fantasy-inducing texts. It had none of the social commentary or blasphemy of its predecessors, though it did not contain the violent and kinky stuff that infused so much later pornography, either. Rather, *L'École* occupied a safe, middle-class world far from religion and politics. The book's sexual actors were neither whores nor aristocrats. They were girls next door, well raised but ready to abandon themselves and more than happy to repeat the magic words "cock," "cunt," and "ass" as long as the printer's ink supply lasted.

The "school" of the title is a girl's bedroom in a bourgeois French house, where two intimate dialogues unfold between the beautiful sixteen-year-old maiden Fanchon and Suzanne, her experienced cousin. Suzanne has been recruited by a young man named Robinet (meaning, appropriately, "faucet") to impart some basic sexual knowledge to Fanchon, whom he fancies. Fanchon has been raised in such perfect innocence that she is unable to understand what Robinet wants from her, or why he "sighs" and "groans" when they are together. Suzanne tutors her admirably. In the first dialogue, she gives Fanchon thorough, detailed descriptions of male and female sexual equipment and of how it is used to "arouse the greatest excitement and pleasure in the world." By the time the conversation is complete, Fanchon is primed and ready to make use of Robinet's "good, stout weapon." Suzanne exits the room and Robinet enters, finding Fanchon on the bed, her heart pounding.

By the start of the second dialogue, Fanchon is innocent no more. She recounts every adventurous detail of her sexual experiences with Robinet. "It is the only thing in the world worth doing, love," she confides, adding that every day she grows "bolder and bolder, my fucking friend assuring me he will so well instruct me that I shall be fit for the embraces of a king." She continues:

> *I believe we were created for fucking, and when we begin to fuck we begin to live . . . Heretofore, what was I good for but to hold my head down and sew? Now nothing comes amiss to me. I can hold an argument on any subject.*

Suzanne is impressed with Fanchon's new attitude, observing that Robinet "must be a good fuckster" and confessing that she was becoming "mad for fucking" just hearing her pupil's stories. And so on.

L'École was clandestinely printed without government approval in Paris. The police learned that the book's promoters, Jean L'Ange and Michel Millot, had copies of the work and had begun selling it. L'Ange was arrested at his rented room, and all his copies of the book were confiscated. The police then went to Millot's residence, where they found a pile of books—but somehow Millot escaped and fled Paris. (Whether his thugs had overpowered the police, as the officer on the scene reported, or whether he paid them off is still the subject of some doubt.) Millot's absence made it easy to pin *L'École*'s authorship on him. At the end of a trial for conduct "contrary to good morals," he was hanged and burned in effigy on Paris's Pont Neuf along with copies of the book. L'Ange was forced to do penance, fined, and banned from Paris for five years.

The spectacle of a man-sized dummy being set alight for writing a sex book is likely to have appeared rather silly to spectators. Everyone knew the monarchy had thus far failed to ban undesirable books, and a little bonfire did not look like success. Paris's seventy-five or so printers had churned out seditious political pamphlets for decades by that point, ignoring laws aimed at controlling the printing trade—such as the 1629 declaration by Louis XIII that the state had the right to censor books prior to publication, including those that "corrupted" morals. Paris was awash in unapproved books and pamphlets. The prosecution of L'Ange and Millot in the same manner reserved for politically subversive writers only highlighted the government's ineptitude.

The book burning on the Pont Neuf was also incomplete: Eight or nine manuscripts had already been distributed, and would soon be reprinted and smuggled throughout Europe. The dirty talk between Suzanne and Fanchon became an underground classic. In 1661, corruption proceedings against Louis XIV's finance minister Nicolas Fouquet revealed that he kept his copy of *L'École* hidden in a locked table in a secret room he maintained for his mistress. Later, in 1668, the English diarist and serial adulterer Samuel Pepys inspected the book in a London shop and found it "the most bawdy, lewd book I ever saw." A few weeks later he went back to the store, where he stayed for three hours to read the book again. Finally, Pepys bought himself a cheap edition, reasoning that he needed to "inform" himself of the "villainy of the world." He spent the next day reading through *L'École* twice more—and achieving at least one orgasm. Pepys burned the book the next day, writing in his diary that he was ashamed to have the book in his collection.

Pepys had conflicted feelings about *L'École des filles*, but at least he did not have to purchase the "idle, roguish book" under the counter. Had he tried to buy it a few years later, though, it would have been much more difficult: In 1677, a London bookseller was forced to close for selling the book in French, not long before another bookseller and a printer were fined for putting out an English translation. The penalties must have been quite mild, however, as both booksellers were charged for the same offenses the following year.[8]

FOR MOST OF the seventeenth century, wrist-slap punishments were common in England for smut peddlers. This is not to say there was a free marketplace of ideas related to sex, only that the government's fury was reserved for troublemaking political or religious material. By contrast, a Protestant cleric was flogged in 1686 for writing a tract urging his coreligionists not to fight for a Catholic cause, and a nineteen-year-old boy was hanged some time later for printing a subversive leaflet. After the ascension of Charles II to the throne in 1660—a monarch of a more liberal bent, as noted earlier—indecency received an informal royal imprimatur. The shows at London's newly reopened theaters were bawdier and more explicit than ever, to the great pleasure of the king. Much of the erotic material being circulated lampooned sexual activity at the court.

In the late seventeenth century, English obscenity law entered its formative stages. One colorful 1663 court case would lay the foundation for legal action against pornographers in the coming decades, though in a rather unpredictable way. It began at the Cock Tavern in London's Bow Street, where roguish nobleman and member of Parliament Sir Charles Sedley was drinking with his mates. After a few too many, they went out onto a balcony and dropped their trousers. According to a contemporary account, the men then "excrementised in the street. Which being done,

Sedley stripped himself naked, and with eloquence preached blasphemy to the people. Whereupon a riot being raised, the people became very clamorous." Sedley was brought into court, where a judge ordered a heavy fine. Sedley observed that he must have been the "first man that paid for shitting." (Charles II himself loaned Sedley the money to pay the fine.) Sixty years later, in 1724, Sedley's conviction gave a London court the precedent it needed to hold a man guilty for publishing two books of pornography. The judge found that the books dirtied up public morals and disturbed the peace just as Sedley had done by "exrementising" off a balcony. The publisher was fined and pilloried, although public opinion seemed to be on his side. No one threw anything at him while he was in the stocks, and after he was freed supporters took him to a tavern.[9]

PESTIFEROUS, PESTILENTIAL, UNNAMEABLE CRIMES: SODOMY, WITCHCRAFT, AND GOATS

Pepys's libido was unusually powerful—he could bring himself to orgasm by just thinking about sex—and his diary, eccentricities notwithstanding, is a fascinating peek into English middle-class sexual habits of the late 1600s. The Navy Office bureaucrat's methods for getting sex were typical, especially his repeated demands for favors from female subordinates. Tavern girls, friends' wives and daughters, almost any female over whom he had some power were game. One seaman's wife came to Pepys several times seeking a promotion for her husband. The seaman got the job, but only after his wife masturbated Pepys in a moving coach and allowed him to kiss her breasts and grope her under her skirt. The chambermaids who combed the lice out of Pepys's hair and helped him dress could expect his hands to travel up their legs while they worked. At the same time, he expressed no shock when his own patron, Lord Sandwich, tried to seduce his wife—that was Sandwich's prerogative.

Pepys was shocked by the stories about Charles II's exploits, although the diarist frequently engaged in similar behavior. There were also rumors of homosexual horseplay at court, and Pepys would undoubtedly have had opportunities to experiment in that direction too, but for him sex was an exclusively heterosexual adventure. In his diary entry for July 1, 1663, Pepys records how he was told that "buggery is now almost grown as common among our gallants as in Italy, and that the very pages of the town begin to complain of their masters for it. But blessed be God, I do not to this day know what is the meaning of this sin."

This attitude was representative of the time. Male-male sex had been openly discussed since at least the reign of James I (1603–25), whose devotion to his male favorites was well-known. Sodomy was a capital offense in England, but few were anxious to see men put to death for it. Unless same-sex behavior was associated with something more troublesome like sorcery, rape, or bestiality, it was mostly overlooked.

England had made "buggery committed with mankind or beast" a civil offense in 1533 under Henry VIII, but that law was passed more to strike a blow against church power than to make drastic new moves against "sodomites." The law stripped religious courts of their jurisdiction over buggery cases even when the defendants were clerics themselves. The statute was reaffirmed several times, but for many years few people were prosecuted under it, even when the offenses were clear. In 1541, for example, the headmaster of the prestigious Eton College, Nicholas Udall, was fired for molesting students, but never charged with a crime. Instead he was given a severance package equal to a year's salary and was eventually installed as the headmaster of a school in Westminster.

It took nearly a century for prosecutions under English antibuggery law to begin, but the luridness of the first prosecutions made up for lost time. In 1622, George Dowdeny of Somersetshire got into bad trouble after he'd pestered a number of his neighbors to have sex with him, possibly raped a boy, and took unnatural liberties with a neighbor's horse. The exact outcome of Dowdeny's case is not known, but given his penchant for bestiality it seems clear that there were few people ready to defend him. According to the depositions, it was his attraction to farm animals rather than boys or men that caused the most horror.

The first known major prosecution under the antibuggery law was against Mervin Touchet, the second Earl of Castlehaven, although homosexual sex made up only part of the case. In April 1631, Castlehaven was convicted of sodomizing one of his servants and helping another to rape his wife. The earl had given prosecutors a lot to work with: The evidence showed that he had regularly sodomized several male household staff members, and pressured one of them into committing the rape. Perhaps worst of all, he had expressed his intent to leave his fortune to a favored male servant at the expense of his eldest son, James.

Castlehaven was especially affectionate toward his page, Henry Skipwith, to whom he had already given a house and much money. It was revealed that he had forced Skipwith on his twelve-year-old stepdaughter Elizabeth (who had, in fact, been betrothed to James when they were both children, making her the earl's daughter-in-law as well). The girl testified that Castlehaven had wanted her to bear Skipwith's offspring as opposed to James's, in order that the servant's descendants could inherit Castlehaven's property. The girl resisted as long as she could, but was ultimately forced to submit. While Castlehaven watched, the court heard, Skipwith inserted himself into Elizabeth's tiny body using oil that his master had supplied. The process was repeated several times, always with Castlehaven in attendance.

Castlehaven inflicted similar brutality on Elizabeth's mother, his second wife, Anne Stanley. He ordered his servant Giles Broadway to rape Stanley in her bed while Castlehaven held her down. Stanley testified that she had tried to kill herself with a knife immediately afterward. (This display of Lucretia-like virtue was in all probability a dramatic ploy, though the crime was ghastly enough. Stanley herself was no innocent, and would take many lovers in the coming years—including Skipwith himself as well as a house page who had also had sex with her husband.)

The jury's vote against Castlehaven for abetting rape was almost unanimous, with just one dissenting vote. For the charge of sodomy, "a crime not to be named among Christians," the vote was closer (15–7), but the majority was enough for him to die. In May, after Charles I refused to pardon him (this Charles being far less open-minded than his son), Castlehaven was brought to the chopping block on Tower Hill in London, where his grave had already been dug. Led to the execution site behind twelve men carrying a black velvet coffin, he ascended the scaffold, proclaimed his innocence for the last of many times, and addressed the assembled crowd: "I beseech you all, when you shall see the axe falling to separate my head from my body, that you will accompany my soul with your prayers to the Kingdom of Heaven where I hope to rest for ever." He took off his collar and laid his head down. With a single blow, the executioner's blade severed his head, which fell into a scarlet cloth held by servants. The head and body were then put into the ground. The fate of his soul is not known.

Castlehaven died for sex crimes, but his legal troubles had begun over money. The case began when James complained to the king that his father was squandering his inheritance on a male servant. James's letter to his father explaining the charges focused on the money rather than morality. He accused Castlehaven of being ready to "sacrifice [their] ancient family to another," and begged his father not to "strike out the difference between a servant and a son." As Castlehaven later correctly pointed out, it was not illegal for him to give property to a servant, but that point was lost amid the storm of sex charges.

The prosecutors pulled no punches. Castlehaven's treatment of his wife was likened to the cruelty of Rome's worst emperors. It was deemed "in the highest degree against the bonds of nature for a husband to consent unto, nay to procure, and assist in the ravishment of his own wife in his own bed." While Castlehaven technically had authority over his wife's body, no one would agree that this prerogative included the right to serve her up for rape by a servant. "[I]t has been reputed one of the miseries of war [for] men to see their wives and daughters ravished and deflowered before their faces," argued the prosecutor, "yet [Castlehaven] esteems this hap a pleasure; he desires it, procures it, en[joys] it, and delights in it."

As for his buggeries, the prosecutor evoked the abominations of Sodom and Gomorrah. The crimes were of such a "pestiferous and pestilential nature," he argued, "that if they be not punished they will draw from heaven heavy judgments upon this kingdom." The king himself was "amazed" at the charges against Castlehaven, the prosecutor reported, and hoped that the "throne and people might be cleared from the guilt of such abominable impieties."

Elizabeth, Stanley, and six servants testified against the vicious earl, painting a detailed picture of a household gone completely mad. Castlehaven's defense strategy made matters worse: He refused to answer any questions put to him on cross-examination. When he did speak, he denied the sodomy, but had no proof other than his own word that it did not occur. His arguments that his son only wanted his money and that his wife was promiscuous herself both backfired, as they reinforced his own lack of control over his household.

Broadway and another servant were also under indictment, and gave the most damning testimony against Castlehaven—they had been promised a deal to help convict their master. The servants kept up their end, but were double-crossed: After Castlehaven was convicted, their testimony was used against them, and they were found guilty and executed. The king pardoned Stanley for her "adulteries, fornication, and incontinency," though, and later granted clemency to Elizabeth. Castlehaven's property went to James after all; the boy became head of the family and the third Earl of Castlehaven.

Castlehaven's case shows the extra element of sin that had to come into play before English courts used their heavy weaponry against same-gender sex. No person of Castlehaven's high rank had been executed for anything other than treason in nearly a century. Moreover, given that the jurors were his social peers and that many of the witnesses against him were merely servants, the result was extraordinary, but the case had become too notorious, and Castlehaven's conduct too outrageous, to let pass. Rather than protecting one of their own, the jury of aristocrats had him killed in an effort to cleanse their ranks. Castlehaven was worse than a rapist, after all: He had encouraged a servant to rape his own family. He represented a dangerously inverted world where servants were favored over sons and noble females forced to yield to the lowborn. Under these circumstances there was no possibility of mercy, whereas if Castlehaven had been guilty only of same-gender, same-class sex, he would probably not have been prosecuted.

A similar principle held in central Europe, where same-gender sex was most likely to bring capital punishment only when it was leavened with some combination of bestiality, witchcraft, and heresy.[10]

Buggerers, Bakers, and Beasts in Germany and the Swiss Confederacy

Nine years before England made buggery a capital crime, Holy Roman Emperor Charles V signed a law proclaiming: "If anyone commits impurity with a beast, or a man with a man, or a woman with a woman, they have forfeited their lives and shall, after the common custom, be sentenced to death by burning." That said, few of the empire's law enforcement units spent their resources chasing down homosexuals. Rather, their efforts were devoted to searching out and punishing adulterers, fornicators, and prostitutes. The city of Frankfurt sentenced just two men for sodomy between 1592 and 1696, but both cases are the exceptions that prove the rule. The sexual habits of the defendants were well-known for years before their trials, with no one trying to put them away.

The first case would not have been brought had the defendant, a Frankfurt baker named Ludwig Boudin, not poached profits from a rival baker named Thomas de Fuhr. Some time before the case was filed, Boudin had hired away de Fuhr's maid, who claimed that de Fuhr had been beating her. The maid convinced many of de Fuhr's customers to transfer their business to Boudin. Only after de Fuhr lost a business competition lawsuit against Boudin did he file sodomy charges. De Fuhr lined up thirteen witnesses against his accused, many of whom repeated long-standing rumors about Boudin's predilections. A few said he had made direct sexual advances on them, and one alleged that he and Boudin had touched each other. There was no issue as to the illegality of Boudin's homosexual conduct, but the townspeople seemed rather tolerant of it. The baker had been groping, propositioning, and jumping uninvited into men's beds for twenty years with no formal complaints, while his business only seems to have grown. Until the trial, most of Boudin's sexual targets were satisfied merely to rebuff him and remind him that he had a wife, not to report him to the authorities.

Neither the unconcerned attitude of Boudin's neighbors nor de Fuhr's economic motives in bringing the case mattered once the prosecution was under way. The law had to be enforced. In Frankfurt, that meant securing a defendant's confession through torture and having witnesses testify in secret. Boudin was never permitted to cross-examine them; he was only allowed to confirm or deny what they had said. If his denials seemed implausible, his interrogators literally turned the screws until he changed his story. When Boudin refused to confirm certain witness accounts, his legs were repeatedly pressed in a rotating torture device and his body hoisted on a rack. Each time the pain was applied, he admitted to no more than being a nuisance while drunk. Under torture, he also demanded: "Why had all these witnesses been quiet for so many years—was it not their duty to report bad deeds to the authorities?" The city's advocates seem to have concluded early on that he was guilty, but they nevertheless tortured him eight more times, to the point where he begged his torturers to kill him. Ultimately he was pilloried publicly and banished from Frankfurt.

The charges brought against Frankfurt shopkeeper Heinrich Krafft were graver than those against Boudin. In 1645, he was accused of targeting animals and boys for sexual pleasure. The most that could be gotten out of witnesses was that Krafft was sexually aggressive with men when drunk, especially when he hosted parties in his basement. Krafft agreed that he had touched men, but denied that his advances had been unwelcome. The case should have ended there; his admission of sex with men was enough to convict him. But the presence of animals in the story made the prosecutors especially aggressive. Krafft was tortured repeatedly while being questioned about the goats he kept in the countryside, and whether or not he had visited a peasant who kept goats. His denials of bestiality in the face of extreme pain probably saved his life. Had he admitted to having sex with goats he would likely have been executed. Instead, he was taken from prison to the city gates and told never to come back.

Religious zeal made authorities in Geneva unusually vigilant in their prosecution of sodomites. From about 1450 to 1540, before John Calvin established a Protestant theocracy in the city, only six known sodomy trials were held there. In the 125 years after Calvin there were sixty, half of which ended in burning, beheading, hanging, or drowning. The Geneva courts also prosecuted lesbianism. In 1568, a woman admitted to having sex with both men and women, for which the judges sentenced her to be drowned. They were so shocked by her confession that they refused to describe her crimes to the crowd at the execution. The official sentence said merely that she had committed a "detestable and unnatural crime, which is so ugly that, from horror, it is not named here."

As time passed, sodomy prosecutions in Geneva focused on cases involving bestiality. Sex with animals was seen as a violation of biblical edicts and, especially when goats were involved, a link to witchcraft. Most jurisdictions had laws on the books condemning bestiality, and these were vigorously enforced. "There is hardly a tribunal in Europe which has not condemned to the fire some miserable ones convicted of this turpitude," Voltaire would later write, although the great philosopher and snob added, rather too carefully: "Young peasants . . . are alone guilty of this infamy and . . . scarcely differ from the animals with which they couple."

In 1601, a sixteen-year-old French girl named Claudine de Culam was charged for carnally knowing a dog, although she passionately denied the accusation. The court came up with an innovative method for uncovering the truth. The girl and the dog were taken to a chamber adjacent to the courtroom, where Claudine was told to undress. The dog immediately leaped up and attempted copulation with her, "which he would perhaps have accomplished had we not prevented him." Both Claudine and the animal were strangled and their bodies burned. Their ashes were "thrown to the winds" to leave no trace of them or their crimes. The execution of animals along with their human lovers was common. Also in France, in 1606, a dog that had scampered away after suffering sexual indignities with a human was condemned and hung in effigy. A few decades later, in Britain's Massachusetts Bay Colony, a teenage boy who was put under arrest was forced to reveal all his sexual partners. The list included a mare, a cow, two goats, two calves, five sheep, and a turkey. The animals were all killed and their carcasses thrown away, and the boy went to the gallows. Occasionally, European courts gave animals the right to confess their crimes, though this took some rather harsh prodding. Their squeals of pain while being held over fires were taken as admissions of guilt.

Scotland had no antibestiality laws as such, so its courts relied directly on the biblical commandment that when "a man lie with a beast, he shall surely be put to death" (Leviticus 18:23, 20:15). In 1654, John Muir confessed that he had committed the "land-defiling sin of bestiality" with a mare on six separate occasions. (The fact that he was spotted copulating with the unfortunate horse on the Sabbath did not help his case.) He and the horse were strangled and burned at the stake. Executed at the same time was William MacAdam, who was made to perish with the cow he had violated.

There was little that accused animal lovers could do to defend themselves if they had been witnessed in the act. When in Scotland one David Malcolm was caught in 1718 by a James Grey while copulating with an animal, Malcolm fell to his knees and begged for mercy. Grey replied that bestiality had become a troubling habit for Malcolm, which Malcolm denied. Oddly, Malcolm said he had tried several times to have sex with animals, but was unable to do so until that very occasion. Like many others so accused, Malcolm also claimed that Satan had forced him to lie with the beast. This last excuse rarely succeeded in getting people mercy in court, but it may have been genuinely believed by some defendants. Animal sodomy was associated at all levels of society with witchcraft.

In the Swiss canton of Vaud in 1595, a peasant was so moved by a sermon he heard on the subject of sin that he sought out the pastor to confess his sexual abuse of a cow thirty years earlier. The pastor promised to pray for the peasant, but went one step further and reported him as a criminal. The peasant was thrown in jail. With no need for torture, the repentant man confessed to bestiality as well as adultery, perjury, gambling, and, most importantly, witchcraft. The devil, he said, had appeared to him recently and told him that his carnal knowledge of the cow had ruined his soul. Now, Satan evidently had told the peasant, the man was obliged to carry out infernal deeds. The peasant's pious resolve to defy Satan's command and tell all may have saved his soul, but it also got him and his family killed. A jury condemned him to burn at the stake along with his wife and twelve-year-old son, both of whom had also confessed to witchcraft. In nearby Fribourg, where cows outnumbered people, bestiality had long been linked with witchcraft. More than a century before the Vaud case, a man there confessed that the devil had appeared to him to demand loyalty after the fellow had enjoyed the company of a cow, a goat, and a deer.[11]

The Witch Hunts

The link between bestiality and witchcraft went deeper than Satan popping up to demand obeisance from people who had copulated with animals. In the witch craze of the sixteenth and seventeenth centuries, when more than seven thousand witchcraft prosecutions took place in Europe and the North American colonies, animals were often characterized as incarnations of Satan himself. Bestial sex was seen as one of many elements of devil worship. Sorcery and witchcraft had been prohibited since at least the Babylonian era, but prior to the Early Modern period, few people were formally charged with the offense. That changed in the late 1400s, when a fever dream began to take hold in legal and religious circles, in which witches were reconceived: No longer were they simply magicians and mischief-makers. The new, much scarier witches were perverse devil worshippers working in league with each other and with Satan to destroy the world. Witches were almost always believed to be female, middle-aged or older, poor, and sexually deviant in the extreme. Accurate figures are impossible to pin down, but there is good reason to believe that more than sixty thousand people were executed for the crime of witchcraft between 1450 and 1750. At least 80 percent of them were women.

The crime of witchcraft hinged on the contract between a given witch and Satan, by which the witch renounced God and agreed to do Satan's work. These pacts, often believed to be written in blood and signed in hell, formally enlisted the witch in the devil's vast army. When the witch caused famine, killed a child, or wrecked crops with hail, she did it in fulfillment of this bargain. When she spat on the Cross, pissed on the Host, and ate children, she was merely keeping up her end of the deal. The law made the contract the most critical aspect of the crime. For example, the influential Saxon criminal code of the 1570s mandated death by fire for people having dealings with the devil, regardless of whether or not they actually hurt anyone. Scottish law went in the same direction. England redefined the crime in 1604 to include communication with evil spirits, even in the absence of an identifiable victim.

The mythology underlying these contracts was complex, but for our purposes they had one common aspect: the devil's demand for sex as part of the deal. Forcing the accused witch to admit she had sex with Satan (or one of his minions) was proof enough that a pact had been made, and was enough to send the witch to death. The seventeenth-century Italian friar and demonologist Francesco-Maria Guazzo told the story of a twelve-year-old girl accosted in the road by Satan in the form of a strange man: "The girl was made to swear an oath to this man, and he marked her brow with his nail as a sign of her new allegiance, and then he lay with her in the sight of her mother." Rather than being appalled at the sight of her daughter being so ravished, the mother became aroused and "offered herself to be defiled by him in the daughter's presence." From that point on, the priest declared, both mother and daughter were Satan's slaves. Other times, the contract was said to be sealed when the devil, in the form of a well-endowed male animal, demanded that the witch-initiate kiss his anus or have sexual intercourse with him. The scenarios were as varied as human nightmares.

In the case of Johannes Junius, burgomaster of the German town of Bamberg, the pact involved sex with a creature of both human and animal form. Under torture, Junius confessed to being in his orchard when a "grass maid" approached him. With "seductive speeches," she convinced him to "yield to her will." Immediately afterward, she revealed herself as a bleating goat that taunted Junius and demanded delivery of his soul: "Now you see with whom you have had to do. You must be mine or I will forthwith break your neck."

By the time Junius was arrested, in 1628, Bamberg was in the grip of a full-scale witch panic in which several hundred persons—including Junius's wife—were condemned and burned. Junius refused to confess despite enduring repeated torture sessions involving thumbscrews, leg vises, and the strappado (a device that suspended victims on a rope with their hands tied behind their back). "Eight times did they draw me up [on the strappado] and let me fall again," he later wrote from jail, "so that I suffered terrible agony." Finally, in "wretched" despair, he broke down and confessed to his seduction by a goat, his later baptism by the devil, and Satan's commands to kill his children.

Junius's tale of Satanic initiation with a woman-goat made perfect sense to his interrogators, but it was not enough to satisfy them. The torture continued until he named other Bamberg residents who purportedly joined him in orgiastic witches' assemblies called sabbats. Each of the innocents Junius identified was most likely also prosecuted and executed. In any event, the good burgomaster's cooperation won him no mercy. After paying a guard to sneak a letter out to his daughter recounting his sufferings, he was burned at the stake.

THE CLERICS AND civil judges (often the prosecutors themselves) who presided over witch trials inevitably pushed accused witches to describe their sexual romps with the devil. The interrogators knew what they wanted and, using torture, usually got it. The image of old beggar women or midwives being pulled to pieces while their interrogators prodded them to "confess" to perverse sexual adventures is impossibly tragic, but it happened time and again. Nothing was too far-fetched, especially for prosecutors who spent their careers layering on the details of their own sadistic fantasies. Said historian Walter Stephens: "Like some forms of drug use and sexual experimentation, fantasies about witches required their addicts to increase the dosage constantly; otherwise, the fantasies lost their ability to satisfy the underlying compulsion, even temporarily."

As the witch trials wore on, the idea of Satan as a sexual supercreature was refined. The prominent French prosecutor Pierre de Lancre, who boasted of sending more than six hundred witches to the stake, told of a seventeen-year-old Basque girl he examined who testified that, whether the devil appeared as a man or a goat,

> *[h]e always had a member like a mule's, having chosen to imitate that animal as being best endowed by nature . . . it was as long and as thick as an arm . . . he always exposed his instrument, of such beautiful shape and measurements.*

The beast's gargantuan sexual organs could be made of scaly flesh, iron, flax, horn, or something else entirely. Some Spanish and Italian witches confessed that these phallic tools satisfied them like nothing on earth, but most others said they caused pain. In his memoirs, the French witch hunter Nicolas Rémy wrote with breathless excitement that "all female witches maintain that the so-called genital organs of their Demons are so huge and so excessively rigid that they cannot be admitted without the greatest pain." One of Rémy's victims, Didatia of Miremont, confessed that the devil's penis caused her to hemorrhage blood.

It must have been a challenge for the accused witches to infer the kind of information their accusers were seeking. One can only imagine the time and effort it took to get one poor girl, tried by the Parlement de Paris in 1616, to describe the devil's horselike member: "[O]n insertion it was as cold as ice and ejected ice-cold semen, and on his withdrawing it burned her as if in fire." Another girl, tried before the Parlement d'Aquitaine in 1594, said she attended an orgy where she was presented to a goat:

> *The goat led her apart as his bride into a neighboring wood, and pressing her against the ground, penetrated her. But the girl said she found this operation quite lacking in any sensation of pleasure, for she rather experienced a very keen pain and sense of horror of the goat's semen, which was cold as ice.*

Satan could apparently turn himself into any animal or insect, but most demonologists agreed he was partial to the goat. "[T]he obscene lasciviousness of goats is proverbial," wrote Rémy, "and it is the Demon's chief care to urge his followers to the greatest venereal excesses." Yet the goat was more than just an animal well "adapted" to seducing people into "revolting obscenities." The association of the devil with goats also tapped into an inexhaustible vein of hatred that ran through the core of European society: The animal evoked the horned Jew as well.[12]

The medieval slander and massacres of Jews as Christ-killers and well-poisoners constituted a kind of basic training for the witch hunts of the Early Modern period. The example of the Jew as a scapegoat for the world's ills was well established by the time the witch craze began. Popular wisdom held, for example, that Jewish rituals involved the blood of Christian children, and that Jews caused outbreaks of plague. Illustrations of the time depicted Jews with goatlike horns, scraggly beards, and tails. Though Jews were not always represented as goats, they were typically depicted as riding them, often sitting backward. In Vienna, Jews were forced to appear in public wearing goatlike horned hats; in thirteenth-century France, Philip III had required Jews to add a horned figure to the customary Jewish badge. Both the Jew and the goat were said to share the same stench of the devil—and goats and Jews were "known" sexual predators.

As Jews and witches were in league with the devil, witch hunters were often on the lookout for Jews as well, even when there weren't many Jews around to hunt. Moreover, medieval laws criminalized sexual relations between Jews and Christians. (In England, sex with Jews was put into the same accursed category as heresy, homosexuality, and bestiality.) Centuries after the expulsion of the Jews from France, de Lancre accused them of doing evil under Satanic protection: "They deserve every execration, and as destroyers of all divine and human majesty, they merit punishment and indeed the greatest tortures. Slow fire, melted lead, boiling oil, pitch, wax, and sulfur fused together would not make torments fitting, sharp and cruel enough." And when, starting in about 1400, the myth developed that witches gathered together to eat children, cook up poisons, and have bizarre sex, it was no accident that those unholy orgies were called "sabbats," after the Hebrew word for the seventh day, or even more directly, "synagogues."

THE EARLY MODERN period saw the development of elaborate legal machinery to root out and execute witches. For lawyers, judges, priests, and inquisitors enterprising enough to make a career out of witch hunting, there was no shortage of work. De Lancre, whose descriptions of sabbats are among the most lurid, claimed that thirty thousand people in the Basque region of southwestern France were taking part in such rituals. The only question for de Lancre and his contemporaries was how to use the law to find and kill as many of them as possible. In France, de Lancre sent more than eighty women to the stake in 1609 alone; Rémy bragged of executing nine hundred witches over fifteen years.

Theories as to the causes of the witch craze are legion: religious intolerance during the Reformation, the chaos of the era's many wars, the state centralization of the legal process, and so on. While almost any event during this tumultuous period could be thrown into the analytical stew, no one in the witch-prosecuting industry was thinking along such lines. Both professional witch hunters and the crowds who gathered to watch the witches burn were focused on the supernatural, evidence of which they saw all around them. People at all levels of society believed unreservedly in the occult. Fighting the devil and his servants was a serious and practical undertaking well within the job description of the learned classes. As they cleared their regions of the devil's accomplices, witch hunters were doing their part for the health of the Christian world.

The main challenge facing witch prosecutors stemmed from this same belief in the supernatural: If witches were using magic to cause trouble, wouldn't they also use it to cover their tracks? They did, replied demonologists, so there should be no reason to expect any eyewitnesses to a witch's activity. Proving witchcraft therefore centered on extracting confessions from accused witches, for which torture was usually required. Persuading elderly women and midwives to confess to the particulars of baby barbecuing, goat copulation, and broom travel was hard work, complained a prominent witch hunter: "[I]t is difficult, or more difficult, to compel a witch to tell the truth as it is to exorcise a person possessed of the devil." Torture was a last resort in other kinds of criminal cases, but when investigating witchcraft, it was employed as the main method of inquiry.

The most important of many handbooks used by witch prosecutors was the *Malleus Maleficarum* (*Hammer of Witches*), written by the German inquisitor Heinrich Kramer, ostensibly in collaboration with his fellow inquisitor of the Dominican order, Jakob Sprengler. (Sprengler is named as coauthor in later editions of the book, but experts now doubt that he had much to do with it.) First published in 1486 and running to about thirty editions by 1669, it provided comprehensive guidance on the fine points of charging, torturing, and executing witches. The book was indispensable for lawyers and judges, but its sexually graphic passages and illustrations also drove sales to a readership outside legal-profession circles. With chapter titles such as "Here follows the Way Whereby Witches Copulate with Those Devils known as Incubi," the *Malleus* and other such books allowed readers to titillate themselves with cruel sexual fantasies and feel pious at the same time.

Kramer did not trouble long on the need to exterminate witches; to disbelieve witchcraft was itself heresy, after all. What the *Malleus* did dwell on was how witchcraft operated, and on this subject it and the other witch-hunting manuals were relentlessly misogynistic. "All witchcraft comes from carnal lust," Kramer wrote, "which is in women insatiable." Women's natural inferiority and alleged sexual weakness made them prime victims for the temptations of Satan. "The Devil uses [women] so because he knows that women love carnal pleasures," agreed French witch prosecutor Henri

Bouget. "[T]here is nothing which makes a woman more subject and loyal to a man than that he should abuse her body." For his part, Rémy found it "not unreasonable that this scum of humanity [i.e., witches] should be drawn from the feminine sex." Even women who were not yet possessed were to be distrusted: "All wickedness is but little to the wickedness of a woman."

The fact that women would themselves be harmed by the devil's sexual abuse was of no concern to the law. Rémy and his contemporaries' endless descriptions of women experiencing agonizing pain upon being pierced by Satan's massive phallus are never sympathetic in tone. The prosecutors seem, if anything, envious of Satan. The real threat of witchcraft was to the sexual pride of men. The vast literature of witch hunting is filled with nightmares of castration and lost virility. Most famously, the *Malleus* told of witches who collected severed penises, twenty or thirty at a time, and kept them hidden while the afflicted men wandered the earth looking for their lost members. It was of "common report," the *Malleus* assured the reader, that witches kept their penis collections in birds' nests, where they wiggled by themselves and ate oats and corn. Perhaps inadvertently revealing too much, the experienced churchman Kramer added that in one case the "big" penis in the nest belonged to a priest.

As the *Malleus* emphasized, mainstream Christianity viewed women as "the Devil's gateway" and their bodies as "white sepulchres." Drawing on ancient Christian wisdom and adding a big dollop of paranoid fantasy, the book (and others like it) turned witchcraft into a female sex crime. Before 1400, about half the people charged as witches were women. By the time the witch craze hit high gear in the seventeenth century, that figure came to nearly eight out of ten. In Switzerland, England, and what is now Belgium, the proportion was even higher.

It was during this period that the cliché of the witch as a hag was crystallized. She was "an old, weather-beaten crone, having the chin and her knees meeting for age . . . hollow-eyed, untoothed, furrowed on her face, having her limbs trembling with palsy, going mumbling in the streets." A beggar woman angry after being refused alms, a midwife presiding over a stillbirth, an isolated widow: These were the types of women most likely to be accused.

Suspects were plentiful. Under torture, accused witches were routinely forced to name both their accomplices and anyone they were meant to have witnessed participating in sabbats. In 1611, Barbara Rüfin of the German town of Ellwangen was accused of witchcraft after objecting to her son's marriage. Her family denounced her for trying to poison her son, and also for killing animals. Officials arrested the seventy-one-year-old and had her stretched on the rack no fewer than seven times. She confessed to copulating and signing a pact with the devil, as well as attempting to kill her son, poisoning livestock, and destroying crops. She also named other witches, who presumably named still more people. The witch hunt in Ellwangen consumed about four hundred souls before cooling off. Among the dead was the wife of a town judge. When the jurist argued that she had been wrongly convicted, he was arrested himself, forced to confess, and executed as well.

The *Malleus* encouraged officials to take whatever steps necessary to neutralize their prisoners' magic powers. The women's houses were to be searched "in all holes and corners and chests, top and bottom . . . [for] various instruments of witchcraft." Kramer also counseled authorities to remove witches from their houses immediately, giving them no opportunity to return, "for they are wont to secure in this way, and bring away with them, some object or power of witchcraft which procures them the faculty of keeping silent under examination."

Even after the search, there remained the risk that witches would work magic on the judges. The *Malleus* warned that physical contact with suspects was to be avoided. If it did occur, then only a concoction of consecrated salt and blessed herbs could protect them. Even a glance from a witch could weaken a judge's resolve. "[B]y so getting the first sight of the

Judge [witches] have been able so to alter the minds of the Judge . . . that they have lost all their anger against them and have not presumed to molest them in any way, but have allowed them to go free." To stop witches from using the evil eye to their advantage, they were made to walk backward into a judge's presence.

Once an accused witch was in custody, her allegiance to Satan could be proved by a number of methods. One process, called "swimming the witch," resembled ancient Babylonian practices: The suspect was stripped and her hands and feet bound together. Then she was flung repeatedly into a river or pond. If she floated, she was guilty and put to death; if she sank, she was declared innocent and allowed to live—that is, so long as she was rescued in time. King James himself believed the method infallible:

So it appears that God hath appointed, for a supernatural sign of the monstrous impiety of the witches, that the water shall refuse to receive them in her bosom, that have shaken off them the sacred water of baptism and wilfully refused the benefit thereof.

Far more common than swimming witches was sexual mistreatment on dry land. Sometimes it was relatively mild, as when the American Puritan minister Cotton Mather publicly groped a girl's breasts while she writhed in demonic possession. More often, though, the abuse was brutal, as when women were searched for "devil's marks." Demonology held that Satan branded witches with telltale signs as people commonly did with slaves or livestock. The marks could be warts, moles, or extra nipples on which baby demons were thought to suckle. Such marks were taken as proof of a witch's infernal pact. The readily apparent ones were found by visual inspection. Others, which were believed to be below the skin and resistant to pain, were discovered by "pricking" the witch with pins and nails. As the devil's relationship with a witch would be sexual, officials would customarily search first for the obliging marks on or around the genitalia.

Prosecutors and professional witch examiners made displays of their searches for devil's marks. The witch's head and genitals were shaven, often in public. Then, while the crowd got worked up, the witches were poked and prodded by their accusers. The *Malleus* and other manuals mandated "diligent and careful" inspections of accused witches' "secret parts." The "witch's tit" was actually, in many cases, the clitoris, upon which inspectors lingered and on which they used metal tools. Even when other parts of the body were scrutinized, such as the legs, arms, or neck, the use of blades to puncture the flesh was itself a form of sexual violence.[13]

Hundreds of inspections for devil's marks took place in the Swiss Confederacy, Scotland, and England. In some cases, accused witches were saved from the stake when no suitable mark was discovered. But prosecutors and probers, who were paid by the conviction, often found what they were looking for. Scottish witch hunter Matthew Hopkins had to hire four assistants to staff his growing business. He believed that devil's marks were a food source for demons, so he held them to attract hungry animal spirits. He stripped his victims naked and tied them to chairs, deprived them of food, and waited. Any animal that walked in the interim constituted proof that the witch was calling a dark spirit to feed off her. If no animal happened by, after a few days Hopkins would have them put there. In other cases, simply leaving accused witches in their cells got the job done. Anne Foster, of Northamptonshire, was reported to have suckled her "familiar" in her prison cell, but what were taken to be the sounds of a witch giving nourishment to a demon were actually her frightened cries as she fought back hordes of rats attacking her in the cell. She was sentenced to hang in 1674.

Once the suspect was identified as a witch, it was necessary to obtain her confession. The law required witches to acknowledge their crimes before they were executed. The *Malleus* advised that torture, deception, and terror be used to extract confessions. The rack, scourging, burning, eye-gouging—all of it was sanctioned. "Whoever comes into the witch prison must become a witch or be tortured until he invents something out of his head," wrote Johannes Junius. Interrogations under torture often followed a standard set of questions, although the "right" answer was sometimes elusive. Walpurga Hausmannin first admitted that she had sex with the devil himself. Later, she was forced to confess that she had given herself to a lesser demon in the form of her human lover.

King James argued that only "the extreme pain of the engines of torture could loosen the devil's grip over his servants." If torture didn't work, it was because Satan was at work right there in the chamber, fortifying suspects against pain. The *Malleus* told of a witch from the town of Hagenau who gave herself the "gift of silence" by killing and cooking a baby boy, thereafter grinding the remains into a powder that she was somehow able to retain during her torture. The Hagenau woman may well have remained silent—if so, it was more likely the result of shock.

IT IS A challenge for anyone today to accept that this kind of superstition and savagery took place under the authority of law. It is too unjust, too perverse, too ridiculous. Yet most of what occurred was done with the active involvement or encouragement of legitimate state governments. Antiwitchcraft statutes were in force everywhere because those at the highest levels of leadership truly believed it existed. According to King James, who personally supervised at least one torture-laced witch trial and also wrote his own book of demonology, witches were everywhere: "The fearful abounding at this time in this country of these detestable slaves of the devil, the Witches or enchanters, who are never so rife in these parts as they are now." Under James's authority, and with instructions to use torture when necessary, a special commission took over witch prosecutions and presided over at least three hundred trials from 1591 to 1597.

On the Continent, Pierre de Lancre's sweep of the Basque country was done under the authority of Henry IV. Nicolas Rémy, who worked for Duke Charles III of Lorraine, had the power to override local magistrates whom he believed too lenient toward the alleged witches. In the German states, where more witches were executed than anywhere else, the process of hunting witches could resemble an official traveling road show. Special judicial witch finders came to towns ready to override any local law or custom standing in the way of convictions. The witch-hunting craze of the sixteenth and seventeenth centuries was imposed from above, not below.

Following the pronunciation of a death sentence for a witch came the spectacle of her execution. In Europe, that usually meant a fire show. Burning witches alive (or sometimes after strangling) was endorsed by Jean Bodin, a respected French philosopher and member of the Parlement de Paris, who regarded the practice as a kind of preparation for an eternity in hell:

> *Whatever punishment one can order against witches by roasting and cooking them over a slow fire is not really very much, and not as bad as the torment which Satan has made for them in this world, to say nothing of the eternal agonies that are prepared for them in Hell, for the fire here cannot last more than an hour or so until the witches have died.*

Typically the witches' misdeeds were announced in detail to the assembled onlookers before the flame was lit. In one Spanish auto-da-fé, whereby twenty-nine witches were set afire (among fifty-nine heretics), the process took two grisly days to complete. The witches had admitted to attending twenty-two sabbats. Said the historian Henry Lea: "All the grotesque obscenities which the foul imaginations of the accused could invent to satisfy their prosecutors, were given at length, and doubtless impressed the gaping multitudes with the horror and detestation desired." In addition to the witches' sexual adventures, their feasts on corpses were detailed, as well as their destruction of harvests and poisonings of their own children. What Michel Foucault called "the spectacle of the scaffold" was a trance-inducing affair.

The imagined sex lives of convicted witches were also retold in cheap illustrated pamphlets peddled to spectators at executions. These early tabloids offered lurid narratives of seductions by the devil, generously illustrated with woodcuts. As so many of the witches' alleged crimes followed set patterns, the printers were able to reuse the woodcuts for multiple executions, changing only the names of the accused in the captions. Armed with images of the witches' crimes, the purchaser/spectator could then listen to the women's screams, experiencing both moral shock and sadistic titillation. When the execution was over, of course, the pamphlets remained, to be reviewed in private again and again.

The witch craze slowed down at the end of the seventeenth century. Why this fury ended is as mystifying as why it began, but one thing is clear: The use of torture to generate new suspects was starting to produce the wrong kind of people for prosecution. In Würzburg, for example, more than 160 people were tried and convicted of witchcraft from 1627 to 1629. The majority of these victims were lower-class women, but soon there were people from all classes in the torture chambers, including clerics, city officials, doctors, and children. The fervor slowed down when the elite began to fear for their own hides.

The last executions for witchcraft in England took place in 1682. Temperance Lloyd, a senile shopkeeper, was accused of casting spells and having sex with "the devil in the likeness or shape of a black man." Lloyd also had "in her secret parts two teats hanging nigh together like unto a piece of flesh that a child had sucked." She readily confessed, adding that she had indeed suckled a black man who had the mouth of a toad but sometimes changed himself into a bird. Her beggar codefendants also confessed to witchcraft. The jury found them guilty despite the skepticism of the judge, who worried that their confessions were in fact a form of suicide. Thirteen years later, an English lawyer had the nerve to argue in court that belief in witchcraft should be seen as a thing of the past. By 1736, the English laws mandating death for witches were repealed. No longer was it a capital crime to be a witch. From that point forward, it was forbidden (under much less severe sentences) to *act* like one. By the mid-eighteenth century, witch hunts on the Continent had also mostly stopped.[14]

6

· · ·

THE NEW WORLD OF
SEXUAL OPPORTUNITY

L ATE ONE NIGHT in 1830, in New Kent County, Virginia, two black
slaves named Peggy and Patrick burst into the house of their owner,
John Francis, bearing weapons. Patrick immediately went after his owner
with an axe while Peggy beat Francis with a large stick. Whether or not
Francis was killed with these weapons we cannot know for sure, as the slaves
set the house on fire as they left and it burned to the ground with Francis
inside. It was not long before Peggy and Patrick were identified (along with
two accomplices) as the arsonists/killers. The evidence—mostly taken from
the verbal accounts of other slaves—soon began to mount against them.
One slave had seen Peggy and Patrick enter the Francis house with their
weapons. Another slave, a girl named Sucky, had been in the house when
Peggy and Patrick had entered and confirmed that they had used straw
to set the structure ablaze. Yet another slave had seen them searching the
remains of Francis's house for money after the attack.

The trial of Peggy and Patrick should have been simple and a guilty
verdict assured: There was no worse crime in the antebellum South than
the murder by a slave of his master, and the law made it almost impossible
for black people to find justice anyway. No black person could ever testify
against a white person, regardless of the circumstances, so even a free black
woman who had been raped by whites had no way of proving the crime

happened. Enslaved women such as Peggy were the most powerless of all. They practically existed to be abused by their masters. "We do anything to get our poor flesh some rest from de whip," explained one Georgia slave woman to an English newcomer. "When [the master] made me follow him into de bush, what use me tell him no?"

Under normal circumstances, Peggy would end up hanged—a sentence judges imposed because it was the only result the law allowed. However, there was something different about this case that made the local white community uncomfortable. Peggy had brutally murdered her master and burned his house down, but she nevertheless gained the support of one hundred local white men, including one of the judges in her trial, who signed a petition to Virginia's governor pleading for her life to be spared.

Slave women were in no position to refuse their owners' sexual demands. As a long-suffering Virginia slave woman explained to her daughter: "[A] nigger 'oman couldn't help herself, fo' she had to do what der marster say." Reprisals or resistance by slaves against their masters often ended in violence. Yet the men who advocated for Peggy knew what the strict letter of the law ignored: that even in the pathological matrix of white-black sexual relations, there had to be limits. This case defined the boundary beyond which even a slave owner such as John Francis must not go.

It was common knowledge among his neighbors that Francis had kept Peggy chained to a block in one of his farm buildings. He demanded repeatedly that she have sex with him, which she refused to do. It was also known that Francis beat her savagely, and that he threatened, if she continued to rebuff him, to thrash her until she was nearly dead, after which he would sell what remained of her in the slave market. Moreover, as everyone from the justice of the peace to Peggy herself knew, Francis was Peggy's father. While Peggy was hardly the first person to have been conceived through master-slave sex, her father's sexual demands were too much to bear for her; resisting them was worth killing and dying for.

Notably, no one did anything to help Peggy while Francis was alive. Slave owners regularly tortured their recalcitrant slave women, as was their prerogative. (Another Virginia slave woman of the same era who had "'fuse[d] to be a wife" to an overseer was suspended by her arms and whipped in punishment.) Any outside meddling in Francis's treatment of Peggy could have been considered as interference with his sacred ownership of property, no different from preventing him from using his land or farm equipment. In addition, despite Francis's cruelty to Peggy, no one who signed the petition believed she should be let off the hook legally. They all expressed "utmost abhorrence" at what she had done. Rather than hanging Peggy as the law demanded, however, they suggested that she be banished from the United States, which they said would "have the same good effect on Society" as her death. In the end, this was indeed Peggy's fate. She and about twenty other slaves (including Patrick) were sold by the state to traders, and never heard from again. John Francis's heirs were then presumably reimbursed by the state of Virginia for the loss of a valuable slave.

Peggy's attack on John Francis sparked a furor among the whites of New Kent County, to be sure, but it never caused anyone to question that state's color-coded system of sexual abuse. Slaves were commonly fathered by their owners, and slave women such as Peggy's mother had no right to resist. Sex between white men and black or mixed-race (commonly called "mulatto") females carried none of the traditional restrictions that governed relations between whites. Furthermore, a slave woman's children were legally illegitimate, regardless of who the father was. While a white master's wife or daughter was held to the high standards of sexual propriety, none of that applied to the women who tilled his fields and cleaned his chamber pots. Peggy had a white father, but she was black enough to be a sexual target. Despite the sympathies her case caused, no one tried to spare her any suffering in the future. She was sold to the highest bidder, and her next master might be expected to take full sexual advantage of his new acquisition.[1]

By 1831, when Peggy was auctioned off, whites had been exploiting women of color in the New World for more than three centuries. Starting with the first arrivals of Spanish and Portuguese explorers and continuing through waves of French, English, and Dutch settlers and profiteers, sexual relations between Europeans and dark-skinned females were both plentiful and charged with power politics. Sex was an instrument of conquest, a prize of victory and a relief from the restrictive mores of home. The New World was not only conquered at the tip of a sword or the barrel of a gun; it was brought down every bit as much (in the choice words of historian R. C. Padden) by the *membrus febrilis* ("feverish member") of white men. White men played out violent sexual fantasies they could never have considered at home without having to fear for their lives.

Copious sex with supposedly insatiable native women was a key lure for libidinous European men to risk their lives crossing the oceans. The contrast with life at home could not have been starker. As the Reformation and Counter-Reformation ground on in Europe, brothels closed everywhere and punishments for even minor sexual transgressions increased. Never before had the disconnect between desire and law been wider or more dangerous to manage. A man might find himself whipped in public for causing an out-of-wedlock pregnancy, banished from his town for committing adultery, or even threatened with death for having too adventurous sex with his own wife. Something had to give, and one escape route was to the lands of the proverbial Amazons. Far from the prying eyes of neighbors and vice patrols, the New World shined with the allure of sexual paradise, a humid playpen filled with panting women ready to serve white men. "They esteem it a breach of Hospitality, not to submit to everything [the white man] desires of them," held one report. For men with little to lose, that was enough.

Of course, it was a puerile myth that any women were waiting to service white men from across the seas. The reality was that violence (either actual or threatened) was usually necessary to convince native women to submit to the Europeans' overheated sexual needs. To choose one example out of millions, Thomas Thistlewood left England in 1750 under the cloud of an arrest warrant for fathering a bastard child. He ended up as a slave overseer (and compulsive diarist) in Jamaica, where he had sex 1,774 times with 109 women over a thirteen-year period—probably every female under his control except the very young and the elderly. Thistlewood was typical in his carnal appetites and readiness to use violence to have his way with slave women. Nowhere in England were such risk-free sexual opportunities available, especially for someone of his low social station. He died in Jamaica after thirty-six consequence-free years of sexual opportunism.

European governments adapted their laws to permit their men to sexually maraud the New World almost unimpeded. Over the centuries, however, the picture became increasingly complicated. The vast territories of the Americas and Africa were not mere enemy towns to be sacked and then deserted. The Europeans had come to stay, and in so doing they were required to develop institutions to permit their men to vent their impure desires while simultaneously building a neo-European society. As the fates of Peggy and the slaves under Thislewood's control attest, that effort was built on the bodies of dark-skinned people.[2]

THE SEXUAL ATTRACTION OF THE WEST

In addition to contributing his name to the landmasses of the Western Hemisphere, the Italian explorer and cartographer Amerigo Vespucci counted among his accomplishments the promotion of the New World as a giant sexual resort. One of his travel accounts, written in about 1504, told of the insatiable women of Hispaniola (the island comprising modern-day Haiti and the Dominican Republic), who used magical insect venom to engorge their men's penises, inflating them to such proportions that they sometimes fell off. With native men unable to satisfy their females, the time was ripe for European men to come and take charge. The women,

Vespucci promised, were ready and waiting for the white men to take them; indeed, they were so fond of "Christians" that "they debauch and prostitute themselves."

Vespucci was not the only pimp for the unwitting women of the New World. According to other early accounts, the entire region was a female body begging to be taken. Emphasizing the interplay of sex and plunder, Sir Walter Raleigh described Guyana as a "country that hath yet her maidenhead, never sacked, turned, nor wrought." The fresh women of Brazil, reportedly given as gifts to Europeans by their fathers, were like "colts who had never experienced a rein." The natives of Virginia were also there for the taking—after an evening's entertainment, a white stranger could hope to find bliss:

> [A] Brace of young Beautiful Virgins are chosen, to wait upon him that night for his particular refreshment. These Damsels are to Undress this happy Gentleman, and as soon as he is in Bed, they gently lay themselves down by him, one on one side of him, and the other on the other.

Other accounts were more candid in reporting that native women needed to be forced to submit to the desires of European men. The women of Brazil, said one explorer, offered "little resistance against those who assault them." The "assault" was most likely rape, but that was no more forbidden than using physical discipline on an unbroken horse. In fact, violence was part of the attraction. An account of an Italian noble who accompanied Christopher Columbus on a voyage to the West Indies, and to whom Columbus had "given" a "very beautiful Carib woman," detailed the way brutal sex was eroticized:

> When I had taken her into my cabin she was naked—as was their custom. I was filled with my desire to take my pleasure with her and attempted to satisfy my desire. She was unwilling, and so

treated me with her nails that I wished I had never begun. But—to cut a long story short—I then took a piece of rope and whipped her soundly, and she set forth such incredible screams that you would not have believed your ears. Eventually, we came to such terms, I assure you, that you would have thought she had been brought up in a school for whores.

SOMETIMES THE FORCE was exerted by local chieftains who gave their girls to the European arrivals as "gifts" and "peace offerings." The girls were then redistributed among the ships' crews according to rank.

Between these encounters and Peggy's murder of John Francis in 1830, white men perpetrated millions of rapes against women of color. All of them, by greater or lesser degrees, affirmed sex as a means of racial and cultural domination. Native and African females were viewed as human in shape, but not in soul: Either they were programmed to crave white flesh or they could be brought to submission readily, and without penalty. One early Spanish conquistador sired thirty children with indigenous women in just three years; had any of the women fought back they would have risked whipping, dismemberment, or—if they could not be brought to heel—death.[3]

For the Europeans, supposed female licentiousness represented opportunity. Male homosexuality, on the other hand, was godless and perverse. The first account of it in the New World came in 1494, just two years after Columbus's first voyage west. The explorer's doctor reported that Carib men castrated the boys they captured from enemy tribes, keeping the eunuchs on hand to abuse sexually. When the boys grew to adulthood, according to the doctor, the Caribs killed and ate them. In 1513, two days before "discovering" the Pacific Ocean, the conquistador Vasco Núñez de Balboa stormed a village in what is now Panama, killing the local king and butchering six hundred of the king's warriors. As he entered the king's house, Balboa reportedly found the king's brother and some of his men dressed as women and engaging in what he called "preposterous Venus." Balboa immediately captured the offending men, about forty in all, and fed them to his dogs.

There was no military need for Balboa to commit these murders. The local king had already been liquidated, and Spanish power in the area established. The story had much more to do with public relations at home than with military strategy. By repressing native sodomy, the conquistadors were able to claim that they were doing God's will. Not only were they rampaging for plunder, they were also righting moral wrongs. Interestingly, the earliest account of this massacre frames the entire affair as a merciful liberation of good natives from corrupt courtiers. When the common folk learned what the king's brother and his men had got up to, they "begged [Balboa] to exterminate them, for the contagion was confined to the courtiers and had not yet spread to the people." The natives reportedly raised their arms to heaven and expressed their understanding that "this sin" caused "lightning and thunder" as well as "famine and sickness."

To believe this story is to accept that the native population of Panama had already read and embraced Leviticus, with its message that God rains down hellfire everywhere sodomy takes place (as he had done to Sodom and Gomorrah), recalling it as they were being attacked by Spanish soldiers. But veracity was not the point. As the destroyer of sodomites everywhere, Balboa was portrayed as morally correct not only in killing the king's brother, but also in protecting the local populace from God's anger.

Upon landing in Mexico in 1519, the conquistador Hernán Cortés described the local populace in blunt terms: "They are all sodomites." In every village he entered, Cortés called for sodomy to be abandoned and Christianity adopted. He was equally frank with the Aztec leader Moctezuma, whom he exhorted to halt the "abominable" sin of sodomy in his lands. Of course, there was no suggestion that the rape of native women

During the age of exploration, the New World was depicted as a humid sexual playground full of willing females ready to "debauch and prostitute themselves" for the pleasure of European men. This image shows Christopher Columbus receiving a comely native girl as a "gift." The other young females seem ready to give themselves to the explorer's companions.
©TOPFOTO

was just as improper; Cortés handed out "Caribs" to his captains just as Columbus had done a generation earlier—although the women were baptized before distribution. (One of them later had a child by Cortés himself.) To Cortés, sexual conquest and the eradication of sodomy were one and the same thing.

The linkage of enemies with ungodly sex was nothing new. In 1492, the year Columbus first sailed to the Western Hemisphere, Christian leaders finally regained full control of the Iberian Peninsula from Muslim rulers after centuries of trying. As the mass expulsions and murders of Muslims and Jews commenced, both groups were broadly accused of committing and condoning sodomy. To the Spanish and Portuguese, the natives of the New World were also cut from sexually incontinent cloth, and deserved no less to be extirpated. While Balboa, Cortés, and their like killed accused sodomites in the West Indies, thousands more were being burned and castrated throughout Iberia.

In the early years of overseas conquest, the New World was, at least for heterosexuals, a lawless place where a man could indulge in sexual adventures. Yet this dynamic could not last. Law abhors a vacuum, and the joys of sex without consequence were short-lived. With the establishment of settlements, trading posts, and ports, Europeans mixing with native populations soon generated offspring. As white, black, and brown combined to create new human incarnations, the laws also had to change color.[4]

GETTING CLOSE TO THE NATIVES

Take a man from his home, put him on a lengthy, dangerous sea voyage, and then drop him on a beach with barely clad native women, and he will forget that fornication and adultery are forbidden. Thousands of miles away from tradition, mothers, and wives, the panoply of European laws limiting sexual behavior (especially those barring sex with non-Christians) was jettisoned as unnecessary ballast. As one thing follows another, the men often came to realize that indigenous women were much more than objects to be raped and discarded. Many colonists and sailors formed deep relationships with them—attachments that demanded that traditional norms regarding sex, marriage, and children be reexamined on the fly.

Throughout the period of European conquest in Africa and the New World, the law was simple: No sex outside marriage was allowed, and sex or marriage with non-Christians was a serious crime. Carnal relations with Muslims, for example, were a capital offense in Portugal and Spain, and sex with Jews was proscribed almost everywhere. The penalties ranged from small fines to banishment and execution, depending on the location and the status of the men and women involved. For example, sex with Muslim women was punished by death in Modena, Italy, except when the women were prostitutes—in which case the male customer was to be merely thrown in jail for the rest of his life and deprived of all of his property.

Of course, the existence of laws does not mean they were always followed, much less vigorously enforced, and there was often a gap between the harshness of the rules governing sex and the punishments actually meted out. The rules against sexual congress with non-Christians were transgressed everywhere such people were encountered, and unless the couplings were too obvious or somehow upset the broader social order, most of them went unpunished. A furtive union between a Christian and a Jew in Spain, for example, was likely to be overlooked so long as it remained quiet. If the affair grew into something resembling marriage, the risk level also grew. While Vespucci and his ilk touted the New World as a paradise of sexual opportunity, they referred only to short-term carnal fulfillment, not lasting marriages. No one disagreed that these relationships crossed every moral and legal boundary, but they happened anyway. What to do?

In West Africa, where many colonists were Portuguese *degredados* (convicts put onto boats rather than executed), official responses to intimate affairs with natives were inconsistent. Many of the men in charge of the Portuguese enterprises were sexual adventurers themselves. Bishop D. Gaspar Cão, for example, was accused of keeping concubines of many races. In the early 1500s the Portuguese Crown began appointing married men to the *capitanías* on the assumption that they would be less inclined to sexual excess, and would set a good example. One such appointee, Fernão de Melo, came to the island of São Tomé to succeed his predecessor, who had lived for years with a slave and a concubine. De Melo brought his wife and children, but kept them locked in a stone tower for their own protection against unruly colonists and foreigners.

The Portuguese who came to Africa were strongly attracted to native women. Time and again, the Portuguese home authorities sent white women to entice the colonists away from natives, but these efforts often met with failure. First, female prisoners were brought over in the hope that they would mate with the *degredados* and populate the settlements with white people. No such luck was to be had. The Crown then sent thousands of Jewish adolescents who had recently been expelled from Spain, hoping that they would marry *degredados* and spawn children. Again, the plan failed. Many of the Jews died, and the survivors proved incompatible with the *degredados*. In fact, both groups preferred the company of natives.

The Portuguese Crown also tried to prevent its colonists from bonding with natives by providing them with cheap prostitutes and slaves. Unattached and well-paid "castle women" were also made available to work in the settlements and, it seems likely, to provide for the colonists' personal physical needs as well. Both of these policies put the Crown in the sex business, but that was preferable to allowing its subjects to form families with Africans. Yet these efforts failed, too. The slaves and castle women did their jobs—they had not been hired for good conversation—but that did not prevent interracial marriages from taking place. As happened elsewhere, religious authorities grudgingly relented and approved the unions provided the native women were baptized and renounced their former lives. But cultural adjustments after marriage sometimes went in the opposite direction. Some of the men left the colonies entirely, settled inland with their wives, and assumed native ways. They became known as *tangosmaos*, a derogatory term implying the worship of fetishes.

Once married white men took up lasting relationships with native women, the question turned to the fates of their families back home. Which family had greater claim to the men? Which children inherited their property? If the African women were technically slaves (which was not always clear, especially when the men had "paid" for their wives), the law always gave preference to their husbands' legitimate families. Once she learned what her husband was up to in her absence, a Portuguese wife could turn to the courts to force him to sell his black wife and mixed-race children. However, in the haze that existed between the European and colonial worlds, the certainties of the law were often obscured. Stationed for extended periods in the tropics, even the most elevated members of colonial society formed profound ties with women who would otherwise have been considered unsuitable as wives, and the law was often at a loss as to how to deal with them.

When the Portuguese captain of São Tomé, Álvaro de Caminha, died in 1499, he left a will that evoked a welter of emotional entanglements. First, he provided for the manumission of Isabel, an African slave to whom he seems to have been deeply attached. He also left her money and a slave child of her own. In the same document, de Caminha left money, furnishings, and several slaves to Ursula, a converted Jew he also loved deeply. Ursula had been in his employ, and while she was not technically his wife, he had lived with her in harmony for some time. De Caminha's will suggested a suitable marriage partner for her and included a letter of introduction to a convent, in the event she decided not to marry and become a nun instead. Most remarkably, the will specified that both Ursula and Isabel were to take their new slave entourages and property and board the first boat for Portugal, where they were meant to support each other in their new lives.

A will is only effective if the courts enforce it. De Caminha was indisputably a man of wealth and influence, but he also must have known that his alliances with an ex-Jew and an African would not necessarily find a willing reception in the staid halls of Portuguese justice. We don't know the fates of Ursula, Isabel, or de Caminha's other slaves and concubines; it seems unlikely that they would have sailed to Lisbon, collected all that he had left to them, and then settled into Portuguese society as wealthy widows. In any case, his freewheeling sex life did not sit well with the Crown: It was after his death that the policy of appointing solid family men to high colonial posts was instituted.[5]

On the other side of the Atlantic, the French in North America found that the more they blended with locals, the better it was for business. Early French colonists were dependent on the aboriginal peoples for their food supplies, as ships from home usually arrived late or came bearing spoiled food. Administrators were frequently forced to disperse their countrymen to local villages, as the resources of the settlements were insufficient to sustain them all. Once the colonists became accustomed to trapping and living with Native Americans, they often refused to work the land as their bosses wanted, preferring instead to conduct commerce with the tribes and hunt for a living.

Most Native Americans made no distinctions between the personal and professional, so sex and marriage often followed commercial relationships. French fur traders, for example, quickly recognized the advantages of forming close bonds with native women. Many kept wives or steady lovers in several locations, both for intimacy and to ensure a consistent supply of pelts. Rather than interdict such practices, French authorities sometimes tried to turn them to their advantage. By cautiously allowing the men to intermarry and produce children with Native Americans, they hoped to housebreak them. Marriage, they believed, would tame the

French colonists' fascination with "savage" life and guide them toward settling down and establishing profitable farms. In the process, they hoped that native women and their children would become Christians and eventually acquire the benefits of French civilization.

This "Frenchification" policy began in the 1660s and continued fitfully for several decades, but it ultimately failed. Rather than remaking aboriginal females into decent Frenchwomen, it was the men who went native. A 1709 letter from a Jesuit in Canada declared: "All the Frenchmen who have married Indian women have become libertines . . . [and] the children they have had are as idle as the Indians themselves; one must withhold permission for these sorts of marriages." The rules then tightened, but relationships with natives and the men's adoption of "lawlessness and idle" ways continued. The choice must have been easy for them. The allure of native women, freedom from repressive French authority, and profits from trading were all too strong to resist, regardless of whether or not they were approved back home. The French explorer Antoine de Lamothe, Sieur de Cadillac, wrote with disappointment in 1713 that his countrymen were "addicted to vice" with Native Americans, "whom they preferred to French women." Worse, aboriginal women were inheriting their husbands' wealth. In 1728, after complaints that native widows were returning to the wild with their dead husbands' property, the law changed to disinherit them if they were to "return among the natives to live according to their manners."[6]

At about the same time, boatloads of African slaves were being shipped to French territories in the Americas, with predictable results in terms of sexual relations with the colonists. In 1724, the French government instituted the colonial *Code Noir*, a landmark piece of official racism that tried to govern, among other things, sex between whites and slaves as well as other people of color. While French law was ambivalent about marriage between whites and natives, no such ambiguity existed in the *Code Noir*'s opposition to black-white and white-mulatto marriages—most likely because there was money to be made from intermixing with Native Americans, while intermarriage with people of African descent (whether enslaved or free) was seen as a drag on the slave-based economy. In colonial Louisiana, blackness signified enslavement while whiteness meant freedom. To tolerate marriages that muddied this equation was, from the French perspective, bad policy. Louis XIV was correct (if heartless) when he observed, in 1670: "Nothing . . . contributes more to the development of the colonies . . . than the laborious toil of the Negroes." The *Code Noir* sought to keep these generators of wealth (and their offspring) enslaved and in their place.

THE RULES ON intermarriage were less strict in colonial Mexico, where the Catholic Church had authority over matrimonial questions. Church officials heard many native women's complaints about their Spanish lovers' broken marriage pledges—promises often made in bed. The women asked the priests to force the men to marry them, but the cases were sometimes resolved with simple cash payments. As sexually unrestrained women had lower "credit" than those considered "honorable," and thus commanded less money in marriage cases, the men usually tried to portray the claimants as promiscuous. Women's chances in court were also limited by their background and ethnicity. A wellborn Spanish woman was awarded one thousand pesos when she complained that her lover had refused to marry her, while a mulatto woman was awarded one-tenth of that sum in exchange for the virginity she had given to a white man.

In 1732, an unusual case arose in Mexico in which a free mulatto man sued a white woman to force her to marry him. The man claimed that they had already been living together for six years, despite her family's dogged opposition to the union. He further testified that one night the woman's male relatives had stormed into the lovers' room and tried to castrate him. The woman agreed that they had lived together, but claimed that she had never had sexual relations with him because he had always been impotent.

The court, no doubt swayed by the man's race and the woman's superior social position, ruled that her marriage promise was null and void. The fact that her family had attacked him was overlooked: Marriage between a mulatto man and a white woman was worse than an assault or a broken promise.

The colonial Venezuelan church's approach toward interracial relationships was unusually harsh, especially after Bishop Mariano Martí arrived in 1770 to take control of its operations. To acquaint himself with the diocese, he took a thirteen-year tour of the region, during which he invited townspeople to tell him about "sinful" activities among their neighbors. The response was overwhelming. By the end of Martí's sojourn, more than fifteen hundred people had been accused of misconduct. Many of the cases involved white men taking sexual advantage of slave and native women, with whom Martí occasionally sympathized. In one case, he ordered the rakish sons of a wealthy family, who had made no secret of their preying on local women, to find wives immediately and settle down. By making such an order, Martí tried to protect powerless females against the predations of the young men.

When sexual relations between slaves and nonslaves got out of hand, Bishop Martí usually made sure that the slave got the worst of it. For example, Sasimira, the domestic slave of Don Francisco Hidalgo, had already borne her master two children when Martí arrived. The bishop criticized Hidalgo for his indiscretions, but ordered Sasimira sold to another landowner. The children, who were the property of Hidalgo, stayed with their master/father. Similarly, when Martí learned that the slave Lucía had given her owner's relative three children and become pregnant with a fourth, he had her auctioned off in another town. Yet another slave confessed to Martí that she had been having sex with her master, but emphasized that he had broken his promise to emancipate her. This was not unusual. Many slave women submitted to sex with their owners on the assurance that they would be freed someday in return. The poor girl most likely believed that

Martí would sympathize with her and free her. He ordered her sold just as he had done with the others.[7]

RACIAL BLENDING IN THE UNITED STATES

In the territories that would later congeal into the United States, the mingling of races was as pervasive as everywhere else. Wherever colonists touched down, children of mixed blood soon followed. Yet there has always been something unique about American interracial relations, something more charged and more contradictory than elsewhere in the New World. The American colonies deeply embraced slavery, so much so that the "peculiar institution" (to use a popular euphemism of the early nineteenth century) remained in place long after it had been abandoned elsewhere. Moreover, while slavery was technically abolished at the close of the American Civil War, in some ways the unequal treatment of nonwhites worsened afterward. It was not until 1967—more than a century after the war—that the U.S. Supreme Court finally struck down state laws barring interracial sex and marriage. Yet despite centuries of such restrictions, the United States had already hosted generations of people whose appearance testified to sex across racial lines. Were they black or white? Whose rights, or bondage, should they inherit? None of these questions were easily answered, especially when a person's race brought with it freedom or enslavement.

The word "miscegenation" came into common use after the 1863 publication, in New York, of a pamphlet titled *Miscegenation: The Theory of the Blending of the Races, Applied to the American White Man and Negro*. The word for interracial sexual congress had heretofore been "amalgamation," but the meaning was the same—as was the widespread contempt for mixed-race children. While abusing women of color was a white man's virtual birthright, the products of black-white unions were generally to be treated as black, even if African American ancestry was many generations removed. In the early nineteenth century, American census workers went house to house looking for people whose characteristics showed signs of past racial mixing. If they found even "one drop" of black blood, the person was stripped of most basic human rights. Two centuries, one civil war, and dozens of civil rights laws later, the United States' obsession with racial distinctions has not disappeared. The 2000 and 2010 census forms allowed people to check more than one racial box, but anyone who did so was automatically relegated to a "minority" category.

The aforementioned French *Code Noir* was instituted to manage the influx of African slaves into Louisiana, and forbade sexual relations between blacks and whites. (It also barred sex between free blacks and slaves.) Under Article 6 of the *Code*, white men living in "concubinage" with their slaves risked having their slave lovers, and any children they had had together, taken away. Additionally, any slaves who had borne children to whites lost the chance of ever being freed. The *Code* was much more restrictive than an earlier version of the law that had been put into place in Haiti by decree of Louis XIV. Under that rule, masters were permitted to marry slave mistresses who gave them children, provided that the marriage was a Catholic one. Once the marriage was performed, the slave and the children became free. That earlier rule produced numerous master-slave marriages, and with them a large population of free blacks with no interest in working on the plantations. It was not long before complaints arose that the policy was "ruining the plantations" and "causing considerable harm to the colony that depends principally on the labor of Negroes." Louisiana's *Code Noir* sought to change that policy. Whether it achieved its intended effects, we cannot know for sure. Certainly the number of slaves who gained freedom through intermarriage diminished but, equally, the fact is that whites continued to take advantage of slaves and to generate mixed-race children.[8]

The English colonies focused on sexual relations between enslaved men and free white females, a much more volatile situation as it tapped into white fears of black men, whom Englishmen believed were irresistible to their wives and daughters. The "beastly" sexuality of black males was the cause of wonderment and fear. Black men were thought to have over-sized genitals, abundant sexual appetites, and the capacity to spark the lust of white females like no one else. Englishmen worried that their women were prone to being "forgettful of their free Condition" by jumping into bed with black slaves. Maryland tried to prevent its daughters from entering into "shameful matches" with slaves as early as 1664, when it decreed that any white woman who married a slave would become a slave herself, serving her husband's master until he died. The offspring of such unions also became "slaves as their fathers were."

The goal of the Maryland law was to halt intermarriage, but it had the opposite effect. Slaves were valuable property, and their owners immediately saw the profit potential in breeding them with white women without sacrificing their daughters. In addition to slaves, many farms had white servants who had worked for a term of years. After the law was passed, planters encouraged and sometimes forced their white female servants and black slaves to marry and produce children, thus generating new generations of slave laborers. The first English governor of Maryland, Lord Baltimore, learned of this tactic upon discovering that his former white servant Eleanor Butler ("Irish Nell") had been married off to an enslaved butler known as Negro Charles—and had therefore become a slave along with their children. To save Nell, Lord Baltimore convinced the legislature to repeal the law in 1681. From that point forward, it was illegal for masters to force their servants to marry slaves, and the children of any such unions were to be considered free.

Irish Nell's own saga would take centuries to resolve, however, as the status of her descendants was continually in doubt. About a century after Lord Baltimore's intervention, a Maryland court ruled that William and Mary Butler, who descended from Nell and Charles, were not entitled to their freedom. Rather, the court said, Nell became a slave when she married Charles and had had her children while the original antimiscegenation law was in force—thus her descendants should be enslaved as well. The same questions came up again in 1787, when William and Mary's daughter sued for her freedom, but she was declared white enough to be free. Later slave masters complained of runaway mulatto slaves who claimed they were descendants of Irish Nell.

Maryland's efforts to halt interracial mingling did not stop with marriage. Soon the state banned all sex between whites and blacks, and ruled that the offspring of interracial sex partners would be slaves. In essence, free white women could give birth to enslaved children if their partners were not purely white, while black women could only give birth to black children, even if the fathers were "English" through and through. In passing such harsh laws, Maryland joined with neighboring Virginia, which also took a hard line. As early as 1630, Virginia's governor ordered Hugh Davis to be whipped for "abusing himself to the dishonor of God and shame of a Christian by defiling his body in lying with a Negro." (The fact that the charge did not refer to a "Negress" could mean that Davis had been caught "lying with" a male, which, if true, would have been another factor in his harsh punishment.) Thirty-two years later, Virginia's assembly imposed fines on interracial fornication, setting the penalties at twice as high as fines for illegal sex among whites. However, the risk of a fine rarely deters anyone's sexual passions, and it apparently had little effect on interracial sex in Virginia. The legislature marched on with ever more severe laws, including a 1691 statute that became a milestone in racist lawmaking:

And for the prevention of that abominable mixture and spurious issue which hereafter may increase in this dominion, as well by negroes, mulattoes, and Indians intermarrying with English, or by other white women, as by their unlawful accompanying with one another, Be it enacted by the authoritie aforesaid, and it is hereby enacted, That for the time to come, whatsoever English or white man or woman being free shall intermarry with a negro, mulatto, or Indian man or woman bond or free shall within three

months after such marriage be banished and removed from this
dominion forever, and that the justices of each respective countie
within this dominion make it their particular care, that this act be
put in effectuall execution.

For nearly three centuries, the Virginia courts indeed took "particular care" in banishing interracial couples from the colony. Such punishments were enforced in one form or another until 1967, when the U.S. Supreme Court finally ruled that all antimiscegenation laws were unconstitutional. Virginia also punished clergymen who performed interracial marriages by hitting them where it hurt most: Any preacher who officiated over such forbidden unions was fined up to ten thousand pounds of tobacco—half of which would go to reward the person who had reported the crime.

For all its interest in keeping the "spurious issue" of all interracial sex out of Virginia, the colony's efforts were concentrated on separating white women from black men. Virginia allowed white men to bed down with black women, and black women were permitted to have white men's babies. The real fear was of white women coming under the spell of dark-skinned sex magicians against whom the masters of the colony felt they had no chance of competing. Punishment in Virginia for consorting across the color barrier became harsher as time passed, and was always imposed overwhelmingly against white women, their black partners, and their children.[9]

Other colonies followed suit, to the point where twelve of the thirteen colonies that declared themselves independent of England in 1776 had already barred miscegenation. Following the American Revolution, laws against interracial sex proliferated, but were never effective, and the "abominable mixture" of such unions continued to multiply. As the "mongrel breed" of mulattos had babies of their own, U.S. states developed a variety of methods for determining a person's race. In many cases, even a "drop" of black blood in one's veins could result in "Negro" status, with all of its attendant disadvantages, but finding that trace was easier said than done. In 1847, a notice regarding a female runaway slave described her as "beautiful girl, about twenty years of age, perfectly white, with straight light hair and blue eyes." The explosive issue of race was thus potentially present in almost every marriage, even between people with Caucasian characteristics: A remote Negro ancestor could invalidate the union. As many as thirty-eight states eventually banned interracial marriages, and some further barred marriage between whites and Hindus, Koreans, Japanese, and Mongolians. An Arizona law, repealed in 1962, prohibited mulattos from marrying *anyone* else—even other mulattos.

Wherever there are laws, especially those limiting sex and marriage, there are people looking to make money off lawbreakers. In North Carolina, where the rules against miscegenation were among the strictest, and where churchmen were fined for performing interracial marriages, Reverend John Blacknall devised an ingenious way to make a profit: He reportedly charged an interracial couple fifty pounds to marry them, and then turned himself in and was fined fifty pounds. However, his reward for informing the authorities about the forbidden marriage was twenty-five pounds—so he walked away from it all twenty-five pounds the richer.

Throughout the nineteenth century and well into the twentieth, the rules mandating separation of the races grew ever more strident. Mississippi went so far as to pass a law—still on the books as of 1965—that made it a crime even to speak out "in favor of social equality or of intermarriage between whites and Negroes." Again, the prohibitions had little effect. As people of increasingly complex racial ancestry continued to produce offspring, the law struggled to define what made someone black, white, or mulatto. For the courts, the question often boiled down to what degree of interracial mingling in people's lineage made them "black enough" to lose their rights. Given that the number of mulattos was growing steadily—reaching, for example, one-third of Pennsylvania's population in 1860—these laws had a broad reach. Marriages and family could be declared legally void years after the fact. Even more bizarrely, a marriage that passed muster under the laws of one state could be held illegal in another, and a husband and wife could be arrested simply by crossing the border into another state with more restrictive laws on the books.

Regulating racial separation was further complicated by the inconsistent methods used by various states to determine race. For example, people with half-Negro grandmothers were considered Negroes in Georgia, but in Florida they were deemed white. Alabama and several other states used the infamous "one drop" rule, which defined a "Negro" as anyone with any ascertainable trace of African blood, while Delaware and Wyoming had no definitions at all. With such shifting standards, and with so many people carrying dizzyingly complex racial ancestries, it was folly to expect a jury or even a judge to make reasoned decisions as to anyone's race. Some states such as Missouri allowed a jury to come to a judgment simply by looking a person over. If the jurors concluded that he or she looked white, black, or a little of both, that decision was final. The consequences were enormous for the people involved in any case, but the jury's gut decisions were, in the end, no less fanciful than many of the quack scientific tests then in use.[10]

Thomas Jefferson fathered a son, Eston, with his one-quarter-black slave, Sally Hemmings. Eston had fair skin, freckles, and red hair, but his background was evidently not black enough to qualify him as "black"; in the early nineteenth century, Virginia law declared people white if they were less than one-quarter black. Nevertheless, the son of a slave was the son of a slave—Eston was only freed on the instruction of Jefferson's will, and lived his life out as a white man in the North. His full brother, Madison Hemmings (born James Madison Hemmings), had no such luck. Though he shared an identical lineage with Eston, and had also been freed in Jefferson's will, Madison had "bronze" skin, which seems to have been enough to condemn him to life as a black man. By law, Madison should have been treated the same as his brother, but no one could accept that someone with Madison's appearance could be considered white, even if his father had been president of the United States. Madison was listed as a "Negro" in the 1830 census and lived his life in Ohio as a black man.[11]

In North Carolina, white-looking William Dempsey spent much of his time hunting in the woods for squirrels and other small animals to feed his family, but the law forbade blacks and mulattos from carrying firearms without a special license—which Dempsey did not possess. At his 1849 trial for violating this law, he argued that he did not need a license because he was legally not black. He showed that he had, at most, one-sixteenth black blood, as only one of his great-great-grandmothers had had any trace of black ancestry. Such a thin residue of color made him white under a strict application of North Carolina law, but the jury convicted him anyway. On appeal, the North Carolina Supreme Court upheld the conviction, ignoring the law and holding, in effect, that *any* black blood in one's ancestral line was enough to deprive one of the rights that came with being white.

Regardless of what the statutes required, Southern juries were confident that they just *knew* how to distinguish people with "pure" white ancestry from those with damning traces of "Negro blood." They could sense it as readily "as the alligator . . . knows three days in advance that a storm is brewing." Going beyond appearances, juries often looked at how the people in question behaved. If they were modest and upstanding, that meant they were "white," and vice versa. Abby Guy, who sued William Daniel in Arkansas in 1855, claimed that she was white, and that Daniel wrongly held her and her children in slavery. The jury's decision came down to her own conduct. Did Guy pass among whites "as an equal"? Did she show the decorum expected of a white woman, or did she exhibit the licentious traits that many whites believed (and some hoped) marked a colored woman?

Guy first argued that her mother, who was Daniel's father's slave, had been freed in the father's will, which made her free as well. However, that point fell apart when Daniel produced documents showing that his father had done no such thing. With her case going down in flames, Guy argued that regardless of what the papers showed, she *could not* be enslaved, because she behaved like—and was accepted as—a white person. Her neighbors testified that despite her "yellow" complexion, she "visited among the whites as an equal" and also attended white church and social gatherings. She was, she claimed, a good woman who had already passed the tests of society. Everyone in the street treated her as white; why should the courtroom be any different?

Guy also claimed that she did, in fact, possess white physical features. She removed her shoes and stockings and displayed her bare feet in the courtroom for all to see—a demonstration that the Arkansas Supreme Court later said was a useful test of one's whiteness: "The experience of every intelligent observer of the race," observed the court's chief justice, "will doubtless attest the truth . . . No one, who is familiar with the peculiar formation of the negro foot, can doubt, but that an inspection of that member would ordinarily afford some indication of the race." Guy's feet passed the test, and so did her comportment, and her children's. She won her case.

IN ANOTHER SUIT by a female slave to gain her freedom, filed in Louisiana in 1845, Sally Miller proved her whiteness by showing "uniform good conduct" and "quiet and constant industry," which was enough to overcome her "polluted and degraded" position. "These traits," witnesses said, "prove her white nature." Her attorney added that "both morally and physically, she shows before the Court that there is nothing of the African about her." She had been in bondage for twenty-seven years, but her whiteness was still evident. The case received a lot of sympathetic publicity, much of it raising the specter of a "true" white woman (she claimed to be of German origin) being forced to suffer the "hardships and privations imposed only on the African race." She was freed.

Alexina Morrison, who had been sold and resold several times before accusing her last owner of unjustly enslaving her, had much going for her, including a fair complexion, blue eyes, and flaxen hair. She also had what doctors described as other "white" physical characteristics, including "double cartilage" and a "hollow foot." However, experts and the Louisiana Supreme Court warned that appearances could be deceiving, and that white features "must yield to proof of a servile origin." The case bounced around that state's courts for about five years, starting in 1858. Morrison's owner sought to use her sexual behavior to prove she was black—specifically, her affair with a white jailer and her post-imprisonment pregnancy. By emphasizing this sexual activity, Morrison's owner insisted that she was conducting herself in a way that white girls did not. Nevertheless, the slave won the public's sympathy, so much so that one of her trials was moved to a different courthouse because a local mob, believing that she was a white woman unjustly held in bondage, had already threatened her owner with violence. Morrison's last trial ended in 1862, two years into the American Civil War, with a hung jury. Her owner appealed to the Louisiana Supreme Court but there was no one around to hear the case; four of the five justices had fled New Orleans in the wake of the Union Army.[12]

All these cases had their roots in white fear and hatred of the "spurious" issue of interracial sex. Mulatto children blurred the color lines that defined American society. As always, dark skin meant slavery, and whiteness signified freedom. Those who straddled the two extremes were living testimony that a strictly biracial society did not, in fact, exist. Worse yet, white women who gave birth to dark babies showed that a virile black man had taken what was surely not his. Not only was the white race purportedly "diluted" by such couplings, the dominance of white men over society was also put at risk. "Hybridism is heinous," declared proslavery advocate Henry Hughes in 1860. "Mulattoes are monsters."

Yet the "monsters" kept coming in droves, and there was nothing the law could do to stop them. In 1877, in a Virginia case involving a married interracial couple prosecuted after entering the state, the judge made his reasoning quite clear:

The purity of public morals, the moral and physical develop-
ment of both races, and the highest advancement of our cher-
ished Southern civilization, under which two distinct races are to
work out and accomplish the destiny to which the Almighty has
assigned them on this continent—all require that they should be
kept distinct and separate, and that connections and alliances so
unnatural that God and nature seem to forbid them, should be
prohibited by positive law and be subject to no evasion.

Except that the races had already been mixing, remixing, and then mixing again in America for more than 250 years. There were no longer, and would never be again, "two distinct races," either in the "cherished" South or anywhere else in the New World.[13]

The law continued to wink at intimate relations between white men and black women, but sex between white females and black males remained a great taboo. A white slave owner was within his rights to sexually abuse a female slave, but should his wife tryst with a black man, the slave owner's humiliation was too much to bear. If he could bring himself to make the matter public by seeking a divorce, he would almost always prevail. Few judges would expect him to tolerate such a blow; infidelity in a wife was bad enough, but when it happened with a black man it became intolerable.

When the Virginian Leonard Owen's wife gave birth to a mulatto baby, he complained that the child was "such a horrid violation of the marriage bed" that "it must be obvious to any person" that he was entitled to a divorce. In the same manner, Joseph Gresham alleged that his wife's infidelity was "aggravated by the fact that it was committed and carried on with a man of colour."

Sometimes husbands lost their divorce cases because they knew, or at least should have known, that their wives were prone to sexual excess. In 1832, in North Carolina, Marville Scroggins sought a divorce after he learned that his wife had been pregnant with a black man's child when they married. During the trial, Scroggins admitted that he and his wife had had sex prior to the wedding. That alone, the court declared, should have made him aware of the kind of woman to whom he was committing himself: "He who marries a wanton [woman], knowing her true character, submits himself to the lowest degradation." Scroggins lost the case, but the judge still sympathized with him: "The stigma in our state of society is so indelible, the degradation so absolute, and the abhorrence of the community against the offender, and contempt for the husband so marked and [i]nextinguishable, that the court has not been able [to deny the divorce] without a struggle."

The North Carolina public disagreed loudly with the Scroggins decision. The controversy benefitted another resident of the state, Jesse Barden, when he sought a divorce on the same grounds later that year. In fact, the case came before the same judge, who adjusted his position and voted to grant the divorce. He admitted that his about-face was "a concession to the deep rooted and virtuous prejudices of the community." These prejudices remained in place in Southern courtrooms long past the antebellum era and into the twentieth century. In 1955, the Virginia Supreme Court declared antimiscegenation laws necessary because "natural law" forbids the "corruption of races" and the "obliteration of racial pride." At that time, more than half of U.S. states still had miscegenation statutes, and 96 percent of white Americans opposed interracial marriage.

American antimiscegenation laws would remain in place in many states until 1967, when the U.S. Supreme Court passed on the marriage of Mildred and Richard Loving. Mildred was a mixture of black and American Indian descent, and Richard was white. She had been eleven years old and he seventeen when they began dating in their hometown of Central Point, Virginia. In 1958, around Mildred's eighteenth birthday, she became pregnant. The couple decided to marry, but as interracial unions were illegal in Virginia, they traveled to Washington, D.C., to exchange their vows. A few weeks after their return to Central Point, a group of police officers invaded their home. Mildred pointed to their marriage certificate on the bedroom wall, but that only made their situation worse. They were charged with, among other things, "cohabiting as man and wife, against the peace and dignity of the Commonwealth." Under the threat of substantial jail time they agreed to leave the state for twenty-five years. The case was then picked up by civil rights lawyers; lawsuits were filed, and years of bruising litigation began.

Fortunately, this was the era of broadening civil rights laws. The U.S. Supreme Court unanimously agreed that Virginia's antimiscegenation law, and similar laws in all states, should be struck down. "The freedom to marry, or not marry, a person of another race," wrote Chief Justice Earl Warren, "resides with the individual and cannot be infringed by the State." That seems rather obvious to most of us now, but for others it remains difficult to swallow. It took South Carolina and Alabama until 1998 and 2000, respectively, to formally repeal their antimiscegenation laws. In 2009, a Louisiana justice of the peace refused to marry a black man and a white woman. "There is a problem with both groups accepting a child from such a marriage," he said. "I think those children suffer, and I won't help put them through it."[14]

Race as a License to Rape

The historian Michel Foucault observed, rather ironically, that "men think that women can only experience pleasure in recognizing men as masters." Had Foucault expressed that idea to the aforementioned shipmate of Christopher Columbus, who whipped a terrified Carib woman into sexual submission, he would have found hearty agreement. Although we have no direct record of the woman's thoughts, we can safely conclude that she only "came to terms" sexually with the Italian upon realizing that her life would end if she did not submit. In other words, she was raped. This onboard encounter was one of the first of millions of rapes perpetrated by European men against women of color in Africa and the New World. Had the rape occurred at home, the Italian would have been exposed to criminal prosecution and possibly even death, but he knew the laws of Europe had no force or effect in the tropics. The fulfillment of his cruel desires was now possible.

As we have seen, European men took native women (and imported slaves) at their violent pleasure in every land they conquered. The laws of the Old World were left behind as soon as it disappeared over the horizon. Occasionally there were directives, such as one by Hernán Cortés, not to treat local women "outside of our law," but they never had much effect. When commanders (such as the Spanish Bernal Díaz) referred to "pretty women" as "spoil," the message was clear: Sex could be had by any means necessary. Not long after Cortés told his men to stop raping native women, another conquistador in Jalisco felt no compunction about chopping off a local woman's hands when she resisted him. When the woman still refused to submit, the man's companions stabbed her to death. Stories like this got around, as did accounts of thirty native women in Chile giving birth about nine months after encountering a company of Spanish soldiers. Vespucci's promise that native women were happy to make themselves available for sex with Christians described a rare occurrence, if it existed at all. Sexual conquest was violent in the extreme and made possible by the absence of any risk of punishment.

The privilege of raping foreigners without consequence did not start with the discovery of the New World. European men had always taken the women of conquered societies, and voyages across the Atlantic Ocean ended in no different a result. These were not sightseeing cruises, but missions of conquest. The men who manned the vessels were, by and large, ragtag treasure-seekers. They were paid in what they were able to take, and indigenous women were prime booty. Additionally, the conquerors' use of natives as slaves in overseas settlements and the development of the African slave trade called up another set of age-old privileges. Slaves were there to be sexually abused, especially when there was general agreement that natives were inferior to whites in all respects. The notion of giving them the right to refuse sex to their superiors would have been viewed as treasonous.[15]

From the beginning of its colonial adventures, the Portuguese Crown assigned slaves to its seagoing men, and even *degredados*, to let them blow off steam and increase colonial populations. The niceties of Portuguese law, which barred the rape of slaves, were easily circumvented. Slaves were forbidden from testifying in court against their masters, so unless a rape took place within sight of a free person, it was as though it had never occurred. Additionally, many of the African societies the Portuguese encountered were themselves slave-owning. In such cases, the use of slave women as sexual playthings matched local traditions. To the Spanish, the children issuing from such rape were a notch superior to the offspring of two natives alone. As observed by Francisco de Aguirre, the conquistador and governor of Tucumán, "the service rendered to God in producing *mestizos* is greater than the sin committed by the same act." Whereas at home rape was a capital crime, in the New World it thus became an act of devotion.

THE OPPORTUNITIES FOR forcible sex multiplied as slaves were shipped from Africa to the plantations of the West Indies. In the Danish colonies, for example, the law equated a slave with a beast, "entirely under the authority of his master, who can treat him as he wishes, just as he might treat any other piece of property." A key aspect of this "authority" was sexual. From the moment they were abducted and stuck in the atrocious seaside holding pens known as barracoons, and then loaded onto the trading ships, African women were subject to exploitation. Officers usually had first pick, while their subordinates waited their turns. Slave ships were, in the words of an eighteenth-century slaver, "half bedlam and half brothel" from the African coast all the way to the New World.

Once ashore, slaves were sold, marked with hot brands, and put to work. Their "pay" usually consisted of small quantities of food and cheap powerful rum known as "kill-devil." In the Danish colonies, as in others, black women who resisted the sexual advances of white men were punished harshly. In one eighteenth-century case, a woman who refused her master sex was imprisoned in a dungeon, beaten, and scorched with hot sealing wax before another white man interceded and persuaded her owner to sell her. Other men used less violent means of persuasion. In the mid-nineteenth century, the Danish manager of a plantation persuaded a slave girl "hardly fourteen years old" to live with him, with the pledge that he would one day free her. She did so, and bore him three children—but he broke his promise and kept them all in bondage. Other, more powerful whites attempted to persuade him to free the slaves, to no avail; there were no laws requiring him to keep his promise, or even to admit that the children were his.

Thistlewood, the English slave overseer who counted about seventeen hundred sexual encounters with black females in Jamaica, also faced no risk of punishment. Sometimes such men were criticized for enjoying the "goatish" embraces of dark-skinned women, but that kind of carping deterred no one. An entry in Thistlewood's diary tells of two of his white acquaintances who "burnt" one of his slaves, a woman named Sarah, for trying to resist them. The men also tried to burn Sarah's hut to the ground. Thistlewood felt no sympathy for Sarah, although he seemed to like her. Rather, he was bothered that the men would try to harm his property. On another occasion Thistlewood's boss, John Cope, joined six drunken men to "haw'l" Eve, a female slave, into a room where they were "Concern'd with her." Thistlewood did nothing to stop the gang rape. Cope was later made chief magistrate for the parish.

Thistlewood and Cope couldn't care less about the opprobrium of whites back home. What terrified them were angry black men. Whites were vastly outnumbered in Jamaica, and the danger of retaliatory violence by slaves against their owners was a daily reality. Thistlewood used terror to keep slave men in line and affirm his absolute control over the plantation. He beat them frequently and without provocation, usually in ways designed to humiliate them to the maximum possible extent. One punishment he invented, called "Derby's dose," involved having one slave defecate into the mouth of another and then wiring the recipient's mouth shut. Thistlewood's constant raping of his female slaves also constituted a humiliation. There could be few experiences more demeaning to the slave population than watching a white man with a whip ride into the fields and take females into the nearest shelter.[16]

When a black man was suspected of sexual violence—at least against white women—no punishment was harsh enough. Several states in the antebellum South passed laws mandating castration for black men who raped or attempted to rape white females, although execution was the more common punishment. The women victims were characterized, whenever possible, as delicate creatures whose beauty and honor were cruelly stolen, while the men were reviled as devils on earth.

Had one young Georgia victim, Mary Daniel, been black, her rape would never have raised notice; but she was white and her attacker was a slave, which changed everything. The judge in her 1852 case (*Stephen v. State*) lamented the "dark cloud" of shame over "the unhappy victim, her family and friends, and . . . society at large," brought on by "the defendant's unhallowed lust." After the Civil War, when racial tensions in the South reached their apex, a man's dark skin was proof enough that he was a rapist. Juries were allowed to infer that any sexual encounter between a black man and a white woman involved intent on the part of the man to commit rape. As one court put it, no black man could assume that a white woman "would consent to his lustful embraces." Between 1700 and 1820, more than 80 percent of the men executed in the United States for rape were of African descent; 95 percent of the females in these cases were white.

BLACK MEN WERE seen as sexual beasts, but the law paid little attention when the violence was directed away from whites. In the 1859 Mississippi case of *George v. State*, a black man's conviction for raping a ten-year-old black slave girl was thrown out, because no law made the attack illegal. "The crime of rape does not exist in this State between African slaves," said the court. Any rights to the girl's body rested with her owner. Had the little girl been white, of course, the defendant would have been put to death. Punishments for black rapists in the South included, in addition to the occasional castration, being burned alive and decapitation followed by display of the severed head on a pole. Some black men were punished even when they were acquitted: One unfortunate slave in Virginia named Prince was given thirty-nine lashes after he had been found not guilty of attempted rape. Instead, he was punished for the hitherto unknown crime of *intending to attempt* rape.

Still, there were cases when black men accused of assaulting white women were treated mercifully. This was especially the case when the women were seen as dubious characters. In the case of Tasco Thompson, a free black man charged in Virginia in 1833 of the attempted rape of Mary Jane Stevens, the jury convicted him as the law required—but recommended that the governor grant him mercy. The jury foreman explained that the Stevens family was "exceedingly disreputable," and that Stevens's mother "had long entertained negroes." There is no doubt, he continued, that Thompson went to the Stevens house believing that Mary Jane's mother "would cheerfully submit to his embraces, as she doubtless had often done before, but finding her absent he probably supposed his embraces would be equally agreeable to her daughter." In the same way, when a slave named Peter was sentenced to death for the rape of a white woman named Patsy Hooker, sixty-two local citizens petitioned the governor in 1808 for mercy, declaring that Hooker was "a common strumpet." The jury had no choice under the law but to convict Peter, but they were clearly uneasy with this result.

In another case, a black man named Fields used creative logic to fight his rape charge. Fields was tried in 1832 for "attempting [to] ravish a white woman," but was freed after the jury found that his attempt to have sex with her had not been forcible. Rather, Fields merely tried "to have such carnal knowledge of her while she was asleep," and used no force except "getting to bed with her and stripping up her night garment in which she was sleeping." Perhaps the drowsy woman was also seen as the sort who would have sex with black men in her sleep, or Fields was an unusually sympathetic character; we will never know. What is apparent is that courts and juries were not always comfortable with the harshness of the laws punishing interracial rape.[17]

HOMOSEXUALITY AWAY FROM HOME

The prevalence of real or imagined homosexuality among natives in the New World was used as a pretext for violent conquest. Sodomy in Renaissance Europe also came to be associated with witchcraft and heresy, so it is no surprise that colonial law adopted the intolerant attitudes of the Old World. In every one of the American colonies, homosexuals and people who had sex with animals risked execution. However, putting harsh laws on the books and enforcing them are quite different matters. In practice, American colonists were more tolerant of this kind of sexual behavior than their counterparts in England, Holland, and France. There was presumably no less sodomy taking place in Boston than in London or Amsterdam, but when such cases came up the New England courts were reluctant to enforce the law to its fullest.

The first known American sodomy case arose in Massachusetts in 1629, when the ship *Talbot* sailed into port with "5 beastly Sodomiticall boys" aboard. The youngsters had already confessed to "wickedness not to be named," so the only task left to the authorities was to formally convict and punish them. Rather than do so, the Puritans shipped the rascals back to England, reasoning that because the "wickedness" had taken place on the high seas they had no authority to punish it.

The colony of Plymouth was slightly more inclined to prosecute sodomy. The first homosexuality trial took place there in 1636, in which John Alexander and Thomas Roberts confessed to "lude behavior and unclean carriage one with another by often spending their seed one upon another." Additionally, there was evidence that Alexander was "notoriously guilty that way." If ever there was an occasion to impose the death penalty for sodomy, this was it. The law had recently been passed, and the time was right to use these men to set an example. However, leniency prevailed. The court ordered Alexander whipped, branded, and banished, while Roberts, a servant, was whipped and sent back to his master.

Several years later, when dealing with a rather convoluted sex ring, the Plymouth courts were even more forgiving. This time, Edward Michell and Edward Preston were found guilty of "lude and sodomiticall practices" with each other. Additionally, Michell had fornicated with Lydia Hatch, and Preston had tried to have sex with yet another man. Despite the range of sex offenses involved, the court treated them all much the same. Hatch was whipped once, and both Michell and Preston, twice. The law mandating execution for Preston and Michell's behavior was ignored, the judge evidently believing that it was only marginally worse than simple fornication.

By contrast, the colony of New Haven was quite intolerant of males having sex with each other, at least in extreme cases. The one execution for homosexuality in colonial New England took place in 1646, when William Plaine was convicted of "unclean practices" by engaging in mutual masturbation with boys "above a hundred times." Plaine also seems to have been a rather vocal atheist, which could not have gained him many friends or supporters. As we have seen, regardless of what the law allowed, a few homosexual acts were not enough to earn anyone the death penalty, and neither were atheist opinions, but with these taken together and leavened with child abuse, Plaine had become a "monster in human shape," and had to go.

Virginia holds the distinction of being the first American colony to execute someone for sodomy, in 1625. Seaman William Cornish had forced himself on a young man aboard an anchored ship. Being "in drinke," Cornish followed his victim into bed, turned him on his belly and "put payne in the [man's] fundament and did wett him." A century and a half later, Thomas Jefferson suggested a series of revisions to Virginia's criminal laws, including the reduction of the penalty for sodomy from hanging to castration. He suggested that the same "proportional" penalty be imposed on men for rape and polygamy. Punishment for a female sodomite, Jefferson advocated, should consist of "cutting through the cartilage of her nose a hole of one half inch diameter at the least." His creative proposals were never adopted, however, and male sodomy was formally made a capital crime in 1792.[18]

The uneasiness American colonists felt at imposing the death penalty for homosexual behavior evaporated when the subject turned to sex with animals, which they usually called "buggery." Bestiality was far more horrible to them than mere homosexuality, probably because they believed that such a union could result in freakish offspring. In 1642, a New Haven sow gave birth to a "monstrous" little premature piglet that resembled the unfortunate farmhand George Spenser. Both Spenser and the little pig had "whitish & deformed" eyes. Spenser first denied, then admitted, then again denied improper relations with the sow. Had the same legal standard in use for homosexuality been applied, his life would have been spared. There were, after all, no witnesses, and Spenser twice had denied the crime, once under oath; but that was not to be. He was put to death.

There was no pretense of fairness in buggery cases, at least so far as the animals were concerned. When young Thomas Granger was indicted for having had sex with "a mare, a cow, two goats, five sheep, two calves and a turkey," the Massachusetts colonial authorities seemed to be making up rules as they went along. As Granger had confessed to buggering the animals, his death was assured, but the law also required that the animals be put to death—and Granger could not recall exactly which ones (especially among the sheep) he had violated. The court solved the problem by staging a lineup of local sheep, from which Granger was expected to point out which ones he had known intimately. Once the offending beasts were identified, they were killed before Granger's eyes. Then he was executed.

In the case of the sadly named Thomas Hogg, accused in Plymouth in 1647 of buggery with a sow who had borne a deformed fetus whose "faire & white" skin resembled his own, the court went to the barnyard to determine the truth. Hogg was ordered to fondle ("scratt") the mother sow. According to official records, "immedyatly there appeared a working of lust in the sow, insomuch that she powred out seede before them." The magistrates then ordered Hogg to fondle another sow, who seemed unmoved. He was then whipped and sent to prison for crimes involving, among other things, "filthyness."

The last known buggery case in early New England involved another unfortunately named man, Thomas Saddeler, who was accused in 1681 of carnal relations with a mare. He was found guilty of the lesser crime of *attempted* buggery, so his life was spared, but he was still whipped, forced to sit on the gallows with a rope around his neck, branded on the forehead with the letter P (for "pollution"), and banished from the colony. Saddeler's treatment was hardly kind, but neither was he put to death as the law strictly required. Eventually, courts in New England seem to have stopped taking bestiality cases, in large part because the harsh sentences on the books failed to deter such unbiblical sex from taking place. In the words of one historian of the era: "Puritans became inured to sexual offenses, because there were so many."

THE RULES FOR dealing with sodomy on the high seas depended on which master one served. During the golden age of English piracy in the seventeenth century, the buccaneers who terrorized the merchant ships and trading posts of the West Indies were almost exclusively homosexual.[19] The reasons for this are many, including prolonged separation from women, the absence of enforceable laws, and the happy rejection of traditional English models for an ordered and respectable life; but more than anything, that was simply how the pirates of the Caribbean wanted to live their lives. As explained by B. R. Burg in his delightful *Sodomy and the Pirate Tradition*, the men who manned pirate ships did not take up homosexuality as a temporary measure until they could return to their lives ashore. The boats were nothing like modern prisons, where men have sex with each other but still regard themselves as heterosexual. Pirates rarely took up opportunities to return home to take up relations with the opposite sex. "They were permanent pirates," Burg tells us, preferring an exclusively homosexual existence over any of the alternatives. For those with authority, the pirate life usually involved the exclusive use of select boys and men with whom they had lengthy, devoted relationships. Some ships discouraged the sexual exploitation of boys because it aroused disruptive jealousies, but nowhere in the pirate world was homosexuality condemned as an evil in itself.

There was also no shortage of homosexuality on English navy and merchant marine ships, but it was handled differently. Henry VIII may have made "buggery with man or beast" a crime punishable by death in 1533, but British admirals waited almost one hundred years to follow the king's decree: It was not until 1627 that the death penalty was formally instituted in the Royal Navy, and even then it was rarely put to use. Perhaps the admirals knew that executing all the homosexuals on their ships would result in a far smaller navy, which England could ill afford. For most of the seventeenth century, the few sodomy prosecutions that actually went to trial usually involved something taking the case beyond just male-male sex. For the defendant to be charged with sodomy, he had to have done something else to earn the enmity of his superiors. For example, sixteen-year-old John Durrant was indicted in 1649 because he had allowed himself to be penetrated by a Hindu named Abdul Rhyme, which made the case far more urgent. Nine Christians and a number of Hindus testified that they had seen the couple frequently buggering and masturbating each other in various places on the ship. For their crimes, Durrant and Rhyme were each given (among other punishments) forty lashes, with the additional command that the wounds be rubbed afterward with salt and water. It was the interracial quality of the sex rather than the sex itself that merited the harshness of the punishment. Significantly, however, despite the volume of evidence against them, the death penalty was not imposed.

Only in the eighteenth century did the British navy start to hand out frequent severe punishments for sodomy. Authorities had noticed a supposed increase in the practice, caused by "foreign" influences. In 1706, James Ball, quartermaster of the *Swallow*, was condemned to death for forcibly buggering a thirteen-year-old boy in his cabin. Five decades later, Henry Bicks was charged with repeatedly buggering a boy who later complained of "soreness in his fundament," and then for molesting a sleeping fellow prisoner while in jail awaiting trial. For his sins, Bicks was given five hundred lashes and was turned out of service with a halter around his neck.

The eyewitness evidence against Bicks was overwhelming, but when that kind of proof was lacking it was difficult to make sodomy charges stick, at least to the extent necessary to put the prisoner to death. Navy judges often required proof of both penetration and emission of semen, which was rarely available. In 1762, Martin Billin and James Bryan were tried for buggery on what seemed like rock-solid evidence. The main witness testified that he saw the two men "behind a chest, Martin Billin with his face to the chest & James Bryan's belly to Martin Billin's back." He continued: "I threw myself down on the chest & run my hand, down between the forepart of Bryan & the hinder part of Billin; Billin's breeches were about half down his thigh, & Bryan's trousers were down on his knees. I laid hold of Bryan's yard and pulled it out of Billin's fundament." The judge asked the witness: "When you had Bryan's yard in your hand, did you observe whether there had been any emission from it?" The witness replied that he was not sure whether there had been emission, but did say that Bryan's penis had left his hand moist. The court pressed the witness further, demanding to know "by what means" he was sure Bryan had penetrated Billin. The response: "Because as I laid hold of part of his yard, the other part came out with a spring, as if a cork had been drawn out of a bottle." Such proof was undoubtedly stronger than the usual case. Few witnesses reached in to touch an offender's genitals or listened to the popping sound of a man's "yard" as it was removed from his partner's "fundament," but the judges were still not convinced that the two accused seamen should be put to death. Instead, Bryan and Billin were each given one thousand lashes—not a slap on the wrist, but (at least theoretically) preferable to hanging.

Because actual buggery was so difficult to prove, navy courts often resorted to charging sailors for less severe offenses such as indecent behavior and indecent liberties, for which the punishments were often quite ferocious. In 1800, one prisoner who had made a habit of cornering boys, groping them, and "with a wonderfully capricious and brutal depravity, making them ease themselves into his hands" was removed from the navy in maximum disgrace and given two hundred lashes on a charge of attempted sodomy. Records of such harsh punishments for relatively minor sexual offenses are extensive. In fact, in the British navy of the eighteenth and early nineteenth centuries, a charge involving homosexual behavior was more likely to result in execution than one for murder.[20]

7
• • •

THE EIGHTEENTH CENTURY:
REVELATION AND REVOLUTION

OPEN MINDS AND SELF-ABUSE

It was in the eighteenth century that life for many in the West began to resemble life as we know it today: urban, mobile, sexually liberal. All things being equal, if a reasonably capable man of the present time was dropped into a crowded London, Paris, or New York street circa 1760, he could have gotten along without too much trouble. The language of the day was different, but not incomprehensible. The streets were full of trash and manure, but at least a few were paved. There were mass-produced iron goods in shops and people wore cloth woven in mills. They spoke less about the Lord above than about money on earth. For a growing number of people, heaven no longer meant paradise after a life well lived; rather, it signified material abundance and physical pleasure in the here and now. If our time traveler were to enter a tavern and strike up a conversation, he would find common ground for chatter. If he were interested in finding sex, it would be likely to be available in the alehouse's back rooms, or close by.

The age of the American and French revolutions began to push God out of the legal business. By century's end, many countries looked to "reason" and to the "people's will" to guide the law. The world was no longer just the product of divine effort, nor was human suffering due to heavenly vengeance. When the new generation of "enlightened" men looked to the night sky, they saw mathematical equations. When they gazed at the mountains, they saw coal for burning in factories. And when they felt familiar stirrings in their breeches, the Father, Son, and Holy Spirit were the last things on their minds.

The transition from religion to reason was patchy and disorderly. France decriminalized sodomy during its revolution—a giant advance in sexual freedom by any measure—but by 1806, England was still putting more sodomites to death than murderers. At the same time, while King George III was warning that divine wrath follows immorality, British publications such as *The Whoremonger's Guide to London* brimmed with adverts for ladies of every description, talent, and price. Some brothels offered women of utmost refinement; others catered to men wanting to be whipped and choked in dungeons. There were paid shows featuring "spotless virgins" copulating onstage, and free peeks could be stolen of couples doing it in the streets and parks. (The rake and diarist James Boswell personally consecrated the new Westminster Bridge by having sex with a "strong jolly damsel" beneath it.) Sex was everywhere, in the open, and in the glow of the new philosophy of the Enlightenment it was natural, reasonable, and right.

The decline of religion sometimes took rather bizarre forms, as when Notre Dame Cathedral in Paris was converted into a "temple of reason" in 1793 (the year after the decriminalization of sodomy), and a showgirl was crowned "goddess" of reason and liberty at the cathedral's altar.[1] In such cases reason became shorthand for hatred of the church and all it represented, but just as often, reason and science were co-opted to justify traditional Christian morals. The problem was that eighteenth-century science was often quite wrong—witness the panic over masturbation. In 1760, the respected Swiss physician Samuel Tissot published *L'Onanisme*, a blockbuster that characterized masturbation as a form of slow suicide. Tissot and his ilk blamed dozens of maladies on the world's oldest pastime. Masturbation, they said, resulted in an irretrievable loss of semen, "the essential oil of the animal liquids." If done with frequency, men were warned, sexual self-abuse depleted the body to the point of madness, illness, and death.

Tissot's obsession with the subject started in 1757 after he learned of a young watchmaker who, the doctor said, masturbated as often as three times per day, resulting in a loss of semen so excessive the man grew fearful for his life. Tissot wrote that upon learning of the case he ran to the man's bedside:

> [W]hat I found was less a living being than a cadaver lying on straw, thin, pale, exuding a loathsome stench, almost incapable of movement. A pale and watery blood often dripped from his nose, he drooled continually; subject to attacks of diarrhea, he defecated in his bed without noticing it; there was a constant flow of semen; his eyes, sticky, blurry, dull, had lost all power of movement; his pulse was extremely weak and racing, labored respiration, extreme emaciation, except for the feet, which were showing signs of edema. Mental disorder was equally evident, without ideas, without memory . . . Thus sunk below the level of a beast, a spectacle of unimaginable horror, it was difficult to believe that he had once belonged to the human race.

Tissot arrived too late to rescue the patient and the experience rattled him deeply. He was already steeped in antimasturbation literature, and troubled by the weakness he had observed in his own self-pleasuring patients, but it was the sight of the watchmaker's hideous state that brought out his true calling: "I felt then the need to show young people all the horrors of the abyss into which they voluntarily leap." He sat at his desk and started to write.

What emerged was a book that used "science" instead of the Bible to justify old-time sexual repression. Masturbation not only violated God's commandments, it was now labeled as medically harmful. Semen was stuff

THE RAVAGES OF SELF-ABUSE

• • •

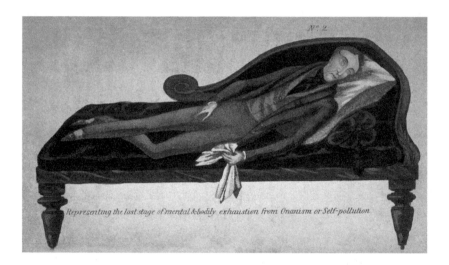

Representing the last stage of mental & bodily exhaustion from Onanism or Self-pollution

Starting in the eighteenth century and continuing for at least 150 years, prevailing sci-
ence held that male masturbation wasted the body's essential fluids, resulting in sickness,
insanity, and sometimes death. This illustration, from 1845, depicts a man in the "last
stages" of exhaustion from "self-pollution." Meanwhile, sales of pornography were soaring.

to be conserved, husbanded, and hoarded. Without an ample supply, the body slowed down and eventually stopped, as dozens of Tissot's gruesome case studies supposedly showed. *L'Onanisme* was an instant hit and made Tissot famous and wealthy. The book quickly became a standard reference work and was translated into English, German, Italian, and Dutch. Tissot became the first major standard-bearer for the 150-year period ending just after World War I, which has been called the age of "masturbatory insanity." A terrified masturbator wrote to Tissot in 1774: "Sir, you are the benefactor of mankind; please be mine as well." The good doctor must have been only too happy to oblige.

NOWHERE DID THE masturbation scare strike as hard as in Germany. A cadre of antimasturbation crusaders emerged, driven by the belief that increasing numbers of males and especially schoolboys were killing themselves. Everywhere they looked, they saw youths rubbing their crotches against trees, arousing themselves on horseback, and even stroking their privates in the classroom under long coats. Those boys who could not be frightened into stopping were sometimes put into mental hospitals or even infibulated—that is, their foreskins were tied shut over the head of their penis and held fast with iron rings. Later preventive devices, used everywhere, were no less crude. Right up to World War I, the U.S. government granted patents for contraptions that restrained, electrically shocked, and pierced penises with the temerity to become erect, even during sleep.

It is unclear whether many males were actually deterred from masturbating. In 1799, one influential German schoolmaster claimed success: "Thousands of young Germans, who ran the risk of ending their abject lives in a hospital, have been saved, and today devote their restored energies to the good of humanity." That statement seems rather optimistic. Most boys and men, even if they were frightened at first, must have discovered that the horror stories simply didn't pan out. Indeed, judging by the high consumption of pornography at the time, it appears that males everywhere were wasting their fluids in volume.[2]

Most eighteenth-century masturbators did their business when no one was looking, of course. Not so among the five-hundred-odd members of the secret Scottish Beggar's Benison society. Strict custom in the centuries-old club required initiates to sit alone in a room and obtain an erection while society members stood in a circle in a nearby chamber. Upon the blowing of a penis-shaped horn, initiates walked into the main room and placed their penises on a pewter "test platter" for the group to inspect and touch with their own genitalia. If all went well and the novitiate was approved, the group would welcome their new brother with the pledge "May your prick and your purse never fail you" and enjoy an evening of bawdy fun with prostitutes. To further cement ties among group members, the test platter and various silver receptacles would be brought out for them all to masturbate upon.

The men of the Beggar's Benison society were respectable businessmen and magistrates. While they shared an interest in raucous drinking, whoring, and masturbating, their approach to their wives was quite another matter. Current mores encouraged the enjoyment of marital sex, but it was something to be managed along rational lines. For sober guidance in this regard, there were a number of manuals available throughout the United States and Europe, most notably *Aristotle's Masterpiece* (published anonymously and having nothing to do with the Greek philosopher) and Nicolas de Venette's *Tableau de l'amour conjugal* (*Conjugal Love*). These books, endlessly reprinted and cannibalized, picked up on the pseudo-scientific tone of the age to instruct married couples how, when, and why to make love. *Aristotle's Masterpiece* went through forty-three editions by 1800. *Conjugal Love* was still in print in the 1950s.

De Venette echoed Tissot's warnings about the dangers of excessive loss of semen, especially the risk of brain damage. At the same time, he taught that females demanded regular doses of semen to prevent their wombs from rotting and their minds from becoming frenzied. Both de Venette and "Aristotle" agreed that sex was required for a woman's health. Even more important, unless a woman experienced orgasm during sex her own "sperm" did not flow and conception was impossible. It was therefore important for the husband to make sex pleasurable for the wife, so long as the goal was preparing her to conceive. (This belief also influenced rape law over the years, as judges often concluded that a pregnancy was proof that the woman enjoyed sex with the accused offender, and therefore no force was involved. See Chapter Four.) A later version of *Aristotle's Masterpiece* also sets out some encouraging verses at the end of each chapter. Chapter Three, for example, provides the following thoughts for a newlywed husband to express to his panting wife:

Now, my fair bride, now I will storm the mint
Of love and joy and rifle all that is in't.
Now my infranchis'd hand on ev'ry side,
Shall o'er thy naked polish'd ivory glide.
Freely shall now my longing eyes behold,
Thy bared snow, and thy undrained gold:
Nor curtain now, tho' of transparent lawn
Shall be before thy virgin treasure drawn.
I will enjoy thee now, my fairest; come,
And, fly with me to love's elysium;
My rudder with thy bold hand, like a try'd
And skilful pilot, thou shalt steer, and guide
My bark in love's dark channel, where it shall
Dance, as the bounding waves do rise and fall.
Whilst my tall pinnace in the Cyprian streight,
Rides safe at anchor, and unlades the freight . . .
Perform those rites nature and love requires,
Till you have quench'd each other's am'rous fires.

De Venette suggested that the man always be on top because that was the best position for conception. Other coital positions, such as woman-on-top, risked producing "dwarves, cripples, hunchbacks, cross-eyed or imbeciles." *Aristotle's Masterpiece* instructed the husband, after lovemaking, "not to withdraw too precipitately from the field of love, lest he should, by so doing, let the cold into the womb, which might be of dangerous consequence." The wife should sleep on her right side and avoid coughing, sneezing, or even moving. Intercourse was to be repeated "not too often," otherwise the husband would "spend his stock" before conception was achieved.

The sex manuals' focus on reproduction excluded other kinds of love-making. Pleasure for its own sake had no place in the biologically balanced marital chamber. Yet fewer people than ever were living their lives that way. Sex, conjugal and otherwise, was increasingly seen as part of the natural order of the world, like the tides, and it was happening everywhere in every possible permutation. The law's task was to balance the weight of fifteen hundred years of restrictive moral teachings with society's carnal demands. The results were anything but neat.[3]

FEMALE LOVE AND LEATHER MACHINES

Can two women love each other sexually? Eighteenth-century morals said no, at least where the females involved were respectable. Among the better classes, lesbian relations were impossible to imagine. Good women could love and embrace each other, sleep together, and write each other passionate letters; all that was noble. But loving and making love were entirely different matters. Unless they were gratifying their husbands, women of "character" were imagined as sexually numb creatures. British judges allowed that females of "Eastern" or "Hindoo" nations might act differently, but not the women of the "civilized" world.

When Marianne Woods and Jane Pirie, the unmarried comistresses of a tony Scottish boarding school for girls, were accused in 1811 of "improper and criminal" conduct with each other, every single student in the school was removed by their parents. Woods and Pirie were ruined overnight. Their primary accuser was a student, the Indian-born grandchild of Dame Helen Cumming Gordon. The girl, who had shared a bed with Miss Pirie, told Dame Gordon that she had been woken up by Miss Woods climbing on top of Miss Pirie and "shaking" the bed. "Oh, do it, darling," Miss Pirie reportedly said as they rolled around together in "venereal" bliss. The girl further reported that the two women cooed as their bodies made the sounds of a "finger [in] the neck of a wet bottle."

Dame Gordon sent out letters telling parents that their children were in "grave danger," and that was it for the school. Pirie and Woods filed a libel suit against Gordon to recover their lost life savings, if not their reputations. Hundreds of pages of trial transcripts later, the two women won, not because they did not sleep together or love each other intimately—they did—but because the judges could not accept that two hardworking, middle-class women such as these could possibly have had sex with each other.

The court saw the stakes as much greater than the personal fortunes of two schoolmarms. For one of the three judges, Lord Meadowbank, the case implicated all well-behaved British women. A world in which women satisfied themselves without need of men was impossible to entertain: "[T]he virtues, the comforts, and the freedom of domestic intercourse, mainly depend on the purity of female manners, and that, again, on the habits of intercourse remaining as they have hitherto been—free from suspicion." As men carried both the sexual machinery and the urge, it was easy for the court to infer that sex would result whenever a man was in bed with another:

If a man and a woman are in bed together, venereal congress would be presumed. And perhaps, even if a man and a man are in bed together without necessity, an unnatural intention may often be inferred.

But that is where Lord Meadowbank drew a bright line. "A woman being in bed with a woman, cannot even give the probability of such an inference. It is the order of nature and of society in its present state. If a woman embraces a woman, it infers nothing."

Pirie and Woods admitted that they slept together often, as many people did, and that their "shifts" had been raised in bed, but nevertheless they claimed to have no idea of what Dame Gordon was accusing them of really doing. The court knew, but it refused to go there. In our time, no one would believe that the relationship between Pirie and Woods was asexual. In Lillian Hellman's 1934 Broadway stage adaptation of the story, *The Children's Hour*, a physical relationship between the two women (cast as mistresses of a snooty New England boarding school for girls) was strongly implied, so much so that the play was banned in several cities. Hellman stressed the viciousness of the young accuser in making the lesbianism charge, and also had the two women deny any sexual contact, but the intimate nature of the relationship was what drove the drama. Without the strong whiff of lesbianism, the play would have been puerile and unrealistic. (To appease censors, the 1936 Hollywood film based on the play was recast as a heterosexual love triangle, although a 1961 remake featured the lesbian relationship intact.)

Hellman came along more than two hundred years after the fact. The critical point that drove the court's decision in the Pirie/Woods case was the conviction that women could not have sex with each other *as women*, meaning that some phallus had to be put to use. Without such a device, sex was as likely as "murder by hocus pocus." "Gross immorality" might result from two females sharing a bed together, even "licentious buffoonery," but without the involvement of something resembling a male, there was nothing illegal to it. Some women, the court allowed, were "peculiarly organized" as hermaphrodites for quasi-male sex—but that was the kind of thing that occurred in Africa or the exotic East. The historical use of dildos was also examined by the court, but there was no proof of that in this case. Pirie and Woods were not, in any event, the sort to do anything like that, the court felt. "I have no more suspicion of the guilt of [Pirie and Woods]," said another of the judges, "than I have of my own wife."[4]

The result of the Pirie/Woods case would have been different had one of them assumed a male role, either by wearing men's clothing or using a penis substitute. In that case, any judge in England would have found a way to punish them severely. In 1746, Dr. Charles Hamilton was convicted in Somersetshire (now Somerset) on charges of fraud and vagrancy for impersonating a man. As widely reported at the time, Hamilton was in fact a woman named Mary Hamilton. For the offense of deceiving another woman into marrying and having sex with her, Hamilton was publicly whipped until her back was "almost flayed" and then sent to prison for six months.

Her criminal life had begun in her teens, when she fell in love with a neighbor girl. The romance ended when the girl became involved with a man and married him. Inconsolable, Hamilton sought a change of scene and identity. She moved to Dublin, where she set herself up as a male Methodist teacher and courted local women. When she was about eighteen, she won the affections of a sixty-eight-year-old cheese seller's widow. The couple married, and she continued to play the role of a man "by means," in the words of one contemporary writer, "which decency forbids me even to mention." The wife's discovery that her young husband was a woman caused a predictable row, resulting in Hamilton fleeing town with a pocketful of the woman's money.

Further adventures landed Hamilton in Wells, Somersetshire, where she assumed the male doctor's identity and began a romance with Mary Price, a naïve eighteen-year-old girl. A two-day courtship resulted in a two-month marriage. Hamilton apparently used a dildo to satisfy Price, as "he" had likely done with other female bedmates. The marriage was sexually satisfying for Price, and might have gone on indefinitely had Hamilton not been recognized by an old acquaintance and denounced. Price tried to defend her husband's manliness, but ultimately she had to admit that she had been deceived. Her neighbors laughed at her and pelted her with dirt.

Hamilton may have been a cad—there was word she had deceived fourteen women into marrying her—but English law did not explicitly punish female sodomy. Henry VIII's buggery statute of 1533 dealt only with sexual relations among men or between men and beasts. Women weren't mentioned. But gaps in the rules have rarely stopped prosecutors from finding something on which to hang a charge. The authorities went after Hamilton under the vagrancy laws for "having by false and deceitful practices endeavored to impose on some of his Majesty's subjects." The case against her was strengthened by the discovery of an object of a "vile, wicked and scandalous nature" found in her trunk. Most likely some kind of dildo, it was used as evidence of the means by which Hamilton "entered" Mary's body "several times." Hamilton was given the maximum punishment the vagrancy laws allowed. By assuming a sexually aggressive male identity, she had usurped the male prerogative of penetration, considered the essence of the sex act.[5]

AROUND THE SAME time the Hamilton scandal was unfolding, a dirty little pamphlet was published about Catherine Vizzani, a female transvestite in Italy. The pamphlet's English translator was England's greatest pornographer, John Cleland, who well knew what the public wanted to hear. As Cleland retold the story, Vizzani had also begun donning men's clothes at an early age, and "incessantly followed the wenches" with "barefaced and insatiable" energy. To affirm her position as an accomplished male rake, Vizzani even sought medical treatment for venereal disorders purportedly caught from "infectious women."

Taking the name Giovanni Bordoni, she finally won the love of a well-born young woman and ran off with her to Rome to get married. They were overtaken en route by a chaplain sent by the girl's uncle to halt the union. Everyone drew their guns, but Vizzani quickly decided it would be safer to give herself up. She was mistaken: The chaplain took Vizzani's gun and shot her anyway. She ended up in a number of hospitals, where her gunshot wound became infected. As her fever grew, she lost control of her senses and took off the cylindrical "leathern contrivance" she kept strapped "below the abdomen of her detestable imposture." A few days later, at twenty-five years old, Vizzani died.

The discovery of Vizzani's "leathern" machine was shocking. Hospital staff members tore the device open. They also examined Vizzani's body and discovered, to their amazement, that she was not only a woman but a virgin, "the hymen being entire without the slightest laceration." Soon a formal autopsy was performed, according to Cleland's account, which resulted in an even more confounding discovery: "The clitoris of this young woman was not pendulous, nor of any extraordinary size . . . on the contrary, hers was so far from the usual magnitude, that it was not to be ranked among the middle-sized, but smaller." Without any kind of deformity to explain Vizzani's "unnatural desires," the surgeon was stumped. The young woman died before legal proceedings could begin, although the local populace's opinions about her may have led authorities not to charge her at all. A fair number of townspeople thought her protection of her virginity "against the strongest temptations" qualified her to be a saint.[6]

Early Modern Germany's sex laws admitted no ambiguity: "Female sodomy" had been an explicit capital crime since 1532. While the law was not often enforced, the threat of the death penalty was real. That was the fate of Catharina Linck, burned in 1721 for living as a man with her young wife, Catharina Mühlhahn.

Before becoming a husband (and an abusive one at that), Linck had been a preacher and a soldier in three armies, among her other personae. Court records from Saxony, where she was tried and executed, reflect the difficulties the judges faced in dealing with a young woman who already assumed no fewer than nine separate male identities.

Linck had grown up in an orphanage, and left it dressed as a young man "in order to lead a life of chastity." She soon fell in with an ecstatic Christian cult given to hitting their heads against walls and speaking in tongues. For two years, Linck traveled with the group as an itinerant preacher and soothsayer, though her predictions did not always materialize—when she urged two men to walk on water and they sank, she fled. She became a swineherd, and later joined the army of Hannover as a musketeer until her desertion three years later.

Next came a stint in the Polish army. Her regiment was captured by French troops, but she managed to escape imprisonment. Her subsequent hitch with the Hessian army lasted about one year. Linck had by now fashioned a leather penis for herself, to which she appended two stuffed testicles made from a pig's bladder. The contraption, held in place with a leather strap, served her well: She used it on a string of young girls, widows, and prostitutes.

Tiring of the military life, Linck reinvented herself as a dyer of fine clothes, met Mühlhahn, and married her. During the wedding, someone called out that Linck already had a wife and children, but she produced a document and two witnesses to prove the allegation false. The newlyweds moved in together, and Mühlhahn would later report that their sex life was active and satisfying, despite the pain she sometimes experienced on account of Linck's large phallus. Their life together out of bed was less successful. Money was always tight, and before long they were begging. Linck also beat Mühlhahn frequently.

One night, as Linck slept, Mühlhahn took a closer look at her husband and discovered the leather truth. Linck awoke and begged Mühlhahn to keep her secret. Mühlhahn agreed, though she demanded that Linck no longer "tickle" her with the device. Finally, Mühlhahn's mother, who had already suspected that her boorish son-in-law was in fact a woman, could bear the union no longer. With the help of another woman, she attacked Linck, tore off her trousers, and confiscated the ersatz genitals, which ended up in court as critical evidence.

Linck's defenders did not let her go to her death before making some creative legal arguments. First, they asked, didn't the Bible only proscribe unnatural acts between women and animals? Moreover, could there be sodomy without semen? But the court was not swayed by such fine distinctions: "The vice is the same for all," the judges pronounced, even if women only engaged in "bestial rubbing and sexual stimulation of their lewd flesh." The court ruled that the penalty was death by fire under both divine and secular law, as both male and female sodomites induced God to rain fire and brimstone down upon the earth. Linck was duly executed. The "simple-minded" Mühlhahn was jailed for three years, and then banished.[7]

MISS MUFF AND INSPECTOR FOUCAULT:
MALE HOMOSEXUALITY ON TRIAL

The Linck case was the last lesbian execution in Europe. Male homosexual conduct would still be punished throughout the eighteenth century, sometimes with execution, but few men seemed to feel an immediate threat. Across Europe and the American colonies, a sprawling homosexual subculture emerged, with no apology. Bars, private clubs, and public cruising zones popped up everywhere, making male-male sexual behavior a visible element of town life. Homosexuality was no less ridiculed than before, and it was still illegal, but its presence was grudgingly tolerated by enough people that it remained in the public eye. Given what we have seen of antihomosexual persecutions over the centuries, and the readiness of people to associate homosexuality with heresy and witchcraft, this was a major advance in itself.

In Stockholm, men met for quick sex in urinals and parks. In The Hague, they signaled each other by stepping on each other's feet, grabbing arms, or waving handkerchiefs. Amsterdam cruisers prowled the

SEX AND PUNISHMENT

city's town hall. Elsewhere, men underwent elaborate rituals in private sex clubs. A group in Haarlem met at night in a forest to choose a "king," while an order of Parisians required initiates to kneel, kiss clusters of false diamonds, and swear fidelity to the others. The more elaborate London clubs, called "molly houses," after the word then used to describe homosexuals, were run by men with names such as Miss Muff, Plump Nelly, and Judith. New members were also given female names, and often married in chapels. The couples would then retire to a nearby chamber and conceive make-believe children, who were then "delivered" in birthing rooms while the group attended with towels and basins of water. In one 1785 raid near the Strand, police found several such "mothers" attending their newborn "children." So well did one of them play the role that authorities were convinced that he was genuine and left him alone with his child—a large doll. For men who could not find a willing husband, male prostitutes were always available.

None of this went unnoticed by the state. By the mid-1720s, at least twenty known molly houses were under investigation. The problem for authorities, at least in London, was that there were few police available to make raids. The constables and justices who were on hand often took money from criminals and bawds. One magistrate in Wapping rented his own home to prostitutes. During this period the city's population was also growing very rapidly. The poor migrants clogging the streets provided new fodder for sex-seekers with money. The church courts, once powerful players in morals enforcement, were now weak. Secular authorities, to the extent they cared, were overwhelmed.[8]

Enter the Holy Rollers. Starting in the late 1600s and lasting for about four decades, a number of groups labeled, collectively, the Society for the Reformation of Manners financed a series of vigilante police actions against behavior deemed immoral, especially among the lower classes. The society was managed by wealthy prigs and members of Parliament, with one overriding objective: Spend what was necessary, pay anyone off, use

THE QUACK DOCTOR
• • •

From the eighteenth century onward, "science," of both the legitimate and the quack varieties, exerted a profound influence on sexual mores and law. Here, a doctor is rebuked by a nobleman for failing to cure the venereal disease he gave to a young girl. Often the remedies for syphilis and other sexually transmitted infections were more harmful than the diseases.

any deception, so long as sexual vice was stamped out in the process. To accomplish this, the society paid informants to infiltrate pockets of sin and then further paid constables and magistrates to arrest and charge people with whatever crime might apply. As lawsuits were costly, the society provided the funds to move the cases through court. For at least a time, the strategy bore fruit: About one hundred thousand people were prosecuted.

Most victims of society purges were hit with garden-variety charges of lewd and disorderly practices such as street soliciting, indecent exposure, and open-air intercourse. However, the society had a special place in its spleen for male sodomy, which it pursued with intensity. Its first anti-homosexual triumph was against Edward Rigby, a navy captain. In 1698, Rigby made the unlucky choice of cruising nineteen-year-old William Minton, who was in the personal service of a member of the society. Rigby approached Minton in St. James's Park during a crowded fireworks display and pressed his erect penis into the young man's hand. Minton could not have been too disturbed by Rigby: He promised to meet him a few days later at a tavern. Nevertheless, Minton had second thoughts about the rendezvous. He told his master and soon agreed to work with the society to trap Rigby into an arrest.

Minton met Rigby at the appointed time, in one of the tavern's back rooms; a constable and four other society members were stationed in the adjoining chamber. Rigby had arrived in a state of high arousal. He told Minton he had already ejaculated in his pants, but was ready for more play. Minton must have seemed hesitant, because Rigby jumped in his lap and begged him for attention, telling him that everyone from Jesus Christ to Peter the Great had had sex with men. Rigby had managed to get inside Minton's pants and had "put his finger to Minton's fundament" when Minton grabbed Rigby's erection and screamed: "I have now discovered your base inclinations!" As the two men scuffled, Minton cried out the signal word "Westminster!" to the officers listening next door. They rushed into the room and took Rigby away.

The captain's conviction for blasphemy and attempted sodomy was a public relations triumph for the society, though Rigby never served out his prison sentence. (After three stints in the pillory, he escaped England to join the French navy.) For its part, the energized society continued to entrap mollies, eventually pulling off its biggest bust ever against a well-known molly house run by a woman known as "Mother Clap." Wedged in between an arch and the Bunch o' Grapes Tavern, Mother Clap's establishment was a kind of molly fantasyland. Its main room was big enough to accommodate dozens of dancing, singing, and drag-wearing men at one time. One society informant described a Sunday night scene in 1725 accordingly:

> I found between 40 and 50 men making Love to one another, as they call'd it. Sometimes they would sit on one another's Laps, kissing in a lewd Manner, and using their hands indecently. Then they would get up, Dance and make Curtsies, and mimick the voices of Women . . . Then they'd hug, and play, and toy, and go out by Couples into another Room on the same Floor, to be marry'd, as they call'd it.

In addition to a wedding chapel, Mother Clap provided her clientele with a variety of bedrooms. While she did not serve alcohol (technically, the joint was a coffeehouse), the Bunch o' Grapes did, and the spirits never stopped flowing.

Mother Clap's club was successful, but not unusual. There were dozens of similar establishments in London, many of which operated in the open without bothering to pay off law enforcement. To the society, the very existence of the molly houses was an outrage, but pulling them down required much more planning than the Rigby operation. Society members needed to secure the cooperation of insiders—hustlers willing to turn in their friends and acquaintances—and gather evidence. Typically, their informers would take constables on fact-finding tours of molly houses.

During one such adventure in 1725, Constable Joseph Sellers accompanied the known sodomite Mark Partridge to several molly houses, where Sellers played the part of Partridge's "husband." One stop that night was the Tobacco Rolls alehouse in Drury Lane. There, an orange-monger nicknamed "Orange Deb" approached Sellers and, as Sellers described it to the court, "put his Hands into my Breeches thrust his Tongue into my mouth swore that he'd go 40 Mile [to] enjoy me." Orange Deb begged Sellers to "go backward and let him," which could mean that he wanted to either bugger Sellers or simply go with him to a backroom. Sellers refused, in either event. Orange Deb then offered to place himself "bare" on Sellers's lap, at which point Sellers lost interest in maintaining his cover. He grabbed a red-hot poker out of the fireplace and threatened to "run it into [Orange Deb's] arse." In a later trial, three men testified that Orange Deb was a good man with a wife and child and never acted inappropriately. The jury disagreed and sentenced him to stand in the pillory at Bloomsbury Square as well as to prison time.

Partridge also helped the society take down Mother Clap, along with two prostitutes named Thomas Newton and Edward "Ned" Courtney. With their help, the constables had enough evidence to show up on a Sunday night in 1726 and round up about forty people, including Mother Clap herself. No one was caught actually having sex (although some of the men had their pants down), but the abundance of informants made that kind of evidence unnecessary. The first of several trials resulting from the raid sent three men to die simultaneously by hanging on a triangular gallows. As ghoulish as that sight must have been, the executions were outdone by another capital punishment at the same time and place. A woman named Catherine Hayes, convicted of murdering and dismembering her husband, was meant to be strangled just before being set alight, but the flames jumped too high and too fast for the executioner to do his job, and she was left to burn alive. Hayes's screams were horrifying, as was the sight of her eyes melting away in the heat. Nor was that the only mishap of the day: More than 150 spectators who had paid to watch the executions from viewing stands fell to the ground in a heap when the stands collapsed, and six people died. Mother Clap was convicted in a later trial and sentenced first to the pillory and then to two years in jail. It is unlikely she survived long enough to serve her jail time, though. The newspapers reported that she was treated with so much "severity" by the crowd while in the pillory that she "swooned away twice and was carried off in Convulsion Fits."

The raids on molly houses stirred their share of public outrage, but so did the underhanded methods used by the society. Its association with lowlife informers such as Newton and Partridge never sat well with many people, nor did the fact that the constables it employed continued to take payoffs, especially from prostitutes. At best, society members were thought of as well-meaning busybodies; at worst, they were reviled as corrupt and vicious. By 1738, the society had lost its luster and was out of business.[9]

The Netherlands also had a large homosexual subculture, but the state's methods of dealing with sodomy made even less sense than England's. In 1730, for the first time in Dutch history, homosexuals suffered heavy state persecutions—a tragedy repeated in 1764 and 1776. In each blast of trials, the confessions of men who were more or less accidentally arrested snowballed into waves of imprisonments and executions, reaching a frenzy toward the end of the century.

In 1764, the drunken Jacobus Hebelaar was drawn to two men urinating in an Amsterdam street. He sidled up, urinated himself, and tried to make a sexual connection with the smarter-dressed of the two. After being told to bugger off, he went to a public toilet under a bridge, where he robbed a man of his money, cufflinks, clothes, and corkscrew. He was arrested shortly afterward by the men at whom he had made a pass earlier in the evening. As luck would have it, they were both in law enforcement. Hebelaar was executed, but not before confessing that for the prior seven years he had committed "the gruesome sin of sodomy" both actively and passively. Moreover, he named his accomplices. Only his robbery was publicly mentioned in connection with the execution, however, most likely to avoid tipping off his sex partners that the police were on their tails. Within one year, seven men were executed, five imprisoned, three exiled, and sixty-four sentenced by default. More than one hundred men had fled the city or committed suicide, all because of Hebelaar's unsuccessful effort to have sex with a policeman.

It is likely that neither Hebelaar nor his accomplices had the money or influence to arrange special treatment for themselves; power and position generally granted immunity from sodomy laws. In Prussia, protection from prosecution for those with means was almost complete. King Frederick II (whose own sexuality was ambiguous, to say the least) wrote that in his state there was freedom of "conscience and of cock," but those words did not translate into action for the lower classes. Typical were the multiple acquittals of Baron Ludwig Christian Günther von Appel for sodomizing his farmhands. One of the baron's accusers was flogged and assessed court costs. Two years later, another farmhand, Jürgen Schlobach, claimed that the baron had "twice stuck his member in his rear and once in his mouth; he'd gotten gooey and had to rinse out his mouth at the fountain." Schlobach was flogged and banished forever from Prussia. As the whipping began, Schlobach's father and brother attacked the flogger with pitchforks, which brought them prison sentences of their own. Schlobach's mother was also jailed after she accused the baron's wife of trying to buy her silence with a new dress.[10]

FRANCE, AS USUAL, cut its own path, suffering neither the vigilante purges of England nor Holland's crazed persecutions. Rather, there was a great deal of police surveillance and record keeping. Sodomy remained a capital offense in France until 1791, and about forty thousand suspected homosexuals were catalogued by special sodomy patrols over the course of the century. However, very few sodomites were executed or even publicly punished. On the contrary, authorities often tried to downplay publicity for fear that spotlighting homosexuality might make it contagious. As elsewhere, those in high places could usually flout the antisodomy laws if they were discreet. The hoi polloi could count on some jail time or even banishment, but even the upper classes were not entirely safe if their sexual adventures were conducted too openly.

One summer night in 1722, among the trees and fountains surrounding the royal palace at Versailles, several young noblemen had sex with each other. The gardens, covering nearly two thousand acres, were certainly big enough for them to find a discreet spot, but they chose instead to have their fun within a stone's throw of the palace—so close, in fact, that several people heard and saw them going at it. Although accounts differ, it seems there were at least six men involved, almost all of them recently married. In the words of a lawyer at the time, the men were not committed to sex only with their own gender; they simply enjoyed "butt-fuck[ing] each other" under the moonlight and "rather publicly." When questioned about their escapades, none of them were contrite, nor did they have reason to be scared for their lives. Most of them were "exiled" to their comfortable estates, later to be joined by their wives. Only one was sent to the Bastille.

When the twelve-year-old future king Louis XV asked why some of his courtiers had been sent away, he was told that they had been tearing down fences in the gardens. Just two years later, Louis (who by then had been crowned) became too involved with the young Duc de La Trémoille, dubbed the "first gentleman of the King's bedchamber." For making a "Ganymede [i.e., a rear-end receptacle] of his master," Trémoille was quickly married off and exiled. Louis was sent on a hunting trip to build up his manly tastes and lose his virginity. He seemed to prefer hunting, however, and—at least then—showed little interest in females.

By 1725, many felt that aristocratic homosexual behavior had gotten out of hand. "All of the young noblemen of the court were wildly addicted to it, to the great distress of the ladies of the court," said Edmond-Jean-François Barbier, a Paris lawyer of the day. Additionally, it was believed that this "aristocratic vice" was spreading to the lower ranks. There "is no order of society, from dukes on down to footmen, that is not infected," wrote the lawyer B.F.J. Mouffle d'Angerville. This belief was both absurd and late. Paris was already crawling with cruising spots and meeting places that catered to homosexuals from every level of society. No one on the street needed sex instruction from his social betters. Nevertheless, it was decided that the time had come for a bloody example to be made.

The scapegoat was the gentleman Benjamin Deschauffors, who was burned alive in Paris for, among other things, selling boys to French and foreign aristocrats and running a "sodomy school." More than two hundred people were implicated in the Deschauffors affair, including a bishop who was banished to his seminary and the painter Jean-Baptiste Nattier, who cut his own throat in the Bastille while awaiting trial. The majority of those accused received jail terms of a few months. Yet if the police hoped that a rare execution would deter others who were "infatuated with the crime against nature," they were very wrong. Paris continued to host more than its share of homosexual action, especially in the Tuileries and Luxembourg Gardens, the city's taverns, and the libertine wonderland that was the Palais-Royal. At least one-third of the men caught by police were married.

By 1750, only three additional men had been put to death for sodomy, two of whom had been caught in the act. If the lives of sodomites were relatively safe, though, their overall legal status remained precarious. The Deschauffors affair was enough to keep people on their toes, especially those with no money or connections. By the 1780s, a special Paris police division was conducting nocturnal "pederasty patrols." Commissioner Pierre Foucault kept a list, in a big book, of tens of thousands of suspected sodomites—as many, he claimed, as there were female prostitutes in the city. The patrols' nightly catches could be as mundane as hauling in a haberdasher for sticking his hand down the pants of a wig-maker during a public execution, or as colorful as an orgy bust in the Palais-Royal. They all went into the book.

By 1791, as the French Revolution raged and King Louis XVI and Queen Marie Antoinette languished in jail, the Constituent Assembly approved a new set of criminal laws that omitted any mention of sodomy and sins against nature. Thus a crime was erased on the books, but not in the minds of many of the people—including the police. The next century would see the heavy use of laws against public decency to harass those engaging in homosexual sex.[11]

VIRGINS AND VD

Venereal diseases had everything to do with the way the law dealt with sex, especially sex for money and sex by force. Current thinking held that "good" girls didn't pass on sexually transmitted diseases; only the "bad" ones did. Men were innocent victims. "[M]en contract this evil from women that are infected," according to one medical source, "because in the [sex] act . . . the Womb being heated, vapors are raised from the malignant humors in the womb, which are suck't in by the man's Yard." In this way, held another authority, "the Pocky Steams of the diseased woman do often evidently imprint their malignity on the genitals of the healthy play-fellows."

The pain and embarrassment of venereal disease, especially syphilis, made people desperate for a solution. The dozens of "cures" available for purchase, such as mercury injections, were often as dangerous as the disease itself. Among the remedies, many agreed that one was superior: intercourse with a young virgin. In London and elsewhere, men sought to cleanse their "pocky" members in the pure fluids of prepubescent girls. Brothels profited by this "defloration mania" by touting purportedly untouched girls. The same girls were sold as virgins time and again, often with "patched up" maidenheads and little blood pellets strategically placed in their vaginas. However, customers with even a little common sense must have known they were not really getting what they paid for. Only truly innocent little girls would do, and to get at them force was usually involved. From 1730 to 1830, at least one-fifth of the capital rape cases in London's Old Bailey involved young children. While the rapists' motivations were not always clear, many were at least in part trying to cure themselves of sexual diseases. The courts never accepted this as a defense, but that did not stop people from believing it to be true.

Consider James Booty, who had raped five or six children less than seven years old by the time he himself turned fifteen. Shortly after being infected by his cousin, a friend told him that "a man may clear himself of that distemper by lying with a girl that is sound." Booty went after every little girl within his reach, including his master's five-year-old daughter. His master had the money and the motivation to push through a prosecution, and Booty was executed, but that result was not typical.

English law never gave much of a hoot about protecting small girls from sexual predators. The traditional age of consent for females was ten, well before the arrival of puberty for most—which allowed men to develop a taste for tender girls. Said one libertine in 1760: "The time of enjoying immature beauty seems to be the year 'ere the tender fair find on her the symptoms of maturity"—that is, before menstruation "stained her virgin shift," and while "her bosom boasts only a general swell rather than distinct orbs." This fetish for taking virgin children became widespread and was, at least tacitly, tolerated.

If a child rape case did make it into court, there was a four-in-five chance the assailant would be acquitted, because the law required proof that the sex had been forced, and that the man had ejaculated inside the victim. Practically, that meant that immediately after a child was raped she had to have the presence of mind to find someone reputable who would, in effect, violate her again to obtain critical evidence. Given that the victimized girls were usually brought down by terror, shame, and physical pain, the reality was that they were there for the taking. Even when there *was* proof of rape, the high cost of a trial effectively slammed the courthouse door in the victims' faces. In one case, the nine-year-old daughter of a servant woman named Margaret East was raped and infected by a man East had trusted. When East could not pay the medical examiner's fees, the examiner hired himself out to the rapist and testified that the girl's hymen was still intact. The man was acquitted.

IN THE UNITED States, a man's social position also protected him against a rape conviction. The 1789 diary of Martha Ballard, a rural Maine midwife, bears haunting witness: Ballard's neighbor, Rebecca Foster, told her that several men had "abused" her since her husband Isaac, a pastor, had left the area on business. One of the abusers was Joseph North, a local power broker, who had broken into Foster's house and treated her "wors [sic] than any other person in the world had." Foster sought Ballard's counsel. "I Begd her never to mentin it to any other person," wrote Ballard. "I told her shee would Expose & perhaps ruin her self if shee did." Foster rejected Martha's advice and told her husband Isaac about the incident. The pastor then took the extraordinary—and risky—step of suing North for the rape.

The trial took place in the tiny river town of Pownalboro. The judges sailed upriver from Boston to the courthouse, as they did twice a year, with valises full of powdered white wigs and black robes. Ballard, who was called to testify, took a boat downriver to Pownalboro—her first visit there in twelve years. The drama was high. Rape cases were rare, and any woman who accused a powerful man of the crime could expect a withering counterattack. Ballard's diary recorded "strong attempts" at trial "to throw aspersions on [Foster's] Carectir." Although it was not spelled out, there is little doubt that North's lawyers would have accused Foster of entertaining men while her husband was away. The matter was further complicated by the fact that Foster had delivered a baby almost nine months after her encounter with North. Most likely, North's "aspersions" of Foster included the charge that she was trying to force a wealthy man to support someone else's child.

On July 12, 1789, North was acquitted, "to the great surprise of all that I heard speak of it," according to Ballard. The Fosters and their children left the area for good and settled in Maryland until Isaac's death in 1800. Rebecca then went to Peru with her youngest son to prospect for gold.[12]

LOVING THE LASH

Samuel Self underestimated his wife Sarah when he sued her for divorce. The Norwich bookseller thought he had a good plan. He had trapped Sarah and her lover, John Atmere, in flagrante delicto, so the court would likely let him out of the marriage without having to pay her anything. Never, he thought, would she have the cheek to strike back by revealing the continuous group sex, erotic whippings, and impromptu sexual shows they had both been hosting in their house for several years. But she did—and by the time the legal proceedings were over Samuel and Sarah were both ruined.

The marriage had never been a healthy one. Samuel was still a virgin at their wedding in 1701, and within a few weeks Sarah had given him gonorrhea. Soon after that she was climbing uninvited into the bed of married neighbors, proposing ménages à trois and presenting a tuft of her maid's pubic hair as a gift. Whether Samuel was aware of Sarah's late-night wanderings isn't known, but by 1706 his own sensibilities were no longer innocent. With the active assistance of Atmere, their maid, and some lodgers, the Self house had become a freewheeling swingers' club, in which sexual partners were traded and whipped each other silly while the others watched.

The most common element of the orgies at the Self house was group flagellation, usually involving Samuel taking a lash to a lodger, Jane Morris. According to the court, Samuel had "indecently, immodestly, lewdly and incontinently" abused Morris "by turning up her clothes and whipping her bare arse, with rods . . . fit instruments for [his] awkward lewdness and devious incontinence." Morris was often held down by others in the house while Samuel gave her a whipping. Each application of the lash brought Samuel to a new level of excitation, so much so that on several occasions he threw the lash down, grabbed his wife, and begged Atmere to whip her.

This was all confusing for the court, and delightful for Norwich's gossipy townspeople. The proceedings dragged on for two years, each new sworn deposition adding a lurid splash of color to the picture. What was the court to do? Given the Selfs' perversions—he an obsessed whipper, she an all-purpose party girl—how could the court judge one more worthy than the other? It was not easy, but judging is what courts must do. Despite the evidence that Samuel was an adulterer himself, the divorce was approved, and Samuel was not compelled to pay alimony, but after two years of court action Samuel's reputation among the respectable folks of Norwich was ruined. His book business fell apart, and in 1710 he was arrested for passing bad financial paper. As for Sarah, she was left homeless and broke.

The Selfs' penchant for whipping was "gross and unnatural" to the court, but it was not atypical. Flogging, both as punishment and as sex play, was common, and most courts were reluctant to penalize it. In 1782, one judge ruled that a man may beat his wife without legal consequence so long as the stick was no thicker than the width of his thumb. The court was referring to discipline, but the line between punishment and prurience is not always clear. Jean-Jacques Rousseau spoke for many of his contemporaries when he wrote, in his *Confessions*, that he grew to love whippings as a child: "I found in the pain, even in the disgrace, a mixture of sensuality which had left me less afraid than desirous of experiencing it again." For the rest of his days, Rousseau wanted to be whipped.

Whipping skills were part of any good prostitute's repertoire. The newspapers were filled with advertisements for brothels offering a good flog. William Hogarth's famous 1732 series of engravings, *A Harlot's Progress*, depicts, among other scenes, a prostitute in her boudoir with a collection of birch rods close at hand. One madam later employed a specially crafted flogging machine onto which she strapped her customers,

THE PLEASURES OF THE BIRCH

· · ·

The British loved their flogging. Whipping skills were part of any good prostitute's repertoire and domestic violence was generally tolerated by the courts, unless it reached "gross and unnatural" proportions. ©THE TRUSTEES OF THE BRITISH MUSEUM

while another machine administered whippings in industrial volume by accommodating forty men at once.

The Selfs' divorce trial roughly coincided with a burst of new pornography devoted to the pleasures of the birch. To choose just two examples, the reprobate publisher and bookseller Edmund Curll did well with the quasi-scientific *Treatise on the Use of Flogging*, while John Cleland's monumental erotic novel *Memoirs of a Woman of Pleasure (Fanny Hill)* devoted much space to the practice. Cleland describes, in loving detail, the prostitute Fanny Hill's harsh treatment of a man she ties to a bench with his own garters. Once she has reduced his "white, smooth, polish'd" buttocks to a "confused cut-work of weals, livid flesh, gashes and gore," Fanny offers up the "trembling masses" of her own "back parts" to the man's "mercy." At first he uses the rod gently, but after a few minutes, "He twigg'd me so smartly as to fetch blood in more than one lash: at sight of which he flung down the rod, flew to me, kissed away the starting drops, and, sucking the wounds, eased away a good deal of pain." Miss Hill finds the experience to be disconcerting at first, but after a glass of wine the "prickly heat" of her wounds puts her into a state of "furious, restless" desire for traditional sex. Her partner gladly obliges.[13]

BEASTS BURDENED

Intimate relations between people and animals (especially goats) were, as we have seen, traditionally condemned as sodomy and associated with devil worship. As the animals involved were considered evil in themselves, they were executed too, often before their human partners' eyes. With the abatement of the witchcraft craze at the end of the seventeenth century, however, a more lenient view toward bestiality emerged. Centuries of cruel punishment had done nothing to dissuade people, especially farmers, from loving their animals. City dwellers had fewer opportunities for such sex, but they nevertheless showed their interest by fuelling the market for bestial pornography.

Somewhere along the line, sex with animals became less radioactive. It was seen as just one category of sex crime among many others.

When, in 1642, young William Hackett was caught in Massachusetts inserting his member in a cow, he told the court that such things were perfectly normal back home in rural England. This defense did not save Hackett from punishment—or the cow, for that matter, who was burned before Hackett's eyes—but it did show a certain nonchalance about the subject that could not have been his alone. When the Prussian king Frederick the Great was told that one of his knights had sodomized a mare, the monarch's reaction was more bemused than horrified: "That fellow is a pig; he must be placed in the infantry."

Animal abusers were still burned at the stake, but less frequently than before. Some courts even started to judge the animals on their own merits. In a 1750 French case, Jacques Ferron was caught making love to a female ass. Ferron was sentenced to death, and while the ass would normally have been condemned as well, this one was acquitted on the grounds that she had been a victim of violence and had unwillingly submitted to Ferron's desires. The court was influenced by a group of religious and civil officials who had signed a petition stating that the ass "is in word and deed and in all her habits of life a most honest creature."

By the close of the seventeenth century, most penalties against human beings for using animals sexually had been reduced, by formal changes either in the law or in practice. Shorter jail terms replaced life imprisonment and execution. In 1791, an English tailor who took liberties with a cow was imprisoned for only two years. The French civil code after the Revolution ignored the subject completely, as did the laws of other countries that fell under French influence. By 1813, the offense would be decriminalized even in such conservative Catholic states as Bavaria.

At the same time, anyone caught in a compromising position with an animal could still count on his or her reputation being destroyed, especially if the offender lived in a city. Rather than take chances, many animal aficionados satisfied their desires with pornography. In 1710, Edmund Curll published a report of a seventy-year-old trial he titled *The Case of John Atherton, Bishop of Waterford in Ireland, Who Was Convicted for the Sin of Uncleanliness with a Cow and Other Creatures, for Which He Was Hang'd at Dublin*. Curll charged a shilling for the four-page pamphlet—an admittedly "very high" price, but one he was confident "would not fail of alluring buyers at any rate." Pornographers also discovered that men enjoyed fantasizing about women and beasts together, especially with household cats and dogs. Whether women ever did the things described in the books is anyone's guess, but there was no shortage of men who liked to think about it.

Tender intimacies with pets held no interest for the Marquis de Sade, whose treatment of animals in his books was nothing less than horrifying. In *The 120 Days of Sodom*, for example, he describes a libertine with a special passion for turkeys. At one point, the man puts his penis in a bird whose neck is held between the thighs of a girl lying facedown. At the same time, another man joins the scene to bugger the man violating the turkey. As the pleasure builds to a climax, the turkey lover cuts the bird's throat. Sade was not personally prosecuted for this scene or, for that matter, the book's passages involving baby rape, torture, and bloodsucking. He was already imprisoned in the Bastille when he composed the work, and never intended for it to be published. It would not be until the 1960s that his works would be published without censorship, by which time intellectuals, such as Geoffrey Gorer, had already hailed him as a revolutionary genius and *Sodom* as "one of the finest works of morals one could hope for."[14]

Dirty Books and Spilled Seed

It was during the French Revolution that the French word *pornographie* assumed its modern definition as a category of "immoral" sex books, but outside the courtroom no one needed a formal explanation. People knew what pornography was when they saw it, and they saw it everywhere. By the end of the century the publication of sexually explicit materials began to resemble the sprawling industry it is today, catering to all tastes and using all available media. Governments tried to repress it, but those efforts usually failed. Many French pornographers charged large sums for not publishing sexual attacks on royals and aristocrats. Never before or since has sexual material packed the political and social wallop it wielded in the eighteenth century. Pornography weakened the French ruling class, especially its kings and queens. It also normalized sex outside the marriage bed and guided the masses out of centuries-old Christian taboos. More than anything, it made some people a lot of money.

Sexually titillating material lurked in unlikely places. While Tissot's *L'Onanisme* denounced pornography's prime objective, masturbation, in the harshest terms—the good doctor said it made people insane, idiotic, hemorrhoidal, impotent, and short-lived—a substantial percentage of his readers used the book itself as an aid to masturbation. In 1835, the American clergyman John Todd published a key passage of his guide to moral behavior, *The Student's Manual*, in Latin, in order not to excite the minds of the very young. The passage warns against the "frequency and constancy" of "the practice of pouring out by hand." Todd also instructs his readers to talk sternly to their hands when they become tempted to touch themselves. (The young men were to say: "Hand—stay your lasciviousness!") The use of Latin probably made the book that much more titillating, if not amusing, to his readers, and surely contributed to the book's success: It ran to at least twenty-four editions and sold one hundred thousand copies in Europe. No less useful as masturbation aids were sex and marriage guidebooks such as *Aristotle's Masterpiece* and Venette's *Secrets of Conjugal Love*. One young man named John Cannon wrote in his memoirs that he regularly masturbated to a midwifery manual until his mother took it away.

The popular press was a major source of pornography, with many of its "reports" concerning divorce and adultery trials. Anyone interested in, say, an illustrated account of a duke's impotence or his wife's infidelity had a variety of choices. There were "sessions papers," reports of sex trials at London's Old Bailey, for example, or the writings of a prison chaplain who took the confessions of sex criminals, collected as *The Ordinary of Newgate, His Account of the Behaviour, Confession, and Dying Words of the Malefactors Who Were Executed at Tyburn*. Yet these publications were often outdone by newspapers and the hacks of Grub Street, a London lane that housed low-end booksellers and impoverished writers. ("Grub Street" soon became synonymous with the disreputable end of the publishing industry.) On Grub Street, printers stole others' material, embellished trial reports with spicy details, and slapped misleading, sexy titles on their products. It was all fair game.

The dean of Grub Street and the father of the modern English pornography publishing business was the aforementioned Edmund Curll. Tall, ungainly, goggle-eyed, and described by Thomas Amory, one of his contemporaries, as a "debauchee to the last degree," Curll noticed that the buying public was more interested in sex than in just about anything else. He also found new, creative ways to take his customers' money. One of his early successes was a 1708 book, *The Charitable Surgeon*, which celebrated a new cure for "venereal distemper." The concoction the book promoted, as well as the equipment for administering it, was on sale at Curll's bookshop.

In 1714, Curll found a gold mine: a two-volume edition of "reports" about a French trial in which an aristocratic wife sought divorce on the grounds of her husband's persistent impotence. The books were larded with detailed "physician's accounts" and special sections on virginity, "artificial maidenheads," and "Examples of some remarkable Cases of natural Impotence." Curll built on this success with a collection of English trial reports about impotence and perversion, including a reprint of court materials about the notorious seventeenth-century bugger and rapist, the second Earl of Castlehaven (see Chapter Five). Curll's success was well noted by his contemporaries, and before long there was no end of books and pamphlets covering polygamy, adultery, and rape cases. One account told of the 1729 rape trial of Colonel Francis Charteris, who was charged with raping his servant, Ann Bond. The cross-examination of Bond was reprinted in full:

> *Being asked whether the Prisoner [Charteris] had his clothes on? She [Bond] reply'd, he was in his night gown. Being asked whether she had not her petticoats on? She reply'd yes; but he took them up, and held her down on the couch. Being asked, whether she was sure, and how she knew he had carnal knowledge of her? She reply'd, she was sure she had, and that he laid himself down upon her, and entered her body. She was asked how it was afterwards? She reply'd that there was a great deal of wet . . .*

By the 1770s, the genre had reached full flower, especially in its use of pictures. A luridly illustrated set of volumes called *Trials for Adultery: Or, the History of Divorces. Being Select Trials at Doctors Commons, for Adultery, Fornication, Cruelty, Impotence, etc.* promised on its cover to provide a "complete history of the Private Life, Intrigues, and Amours of the many Characters in the most elevated sphere: every Scene and Transaction, however ridiculous, whimsical, or extraordinary, being fairly represented, as becomes the faithful historian, who is fully determined not to sacrifice the Truth at the Shrine of Guilt and Folly."[15]

The next decade saw dozens more of such accounts, one of the most widely distributed being of Sir Richard Worseley's £20,000 suit against one of his wife's lovers, George M. Bisset. Worseley technically won the case, but the jury had no love for him—he was awarded just one shilling. The evidence showed that he had enjoyed showing off his wife to friends when she was undressed. On one occasion, while she was taking a bath, Worseley raised Bisset on his shoulders to let him take a peek at her through a crack in the wall. "On coming out . . . [the wife] joined the Gentlemen; and they all went off together in a hearty laugh." The popular accounts of this scene were, of course, graphically illustrated.

Curll not only helped create a new platform for pornography, he was also the key player in the lawsuit that set England's legal standard for obscenity—a precedent that lasted until 1959. His trial reports were mostly safe from legal challenge because they focused on the foibles of real people in real courts, but that was not all he produced. He also put out the *Treatise on the Use of Flogging*; tracts dealing with masturbation, hermaphroditism, and sodomy; and collections of sexy poems such as *The Peer and the Maidenhead*. In 1724, he released an English translation of the French book *Venus in the Cloister, or the Nun in Her Smock*, which purported to describe certain "goings on" in French convents. The book went into two editions before Curll was taken into custody and brought to court on a charge of publishing "lewd and infamous books."

The trial concerned both *Venus in the Cloister* and the flogging treatise, but it was the former that most concerned the court. With its descriptions of bed-hopping, masturbating, bisexual nuns, this book was as lewd as any Curll had published. To his advantage, English law at the time had no clear standard for determining which kinds of books were too bawdy to sell. In fact, what law did exist on the subject seemed to favor Curll. In a 1708 case concerning the book *The Fifteen Plagues of a Maidenhead*, a court ruled that obscenity cases should be dealt with by the church courts, as no secular law forbade material of a sexual nature, even if it "tends to the corruption of good manners." If the courts had refused to punish *Maidenhead*, argued Curll's lawyer, they should let Curll off as well.

The government's attorney disagreed, arguing that Curll's book corrupted the morals of the king's subjects and disturbed the peace. If the courts had any interest in guarding the realm's good order and general morality, he told the court, it was their obligation to take the situation in hand. Meanwhile, Curll did everything he could to exacerbate the situation. While he was out on bail, as the court was trying to figure out what course to take, he published *The Case of Seduction . . . The Late Proceedings at Paris against the Rev. Abbé des Rues for Committing Rapes upon 133 Virgins*, and also put out the memoirs of a notorious spy. After these works appeared, he lost his case. The court agreed with the government's attorney that if a book "tends to disturb the civil order of society . . . it is a temporal offense." Interestingly, in its ruling the court was influenced by an earlier case (discussed in Chapter Five) concerning Sir Charles Sedley, who was fined for disturbing public order after he defecated out the window of a tavern. Sedley had soiled the realm with excrement; Curll was staining England with words about oversexed French nuns.

Curll was ordered to pay a small fine and stand in the pillory for one hour. Depending on the public's opinion of an offender, even such a short stand in a pillory could be a terrible ordeal. Sodomites were pelted with filth and dead cats. Mother Clap, the notorious molly house keeper, nearly died there. Ann Morrow, who was found guilty of marrying three women while impersonating a man, was blinded in both eyes by objects flung at her by spectators. Yet Curll had thought ahead, and made sure he would suffer no such indignities. According to one contemporary report:

> *This Edmund Curll stood in the pillory at Charing Cross, but was not pelted nor used ill; for being an artful, cunning (though wicked) fellow, he had contrived to have printed papers dispersed all about Charing Cross, telling the people that he stood there for vindicating the memory of Queen Anne; which had such an effect on the mob, that it would have been dangerous even to have spoken against him; and when he was taken down out of the pillory, the mob carried him off, as it were in triumph, to a neighboring tavern.*[16]

Curll died in 1747, just before a no-account writer and civil servant named John Cleland was sent to jail. Cleland, future reteller of the Catherine Vizzani story and author of *Fanny Hill*, had returned to England several years earlier from a failed career with the British East India Company and had found no success at home. His debts multiplied, leading to his arrest and a one-year stretch in debtor's prison. While incarcerated, the bookseller Ralph Griffiths offered him a small sum to write some drivel about a fictional London prostitute. The work—*Fanny Hill*—was published with huge success while Cleland was still behind bars and became the key event in the history of English-language pornography and a flashpoint in Anglo-American obscenity law for more than two centuries. It was not until 1966 that the U.S. Supreme Court ruled that the book was protected from censorship. England first permitted the entire book to be sold in unabridged form in 1970.

Reading through *Fanny Hill*, it is hard to see what all the fuss was about. There is not one obscene word in the work, the sex is mostly conventional, and the story resolutely middle-class. Fanny is a young girl from the hinterland who comes to London as an orphan and ends up in a brothel. There she loses her virginity to Charles, with whom she falls in love but to whom she must bid goodbye when he is sent to the South Pacific. In his absence, she achieves success in the business of pleasure, eventually opening her own establishment and inheriting the fortune of one of her clients. Finally, Charles returns, they marry, and Fanny lives out her life "in the bosom of virtue." The book ends on a suitable tone, with Fanny telling her readers that the sensations of vice are "spurious," "low of taste," and "inferior" to the joys of a moral life: "If I have deck'd [vice] with flowers, it has been solely in order to make the worthier, the solemner sacrifice of it, to Virtue."

Pretty mild stuff, but after the Curll case the publisher took no chances. Griffiths had kept his name off the book, while Cleland was represented only as a "person of quality." Neither measure fooled the authorities for

long. In 1749 a warrant was issued to seize the author, printer, and publisher. Cleland had none of Curll's courage. He told the court he regretted
writing *Fanny Hill*, and that he had only done so to escape poverty. The
indignities he had already suffered were, he claimed, punishment enough:
He was "condemned to seek relief . . . from becoming the author of a Book
I disdain to defend, and wish, from my soul, buried and forgot." Cleland's
groveling worked, and he was given a hundred-pound annual pension in
exchange for his agreement to stop writing pornography. For Griffiths's
small investment, he had made about ten thousand pounds.

From that point forward, unexpurgated versions of *Fanny Hill* went
underground and multiplied. Repeatedly abridged, translated, illustrated,
and confiscated, no work of pornography has ever been as popular. It was a
favorite of soldiers and snobs, a barracks-room staple during the American
Civil War, and even a token of international goodwill: The future Duke
of Wellington took along eight copies on an extended voyage to India,
presumably both for his own shipboard pleasure and to give as gifts. In
1819–20, *Fanny Hill* was the subject of the United States' first prosecutions
for the sale of obscene literature, when two traveling booksellers were fined
and imprisoned for trying to sell the novel to Massachusetts farmers. By
1966, the U.S. Supreme Court would be sharply divided over the question
of whether or not the book should be sold. Long after much more explicit
material had survived obscenity charges, *Fanny Hill* was still too much for
three of the nine justices to stomach. "Though I am not known to be a pur-
ist or a shrinking violet," wrote Justice Tom C. Clark in his dissent, "this
book is too much even for me." Despite Clark's qualms, the Court's majority ruled that the book had some merit, and therefore could not be banned.

After the *Fanny Hill* decision, a book could claim protection under
the First Amendment if it had an iota of "redeeming social value," even
as a curiosity. The *Fanny Hill* case was all the more critical because it
concerned such a substandard piece of writing. Other works that had
squeaked through the courts over the years, such as Henry Miller's *Tropic*

of Cancer and James Joyce's *Ulysses*, were ambitious works of literature. *Fanny Hill*, by contrast, was "nothing but a series of minutely and vividly described sexual episodes." If it had social value, then social value was very easy to find.

No one would have been more surprised by the *Fanny Hill* decision than John Cleland himself. When he wrote the book in a stinking jail, he never could have imagined that its artistic merits would be seriously scrutinized by the most august court in the English-speaking world. Based on Cleland's later disavowal of the book, he would have been the first to agree with Justice Clark that it was "bankrupt" in "both purpose and content."[17]

AS PROBLEMATIC AS *Fanny Hill* has been over the years, it is completely apolitical. Nowhere does Fanny or any other character show any interests beyond their next erotic adventure, which well suited the tastes of Cleland's readership. English pornography was a private affair; the middle and lower classes could enjoy reading about the sexual foibles of the aristocracy, and books about fantasy prostitutes such as Fanny Hill were appealing to all, but no harm was done. No one really believed that the state was ever put at risk by a sexy book.

Not so in France, where pornographic attacks on the upper crust were weapons of rebellion. The tradition of printing pamphlets about the real or imagined debauches of the powerful, called *libelles*, started in the mid seventeenth century when thousands of them clogged the shops of Paris. The main targets were the Italian cardinal Jules Mazarin and Anne of Austria, the mother and regent of Louis XIV. Mazarin and Anne were charged with running the country while the future Louis was still a boy, and lost no time in making enemies. By characterizing them as perverts intent only on satisfying their unnatural desires, the pamphlets were accusing them of being unfit to govern. Their passions were, said the *Mazarinades* (as the early *libelles* were known), satisfied to the ruination of the state. Mazarin and Anne were often depicted as indulging in anal sex, which to French audiences served as shorthand for the basest form of immorality. As one *Mazarinade* put it:

The Cardinal f[ucks] the Regent;
What's worse, the bugger boasts about it
And steals all her money from her.
To make the offense less grave,
He says he only f[ucks] her in the a[ss].

The poet's solution to the scourge of Mazarinism was simple enough: "Cut off his balls." The "Sicilian bugger's" abuse of his genitals was the same as his misuse of his authority:

Constable with a rod of Sodom,
Exploiting the kingdom left and right,
Buggering bugger, buggered bugger,
And bugger to the highest degree,
Bugger this way and bugger that way,
Bugger in large and small size,
Bugger sodomising the state,
And bugger of the highest carat,
Investing the world in the stern,
That is to say, in the rump,
Bugger of goats, bugger of boys,
Bugger in all ways,
Bugger directly descended
From Onan, the notorious masturbator,
Doctor of buggery in both kinds,
Swindler as well as sorcerer,
Man to women and woman to men.

The *Mazarinades'* charges against Anne were only slightly less extreme: She was, they said, a serial adulteress who abandoned the state and her royal son. Mazarin was her god, for whom she would sacrifice every Frenchman:

Jules, whom I love more than the king of the state,
I want to show you my intense passion
By ruining the realm, by ruining myself.

Sexual misconduct at the top of the state was worse than simple bad behavior; it was a contagion. The "cursed pus" that flowed from Mazarin's "tool" into Anne was infecting the kingdom. The only cure, according to the *Mazarinades*, was to castrate him, torture him, or administer the legal penalty for sodomy and burn him alive.

That never happened. Mazarin and Anne both died peacefully, and France survived their rule with the monarchy intact. Louis XIV assumed personal control of the kingdom in 1661 upon Mazarin's death, and led it into an age of unparalleled grandeur and influence. The chief emblems of royal power were the vast palace and gardens Louis built at Versailles. It was no accident that the center of the palace—the vector from which all power in France emanated—was Louis's bedroom.[18]

The Sun King's prestige and relative sexual restraint helped him avoid the worst of the *libelles*. His successor, Louis XV, who ruled from 1715 to 1744, had no such luck, nor did he deserve it. A lackluster monarch, he devoted himself to sensual pleasures, especially in his later years, turning the court into a massive seraglio. The king's many mistresses, especially the notorious Madame de Pompadour and Madame du Barry, were repeatedly accused (with some good reason) of controlling the king and leading the country toward despotism.

While France feared that it was coming under the rule of corrupt whores, the king retreated to a country estate known as the Deer Park, where he led the life of a dirty old man. There, Madame de Pompadour supervised the delivery to him of a steady flow of young virgins for deflow-ering. Many of them lived at Deer Park, where they were given maids and footmen and taught singing, dancing, and painting in their spare time. They were told that the man they serviced was a Polish nobleman, a relative of the queen. To believe otherwise, the girls discovered, was risky indeed. One of them, who had mentioned that her lover was actually the king, was sent to a madhouse. If a girl excited more than just a passing interest for Louis, she was given a special house of her own and sometimes jewelry and other expensive trinkets. He sired at least six royal bastards in the early 1760s alone. (The upkeep of Deer Park was costly, as was the maintenance of the service staff to keep the operation going, though the actual expense came nowhere near the *libelles'* accusations.)

The *libelles* went into overdrive when Madame du Barry, an ex-prostitute and the illegitimate daughter of a defrocked monk, replaced Madame du Pompadour as the king's mistress. The king was accused of being senile, servile to a whore, and unconcerned that the resources of the state were being wasted:

> Who'd imagine that a clique,
> In the teeth of all critique,
> Could turn a wanton, public whore
> Into a brand new potentate?
> Who'd ever think that, without shame,
> Louis would give up the helm
> To such a bitch, and let
> Founder the imperilled ship of State?

By the time Louis died of smallpox in 1774, it had become unsafe for him to go to Paris at all. The *libelles* followed him to the grave and beyond. One told the story of his departed soul's search for paradise: On his jour-ney, he asks directions from Saint-Denis (who had been decapitated) and Mary Magdalene, both of whom point him in the wrong direction. When he finally reaches the heavenly gates, Saint-Pierre ridicules him for taking advice from "men with no brains and whores."[19]

STARTING IN THE 1750s, many of the *libellistes* based themselves in London. England did not allow foreigners to come to its shores and file lawsuits, which made England somewhat of a safe haven for pornographers looking to attack anyone on the Continent. If French foreign agents were unable to kidnap or kill the *libellistes*, the only means of silencing them was to pay them off. This happened often enough to make pornographic blackmail a lucrative profession. Many of the *libellistes'* works found their way into France anyway, where they were widely read. In many cases, French officials paid London-based *libellistes* to launch sex-slander attacks on their rivals.

One of the best-known *libellistes* was Théveneau de Morande, an adventurer and petty criminal who awarded himself the title "chevalier" to gain admittance into high society. While living in Paris from 1765 to 1770, he made contacts at Versailles and acted as a pimp for high-class courtesans and court mistresses. During these years he also gathered incriminating material for his later career as a blackmailer. In 1770, after his release from jail for loan-sharking, he fled to London, where he drew on his wealth of experience to remake himself as a scandalous writer. The following year he published the *Gazetier cuirassé*, an archetypal *libelle* brimming with salacious anecdotes about the rich and powerful in France.

One of Morande's most successful ventures was a scandalous biography of Madame du Barry, titled *Secret Memoirs of a Public Woman from Her Cradle to the Bed of Honour*, which he threatened to publish unless he was paid a handsome sum. The French royal court tried several times to have him eliminated, yet he was not to be intimidated. At one point, he incited a London mob against two of du Barry's thugs, forcing them to flee for their lives. Finally, when the *Secret Memoirs* was printed and ready for shipment, the great dramatist Pierre-Augustin Caron Beaumarchais was sent to negotiate with Morande. The *libelliste* agreed to give up the entire print run of the book in return for payment of all of his debts, plus a lifetime annuity.

Morande also agreed to stop libeling French ministers and monarchs, but that promise soon evaporated. Louis XV died a few weeks after the contract was signed, and before long Morande was scribbling a new pamphlet claiming that the new king, Louis XVI, was impotent and that his Austrian queen Marie Antoinette was taking lovers to produce an heir. Beaumarchais was dispatched again to bribe Morande, which he did— but evidence suggests that he may have actually plotted with Morande to produce the work in order to share the payoff. Later, it was rumored, Morande was paid by Marie Antoinette and Louis XVI themselves to libel the Duke of Chartres.

The royal couple may have made their peace with Morande, but they had no such luck with other *libellistes*, who produced a nonstop flow of scabrous books about them. So harsh, so dirty, and so plentiful were the attacks on the king and queen that they seriously undermined the monarchy and played an important role in moving the French Revolution forward. The attacks on Marie Antoinette were the worst, and the most widely distributed. By the time they reached their peak in the early 1790s, she had been branded a lesbian, prostitute, sodomite, nymphomaniac, and even a lover of incest. With such a queen, popular disgust for Louis XVI as a hapless impotent grew steadily worse. Marie Antoinette was, according to the *libellistes*, poisoning the royal line (and thus France itself) with the stray seed she gathered at her orgies. Whereas Louis XV had been criticized as being unable to control his libido, Louis XVI was worse: He could not even manage his wife. As the calumnies piled up, it became easier to imagine obliterating the monarchy and, eventually, executing the king and queen.

The *libelles* against Marie Antoinette were like nothing ever seen before in France. With names such as *The Austrian Woman on the Rampage, or the Royal Orgy* (1789); *The Royal Bordello* (1789); and *The Vaginal*

Fury of Marie Antoinette, Wife of Louis XVI (1791), the queen was transformed into a source of national infection, a channel for foul rumors to flow directly into the heart of the Bourbon household. In the chaos following the start of the Revolution in 1789, some *libelles* were printed in France, but London was still the safest place for their authors to operate, especially when they were already in trouble with the law at home.[20]

One of the first *libellistes* against Marie Antoinette was the "Comtesse" de la Motte, a part-time prostitute and former fringe character at Versailles. La Motte, born in 1756 as Jeanne de Valois Saint-Rémy, had started life on the streets of Paris as a beggar. Her situation changed when a hint of nobility was discovered in her lineage; she was later adopted by a marquise. Finishing school smoothed over her rough edges, but did nothing to change her character. By the age of twenty-three she was married to an impoverished noble and well into a life of crime. Always living one step ahead of the police and creditors, in 1785 the la Mottes pulled off one of the greatest confidence schemes in French history—and one that would further tarnish the reputation of the queen.

The la Mottes lived for a time at Versailles, where they submerged themselves in the dull intrigues of court life. The Comtesse de la Motte may have met Marie Antoinette, but never knew her well enough to make a successful living selling royal influence. What she lacked in connections, however, she made up in ambition. She devised a complex plan by which she and her husband conned a jeweler out of a fabulous diamond necklace, and a cardinal out of his honor. She told Louis René Édouard, the Cardinal de Rohan, that the queen wanted him to procure a certain necklace—but secretly, for fear of having her extravagance exposed. Relations between de Rohan and the queen had soured of late, and while the cardinal wanted to regain her goodwill, he needed to be sure that it was in fact Marie Antoinette who was making the request. With the help of a forger, the comtesse concocted a series of fake letters from the queen to de Rohan, as well as a contract supposedly bearing Marie Antoinette's signature. The la Mottes also arranged a secret nighttime meeting in the palace gardens between the queen and the cardinal—though it was not Marie Antoinette whom de Rohan met, but a prostitute the comtesse had chosen because she resembled the queen. The ruse worked; the cardinal obtained the necklace and delivered it to the la Mottes, who promptly took it apart and sold the stones around Europe.

The scheme unraveled when the jeweler who sold the necklace demanded payment from Marie Antoinette. Rumors circulated that the queen was secretly squandering the state's money on elaborate baubles. To clear his wife's name, Louis XVI demanded a trial, but that spectacle only served to degrade her further. The cardinal eventually admitted that her signature on the contract had been forged, but argued that it was reasonable for him to have believed she would acquire jewels in a backhanded way. He was acquitted as an innocent dupe, but the king banished him anyway. Although Marie Antoinette was not found guilty of anything, the cardinal's acquittal implied that she was up to no good. The Comtesse de la Motte was whipped, branded, and jailed for life, but she eventually escaped to London, where she set to work on a *libelles* justifying her actions and slamming the queen.

The first of la Motte's *libelles* was a set of memoirs in which she portrayed herself as an innocent in the diamond-necklace scandal and described her purported lesbian love affair with Marie Antoinette and their "moments of delirium together." A later version of the memoirs provides the details:

> *[The Queen] deigned to embolden me by non-equivocal caresses and by the sweetest words . . . Soon, the ingenious libertine ran her devouring eyes over what she called my charms; her enflamed mouth, pasted kisses of fire everywhere, and I blush to admit that I was sated.*

Allegedly helpless before the scheming queen, la Motte claimed that she was used as a royal tool to acquire the necklace.

La Motte's material was outdone by the *libelles* that turned up once the Revolution started in 1789. Right under the windows of the Tuileries Palace, where the king and queen lived, it was possible to buy materials that depicted Marie Antoinette as a sexual monster. Just behind the windows of the palace, according to one of the *libelles*, she lay on her bed, masturbating and waiting for all comers:

> *Sometimes dying of boredom in the midst of a lovely day,*
> *She writhed all alone on her bed,*
> *Her palpitating tits, her beauteous eyes and her mouth*
> *Gently panting, half opened,*
> *Appeared to invite the challenge of a proud shagger.*

The queen was branded as a living example of royal decay. In one poem, *Le Godemiché royal* (*The Royal Dildo*), Marie Antoinette demands that a bishop "baptise my cunt" with holy water to wipe out original sin. In another *libelle*, she speaks of the "lascivious twitching in my randy cunt" while she waits for sexual fulfillment to come. "Fuck virtue," she hisses, "that's merely a chimera; A really amorous cunt can fuck its own father." And what, according to the poet, was her husband doing while she amused herself with others? Not enough. His "matchstick" was "no fatter than a straw" and far less sturdy. The king was impotent and useless.

By the time Marie Antoinette stood trial herself, the royal couple's reputation had been damaged beyond repair, and the social order turned upside down—spurred in large part, said the *libelles*, by the breakdown in *sexual* order at the top of society. Marie Antoinette was fair game for any kind of accusation. She was charged with committing incest with her son, the young Louis XVII, and causing him to commit the filthy sin of masturbation. According to the reports of her prosecutors, the child "learned [masturbation] from his mother and his aunt (Marie's sister), who often put him to bed between them, and there the most unbridled debaucheries were committed." The result, it was understood, was that the boy's physical constitution—and by extension France itself—was growing weaker by the day. Marie Antoinette was beheaded for treason on October 16, 1793, soon after the trial.

When she was asked why she had, at first, refused to reply to the incest accusation, Marie Antoinette retorted that the charge was too awful to dignify with an answer. "I appeal to all those mothers who might be here today," she said in court, expecting everyone to agree that no mother could do such a thing to her son. This appeal did not save her, but it did affirm the presence of sexual boundaries. Even a woman as "evil" as the queen would not admit to crossing them.[21]

HAD THE MARQUIS de Sade been asked about "excessive" carnal behavior, he would have laughed. To Sade, the very notion of sexual limits was foolish. Pleasure defined morality. The craving for orgasmic sensation is natural, Sade argued, and as such it is right and good regardless how one satisfies it:

> Will it never be understood that there is no variety of taste, however bizarre, however outlandish, however criminal it may be supposed, which does not derive directly from and depend upon the kind of organisation which we have individually received from Nature? . . . Even were one to desire to change those tastes, could one do so? Have we the power to remake ourselves? Can we become other than what we are?

In short, pleasure was worth the price. Coming from one who spent twenty-seven years of his life behind bars, mostly for his own sexual misconduct, we can at least admire Sade for having the courage of his convictions. When he celebrated sex with babies or the dead, or dismemberment, or prodigious anal abuses, he wasn't kidding. Sade didn't come close to doing everything he described in his writings, but his life gives the impression that this may have been because he didn't have the time or the opportunity.

Despite the volcanic nature of Sade's books—they are far better read about than read, because they are truly disgusting—most of his legal troubles were not caused by his writings. *Philosophy in the Bedroom, The 120 Days of Sodom,* and his other major works were written while he was already in prison. To the limited extent his erotica was published during his lifetime, it came out anonymously, and when his work became the target of obscenity proceedings, he tried to protect his own safety by denying authorship. Sade was a pervert's pervert with an imagination as sprawling as his libido, but he was also a man of his times. No civil society could tolerate someone who would not think twice of using hot iron or molten lead as a sexual aid.

Donatien Alphonse François, Marquis de Sade, was born in 1740 to a minor aristocratic family from Provence. After becoming too intimate with his female caretakers, he was sent, at ten years old, to the Lycée Louis-le-Grand in Paris, where he presumably learned the fine points of flogging. Sade's taste for sexual violence bloomed while he was in the army, where he distinguished himself in the Seven Years' War with England and rose to the rank of captain. His arranged marriage in 1763 did nothing to quell his quirks. Five months after his nuptials he was briefly imprisoned for mistreating a young prostitute. He got into much worse trouble five years later, when he picked up a thirty-six-year-old widow and brought her home on Easter Sunday under false pretenses. The poor woman was tied to a bed and whipped with a birch switch. Sade then cut her flesh with a small knife and poured hot wax into the incisions. Even worse, he offered to hear her Easter confession, a blasphemy that seemed to help him achieve orgasm. This frolic brought him a seven-month prison stint. It also led police to caution brothels not to supply him with girls.

That warning was not heeded. In 1772, after a multiday debauch with his manservant and four prostitutes in Marseilles, he faced charges of poisoning and sodomy. He spent four months in prison and then fled to Italy with his sister-in-law (whom he always preferred to his wife). The case led to the issuance of a death sentence against him, which was carried out in absentia while he acquired further sexual experience in Florence and Naples. He slipped back into France and took up residence at his château at La Coste, where more excessive orgies took place. Somehow, he remained at large for four years until he was plucked out of a Paris hotel and put in jail again—this time for thirteen years—thanks to the efforts of his outraged mother-in-law, Marie de Montreuil. As a result of her boundless hatred and that of other members of his family, he would spend most of the rest of his life incarcerated in prison and mental hospitals.

It was in the Bastille in 1785 that Sade wrote the seminal *120 Days of Sodom*, with the goal of cataloguing six hundred separate perversions. The work was composed on small bits of paper that he stuck together into a forty-foot-long roll. That is a lot of misbehavior, but nowhere near enough to meet his objective. Sade never finished the book, and left his most hideous ideas in note form only. The manuscript was presumed lost after he was moved out of the Bastille in 1789. The work was later rediscovered, but a French version would not be published until 1931. Sade's work was censored well into the twentieth century. At late as 1956, the French publisher Jacques Pauvert was convicted on a charge of "outrage to public morals" for his publication of the novel *Juliette*.[22]

THE TRIUMPHANT WHORE

Sade's Juliette was a prostitute—a good girl who went very bad, eventually having sex with heads of state and the pope himself. While anything coming from Sade's pen must be taken on its own terms (one of Juliette's lovers fantasized about starting a famine that would wipe out half of France), the author's love of prostitutes well fit the eighteenth-century mold. The whore ruled the age. She was worshipped, pampered, adored, and hated. More than ever before or since, prostitutes were objects of popular fascination, limitless tableaux on which men painted their most intense aspirations. Fanny Hill was a male fantasy of a personal sex servant, but her flesh-and-blood doppelganger was available just down the block.

The whore was everywhere, especially after Reformation-era laws were relaxed in the late 1600s. The mass brothel closings that were the keystone of Protestant and later Catholic governance failed; prostitution simply went underground. By the early 1700s, the demand for quality whorehouses and the opportunity for large graft payoffs led to a mass resurgence of commercial sex establishments. In Paris, prostitution was prohibited, enabling police authorities to command larger and more selective bribes. In fact, in some instances regulation technically became stricter. Laws were passed prohibiting unmarried people from rooming together in a hotel, which had the effect of protecting brothels against competition from streetwalkers.

Parisian bordellos reached mythical proportions. In one, patrons were greeted in a central seraglio area where fifty girls awaited, each bearing ribbons denoting their talents. Another brothel could be accessed by a secret tunnel system and featured peep rooms and a dungeon for flogging. Others specialized in black prostitutes, the special needs of clergymen, and the sale of "virgins." To keep the supply of girls up, parents sold their daughters to brothel-keepers, signing formal written contracts by which they abandoned all claims to the girls or their offspring. Neither the brothels nor the fifteen hundred or so streetwalkers around the Palais-Royal could have operated without the sanction of the police.

Similar conditions prevailed in Boston, where Puritans complained bitterly about the prevalence of prostitutes, and also in London, where the efforts of the Society for the Reformation of Manners and other such groups were ultimately a bust. Prostitutes advertised in newspapers and magazines, using ads that might be blunt (one declared that the woman it touted had "noble elasticity in her loins") or rather clever in their use of double entendres, such as the following:

Miss Rattletrap, from Pall Mall, London, is calculated for first rates; the rider must be very careful of her, as she starts at full speed. Price 15s.

Always more numerous than the glamorous girls of the finer brothels were the poor wretches, past their prime, ill with venereal and other diseases and begging passersby for business. The high-end courtesan, moreover, could turn into a tragic figure at any moment. Over the years, the image of the prostitute was imbued with the somber hues of a fallen woman, often portrayed as a middle-class girl driven down by bad luck into the hands of predatory men. Starting in the 1740s, several hospitals for "penitent prostitutes" were founded in London, built on the assumption that whores led immoral lives not because they were inherently evil or lusty, but because they had been debauched and abandoned. They needed only to be "reclaimed" to lead productive lives.

The life offered by the hospitals made prostitution look easy by comparison. Morals were drilled into their inmates through strict work regimens, quick punishment for insubordination, and endless prayer. The first month of confinement in an English institution of this sort was spent in complete isolation. Life in the reforming hospital of Montpellier, France, was even more spartan. Its inmates had their heads shaven and their possessions confiscated upon entry. For the first two weeks they were kept in dungeons, during which their only human contact was with the nuns who brought them food and chastised them with whips. Throughout their stay, inmates were mentally isolated from each other through a strict rule of silence; even whispering was punished.

Whether any of these measures had a lasting social impact is doubtful. In Montpellier, it was agreed by all that the reform movement had failed to stem prostitution or sexual license generally. Even the city's mayor conceded that it was "the most dissolute city in the world." Many of the tens of thousands of women who entered the London hospitals made shows of penitence just to secure care for their children. Throughout this period, prostitution itself was still not illegal in England, even if brothel-keeping and disorderly behavior were. Where the line lay between these two rules is anyone's guess.

The mixed messages about both prostitutes and prostitution continued as they had for many centuries. No number of laws, speeches, or sermons from the pulpit could change the reality that the sale of women's bodies remained a viable choice for them to earn money, and for men as a common way to spend it. For law enforcement, the skin trade remained a source of income and, sometimes, pleasure. (The Parisian inspector M. Berryer found it necessary to patronize brothels himself in order to ensure that he knew what was going on in them.)[23]

BY THE CLOSE of the eighteenth century, people at all levels of society were demanding liberties previously allowed only to the ruling classes. The world was becoming more crowded, less religious, and, by several orders of magnitude, more sexually permissive. In the coming decades social classes would mix unprecedentedly, both in the streets and in bed. However, new legal issues would arise, by which the upper classes would be forced, for the first time, to pay a steep price for sexually abusing their inferiors. A wealthy man's age-old prerogatives of taking liberties with his servant girls or male laborers would come under scrutiny as never before.

Everywhere there were trials, gleefully covered by the penny press, in which one snob or another would be called to task for sexual indiscretions with the lower orders. The notion was starting to take hold, ever so slowly, that a young girl could refuse sex to an older man—even her employer— and that a handsome young man was not easy prey for any gentleman. Of course, the process was untidy, and old habits would die hard, but by the beginning of the twentieth century the popular idea of liberty began to encompass freedom from sexual predation.

8

• • •

THE NINETEENTH CENTURY:
HUMAN NATURE ON TRIAL

IN SEPTEMBER 2009, the acclaimed film director Roman Polanski was arrested at Zurich airport. The seventy-six-year-old, Polish-born French citizen was on his way to collect a lifetime achievement award at a film festival, but U.S. police authorities—who had been chasing Polanski for decades, and who urged Swiss police to detain him—viewed his accomplishments differently. Polanski had fled the United States in 1978, just hours before a Los Angeles judge would likely have sentenced him to prison for having "unlawful sexual intercourse" with a thirteen-year-old girl.

Polanski's flight from American justice caused a big stir at the time, but the story calmed down after he settled in Paris and continued to make films. His arrest in Switzerland, however, rekindled the old controversy with a vengeance—now, just a few years after he had won the Academy Award for Best Director for *The Pianist* (at a ceremony he did not attend, as doing so would have meant certain arrest), Polanski was again reviled as a sexual monster so dangerous that no jail sentence was long enough to contain him. Any arguments to the contrary were attacked with equal fury. When the actress Whoopi Goldberg said on U.S. television that Polanski was not as bad as a man who commits "rape rape"—meaning that Polanski had not physically forced himself on the girl—she suffered a furious public-relations backlash. The message was clear: To have sex with a girl that young was perverted under any circumstances, and to think otherwise was wrong in itself.

Omitted from the brouhaha was one salient fact: Polanski's crime was an accident of history. It was only recently that encounters between men and girls that age became illegal at all. Had he been caught less than a century earlier, the law would have looked the other way. California's legal age of consent during the nineteenth century was ten, as in most other states in the Union (in Delaware, it was seven). The state raised it to fourteen in 1889 after a tussle between Christian pressure groups and male legislators, whose main concern was avoiding blackmailing schemes by cagey young girls and their families.

Given that Polanski's victim was not a virgin when they had sex, there is every reason to believe that, in the not-too-distant past, he would not have been given jail time, much less become an international fugitive. Even after the age of consent was raised, most white California men were sentenced to probation for sex with minors, even when they were caught dead to rights. (Black men, on the other hand, were usually incarcerated.) Girls with any kind of sexual history were routinely branded as temptresses and aggressors. In one California case, the judge observed that "it would be a pretty strong man" who could "escape" the temptation of the teenage girl in his apartment with whom he had had sex, even though she had refused his advances. In another prosecution, a man's violent rape of a fourteen-year-old female cannery worker got him only probation. The judge observed: "Her willingness to accompany [the defendant] into the office alone placed him under special temptation."[1]

Polanski's case never actually went to trial, but had he been pushed to the wall he would have had much to say in support of the "special temptation" defense. Court and grand jury records show that the girl had met him with her mother's consent; had let him photograph her nude, in a hot tub, in suggestive poses; and had drunk the champagne he had given her (although she did not know he had spiked it with drugs). The girl told prosecutors that while she did ask Polanski to stop, she did not fight back, scream, or try to flee.[2] The filmmaker claimed that he had had good reason to believe that the girl knew what she was doing sexually.

As infuriating as arguments in Polanski's defense may strike us now, they still had some force in 1978. Polanski was guilty, but he was about to receive the leniency given to so many men before him. His lawyers and prosecutors had agreed to a plea-bargain deal by which he would be spared prison. Judges normally honored these arrangements and, for a time, there was no reason to believe that Polanski's judge would stand in the way of the deal—but that was not to be. The judge reportedly decided to disregard the deal after he was shown recent pictures of Polanski partying in Munich with his arms around young girls. It was only after he signaled that he would impose jail time on Polanski or deport him that the director fled to France, where his citizenship protected him from extradition.

No one disputes that the legal climate has grown more intolerant since Polanski's 1978 flight to France, but when did sex with girls become sinister at all? Is sex with a fourteen-year-old girl in Germany, which is still legal, any worse than sex with a girl of the same age in California? As with everything involving sex and power, the answer is unclear.

THE QUESTION OF what age should be considered "underage" for sex was one of the most explosive issues in nineteenth-century sex law. As moral reformers in Europe and the United States sought to raise the age of consent, they pressed a number of hot social buttons, including the double standards applied to people of different races and classes, the sexual prerogatives of men, and the public health threats of the prostitution trade. Had Polanski been caught having sex with a thirteen-year-old in London in 1878, he would have been well in the clear. The traditional English age of consent, twelve, had recently been changed to thirteen, and only after a bruising fight in Parliament during which proposals to raise the age further were repeatedly struck down.

For English legislators, the idea of jailing men who took young girls for pleasure made no sense. For centuries, young girls—especially maids and preadolescent prostitutes from the lower classes—had been theirs for the taking. To criminalize this kind of sexual encounter, as a growing coalition of Christian and proto-feminist activists advocated, would be to rob Parliament's sons of their birthrights and open future generations to blackmail. As the House of Lords struggled in 1884 to decide whether or not to raise the age of consent to fourteen, one Lord appealed to his colleagues' loyalty to their own kind: "Very few of their Lordships . . . had not, when young men, been guilty of immorality." He went on to express the hope that they "would pause before passing a clause within the range of which their sons might come . . . the more they attempted to prevent the indulgence of natural passion, the more they would face unnatural crime." Pause the Lords did; the bill died.

Nothing could have infuriated the morality lobby more. Early feminists such as the evangelical Josephine Butler argued that retaining such a low age of consent condemned "a large section of female society" to lives of "administering to the irregularities of the excusable men." For Puritans such as the publisher Alfred Dyer, the purpose of law was to force everyone to do right, regardless of their rank or gender. Without laws requiring moral behavior, a just society was impossible. The failure of bill after bill to raise the age of consent and protect girls from exploitation revealed the entire country to be immoral at its core. Despite thousands of books, pamphlets, and petitions, and hundreds of public meetings calling for changes to the law, the social-purity lobby was unable to get Parliament to budge. For MPs, raising the age of consent to thirteen was bad enough. No amount of tiresome rabble-rousing could get them to legislate against their own sexual prerogatives, and by 1885 the English age of consent appeared to be stuck at that age (which was not significantly different than anywhere else in Europe). Unless something drastic happened, the chances of securing legislation to protect older girls from men's "irregularities" were dim at best.

Deliverance finally came that summer in the form of a massive publicity stunt known as the "Maiden Tribute of Modern Babylon" affair, which was orchestrated around a series of articles in the *Pall Mall Gazette*. The investigation—in which the *Gazette*'s editor, W. T. Stead, purchased a young girl in London and had her drugged and shipped off to France— caused such a popular outcry that Parliament had no choice but to take action. The main players of the "Maiden Tribute" affair were Josephine Butler, Salvation Army leader Catherine Booth, and Stead, who together formed a secret "commission" to investigate and expose London's trade in young girls. Stead was the right man for the muckraking end of the job: He had been moved to antivice activism by a recent encounter with two girls, aged seven and four, who had been repeatedly raped in fashionable London brothels. Because the girls were so young, English law disregarded any testimony they might have given against their attackers, so the men were safe from prosecution. (The girls were left in a shelter.) Stead then resolved to use his paper to "damn, and damn, and damn!" sexual predators until something was done.

The commission developed a fat dossier on cases of abused girls, but it had nothing conclusive or sensational enough to break the deadlock in Parliament. It decided to stage its own heartrending sex crime and then relentlessly publicize it to stir maximum outrage. Stead became a white slaver himself, and a nasty one at that. Butler introduced Stead to a former procuress, Elizabeth Jarrett, whom he browbeat into finding a suitable thirteen-year-old virgin. Jarrett put the word out on the street, and before long she found little Eliza Armstrong, whose mother was willing to do business. Jarrett paid the mother, and the girl was delivered to a boarding-house. There, Eliza was chloroformed and inspected by a crooked midwife to confirm that she was a virgin. Jarrett then took the girl to another house, where she was placed alone in a locked room. The door swung open and in walked Stead, disguised with a false moustache and enthusiastically playing the part of a lecherous old man. The drowsy girl cried out in terror, and

Jarrett rushed in to "rescue" her. Again, Eliza was inspected for proof of virginity (this time to protect Stead's own reputation), after which she was transported across the English Channel and delivered to the Paris chapter of the Salvation Army. The story had thus been made.

Neither Jarrett, Eliza, nor the girl's mother knew they were being used by Stead and the commission, but honest dealing was the last thing on the newspaperman's mind. He now had the goods to prove how easy it was to abduct, rape, and transport a girl to the Continent for further exploitation. On July 6–8, 1885, he published the three "Maiden Tribute" articles, using his own mistreatment of the girl (dubbed "Lily") to expose London's sexual "inferno" in the most shocking terms possible. By the publication of the third installment, riots erupted outside the *Gazette*'s London offices as people struggled to get copies. The paper's staff had to press desks and cabinets against the doors to keep out the stampede. By the end of the month, and despite the arrests of newsboys for trafficking in obscenity and the refusal of many newsstands to sell the paper, it had become Britain's journalistic sensation of the century. A later pamphlet version would sell 1.5 million copies.[3]

The "Maiden Tribute" series was not the only sexual-exploitation story in circulation, but it was the most masterfully stage-managed. Several days before the articles came out, Stead issued a "frank warning" to his readers, especially "all those who are squeamish . . . prudish . . . and all those who live in a fool's paradise of imaginary innocence . . . selfishly oblivious to the horrible realities," to stay away from his paper. Nothing could have sparked a better buzz. Butler's many antivice allies were also put on alert. "We want to make all possible use of the wave of indignation which will be aroused," Butler wrote to her confederates, "so I ask you all to be ready . . . I think the public will be greatly roused and we must take advantage of the awakened feeling." This turned out to be an understatement. The "Maiden Tribute" stories not only "exposed" a cruel dimension of the sex trade, they also attacked English society generally—especially the men whose money and sexual proclivities financed the commerce in young flesh:

> *London's lust annually uses up many thousands of women . . . If the daughters of the people must be served up as dainty morsels to the passions of the rich, let them at least attain an age when they can understand the nature of the sacrifice which they are asked to make. And if we must cast maidens . . . into the jaws of vice, let us at least see to it that they consent to their own immolation, and are not unwilling sacrifices procured by force or fraud.*

In column after column of frenzied prose, Stead concocted a number of mistruths. First, his claim that "many thousands of women" were being "killed and done away with" in the white slave trade was untrue, and the abduction of "Lily" was not, as Stead had portrayed it, the result of a cruel mother "indifferent to anything but drink" (the mother later testified in court that she had believed she was providing Eliza with a job in domestic service). Most importantly, nowhere in the "Maiden Tribute" articles did Stead ever mention that it was he who hired a procuress to find the girl, drugged and repeatedly "inspected" Eliza, and terrorized her out of her wits. Rather, he allowed that he "can personally vouch for the accuracy of every fact in the narrative."

Stead's fraud was discovered, but not before a stunned Parliament was goaded into action. On July 9, just one day after the stories were published, a bill to raise the age of consent was reintroduced. By July 30, the Salvation Army had delivered a petition to the House of Commons in the form of a 2.5-mile-long scroll bearing three hundred and ninety-three thousand signatures. Lest anyone fail to pay attention, the document was brought to the Commons in a carriage drawn by white horses, accompanied by a fifty-piece brass band and hundreds of Salvation Army officers. In a matter of days, the law changed. Under the 1885 Criminal Law Amendment Act, the age of consent was raised to sixteen. A number of penalties for indecent assault were also put into place, and for the first time it became illegal to procure *any* woman, regardless of age, for the purposes of prostitution.

Stead's crusade and especially his methods earned him no shortage of enemies. Before long he would stand trial under the very abduction laws he had helped to bring about. Eliza Armstrong was still missing when the "Maiden Tribute" articles came out. Her mother soon made the connection between her daughter and the ill-fated "Lily," and asked local authorities to help find her daughter. The whole scheme unraveled quickly, and Eliza was returned to her parents about two months after her abduction. Stead was quickly transformed from master reformer to public scoundrel, as hostile crowds surged around his home and the courthouse, hanging wax effigies of him from trees. Jeering mobs also hurled abuse at his wife. Stead's defense—that he had taken Eliza based only on pure motives—was dismissed by the court as irrelevant. He served three months in jail.

The judge who sentenced Stead said he was a "disgrace to journalism" for releasing a deluge of "filth which I fear tainted the minds of the children you were so anxious to protect." Maybe so, but after the affair died down Stead reemerged as a worldwide hero, especially to antivice reformers in the United States. In the decade following the "Maiden Tribute" scandal, thirty-five U.S. state legislatures raised their age of consent. (California raised its own to sixteen in 1897.) However, the justice handed out in court is very different from that written in the statehouse. Regardless of the new laws on the books, both judges and juries had a hard time accepting that men should be penalized for having sex with girls, especially when they saw signs that the girls either "wanted it" or were looking to make money off a lawsuit.[4]

BY THE EARLY twentieth century, New York law stated that men who had sex with girls under eighteen should be sentenced to a maximum of ten years' jail time, regardless of whether the girls had consented. This "zero tolerance" message from the legislature was clear enough, but the courts did not want to let girls off that easily. In 1933, an appellate panel ruled that underage girls could still be found at fault if there was a suspicion that they had wanted the sex to take place. In the case that led to this decision, a fifteen-year-old girl had convinced a jury to award her $3,000 against a bus driver who had raped her while she was a passenger. The higher court threw the case out. To the appellate judges, it was one thing to jail men for taking girls by force, and quite another to "reward" girls for "enticing" men and then suing them. If that was allowed, they said, "we should unwarily put it in the power of the female sex to become seducers in their turn."[5] Translation: All girls are potential "seducers," and if a man feels he has been enticed, the girl will be made to pay the price.

North Dakota's courts went even further, holding in 1932 that an underage girl could still be charged with criminal fornication even in cases of statutory rape. The case in question involved a roll in the hay between an underage farm girl and a neighbor boy. The girl became pregnant, but the baby died a week after being born. The girl's father sued the boy's father for the costs of the pregnancy and the "lost services" of his daughter while she was laid up. Again, the case was thrown out. According to the North Dakota Supreme Court, "she is guilty of violating the law even though she be under the age of consent . . . It is not possible to regard her as legally innocent."[6] In Depression-era North Dakota, then, one could be a rape victim and a criminal delinquent at the same time.

It was impossible for many to accept that females would not have wanted sex with the men who took them, or at least would not want to profit from it. Back in England, during the same summer of 1885 when Stead's "Maiden Tribute" articles caused such a fuss, a nine-year-old errand girl testified in court that she had been forcibly raped by a middle-aged man. Using an old courtroom tactic, the defendant's attorney directed the inquiry away from the man's actions and toward the little girl's moral character. The judge threw the case out after the girl admitted in court "that she had been complained of for her forward manners." The judge observed that the charge "was one of those which might be made with the most terrible facility against men by little girls of unclean imagination." So much for protecting society's most vulnerable citizens.

Courts were often no more sympathetic to boys who had been sexually assaulted, especially when class issues were involved. A guilty verdict was certain to damage a respectable man's reputation, which was seen as a far worse result than the ruin of a common child. In 1870, a wealthy gentleman was accused of indecently assaulting a fifteen-year-old boy, who claimed that the man had plied him with wine, taken sexual liberties, and then paid the boy to keep his mouth shut. For the case to go away, the defendant merely had to ask the court: "Good God, do you intend to take me on the boy's statement?" Ten years later, a barrister's clerk (a position of some status then) was charged with sexually assaulting a common boy who lived in a lodging house. After a string of lawyers lined up in court in support of the clerk, the jury found in his favor. Jurors even extended their sympathies to the man in his time of distress.[7]

AN INDIAN CHALLENGE

The debate over the age of consent roiling England was built on the assumption that underage victims of sexual assault were "daughters of the people"—that is, that they were homegrown and therefore worth protecting. Had the "Lily" of the "Maiden Tribute" articles not been an English lass, the story would never have resonated with the public as it did. There would have been no riots and no inquiries or lawsuits, and the law would have remained unchanged for at least some time.

Neither Stead nor many of the other English sex-law reformers gave a damn about the millions of girls under British rule in India, even the ones taken daily as child brides. Everyone applied different standards where the colonies were concerned. The idea of imposing an age of consent of sixteen on India, in line with England's new law, never came up. In fact, the age was only raised to twelve (from ten) in 1891, after a furious debate and the well-publicized travails of a "Hindoo lady" named Rukhmabai, who was sued in Bombay for refusing to submit to a marriage forced on her as a child. The trials of this media-savvy woman, and the intense publicity her case received worldwide, showed the difficulties of applying English sexual standards in the colonies. In this case, British support for a low age of consent for Indian girls was tied to its efforts to hold on to its most prized foreign possession.

Rukhmabai, the daughter of an educated Hindu family, had been married off to Dadaji Bhikaji (variously described in the press as "ignorant," "idle," a "boor," and a "coolie") in 1876, when she was eleven and he nineteen. The marriage was never consummated, and she remained with her stepfather until 1884, when Dadaji demanded that she come to live with him. Bucking thousands of years of tradition, she refused. He then went to the Bombay High Court to get an order forcing her to comply. Dadaji lost the first stage of the case, when the British judge ruled that there was no marriage because there had been no sex, and because his claim for "restitution of conjugal relations" had no root in Hindu law. Dadaji appealed and won; the higher court found that while native law didn't approve such a suit, it didn't forbid it either. Rukhmabai was ordered to go to her husband, or to jail for six months. Her stepfather then paid Dadaji two thousand rupees to drop his suit, after which Rukhmabai traveled to England to study medicine and become a physician. She eventually returned to India to head up a women's dispensary.

The case was picked up in midstream by the *London Times* and immediately became a political and media football. Everyone had an opinion. Not only were Rukhmabai's stream of letters about her case and the dark fate of Indian child brides generally published and intensely discussed, but so were the opinions of Hindu nationalists, marriage-law reform advocates, and various members of the British ruling class. The controversy tied the bodies of Hindu girls to the stability of British

A HINDU WEDDING

· · ·

In the late nineteenth century, the age at which a girl could legally consent to sexual relations was a contentious question in England and the United States. The issue put male upper-class sexual prerogatives against popular fears of young girls being sold into "white slavery." The age-of-consent issue was also at the center of a major legal case in India, where a "Hindoo" girl refused to submit to a marriage forced on her as a child. The case, which was followed closely by newspapers in England, resulted in the Indian age of consent being raised from ten to twelve. ©THE TRUSTEES OF
THE BRITISH MUSEUM

rule in India. To Rukhmabai, the issue was inequality: Indian girls were being sacrificed to a system that robbed them of an education and personal freedom. Given that "there is not the smallest chance" that Indians would change their "abominable customs" on their own, she agitated for the British government to step in and raise the legal age of marriage. Rukhmabai's views were not shared by Indian nationalists, who regarded British tampering with local marriage practices as an assault on Indian pride. Britain had earlier pledged not to interfere with local religious practices, and in their opinion Rukhmabai's troubles were no cause to reverse that policy.

British opinion on the Rukhmabai case was divided. Even as the British viceroy cabled messages to his colleagues that "it would never do to allow her to be put into prison," a British ex-judge in India opined in a letter to the *Times* that "in Eastern climates girls are precocious, and, unless early settled in her home, the girl is almost certain to disgrace her family." He went on to observe that the "real mistake was educating [Rukhmabai] so as to make her unfit company for her husband." On balance, the Rukhmabai affair probably hardened English resistance to Indian self-rule. If Indian men could not manage their domestic lives better than this, the thinking went, then they had no business taking on the more subtle challenges of statecraft.

Then another story came along that changed minds. In 1890, the British media reported that an eleven-year-old Indian bride named Phulmonee had been literally "raped to death" by her thirty-five-year-old husband. This case had the requisite blood and guts to give reformers what they needed to convince the colonial government to take action. Under a new law, girls could still marry as young as ten, but consummation would have to wait for two years. The law was a victory for reformers, but whether or not it was ever seriously enforced is another question. Hindu nationalists continued to mount intense resistance, resentful of what they saw as top-down interference in the life of their country.

Returning for a moment to Roman Polanski: While he was fighting for his freedom in California in 1977, loud and influential voices in France were agitating to *lower* that country's age of consent from fifteen to thirteen. At the time, several men were in custody for having sex with thirteen- and fourteen-year-old boys and girls. Intellectual heavyweights Jean-Paul Sartre and Simone de Beauvoir, Médecins Sans Frontières cofounder and later foreign minister Bernard Kouchner, and Jack Lang, later minister of culture and (still later) education, all described the arrests, and the age of consent law under which they were made, as scandalous. The law did not change, but Polanski nevertheless found a safe haven in Paris.[8]

THE SCIENTIFIC RESPONSE TO PROSTITUTION

Nowhere has science (quack and otherwise) been more mixed up with morals law than with regard to prostitution. In the Middle Ages and the Renaissance, prostitution was tolerated because brothels were seen as public sanitation facilities—in effect, disposal units for sexual sin. No less a moral force than Saint Thomas Aquinas likened whorehouses to cesspools in a palace: "Take away the cesspool," he warned, "and the palace will become an unclean and evil-smelling place." Prostitutes themselves were damned, but they served an important purpose. Rather than taking a boy for pleasure or wrecking the honor of decent women, sexually restless men deposited their shameful desires into those whose bodies were for sale, leaving the rest of female society unstained. Better that a few prostitutes be infected with sin and descend to hell than everyone else, and better that brothels should be owned by the state and the church than to let the profits go to private operators.

By the nineteenth century, those perceptions had changed completely. The intolerance of the Reformation and Counter-Reformation left authorities with little room to permit, much less participate in, the flesh trade. Intense outbreaks of venereal diseases (primarily syphilis), especially among military troops, also changed public perceptions of prostitutes. No longer were they viewed as lockboxes for vice and infection, but as the *sources* of disease—distributors of contagion into respectable society. Unlike as in earlier periods, when authorities had tried to eradicate prostitution completely, governments and police took a new approach. The question was not whether prostitutes could be wiped away—everyone agreed that was never going to happen—but how to contain the health hazards they posed. In Europe, and for a brief moment in the United States, that meant legalizing them by various degrees and subjecting them to punishing medical inspections.

That these efforts were hypocritical is an understatement. Male customers (who were no less likely to be carrying venereal diseases) were never targets of government public-health regulation. The focus was on lower-class females. On nothing more than an anonymous tip from a neighbor, a poor girl or woman could be officially labeled a whore and subjected to humiliating (and often infectious) medical exams while her customers faced no risk. This double standard, by which male promiscuity was treated as a normal impulse and female prostitution a public health hazard, was an accepted fact of life. Also seen as natural, at least by lawmakers, was the fact that poor and working-class females, who made up the bulk of the prostitute population, should bear the brunt of official torment. Good women were passive, with no sexual needs; the bad ones were sexually aggressive. The law was there to protect men from the women men paid to service them.

France was the first country to institute a comprehensive state regulation system after its soldiers returned infected from the Napoleonic wars. All females suspected of prostitution—which included girls as young as ten—were required to register themselves and submit to periodic medical exams, for which they were charged. The inspections were savage and the treatments poor. The cold, filthy metal instruments used by police doctors probably resulted in the transmission of a variety of harmful infections. Any female who was found to be carrying venereal disease (or who could not pay the doctor to write up good results) was incarcerated in a grim hospital for treatment. Women who plied their trade without being registered were to be jailed.

The French system was broadly copied throughout Europe, but it did little to slow the spread of sexually transmitted diseases. Men remained outside the system, and thousands of prostitutes evaded inspection. By 1870, there were at least as many unregistered prostitutes operating in France, Belgium, Russia, Poland, and Italy as there were on the official lists. The proximity of government bureaucrats to a trade that was still in the legal shadows also begged for corruption: The bribing of police, doctors, and judges was commonplace. Police protected well-paying brothel-keepers and came down hard on freelance streetwalkers. Townspeople also made secret accusations against neighbors they disliked, resulting in police dragging the accused women through the streets to be registered and inspected. In Warsaw in the 1880s, police detained and examined four thousand to five thousand women every year, but only about seven hundred to twelve hundred ended up on the lists. The rest were simply women caught in the wrong place and time.

In Prussian Berlin, three months in jail awaited both unregistered prostitutes and those on the list who infected their customers. As everywhere, the burden fell on the women, and those unlucky enough to find themselves on the list had to undergo (in the words of opponents of the French system) "instrument rapes" every week. Additionally, registered prostitutes were obliged to let police into their houses at any time, and were banned from theaters, schools, and other places where respectable people gathered. There were penalties on the books for clients who passed diseases on to the women they paid, but the charge was impossible to prove. Any man so accused could simply ask: "How do you know it was me?"

The Berlin system invited abuses, but at least it stuck to the goal of disease prevention. The scheme in Vienna, on the other hand, was more nuanced and misogynistic. Many there held to the "scientific" view that females were prone to irrationality and were weak in the face of their carnal needs. Women with honor overcame this by limiting their sexual activity to the dry business of producing legitimate children, but their reputations could be lost whenever they displayed sexual desire. According to an 1851 police policy statement, every woman in the city with an active sex life was a potential whore and a threat to public morals. The statement broke prostitutes down as follows:

1. *Normal prostitutes, who made their living by selling sex for money;*

2. *Occasional prostitutes . . . who had sex with men with no expectation of money, presents or lasting relationships;*

3. *Mistresses;*

4. *Concubines.*

That did not leave many women out. By the end of the century, police estimated that thirty thousand to fifty thousand Viennese women fit into one of the above categories, but only about two thousand were under medical control. All female prisoners, regardless of whether or not they had been jailed for morals offenses, were put on the list, but that still was not nearly sufficient to remedy the discrepancy. Police therefore started a bizarre hunt for "hidden prostitutes," in which most women in the metropolis were at least potential targets. The police used agents provocateurs to flirt with women in the streets. If the women responded with interest, they were arrested, jailed, and put on the list. Additionally, anyone with a bone to pick with his or her neighbors was invited to make accusations.

On one occasion, a "young girl" was reported by her neighbors for leaving her house in "striking" clothes and coming home late. The girl was taken to court, where it was revealed that she had once had an older lover. She went on the list. Another girl who had been anonymously accused of secret prostitution had the support of all her neighbors, but that did little good. When the caretaker of her house defended her in court, the police threatened to arrest him. The girl was put in jail for two days. Men who received women in their homes were also questioned, though they were never arrested for consorting with prostitutes. One man complained that police had demanded to know the names and addresses of all the women who had visited his apartment. When he refused, he was told he would be brought to court for questioning.[9]

ENGLAND: THE BIG TEST

The sleepy members of the House of Commons can be excused for not having paid much attention to the last item of official business late one night in June 1864. The legislation, called the Contagious Diseases Act (CDA), seemed like one of a series of recent measures aimed at preventing illness among cattle. The bill was read without debate and became law on July 29. Although the CDA was passed quietly enough, it would soon set off a noisy twenty-year national debate that galvanized Britain's early feminist movement, energized the careers of muckraking journalists, and focused the world's attention on the different sexual standards the United Kingdom applied to its men and women. For the first time ever, Britain had a law establishing state regulation of prostitution.

During the first few years of its existence, the CDA seemed like a reasonable tool for improving public health. British troops had returned from the Crimean War in sorry shape. More of them had died in the hospital than on the battlefield, and one out of three soldiers had a sexually transmitted disease. The problem was especially bad in the port and garrison towns, where returning troops and sailors had only one thing on their minds. Said one admiral:

Let those who have never seen a ship of war picture to themselves
a very large and very low room with 500 men and probably 300

or 400 women of the vilest description shut up in it, and giving
way to every excess of debauchery that the greatest passions of
human nature can lead them to, and they see the deck of a gun
ship upon the night of her arrival in port.

There were efforts to raise the moral character of soldiers, but they
were as ineffective as might be expected—especially as enlisted men were
forbidden from marrying. Efforts to enforce the compulsory inspection of
soldiers for venereal disease had been abandoned in 1859 because officers
feared a backlash from their men. The logical alternative was to focus on
the prostitutes who serviced soldiers and sailors, which is what the CDA
set out to do.

Under the CDA, police in eleven military towns could force the inspection and treatment of any women they suspected of being diseased prostitutes. If the women refused, they were taken before a magistrate who could
lock them in hospitals for three months. In 1869, five additional districts
had been added, "detention" times increased, and police powers expanded
to make sure that more women were put through the system. The police
were allowed to take aggressive measures to enforce the law, in no small
part because the law was so vague. The key word in the legislation, "prostitute," was nowhere defined. As abuses mounted, it became clear that
almost any woman could be processed as a prostitute, with all the shame
that entailed. As on the Continent, police began to blackmail and intimi-
date innocents as well as streetwalkers. Moreover, once a woman was put
on the list, only a magistrate's order could get it removed. For the unedu-
cated and the poor, this was almost impossible to accomplish.

In a very short time, the British government had marshaled its regula-
tory power as a forceful weapon against lower-class women. The soldiers
and sailors who used registered prostitutes could take some comfort that
they were bedding down with women with "clean" bills of health, but that

goal was soon obscured as droves of innocent women found themselves ensnared in a system that robbed them of their freedom and reputations.

On New Year's Day 1870, the *Daily News* published a letter signed by 140 women, including Josephine Butler and the beloved Florence Nightingale, that attacked the laws on a number of fronts: The CDA condoned the ill-treatment of women while benefiting men, the letter argued; it created state-sanctioned vice; and it was a threat to civil liberties in that excessive powers were granted to police, doctors, and magistrates. The document was the start of a heated, melodramatic conflict that would take another fifteen years to resolve.

Opponents to the CDA were first dismissed as a collection of female cranks and religious zealots, but eventually they gained steam and, in the course of hundreds of demonstrations, publications, and even street battles, grew into a formidable voice for the repeal of the act. The fight was not easy. CDA proponents were every bit as driven as their nemeses. CDA supporters believed it was indecent for women to speak out about sex and state governance at all, much less try to influence legislation. Tempers rose. The deeply religious Butler was no feminist revolutionary (she had formally asked her husband's permission before taking up the anti-CDA case), but even her religious bona fides did not shield her from violent attack. In 1870, Butler and other repeal advocates spoke out against Henry Storks, a pro-CDA candidate running for office in the military town of Colchester. Butler's group distributed handbills accusing Storks of endorsing a plan to haul in military wives for humiliating inspections. In response, Storks's support base (which included brothel-keepers and hired toughs) formed a mob and gave a solid thrashing to Butler's preferred candidate. Later that night, the crowd surrounded Butler's hotel and threatened to set it on fire. She escaped out the back door and hid among the food stocks of a sympathetic grocer. During an election a couple of years later in Pontefract, while Butler led a women's meeting in a hayloft, a gang of paid hooligans set the barn afire. Local police did nothing—Butler and her colleagues escaped

In the nineteenth century, England's dockside prostitutes
became the focus of government efforts to control venereal
diseases. In a series of laws called the Contagious Diseases
Act, women could be forced to undergo cruel inspections
and treatments if they were suspected of being prostitutes.
If the women refused, they were subject to imprisonment.
The corruption and abuses the laws engendered, especially
against lower-class women, galvanized England's early
feminist movement. ©THE TRUSTEES OF THE BRITISH MUSEUM

being burned alive by jumping through a trapdoor. Her reaction to the attack was telling: "It was not so much the personal violence that we feared as what would have been to any of us *worse than death*; for the indecencies of the men, their gestures, and threats, were what I prefer not to describe" (italics original). For Butler, the immorality of prostitution was nothing next to the "indecencies" of her opponents.

In their journals and pamphlets, the pro-repealers told story after heartbreaking story of girls destroyed by the CDA. One pamphlet spoke of a cabaret singer so tormented by police she threw herself into a canal and drowned. To the police, the case was one of simply another dead whore; to the anti-CDA agitators, the girl was one more of God's children broken on the wheel of an unjust law. At public meetings, the blunt instruments used in medical inspections were displayed to horrified audiences. Women both virtuous and fallen gave witness to what they had endured:

It is awful work; the attitude they push us into first is so disgusting and so painful, and then those monstrous instruments—often they use several. They seem to tear the passage open first with their hands, and examine us, and then they thrust in instruments, and they pull them out and push them in, and they turn and twist them about; and if you cry out they stifle you . . .

BUTLER ALSO WENT for the jugular of hypocritical government officers. She trumpeted the case of one "unfortunate" woman committed to prison by a magistrate. "It did seem hard, ma'am," the prostitute said, "that the Magistrate on the bench who gave the casting vote for my imprisonment had paid me several shillings a day or two before, in the street, to go with him."

By 1883, with the help of accumulating data that the CDA was failing to stop the spread of disease, the pro-repealers managed to convince Parliament to suspend compulsory inspections. However, the laws remained on the books, and the battle was far from won. It must be remembered that this issue was being played out at the same time as the age-of-consent drama was unfolding. This Parliament was the same body that had recently *rejected* a proposal raising the age of consent to fourteen. For parliamentarians, any changes to the rules of sexual behavior, especially those that went against their prerogatives to choose any female they wanted, were unacceptable.

By 1885, the issues of CDA repeal, age of consent, and white slavery had become intertwined and doomed to legislative Siberia. There was even a possibility the CDA would be reactivated and extended. It took the convulsive scandals triggered by W. T. Stead's "Maiden Tribute" articles to push Parliament not only to raise the age of consent but also to repeal the CDA the following year. Anti-CDA activists were bothered by Stead's methods, but they liked the results. Britain had finally gone out of the legalized prostitution business.[10]

THE AMERICAN RESPONSE

American society in the nineteenth century was defined by the multitudes of immigrants spilling onto its shores, whether Chinese laborers in the West or the boatloads of poor Europeans filling New York City's tenements. The first waves of immigrants were often young men who worked for years in isolation while saving to bring their loved ones over. In the meantime, many sought the solace of prostitutes. On the California frontier, men outnumbered women fifty or a hundred to one during the early years of the Gold Rush, which made life busy for women working the sex trade. Daily shipments of prostitutes sailed to San Francisco from Latin America. In 1849, Patrick Dillon, later the French consul in San Francisco, observed that "weeks never pass that some Chilean or American brig loaded by speculators does not discharge here a cargo of women. This sort of traffic is, they assure me, that which produces at the time the most prompt profits." Many of the women stayed to work in brothels on the Barbary Coast, but others went on to the mining camps where they adopted names like "Kittie," "Wicked Alice," and "Little Gold Dollar." (One Wichita prostitute called herself "Squirrel-Tooth Alice.")

Immigrant men were not the only patrons of prostitutes in the United States, of course, but foreign-born women did make up a big part of the sex-worker population. More than half of mid-century prostitutes in New York, for example, came from Ireland and Germany, the two countries supplying the most immigrants at the time. The demand for commercial sex was inexhaustible, and for unsupervised factory girls living in board-inghouses the temptation to make extra money was strong. By 1858 there were an estimated 7,860 prostitutes in New York City alone—one for every 117 people. Hundreds of brothels and saloons with back rooms blanketed the city, each catering to men of particular income levels and tastes. Cigar stores commonly served as fronts for whorehouses, in which the salesgirls were the establishments' true merchandise. Theaters also served as tryst-ing places. As the house lights were always kept on during performances, everyone could see what everyone else was doing—and there was a lot to see. No one kept still or quiet even in the most respectable theaters, and as audiences hooted and threw food onto the stage, prostitutes serviced clients in the galleries.

Criminality always follows the prostitution trade, and in the United States a visit to a prostitute was a risky affair. Customers in lower-end establishments were often beaten, blackmailed, or simply robbed. Houses were equipped with sliding panels that allowed hands to appear and take customers' wallets while they were occupied. If a client was well-to-do, the woman's fake husband or brother would sometimes storm in and demand money. Any man appearing out of place in a low-end brothel could expect to be roughed up, if not attacked, but while customers took their chances, it was the prostitutes themselves who bore the greatest risks. Chinese women working in the famous cribs of San Francisco were no better off than slaves and were often worked until illness and exhaustion killed them. An 1869 story from the *San Francisco Chronicle* described Cooper Alley, the last stop for many:

> *The place is loathsome in the extreme. On one side is a shelf four feet wide and about a yard above the dirty floor, upon which there are two old rice mats. There is not the first suggestion of furniture in the room . . . When any of the unfortunate harlots is no longer useful and a Chinese physician passes his opinion that her disease is incurable, she is notified that she must die. Led by night to this hole of a "hospital," she is forced within the door and made to lie down upon the shelf. A cup of water, another of boiled rice, and a little metal oil lamp are placed by her side. Those who have immediate charge of the establishment know how long the oil should last, and when that the limit is reached, they return to the hospital, unbar the door and enter. Generally the woman is dead, either by starvation or by her own hand; but sometimes life is not extinct; the spark yet remains when the "doctors" enter, yet this makes little difference to them. They come for a corpse and never go away without it.*

Working conditions for upper-class hookers were better, but the law still placed little value on their lives. In 1836, a beautiful young New York prostitute named Helen Jewett was bludgeoned to death, most likely by the nineteen-year-old socialite Richard Robinson, whose cloak and hatchet were found with her body in a luxurious brothel. Robinson was arrested that day and put on trial for her murder, but he was never really at risk of punishment. Despite the strength of the circumstantial evidence—he was a regular customer of the brothel, and was served champagne in Jewett's chamber not long before she was found dead—Robinson was acquitted. Most of the testimony came from other prostitutes, and was thus easily disregarded by the jury.

The trial was heavily covered by the penny press and became a topic in the growing national discussion about what to do with "fallen" women and the men who used them. One loud urban missionary, John R. McDowall, focused his efforts on the "silly and inexperienced youth" who visited "these infatuating furies." Neither McDowall nor his publications would have been noticed much had he not voiced his intention to identify men and boys who visited prostitutes, whom he called "the companions of the polluted." He also threatened to name men who profited by investing in the sex trade. Ironically, he was brought down on charges of doing exactly what he fought hardest against: A grand jury found that McDowall's newspaper was "calculated to promote lewdness," and soon he was convicted of corrupting public morals and committing other acts "too bad to name."

The first serious effort to control prostitution in the United States was initiated in 1870, when the city of St. Louis passed a "Social Evil Ordinance" based on the European model of weekly health inspections. Prostitutes found to be infected were to be locked up until a doctor could certify their cure. The plan caused an immediate uproar. Moralists attacked what they saw as official approval of prostitution, while feminists objected to the intrusiveness and violence of the inspections. One protestor, Frances Willard, had been to Paris and warned that St. Louis would end up like the French capital, where black-shrouded wagons ferried prostitutes to their examinations: "Those awful wagons seemed to me . . . the most heart-breaking procession that ever Christian woman watched." The Social Evil Ordinance was repealed after one hundred thousand people signed a petition against it in 1874. (Those ushering the massive document into the Missouri legislature were flanked by young girls in white gowns.)

Other U.S. cities considered similar ordinances, but the issue died after the problems in St. Louis and the well-publicized repeal of the CDA in the United Kingdom. From that point forward, urban red-light districts were often tolerated, but were always illegal and subject to police raids. As everywhere, prostitutes were blamed for the spread of venereal disease, especially those who came from "degenerate racial stocks." Doctors and politicians alike characterized sex-trade zones as "venereal swamps" where immigrant women spread sexual infection. None of the warnings to stay away interrupted the flow of customers into the brothels, but the ethnicity of prostitutes was often figured into their prices. For example, the San Francisco brothel run by Nell Kimball had a price sheet that read, as she later recalled: "Two bits for Mexican, Nigrah, Chinese or Japanese asked 50 cents. French asked 75 cents, and the American Yankee was $1.00." (A Nevada hooker named "Big Matilda" promoted herself as "300lbs. of Black Passion," and priced her availability at 50 cents for one hour or three hours for $1.)[11]

Chinese women, especially prostitutes, were targets of some of the United States' worst racial xenophobia. They were thought to carry deadly germs, sexually transmitted and otherwise, to which they were immune but the white population was not. This view was not confined to a racist fringe. The American Medical Association studied whether or not Chinese prostitutes were poisoning the American bloodstream. A doctor's report to Congress warned: "[T]he virus of the cooly, in my opinion, is almost sure death to the white man. That is my opinion because I have seen it. There are cases of syphilis among the whites that originated from these Chinese prostitutes that are incurable."

In 1865, the city of San Francisco passed an "Order to Remove Chinese Houses of Ill-Fame Within City Limits," and the following year California enacted "An Act for the Suppression of Chinese Houses of Ill-Fame." These laws were, in equal measure, the product of quack science and the visceral hatred Californians nursed for Chinese laborers—but their geographical reach was limited. That changed in 1875, when Congress passed the Page Act, which barred entry into the United States of all Asian women brought for "lewd and immoral purposes." The act theoretically allowed genuine Chinese wives to immigrate while keeping out only sex workers, but in application it barred almost all Chinese women from entering the country. Out of 39,579 Chinese who entered the United States in 1882, for example, only 136 were women.

Before Chinese women could be admitted, the Page Act required that they undergo a grueling evaluation process both in China and at port in the United States, which was skewed toward showing that they were coming for immoral purposes. Long interrogations were routine, photographs were taken, and examinations were conducted for "clues" to the women's immorality in their bodies and clothing. A negative report on any of these factors was taken as a sign of a woman's intention to work in the sex trade. Ironically, the shutoff of Chinese female immigration in the wake of the Page Act made it that much more difficult for Chinese men to find wives—so prostitution geared toward Chinese population increased. It would take about seventy years for the immigration authorities to allow an appropriate gender balance among Chinese Americans.

IMMIGRANTS AND DESPISED minorities, particularly Jews, were also blamed in the white slavery panic that swept the United States just after the turn of the twentieth century. Unlike the "Maiden Tribute" furor in Britain, where the villains were Englishmen accused of exploiting native girls and exporting them to the Continent, the white slavers feared in the United States were foreigners. The panic was sparked by a 1909 exposé in *McClure's* magazine, which accused immigrant Jewish "scum" (among other groups) of "cruising" the American heartland looking for innocent girls and then plucking them up for deposit into a "closely organized machine" of sin from which there was no escape. The two articles described girls smoking opium, drinking, and shrieking from their makeshift urban prisons: "My God, if only I could get out of here!" Who, *McClure's* asked, allowed this horrid business to continue? The answer was corrupt city political machines such as New York's Democratic Party organization, known as Tammany Hall, which the magazine accused of protecting prostitution rings and skimming profits.

The *McClure's* articles were as sensational as the "Maiden Tribute" series had been in Britain. Shortly thereafter, President William Howard Taft started giving speeches about "the urgent necessity for additional legislation and greater executive activity to suppress" the trade. In the bundles of literature that amplified the general alarm, the responsible parties were repeatedly characterized as foreign, particularly "Jew traders" and "typical Jew pimps," the "outcast filth" who fed corruption and immorality in the cities. The legislative result of the panic was the Mann Act of 1910, a measure its sponsors said was necessary for a trade "more horrible than any black-slave traffic ever was" to flourish. The law created a new form of criminal: one who "knowingly transport[s] in interstate commerce . . . any woman or girl for the purpose of prostitution or debauchery, or for any other *immoral purpose*, or with the intent . . . to induce, entice, or compel" any female to do something immoral (italics added).

The law could not have had a broader reach. The phrase "immoral purpose" covered much more than white-slave traffic, which was never widespread in any case. For example, the prizefighter Jack Johnson angered many when he became the first black heavyweight boxing champion in 1908. That victory led to a search for a "Great White Hope" who could defeat him. Two years later, in a match called "The Battle of the Century," Johnson beat Jim Jeffries, a white former champion who had been coaxed out of retirement. Deadly riots ensued, and Johnson was arrested and convicted under the Mann Act for his multistate relations with a white woman. As crowds shouted for a lynching, and after the Chicago district attorney called for a tough sentence "to set an example to Johnson's race," the boxer fled the country. He returned in 1920 to serve a yearlong prison term.[12]

STERILIZATION, CASTRATION,
AND THE CURE FOR SOCIETY'S ILLS

Starting in about 1850 and continuing for well over a century, American physicians lawfully and forcibly sterilized about sixty-three thousand people. The goal was preventing crime and improving the human race by removing the criminal and the weak from the reproductive pool. By the turn of the twentieth century, two-thirds of U.S. states had passed laws authorizing the sterilization of a wide variety of society's outcasts, including criminals, the mentally challenged, and chronic masturbators.

In some ancient societies, as we have seen, sexual violence was used as punishment—recall the Egyptian violators of property markers who were forced to deliver their wives and children to be raped by donkeys, or the Romans and Greeks sentenced to endure the insertion of objects in their anus for having sex with other men's wives. In the United States, the thinking was reversed: The answer to wrongdoing was not to force sex on offenders but to desexualize them entirely. From the beginning, the sterilization movement advocated that deactivating the sexual functions of the unfit served the greater good.

"Like begets like," wrote Gideon Lincecum, a Texas doctor who was one of the first to agitate for forced-sterilization laws. "To have good, honest citizens, fair acting, truthful men and women, they must be bred right. To breed them right we must have good breeders and to procure these the knife is the only possible chance." The idea resonated in Texas: Doctors there practiced sterilization even before the law formally permitted it. In 1864, after a Texas jury found a black man guilty of rape, the trial judge sentenced him to "suffer the penalty of emasculation." In several other states, doctors began to forcibly sterilize prison inmates and mental-health patients. For example, a panoply of new mental disorders found in women—grouped together as "hysteria"—were traced (falsely) to malfunctioning reproductive systems and treated with hysterectomies. The same procedure was used on a Tennessee woman diagnosed with "sapphism" (i.e., lesbianism) who had cut her female lover's throat.

Sterilization was also forced on mental patients who were plagued by the compulsive urge to masturbate. As we have already seen, masturbation had been classified as a dangerous mental disorder at least since the 1760 publication of Samuel Tissot's seminal treatise, *L'Onanisme*. However, the cures were far more dangerous than the "sickness." Between 1893 and 1898, doctors at one Kansas mental asylum severed the testicles of forty-four masturbating male inmates and performed hysterectomies on fourteen self-abusing females. Said one Ohio doctor at about the same time: "That insanity exercises a peculiar influence on the sexual organs of women there can be no doubt. This can also be said of insanity in men."

Across the Atlantic, a French surgeon in 1864 reported a procedure he used to halt a five-year-old girl's "deplorable habit" of touching her clitoris. The doctor sewed the girl's labia shut, leaving only a tiny opening for urine and, eventually, menstrual fluid to pass. In this way, "the clitoris is placed out of all reach" and the need for a clitoridectomy was avoided. The doctor's colleagues were not convinced, though. "In one way or another, the child will continue her vicious behavior," said one surgeon, although even that doctor allowed that masturbating boys did not always need to be castrated. In one case, the doctor cauterized a young boy's penis for an entire year, with an admitted "persistency that was almost cruel." The irritation to the penis was "sufficiently painful to render any touch impossible," he said, which forced the boy to direct his attention away from self-gratification. "Today, the young boy is a young man who thanks me for my tenacity," he boasted.

In the period following the American Civil War, many U.S. doctors advocated castration as a response to sex crimes by black males. In a 1906 speech to the Medical Society of Virginia, a doctor named Jesse Ewell announced that forty years after the emancipation of African Americans from slavery, the "negro . . . has retrograded physically, morally and mentally." Ewell called on the Virginia legislature to empower doctors to "protect our loved ones" by castrating black men who sexually assaulted white women.

Ewell was not alone. No less a mainstream voice in American jurisprudence than *The Yale Law Journal* argued, in 1899, for the castration of black rapists, whose sexual assaults, it said, were a "daily terror" to Southern women and caused "uneasiness" to their "Northern sisters." Without questioning the fear and racism that motivated the many lynchings of black men taking place at the time, the article concluded that the violence was "caused" by sexual assaults perpetrated by these "ruffians." It also advocated the castration of "imbeciles," "paupers," and "feeble-minded" children, whom it called "the progeny of a worthless stock." Only castration, opined the anonymous author, could simultaneously prevent sex crimes and end the family lines of people who were "misusing the earth" by existing.

Castration as punishment was not new to the United States. Men of color accused of sexually assaulting white women had been mutilated and castrated for many years. Virginia castrated more than a dozen black men for sex attacks in the late eighteenth and early nineteenth centuries. Yet those acts had been performed more in the spirit of punitive rage than anything else; now, sterilization was becoming accepted as a scientific breeding technique. Laws were already in place forbidding interracial intercourse, as well as sex with epileptic or mentally challenged people. Soon, state after state would pass legislation outlawing sex with undesirables. The American Medical Association enthusiastically endorsed the trend, saying that sterilization "restrict[ed] crime by restricting the breeding of our criminals." By 1937, two-thirds of the country's states had compulsory sterilization laws on the books.[13]

PORNOGRAPHY AND THE CONTROL
OF PRIVATE PLEASURES

The early years of the nineteenth century were a low point for English morals agitators. The mostly evangelical members of the new Society for the Suppression of Vice were disappointed at the government's failure to control unchristian behavior. Obscene literature was hawked on London corners, brothels operated in the open, and people were even working and playing on Sundays. It was "a truth too evident to be denied," held one of the society's early publications, "that vice has of late advanced upon us with almost unexampled rapidity." Earlier antivice societies had petered out in a hail of ridicule for their sleazy methods and snobby biases against working-class amusements.

Now, the society was ready to try again. It would not be easy. Of the 678 convictions it pushed through in its first couple of years in existence, 623 were for doing business on Sunday. The sex trade was untouched. The society became the butt of jokes at London theaters, and by 1810 its membership had dwindled to three; but press on it did, with the zeal of the righteous. In the coming decades, the society became a powerful force, largely by paying spies to buy smut and then funding prosecutions against the merchants who sold it. Thanks to the society and its paid agents, for example, the suppliers of sex-themed prints to a girl's boarding school were put behind bars, as were the sellers of an illustrated toothpick case that featured "on the inside lid thereof one obscene, filthy and indecent picture representing the naked persons of a man and woman in an indecent, filthy, and obscene situation, attitude and practice."

Despite the society's boasts, its efforts did little to suppress the flow of pornography. British law was expensive and moved slowly. The one-by-one process of obtaining warrants and then arresting and imprisoning smut peddlers guaranteed the continued supply of sexy material on the streets. In 1845, the society managed to nab a London dealer with 12,346 obscene prints, 393 books, 351 copper plates, 188 lithographic stones, and bundles of letterpress—a good bust, to be sure, but with such volume being traded by just one man (and this was *before* the easy reproduction of photographs became possible), it stands to reason that many others were pursuing the same line of work with equal success.

The society decided that changes in the law were required, so it began to lobby Parliament. In 1857, it pushed through the Obscene Publications Act, a landmark statute that empowered magistrates to confiscate and eradicate obscene material on the spot. In effect, the law turned magistrates into all-purpose censors, fully able to declare any literary or artistic work obscene and order it destroyed. The law had teeth: Hundreds of shops were shut down, as were the "low class, cheap [and] obscene papers hawked by boys" on the streets. As pornographic photography and three-dimensional stereoscopes came into vogue in the 1870s, the society worked with the police to confiscate hundreds of thousands of photos and viewing devices. (One photographer, Henry Hayler, escaped to Berlin in 1874 just as he was about to be arrested. In his studio were thousands of photos, including images depicting Hayler having sex with his wife and sons.)

The law never strikes with surgical precision, especially when sex is involved. Despite the society's pledge to target only hard-core material, zealous authorities went after anything that smelled of sex, regardless of whether or not it was a serious work of art or scholarship. Ironically, one of the key early prosecutions under the Obscene Publications Act, in 1868, targeted a quasi-religious work published by a militant Protestant society that "exposed" the corruption of Catholic confessionals. It was called *The Confessional Unmasked: Showing the Depravity of the Romish Priesthood, the Iniquity of the Confessional and the Questions Put to Females in Confession.* This anonymously authored pamphlet was sold on street corners by an anti-Catholic zealot named Henry Scott, who seemed to be acting on genuinely religious motives. After a series of appeals, Lord Chief Justice Sir Alexander Cockburn affirmed that *The Confessional Unmasked* should never see the light of day. More importantly for pornography law, his written opinion laid out the method for determining what was obscene:

> I think the test of obscenity is this, whether the tendency of the matter charged as obscenity is to deprave and corrupt those whose minds are open to such immoral influences, and into whose hands a publication of this sort may fall.

This decision, known as *Queen v. Hicklin*, set the standard for British and, later, American pornography law well into the twentieth century. Under *Hicklin*, an entire book could be banned so long as a judge was convinced that one isolated passage could "deprave and corrupt" even one group of readers. *Hicklin* was a censor's dream. Not only did it cover hard-core pornography, it also allowed the government to ban books by such literary luminaries as Rabelais, Zola, Joyce, and Lawrence.[14]

The year 1857 was also a watershed in French pornography law. Gustave Flaubert was put on trial for his novel *Madame Bovary*, and Charles Baudelaire was hauled into court for his collection of poems, *Les Fleurs du Mal* (*The Flowers of Evil*). While Flaubert got off with a stern warning, the court ordered some poems from Baudelaire's collection excised. The two trials provide interesting glimpses into France's market-based definition of indecency.

The key issue in the *Madame Bovary* trial was not explicit descriptions of sex in the book—there were none—but the presumed moral frailty of Flaubert's female readership. "Who," asked the prosecutor, rhetorically, "are the readers of M. Flaubert's novel? Are they men interested in political and social economy? No! The light pages of *Madame Bovary* fall into even lighter hands, into the hands of girls, and sometimes married women." For that reason, the prosecutor argued that it was Flaubert's responsibility to use his literary gifts to raise, rather than debase, women's morals. When confronted with a fictional adulteress such as Emma Bovary, the fear was that women would be steered toward sinful behavior, especially as there were no characters in the novel who forcibly argued that adultery was wrong. As *Madame Bovary* did not elevate the morals of its female readers, the prosecution argued, it degraded them.

Flaubert's defense attorney agreed with the premise that literature should be uplifting, but he also claimed that the author depicted vice only to show how wrong it was. The argument worked to the extent that Flaubert was acquitted and publication of the book permitted, but the court still had this to say:

> *The work in question merits severe blame, since the mission of literature should be to beautify and enhance the spirit by elevating the intelligence and purifying morals rather than to inspire disgust for vice by offering a portrait of the disorder that may exist in society.*

Flaubert's first published masterpiece may have been too "real" for respectable French tastes, but the controversy was a winning formula for launching his literary career. The trial made him famous, and the book a hit.

Baudelaire's *Les Fleurs du Mal* was seized soon after it was released, in June 1857. The poet went to trial on the same morals charges as those leveled a few months earlier against Flaubert, with the same prosecutor in charge, but the two cases went in different directions. Unlike the new literary form of the novel, which was associated with female readers, poetry in mid-nineteenth-century France was thought to be read by men, who were thought to be less easily corrupted. Baudelaire agreed: "This book was not written for my wives, my daughters or sisters; nor for my neighbor's wives, daughters or sisters. I leave that task to those interested in confusing virtuous acts with beautiful language." Because Baudelaire's market was presumed to be masculine, the prosecution could not argue that he threatened delicate female souls. At the same time, *Les Fleurs du Mal* was far sexier stuff than *Madame Bovary*, and the prosecutor still had a lot to work with.

In the end, six of Baudelaire's most explicitly erotic poems were suppressed. Given the moral climate of the times, it is impossible to see how a poem describing the sucking of hemlock from a woman's "sharp breast" (*La Léthé*), or one in which the poet threatens to drip venom into a woman's labia (*À celle qui est trop gaie*), or poems depicting lesbianism (*Delphine et Hippolyte* and *Lesbos*) could have escaped the censor's knife. It would take nearly a century before Baudelaire was officially exonerated and the six forbidden poems allowed back into French editions of the book. In the meantime, his poems have become, like *Madame Bovary*, part of that select group of canonical works that few educated people in Europe or the United States would admit to not having read.[15]

THE CRUSADE AGAINST pornography in the United States was dominated by one outsized character: the Brooklyn dry-goods salesman and Olympian busybody Anthony Comstock. The United States' most intrusive antiobscenity law was named after him, and for decades he held a powerful position with the government in order to enforce it. His strict and often bullying methods also earned him a place in the English lexicon with the word "Comstockery." During his forty-year career as an antismut crusader and protector of American youth, Comstock proudly claimed to have confiscated sixteen tons of "vampire literature," organized more than four thousand arrests, and caused the conviction of enough people to fill sixty train coaches. He also caused the suicide of about fifteen people.

As a young Union soldier during the Civil War, Comstock quickly earned the enmity of his peers for pouring his whiskey rations onto the ground and needling officers to sanitize soldier entertainments. "Seems to be a feeling of hatred by some of the boys," he wrote in his diary, "constantly falsifying, persecuting, and trying to do me harm." The hostility of his fellow soldiers only fanned Comstock's desire to do God's work. When he returned from the war, he set himself up in the dry-goods business, but that never went very well. His true métier was prying into the lives of

Building on "scientific" theories about the harmfulness of masturbation, New York's Society for the Suppression of Vice was responsible for the confiscation of sixteen tons of "vampire literature" and the conviction of obscenity of "enough persons to fill a passenger train of sixty-one coaches." The society, which had its heyday in the late nineteenth and early twentieth centuries, also targeted purveyors of birth control information and medical handbooks. ©TOPFOTO others and getting them put in jail. At this he excelled more than just about anyone. As soon as he moved to Brooklyn, he went to work on closing saloons that were doing business on Sunday. He also developed a lifelong obsession with pornography, and set it as his personal mission to end the trade by any means necessary.

Comstock did reasonably well and bagged several convictions, but two things were holding him back: money and the law. Bringing down an entire industry was not cheap. Purchases had to be made, raids organized, and lawsuits pursued. He needed an underwriter. He also needed to surmount the pesky civil rights of citizens. Federal obscenity law was already restrictive, but it excluded newspapers and, to Comstock and his fellow moralists' horror, did not ban traffic in "rubber goods," contraceptive information, or advertisements by abortionists. Even worse, federal law did not mention search and seizure. As described, British law had already been changed to allow authorities to nab and burn obscene materials almost at will. Comstock wanted the U.S. government to adopt similar laws. In 1872, he found the perfect partner in the New York YMCA, which had money and was no less driven to purge society of immorality.

The match could not have been better. The YMCA had long been in the smut-bashing business. While Comstock was irritating his fellow Union soldiers with his moralizing, the YMCA was pushing for a ban on the use of the U.S. mail to send "vulgar" or "indecent" materials to military camps. In 1868, it had also lobbied for a stiff New York state law against trading in pornography. Comstock went on the YMCA payroll, taking in twice what he had earned in his day job, plus expenses. They also worked together to charter the New York Society for the Suppression of Vice in 1873, with Comstock as its secretary and public face. Comstock was only twenty-eight years old when the society was formed, but he had already found his place in life. He would remain there for forty-three years and would soon become a nationally known—if often reviled—figure.

The New York Society for the Suppression of Vice and Comstock put their efforts in terms of saving the nation's youth from the devil. In his monumentally tedious manifesto, *Traps for the Young*, Comstock declares:

> *Satan is more interested in the child than many parents are. Parents do not stop to think or look for their children in these matters while the arch-enemy is thinking, watching, and plotting continually to effect their ruin. Thoughtless parents, heedless guardians, negligent teachers, you are each of you just the kind that old Satan delights to see placed over the child. He sets his base traps right in your very presence, captures and ruins your children, and you are all criminally responsible.*

Comstock's ideas did not come out of the clear blue sky. The fear of pornography was closely related to the ongoing mania against masturbation. Comstock himself had masturbated so furiously in his youth that he believed he might be driven to suicide. His own experiences seem to have strongly influenced his later work. In his book *Frauds Exposed*, he wrote that obscenity is like a cancer: It "fastens itself upon the imagination . . . defiling the mind, corrupting the thoughts, leading to secret practices of most foul and revolting character, until the victim tires of life and existence is scarcely endurable." He warned: "Every new generation of youth is sent into the world as sheep in the midst of wolves. Traps are laid for them in every direction . . . [O]nce in the trap, the victim will love it and press greedily forward."

Few at the time disagreed that masturbation caused insanity, sickness, and death. Well-meaning parents everywhere were warned to look for signs of self-pollution in their children, including bashfulness, acne, and pencil-chewing. Among the profusion of "authorities" on the subject was Sylvester Graham, who advocated a sex-drive-diminishing diet of coarsely ground grain combined with molasses or sugar—the same ingredients that later went into his signature Graham cracker. John Harvey Kellogg promoted his Corn Flakes as antimasturbation fuel as well.

Comstock and the society were not interested in improving diets. They saw only one course of action, to "[h]unt [smut dealers] down as you hunt rats, without mercy." They wrote a new bill, which they offered up to the government, to give them almost complete freedom to move against the pornography industry. The plan was to use federal control over the mail—through which most commerce passed at some point—to seize Satan's handiwork and imprison smut dealers.[16]

Comstock went to Washington, D.C., in 1873, where he lobbied hard for the new federal antipornography law. He brought with him fifteen thousand letters purportedly "written by our students of both sexes . . . ordering obscene literature" and set up an exhibition of pornographic materials students had received by mail. This popular "chamber of horrors," set up in Vice President Schuyler Colfax's office, included "lowbrow publications and their advertisements, gadgets purportedly designed to stimulate sexual potency, and 'fancy books' and . . . other abominations which were sold through the ads." The bill's official sponsor, Rep. Clinton Merriam of New York, argued that the fate of the country was at stake, and claimed that "low brutality" threatened to "destroy the future of the Republic by making merchandize of the morals of our youth." *The New York Times* joined in, expressing its disgust at the sexual materials "sent by post to the girls and boys in our schools" and lionizing Comstock for having already seized tons of "the most loathsome printed matter ever sent into the world to do the devil's work."

After months of effort, Comstock and the New York Society got exactly what they wanted. In 1873, President Ulysses S. Grant signed an act for the "Suppression of, Trade in, and Circulation of Obscene Literature and Articles of Immoral Use." The law, commonly known as the Comstock Act and modeled on the United Kingdom's 1857 Obscene Publications Act, empowered the U.S. Postal Service to seize just about anything its new special agent—Comstock himself—thought was indecent, and to arrest the senders. As worded, the law was unbelievably broad, prohibiting erotic, contraceptive, and sometimes purely medical materials:

> *That no obscene lewd or lascivious book, pamphlet, picture, print or other publication of an indecent character or any article or thing designed . . . for the prevention of conception or procuring of abortion, nor any article or thing intended or adopted for any indecent immoral use or nature, nor any written or printed card, circular, book, pamphlet, advertisement or notice of any kind giving information directly or indirectly, where, how, or of whom, or by what means, either of the things before mentioned may be obtained or made . . . shall be carried in the mail.*

Comstock was off to the races. In the law's first six months of operation, he claimed to have confiscated massive amounts of bad stuff, including fifty-five hundred sets of naughty playing cards and 31,151 boxes of pills and powders (mostly aphrodisiacs). However, as much as Comstock loved to quantify his achievements, numbers alone do not say enough about the effects of his crusade. It involved living, breathing individuals, many of whom did not fit the demonic image of the smut dealer preying on American youth.

The reach of the Comstock Act beyond the erotic became clear when Comstock put a physician on trial for disseminating birth-control information. Dr. Edward B. Foote had already sold hundreds of thousands of copies of his physiology book *Medical Common Sense* when he came out with the popular *Plain Home Talk*. The edition of the book that Comstock bought in 1876 suggested that readers could obtain birth-control information from another Foote pamphlet called *Words in Pearl*. The pamphlet merely contained advice to married couples on how to prevent conception, but the judge ruled that it was obscene—so much so that he did not let the jury look at it. As many courts would later rule, the judge in Foote's case refused to let the case record be "polluted" with "obscene matter." The fact that the book was medical and not meant to arouse its readers made no difference. The judge ruled that even medical advice given by a doctor could be illegal if it was mailed. Foote received a ten-year suspended prison sentence plus a big fine.

The following year, Comstock bought a twenty-three-page mail-order pamphlet called *Cupid's Yokes*, written by the socialist and free-love advocate Ezra Heywood. Predictably, Comstock hated Heywood and thought the book "loathsome" and "too foul for description." In reality, it was a rather clumsy polemic for keeping the government out of marriage and letting individuals regulate their desires as they pleased. "If government cannot justly determine what ticket we shall vote, what church we shall attend, or what books we shall read," Heywood argued, "by what authority does it watch at key-holes and burst open the bed chamber doors to drag lovers from sacred seclusion?" Nothing erotic there, but it was too much for Comstock. As he sat in the audience of a Boston free-love rally at which Heywood and his wife spoke, Comstock saw the horror of "lust in every face." He stayed to the side of the stage, silently praying to God for the strength he needed to stop this "horde of lusters."

As soon as Heywood left the stage, Comstock had him arrested and charged with mailing an obscene publication. The Boston judge, Daniel Clark, made no secret of where his sympathies lay. He told the jury that Heywood's ideas would transform Massachusetts into a vast house of prostitution. Refusing to let the jury see *Cupid's Yokes* during the trial, Clark read just two bits of the pamphlet for the record and then asked jurors: "What could be more indecent than those?" "Nothing," it seems, was the jury's reply, although Heywood won in the end: President Rutherford B. Hayes later pardoned him because the U.S. Attorney General failed to find anything obscene in the little book.

Unmoved by this setback, Comstock pressed his campaign against *Cupid's Yokes*. He trained his sights on one of Heywood's friends, D. M.

Bennett, who published a freethinking newspaper called *Truth Seeker*, which advertised the pamphlet. Bennett was convicted at trial and given thirteen months' jail time. This time, the president was not forthcoming with a pardon, and Bennett was forced to take the case up on appeal. The higher court not only affirmed the conviction, but also issued a written opinion that, along with *Hicklin*, would help define what was "obscene" in America for about fifty years. Comstock could not have written the definition better himself. Under the *Bennett* opinion, an entire book could be censored if only a small part of it—even a few sentences—tended "to deprave and corrupt" the most susceptible readers. In other words, a work could be outlawed and its sellers put in jail if any part of it could arouse an excitable adolescent boy.

With the passage of the Comstock Act and the *Bennett* opinion, the U.S. government became, in the words of a proud prosecutor, "one great society for the suppression of vice." During the 1880s, Comstock won 90 percent of his cases, but eventually the public began to tire of him and came to regard him as a monomaniacal buffoon. Even *The New York Times*, which had supported him strongly at first, began to express reservations: "Our voluntary associations for the prevention of various evils resemble vigilance committees, regulators or lynch policemen." Comstock's crusading also earned him enemies when he moved against popular amusements such as Sunday concerts in Central Park, which he claimed were violations of the Sabbath. Yet his zeal never wavered.

In 1902, a shorthand teacher and self-described "divine science" authority named Ida Craddock slashed her wrists after being sentenced to five years in jail under the Comstock Act. Her crime was selling a pamphlet she wrote called *Advice to a Bridegroom*, which counseled young men on attaining "sweet and wholesome" satisfaction with their brides. Craddock's previous work, *The Wedding Night*, had also brought a prosecution by Comstock. Her lawyer's appeal for mercy in that case—that "no one in her right mind would write such a book"—had done Craddock no good, and she was convicted. As soon as she was released from jail she found herself under indictment again. This time it was even worse. The judge found *Advice to a Bridegroom* so "indescribably obscene" that he also kept it from the jurors, who convicted her without ever leaving their seats. She ended it all the day before she was to report to prison, leaving a note: "I am taking my life because a judge, at the instigation of Anthony Comstock, has declared me guilty of a crime I did not commit—the circulation of obscene literature."

Craddock was not the only person to die under such pressure, but she was probably the last. Among the fallen who preceded her was the well-known abortionist Ann Trow Lohman, known professionally as "Madame Restell." In 1878, Comstock went to Lohman's home and told her he needed birth-control devices for his wife. When she supplied them, he arrested her on the spot. On the morning of her court hearing, she slit her throat. Comstock's reaction: "A bloody ending to a bloody life." Neither marriage counseling, birth control, nor abortions had anything to do with pornography, nor did they bear on the corruption of youth, which was the original rationale for the Comstock Act, but focus always gets lost in morality campaigns.[17]

Sapphism in France

Pornography was easy to obtain in fin-de-siècle France, although authorities occasionally conducted raids against materials and performances that crossed the line. As no one had clearly defined where the line was, it was often a matter of chance whether a book, picture, or play would draw legal fire. Depictions of male homosexuality were risky even though private homosexual sex was no longer strictly illegal. There were more prosecutions against homosexual pornographers than there were against homosexuals. "Sapphism" was particularly irksome to the police. Absent special certification, women were not even permitted publicly to wear men's clothing in public.

The French music-hall scene was famously bawdy. In 1907, at the Moulin Rouge, the writer Colette and her lover, the cross-dressing Marquise de Morny, performed a pantomime called *Rêve d'Egypte* (*Egyptian Dream*). In it, a male archaeologist discovers a female mummy who seductively unwraps herself and kisses the startled explorer. The first performance sparked an immediate uproar. Under pressure from the de Morny family, the Paris police prefect threatened to close the show if the two women performed together again. The marquise buckled to her family's demands, but the show was shut down anyway the following day, after Colette performed it with another woman. In 1908, after a more explicit sexual performance between two scantily clad women called *Rêverie d'éther* (*Ether Intoxication*), the court fined the Moulin Rouge's manager two hundred francs and sent him to prison for three months. The performers were also fined for exposing their "bare flesh" and acting in a way the judge said "appealed to the grossest, most excessive and dangerous lubricity" and "nervous passions."

The judge was fighting an uphill battle: The French public was hungry for anything that might stir "nervous passions." Lesbian-tinged public performances might be shut down, but there was no shortage of sapphic material in print. Back in 1857, when Baudelaire's poems *Lesbos* and *Femmes damnées* were censored, the subject was rarely addressed in literature, but by the end of the century lesbian-themed pornography was much in vogue. There was no way to halt the trade entirely, so authorities prosecuted authors and publishers on a selective and rather arbitrary basis. For example, the mildly erotic novel *Zé'Böim* (named after one of the ill-fated five Cities of the Plain along with Sodom and Gomorrah) had already been in print for twelve years without incident when, in 1889, the book's publisher decided to spice up the cover. The new artwork, which featured a woman with parted legs and a flash of light where her crotch would be, was too obvious. The entire stock was seized, and the writer and publisher punished. A later revision to the cover illustration, which put an image of a cat in place of the pubic light flash, led to another indecency charge.[18]

THE EMERGENCE OF THE "HOMOSEXUAL"

On April 30, 1870, two young men dressed as women were arrested at the Strand Theatre in London. Earnest Boulton, twenty-three, and his companion Frederick Park, twenty-two, had been parading around town in drag for some time, especially at theaters and nightspots, where they always caused a stir. On the evening of their arrest, they were occupying their private box at the theater as usual, nodding and smiling to their admirers. They were apprehended after the show as they got into a cab with a man they had picked up earlier in the evening. The charge was impersonating women "with the intent to commit a felony." However, the question was "what felony?" Blackmail of their new friend? No: Their companion later told the court that there had been no such impropriety. Sodomy? Perhaps, but wearing women's clothing does not necessarily mean that one "intends" to have homosexual sex. Their drag display could, as their lawyer argued, signify nothing more than a harmless "lark." No one was sure, least of all the police.

After their arrest, Boulton and Park were stripped and examined by a police doctor, who looked for physical "signs" of homosexuality, but the doctor later admitted that he had no idea what kind of markings he was seeking. There was no textbook describing what the physical markers of homosexuality were. Clearly, the prosecution thought they were homosexuals—the "molly" tradition of cross-dressing gay men had not been forgotten—but being a transvestite was not illegal in itself. There was no evidence that Boulton or Park had had homosexual sex at all.

The case drew a lot of press coverage. On their first day in court, as the *Times* of London reported, "Boulton wore a cherry-coloured evening silk dress trimmed with white lace; his arms were bare, and he had on bracelets. He wore a wig and plaited chignon. Park's costume consisted of a dark green satin dress, low necked and trimmed with black lace, of which material he also had a shawl round his shoulders. His hair was flaxen and in curls. He had on a pair of white kid gloves." The following day they appeared in court in men's clothing, much to the disappointment of the assembled crowd. The evidence showed that Boulton and Park often dressed up as women—and very convincingly—but that was the most that could be proven. No fewer than six court hearings only managed to show what many already knew: They were merely two of many London "young men who, for years past, have been in the habit of visiting places of public resort in feminine attire."

It took the jury just fifty-three minutes to decide that Boulton and Park were not guilty, which was greeted with shouts of "Bravo!" and other loud cheers. The two were dismissed as harmless eccentrics, which they clearly were, but the case also shows a critical early effort at defining a homosexual as a kind of person with certain telltale characteristics, rather than just considering homosexuality a type of sexual activity. In 1870, the view of homosexuality as an inbred (or deeply ingrained) pathology had not yet fully sunk into legal, medical, or popular thought, though before long it would. Had Boulton and Park been put on trial, say, in 1895, when Oscar Wilde was thrown in jail for his relations with young men, they would not have done nearly as well. By then, the image of the effeminate, monstrous, and predatory homosexual was well ingrained, and with the label came powerful hatred and fear at nearly all levels of society.[19]

Around the time of the Boulton and Park trial, when the word "homosexual" was first put to use, medical researchers began to study and label every conceivable abnormal sexual trait. This was when coprophilia (arousal by feces), urophilia (arousal by urine), and mysophilia (love of filth) were identified as separate pathologies, along with necrophilia (sex with corpses), gerontophilia (sex with the aged), and exhibitionism. Homosexuality was just one of dozens of new avenues of research, although its association with sodomy and its ubiquity set it apart. Because homosexuals "wasted" their seed by having sex with no chance of procreation, they were originally likened to the compulsive masturbators diagnosed by Tissot and others as potential psychotics. By the mid-nineteenth century, it was widely accepted that the loss of an ounce of semen was equivalent to the loss of several times that amount of blood; in this light, men who ejaculated with each other were considered as either having been born weak and insane or having engaged in the process of making themselves so. (In France, one medical "expert" cautioned police to look for "signs" of masturbation—tantamount to proof of homosexuality—in all men arrested for public indecency.)

The Boulton and Park trial highlighted the existence of a group of dedicated transvestites, but the link had not been made between homosexual sex and cross-dressing. Soon it would be, however, along with upper-class depravity and an "artistic" temperament. Homosexuals were no longer just sinners. In the late nineteenth century, they were seen as plagued, fulltime, with what historian Michel Foucault later called a "hermaphroditism of the soul." As homosexuality emerged as a full-fledged mental disease, the law responded by reducing the penalties. Yet while it was less risky, legally, for men to have sex with each other, it now became, if possible, even less socially acceptable.

The 1861 Offences Against the Person Act in the United Kingdom took the punishment for sodomy down from death to a prison sentence of ten years to life. Twenty-five years later, "gross indecencies" between men would be punished as misdemeanors with a maximum punishment of two years' hard labor. These changes were double-sided. On one hand, they showed a measure of mercy for a group of people now thought to be sick rather than blasphemous. On the other, lighter sentences made it easier to secure convictions and opened the door to stepped-up prosecutions against men such as Wilde. People no longer wanted to burn homosexuals alive, but a little prison time seemed appropriate.

AS POPULARLY CONCEIVED, the new homosexual personality had a powerful class aspect. Upper-class homosexuals did it for perverted fun (the result of "erotomania," as Wilde would claim), while lower-class men were pulled into it for money. Many trials against homosexuals were rooted in the belief that well-heeled men were corrupting rough boys, what Wilde later called "feasting with panthers." There was some truth to this. In an 1881 semifictional autobiography, *The Sins of the Cities of the Plain; or the Recollections of a Mary Ann*, the pseudonymous London hustler "Jack Saul" described a broad subculture of brothels in which rich men paid well for the company of lower-class adolescents, often soldiers. The young men, known as "rent boys" for their tendency to blackmail their customers for rent money, were objects of dangerous and intensely erotic fascination for aristocratic men. Wilde himself read Saul's book and explored this underworld with gusto; so did a group of aristocrats, whose patronage of a male brothel in London's Cleveland Street comprised one of the largest scandals of the century.

The Cleveland Street case began in July 1889 at a post office, where a telegraph messenger boy named Charles Swinscow was caught with more money in his pocket than his job warranted. He admitted to police that the money came from "gentlemen" who paid to touch him. He then volunteered that other telegraph boys were doing the same thing, mostly at a brothel run by a man named Charles Hammond. Hammond got wind of the bust and escaped to Paris, leaving his angry young charges to deal with the inquiry by themselves. One of them told police: "I think it is hard that I should get into trouble while men in high positions are allowed to walk free." When asked whom he was referring to, he responded that Lord Arthur Somerset went regularly to Hammond's Cleveland Street house, as did the Earl of Euston.

These were two names the police did not want to hear. Somerset was an intimate of the Prince of Wales and ran his stables. Euston was the eldest son of the Duke of Grafton, and a high-ranking Freemason. The case became a hot potato for police investigators, who referred it to ever higher levels of command. Meanwhile, the Cleveland Street brothel was put under observation and within days Somerset, a member of Parliament, and other notables were seen skulking in and out. There was sufficient evidence to arrest Somerset, but to do so would imply that the heir to the British throne—the ambiguous Prince Albert Victor (known as "Eddy")— also enjoyed "feasting with panthers." The matter went all the way up to the prime minister, Lord Salisbury, who seems to have barred prosecution of the brothel's loftiest patrons—especially Somerset. However, the case could not be contained. The conviction of a rent boy and a street-level procurer stirred newspapers to claim that a cover-up was being orchestrated. In the *Pall Mall Gazette*, the two convicted men were portrayed as "wretched agents" who were "run and sent to penal servitude" while "the lords and gentlemen who employ them swagger at large and are even welcomed as valuable allies of the Administration."

Finally, names were named. *The North London Press* published an article directly implicating Somerset and Euston, and asking why no official charges had been made against them. The paper also hinted that Prince Eddy might be involved. Somerset left the country, never to return, but Euston immediately sued the paper and its editor, Earnest Parke, for criminal libel. At that trial, the newspaper called several witnesses who confirmed that they had seen Euston enter the Cleveland Street brothel, although their stories differed as to details. Euston agreed that he had gone in, but forcefully claimed that he had done so while looking for a female sex spectacle and not a romp with rent boys. Jack Saul was also called to the stand by Parke, which turned out to be a big mistake. By this time he was a weathered thirty-five years old, and his "queen" shtick and braggadocio in describing a life spent servicing rich men only made Euston look that much more like a solid citizen. It took the jury little time to rule against Parke. The judge gave him twelve months in prison.

The verdict did not calm the controversy, however. The outraged newspaper headlines kept coming, this time joined by a homophobic member of the House of Commons, Henry Labouchere (of whom we will learn more soon). It was out of the noise of the Cleveland Street affair, and the growing feeling that perverted rich men were taking advantage of under-privileged boys, that Wilde was put on trial in 1895. The great writer, wit, and snob had been publicly accused of being a sodomite and, like Euston, sued his accuser for libel. However, the Wilde case turned out much differently. Unlike Euston, who returned to his life with his reputation as a heterosexual intact, Wilde ended up in jail doing hard labor.[20]

MUCH WAS ALREADY aligned against Wilde when his sexual life came up for public review. Times had changed since the simpler days of the Boulton and Park trial, when the flirtatious habits of two transvestites were treated as a light joke. Now the mood against homosexuals had turned dark indeed. They were seen as predators ready to waste the country's youth with "unnatural" lusts. Wilde fit that mold, and added to it a flamboyance and a knack for making enemies as easily as he tossed off witticisms. His only novel, *The Picture of Dorian Gray*, oozed with decadence and boy love. The book tracks the life of a gorgeous young man who trades his soul to keep his beauty. As Gray chases a life of sexual dissipation, his sins are etched magically onto a painted portrait he keeps locked in a closet. Gray comes to a bad end, but that was lost amid the book's thick homoeroticism.

Dorian Gray was first published in *Lippincott's Monthly Magazine* in 1890, to deadly reviews. Said *The Scots Observer*:

> *Mr. Oscar Wilde has been writing stuff that were better unwritten; and while* The Picture of Dorian Gray *... is ingenious, interesting, full of cleverness and plainly the work of a man of letters, it is false art for its interest is medico-legal; it is false to human nature—for its hero is a devil; it is false to morality—for it is not made sufficiently clear that the writer does not prefer a course of un-natural iniquity to a life of cleanliness, health and sanity ... Mr. Wilde has brains, and art, and style; but if he can write for*

none but outlawed noblemen and perverted telegraph boys, the
sooner he takes to tailoring (or some other decent trade) the better
for his own reputation and the public morals.

The reference to the Cleveland Street affair was direct: Wilde was yet
another dirty man lusting after England's youth. *Lippincott's* wholesaler
pulled the issue out of circulation immediately. The novel was published
in book form, with six additional chapters, but carried the same scandalous message. Wilde's indiscretion about his sexuality, plus his dandyish
arrogance, would ensure that he paid the price for all men with a taste for
the likes of "perverted telegraph boys." To Wilde, the intimate company
of adolescent boys was stimulating. To most others it was simply a crime.

Wilde met his own Dorian Gray in the person of Lord Alfred Douglas,
a uniquely handsome Oxford dropout he affectionately called "Bosie."
Until his trial in 1895, Wilde and Bosie lived the life described by Saul in
Cities of the Plain. Wilde was married with two children, but that did nothing to interfere with his escapades. He rented rooms in Piccadilly, ostensibly to work undisturbed but also to entertain the rent boys he and Bosie
met through a pimp, Alfred Taylor. Wilde's recklessness was matched
only by his triumphs as a writer and personality. *Dorian Gray* was not an
instant hit, but Wilde's plays did very well. During the same period when,
as he later wrote, he "went to the depths in search for new sensations," he
reached the apex of commercial success. Wilde cut a unique public figure,
but from his perspective it was working. He was the toast of the society
that mattered to him.

Not everyone was charmed. Bosie's father, the ninth Marquess of
Queensberry, a truculent little man best known for penning a set of boxing
rules, developed an obsessive hatred for his son's companion. His threats
to cut off Bosie's money unless he stopped seeing Wilde were unsuccessful, so Queensberry started to threaten Wilde himself. One day in June
1894, he appeared without warning at the London house Wilde shared

with his family, accompanied by a prizefighter. The interview did not go well. Queensberry threatened to "thrash" Wilde if he showed his face in public with Bosie again; Wilde threatened to sue him for libel.

Not long before that, Wilde had had a series of other visitors: rent boys looking to blackmail him over some passionate letters he had written to Bosie, which had gotten into their hands. One of the letters, addressed to "My own boy," later found its way into court as evidence against Wilde. The writer appeared unfazed, telling one of the blackmailers that the letter was a "prose poem," the "art" of which "is rarely intelligible to the criminal classes." Nevertheless, Wilde paid, and then he paid some more, but the letters had already been copied. A duplicate of one of them, in which he tells Bosie that "it is a marvel that those rose-red lips of yours should have been no less for music of song than for madness of kisses," eventually fell into Queensberry's hands. He was not amused.

For the moment, however, the visits by the rent boys and Queensberry's rage must have seemed to Wilde like the kind of surreal encounters an enriched life such as his would naturally invite. He had much bigger matters at hand, not least of which the fact that two of his plays, *An Ideal Husband* and *The Importance of Being Earnest*, were running simultaneously on both sides of the Atlantic. Yet Queensberry could not rest while his son pursued a "most loathsome and disgusting relationship" with the playwright. He showed up to the opening of *The Importance of Being Earnest* with a "grotesque bouquet of vegetables," evidently for hurling at the stage, but guards at the theater had been warned of his arrival and he was refused admittance. A few days later, he went to Wilde's London club, the Albemarle, where he left a calling card reading: "To Oscar Wilde posing as a somdomite" (the last word misspelled in his angry haste). Wilde read the card about ten days later, after which he made the single worst decision of his life.

Rather than ignore the scrawled message, Wilde consulted a lawyer, who asked him point-blank if the accusation was true. In the first of several

fateful lies that would sink him, Wilde solemnly said no. "If you are innocent, then you should succeed" in court, the lawyer replied, and a lawsuit
for criminal libel was filed. Interestingly, despite his appearance of wealth,
Wilde was insolvent at the time. His debts to the posh Avondale Hotel, for
example, had gotten to the point where the hotel had impounded his lug-
gage and refused to release it—thus it would have been difficult to flee the
country even if he had wanted to, and as friends such as George Bernard
Shaw advised him to do. Bosie, no less implacable than his father, offered
to foot the legal bill. The Douglas family "had often discussed the possibility of getting [Queensberry] put into a lunatic asylum so as to keep him
out of the way," according to Bosie, and a jail sentence for libel seemed
just as effective.

Perhaps Wilde thought he could succeed as Lord Euston had done;
perhaps he also thought his brilliance could win over anyone in court,
especially when matched against Queensberry's buffoonery. Most likely,
he saw the trial as a set piece for good dialogue, one that could even further
elevate his reputation as a genius and drive crowds to his plays. However,
Wilde had sealed his fate by taking a false position: He was not only "posing" as a sodomite, by law he *was* one, and he had seriously underestimated the fury of his opposition. With the help of private investigators and
some of Wilde's more spiteful enemies, Queensberry lined up incriminating
letters and a stable of pimps and male prostitutes to testify against Wilde.
He also planned to take Wilde to task for some of the more turgid passages
in his writings.

Everyone except Wilde himself seemed to know that the libel case
would be a disaster, but he found out soon enough. His penchant for lying
didn't help his credibility in court, either. (In Wilde's aesthetic universe,
a lie was almost more valuable than the truth because of its creative possibilities.) In the first minutes of his testimony, Wilde stated that he was
thirty-nine years old, which was two years shy of the truth. He may have
thought it just and harmless to trim a couple of years from his age, but it

was exactly what Queensberry's superb lawyer, Edward Carson, needed to kick off a brutal, multiday cross-examination that ensured Wilde's defeat. Carson used Wilde's birth certificate to show that not only was he older than he admitted, he was also much older than Bosie, who was in his early twenties when their relationship began.

Carson pressed Wilde like a well-spoken steamroller, demanding that he explain homoerotic passages in his work—particularly in *Dorian Gray*. Wilde deftly parried many of Carson's early questions at first, and the match of minds seemed to be a draw until the subject turned to Wilde's own sex life. When the questions started to focus on rent boys and the pricey gifts he had given to a pier-side newsboy, "the faces of the twelve good men and true in the jury box plainly showed signs of surprise," according to one observer. As Carson named boy after boy whom Wilde had known in questionable circumstances, the jury's countenance grew grimmer.

Everything fell apart when Carson referred to a young servant of Bosie's and asked Wilde if he had ever kissed the boy. Unable to resist a sharp response, Wilde replied: "Oh, dear, no! He was a peculiarly plain boy. He was, unfortunately, extremely ugly." That was it. Carson pressed him relentlessly, demanding: "Why, why, why did you add that?"

On the advice of his lawyer, Wilde gave up the libel case before the rent boys began to give their testimony, but only after Carson forced Wilde's side to admit that Queensberry's actions had been justified. In effect, Wilde admitted that he was a homosexual. When Queensberry was acquitted, there were cheers in the courtroom's public gallery, and prostitutes danced in the streets. However, that was only the beginning of the end. On the very afternoon the libel case collapsed, a warrant was issued for Wilde's arrest. He was taken into custody that evening, just as the late-edition newspapers gloated that he was "damned and done for."[21]

The charge, "gross indecency," came under the same law the moral reformers had pushed through in 1885, during the frenzy of the "Maiden

Tribute" scandal. It had primarily been intended to protect girls from white slavery, but its fine print went much further than that. In the moments just before the bill passed in the House of Commons, Henry Labouchere had inserted a clause creating a new offense: indecency between men. The bill passed with almost no discussion about that addition.

It is doubtful whether anyone in Parliament realized at the time just how much they had changed English criminal law. It had always been illegal for adults to act indecently in *public*, or to corrupt youth, but under what became known as the "Labouchere Amendment," the *private* pleasures of men with other men became public crimes:

> *Any male person who, in public or private, commits, or is party to the commission of, or procures or attempts to procure the commission by any male person of, any act or gross indecency with another male person, shall be guilty of a misdemeanour, and being convicted thereof shall be liable at the discretion of the court to be imprisoned for any term not exceeding two years, with or without hard labour.*

Wilde's loss in court sparked what a friend called an "orgy of Philistine rancour" in which "everyone tried to outdo his neighbour in expressions of loathing and abhorrence." Almost immediately, Wilde went from being one of the world's most sought-after playwrights and dinner guests to the most hated man in England. His plays were shut down, he ran out of the little money he had left, and in less than a few weeks the entire contents of his household were sold to pay off his creditors.

Two criminal trials against him followed. In the first, the jury failed to agree on a verdict after Wilde made an exceptional speech in which he likened his affection for young men to the exalted male-male relations of the ancient Greeks. The second brought a conviction and a sentence of the maximum two years' imprisonment with hard labor, although the judge opined that it was "totally inadequate for a case such as this."

More expressions of joy followed on the streets. One woman, referring to the writer's famous foppish coif, provoked laughter outside the courthouse when she exclaimed: "'E'll 'ave 'is 'air cut reglar now!" *The Daily Telegraph* expressed the same sentiment in finer language: "[W]e have had enough of Oscar Wilde," it announced. He "has been the means of inflicting . . . as much moral damage of the most hideous and repulsive kind as no single individual could well cause." *The London Evening News* agreed: "England has tolerated the man Wilde and others of his kind too long . . . [W]e venture to hope that the conviction of Wilde for these abominable vices, which were the natural outcome of his diseased intellectual condition, will be a salutary warning."

The suddenness and depth of Wilde's fall from grace are still a stunning thing. After his arrest, his supporters put up his bail, but he was unable to find repose for one minute. When he and Bosie checked into a London hotel (presumably under false names) and were about to sit down to dinner, the hotel-keeper rushed into the dining room and told him he must leave at once. At another hotel later that night, guests threatened to tear the place apart if Wilde were permitted to stay. Wilde ended up at the house of his mother and brother, where he begged for shelter and then collapsed on the threshold. Depressed, confused, and ill, he rejected the advice of his remaining friends and his wife to flee the country. Again, we are left with "perhaps" questions. Perhaps he stayed on account of his mother's threat never to speak to him again if he fled. Perhaps it was his fear of a fugitive life "slinking about the Continent." Whatever it was, he drifted around France and Italy for two years after his jail term, finally dying in a dingy Paris hotel room in 1900.

The Wilde trials [22] helped to perfect the image of the new English homosexual: pretentious, unmanly, and decadent. Homosexuals were, in the later words of an English judge, "stamped with the hallmark of a specialised and extraordinary class as much as if they had carried on their bodies some physical peculiarities." Because the likes of Wilde were seen as

threats to the "wholesome, manly and simple ideals of English life," there
was no option but to put them away. "Open the windows," exclaimed one
newspaper upon Wilde's arrest, "Let in the fresh air!" The Labouchere
Amendment, which slammed shut the doors of liberty to homosexuals,
would remain in place until 1967.[23]

IN FRANCE, THE movement to classify people and especially homosexuals
by their sexual habits was as strong as it was in England. Sodomy had been
decriminalized since the French Revolution, but that brought little peace to
men continually hunted under public indecency laws. One police inspector developed an elaborate taxonomy for homosexuals. There were the
effeminate *périlleuses*, who sold sex for money or blackmail; the *travaill-
euses*, working-class men in traditional occupations; and the *honteuses*,
men of all classes who went to cruising spots but were ashamed of doing
so. There were also the part-time *amateurs* and the *renifleurs* ("sniffers"),
who enjoyed the ambiance of public urinals. In one month alone in the
1850s, police made more than two hundred arrests in the water closets of
the Les Halles markets alone.

As in England, the French public's special ire was reserved for upper-
class men who preyed upon their young inferiors. When one was caught,
newspaper sales soared on a wave of middle-class and moral superiority.
Such was the case when the nobleman and wealthy lawyer Charles-Eugène
Le Bègue de Germiny, known as "le Comte de Germiny," was arrested in
1876 at a notorious Paris urinal along with an eighteen-year-old working-
class boy, Edmond-Pierre Chouard. The de Germiny case was among the
most sensational of its day, to the point that the count's very name morphed
into a synonym, in popular speech, for homosexuality—"Germinisme."

From a press perspective, the case started out well and just got better. It
took four police officers to subdue de Germiny, which earned him charges
of both indecency and resisting arrest. His flailing also undercut his later
story that he was merely conducting his own civic-minded investigation

into the "scenes of immorality" that unfolded in public urinals. He later said that, while taking a stroll, "the idea came to me that I should conduct a sort of inquiry in regards to the activities of certain habitués of these areas, of which the indecency revolts the residents of the neighbourhood." When he went in, he indeed saw people of "suspicious appearances," including Chouard, whom he claimed only to have "observed" for some time before police came on the scene. As for resisting arrest, he said he believed he had been set up by local ruffians for a blackmail charge, against which he naturally put up a fight.

No one believed that story for a second, especially when it was lined up against the other evidence in the case. In truth, when the police entered the urinal, de Germiny had already been engaged in "obscene touching" with Chouard, and he had admitted as much in a signed statement before the trial. Chouard testified that de Germiny was the sexual aggressor, and he had refused the older man's advances only to be caught when buttoning his pants after a "natural act." For the public and the press, it was less a question of who made the first move than one class taking unfair advantage of another. The papers contrasted the "almost infantile countenance" of Chouard with the aristocratic bearing of his older, well-connected codefendant. The count's many more advantages in life were repeatedly pointed out, as if to show that the cards of justice were already stacked in favor of a lawyer from an old family. Chouard was an innocent youth, despite his prior vagrancy conviction; de Germiny, a dirty middle-aged man.

The court seemed to agree, at least in part. Despite his considerable connections with the Paris courts, de Germiny was sentenced to two months in jail and a fine of two hundred francs—a heavy sentence by contemporary standards. Chouard got a fifteen-day jail term and a fine of sixteen francs. (Only a few weeks after Chouard did his prison time, he was named in a police report with a number of "vagabond" criminals, and six months later he was arrested on the Champs-Elysées for "obscene touching" with another man.)[24]

Had they ever met, de Germiny and Wilde would have probably hated each other. One was a true aristocrat and proud member of the ruling class, while the other was an extravagant bohemian who took every opportunity to insult respectable society and its values. However, in the realm of homosexual stereotypes, they were similar in key respects. Both were men of position with sexual tastes for rough young lads. Wilde caused his own ruin when he told his attorney "on my honour as a gentleman" that Queensberry's accusation against him was untrue. Trouble came to de Germiny in the form of a vice squad, but it was the lawyer's stupid decision to attract attention by walking in a notorious cruising spot six times in one evening.

By 1903, the French stereotype of the upper-crust homosexual had been leavened to take on a distinctly effeminate aspect. In July of that year, the papers burst with reports of two men from "excellent families" who were charged with corrupting schoolboys in a posh Paris apartment with "Satanic Masses" and "orgiastic bacchanalias." In truth, Baron Jacques d'Adelswärd-Fersen and Count Albert Hamelin de Warren were more aesthetic dilettantes than devil worshippers, but that did them little good in the public eye or in court. Their "Black Masses" were little more than bizarre reenactments of decadent French literature. D'Adelswärd-Fersen stated that he "wanted to put on stage what [he] had read in Baudelaire," which he accomplished on one occasion by reading the poet's La Mort des amants while incense burned, flutes played, and young men took poses draped only in shawls and togas. "[I]n truth," according to one newspaper during the trial, "this pathetic and downright filthy case doesn't live up to its name . . . [the defendants'] aesthetic tableaux vivants . . . are really no more artistic than the revolting taste of a pansy hairdresser."

Artistic or not, such scenes generated intense interest and newspaper sales. Every element of the defendants' "nature" was examined in detail, from their flowing, tinted hair and taste for jewelry and delicate clothing to their psychological "corruption" by literature. The trial allowed the public to vent its hostility against homosexuals just as the Wilde trials had done. Yet these defendants were nowhere near being in Wilde's artistic league. The latter was, at least for a time, a successful public figure and respected writer. D'Adelsward-Fersen and de Warren were grotesques from the fringe, debased aristocrats with nothing to do but ape the accomplishments of their creative betters. In the opinions of court experts, they were either mentally ill or had made very bad choices. Either way, they were criminals. "If our laws no longer permit us to punish the sin, as they did in the Middle Ages," argued the prosecutor, "we can still punish the wrong-doers, so that this will not happen again." Sodomy was no longer a crime, but being too obvious a sodomite was not permitted.

The judge gave them both six months in prison and a fifty-franc fine. De Warren later disappeared from view, but d'Adelsward-Fersen's name reappeared when he tried to shoot himself. He then went into self-imposed exile on Capri with a young Italian lover, where he smoked copious amounts of opium at his villa, wrote poetry, and financed France's first homophile literary journal, *Akademos*. In 1923, he died of heart disease, a victim of drug abuse and what the judge at his trial had called "very unhealthy literature."

Wilde's troubles had helped set the stage for d'Adelsward-Fersen and de Warren's rough treatment in France, as did the creeping feeling that their inclinations were due to congenital problems exacerbated by bad habits. After reviewing the "defects" in d'Adelsward-Fersen's bloodline (insanity, epilepsy), a mental disorders specialist at his trial suggested that "we ought to recognize his diminished responsibility because of certain hereditary factors. That merits a certain indulgence." Compared to the two years of hard labor given to Wilde, it seems that the baron received just that, but the ambivalence toward homosexuality, especially the question of whether or not it is a "lifestyle choice" or a congenital characteristic, would continue until the present day.[25]

NOTES

INTRODUCTION

1   Epstein, *Urbanization and Kinship*, 86–89.

2   *Gettysburg College Student Handbook*, accessed September 30, 2011, http://
    web.archive.org/web/20060904040430/http://www.gettysburg.edu/about
    /offices/college_life/srr/whps/0607handbook.pdf. The 2010 version of the hand-
    book is slightly different.

3   Antioch College Sexual Offenses Prevention Policy, accessed September 30,
    2011, http://antiochmedia.org/mirror/antiwarp/www.antioch-college.edu
    /Campus/sopp/index.html.

4   "Justice Department Covers Partially Nude Statues," *USA Today*, January 29,
    2002.

5   Herdt, *Sambia Sexual Culture*, 58–59; "Convicted Child Molester Gets 800
    Years," Associated Press, February 9, 2007.

1
. . .
CHANNELING THE URGE:
THE FIRST SEX LAWS

1   Jacobson, *Toward the Image of Tammuz*, 196–202 (see also Gibson,
    "Nippur"; *Middle Assyrian Law [MAL]* 40, cited in Roth, *Law
    Collections*; and Driver and Miles, *Assyrian Laws*); Roth, "Case Study from
    Mesopotamia," 177–78.
    When U.S. and allied troops invaded Iraq in March 2003, the Nippur
    archaeological mound sat in the battle zone between the modern cities of Basra
    and Baghdad. The painstaking work done at Nippur, where 80 percent of all
    Sumerian documents have been discovered, was nearly obliterated. Hours after
    the U.S. invasion, the Nippur mound was overrun by swarms of looters looking
    for treasures to sell on the black market. The damage caused by this riot of greed,
    both to Iraq's patrimony and to our own understanding of our common history,
    is incalculable. How many Nin-Dadas have now been silenced forever? How

many assemblies forgotten? What murderers, lovers, adulterers, gods, and children will we never meet? We can never know, and must now content ourselves instead with the archaeological work already done and the shreds of material left in the wake of the war. Our picture of the ancient Near East is like a child's stick-figure drawing: The basics are there, but there are few reliable details.

2   Taylor, *Prehistory of Sex*, 1–3; see also "Iceman's Final Meal," BBC News, September 16, 2002. *Laws of Ur-Nammu (LU)* No. 7, cited in Roth, *Law Collections*: "If the wife of a young man, on her own initiative, approaches a man and initiates sexual relations with him, they shall kill that woman; that male shall be released"; Saggs, *Civilization*, 156; *MAL 8*, cited in *Ancient History Sourcebook*, www.fordham.edu/halsall/ancient/1075assyriancode.asp; see the list of other similarities between Assyrian and Hebrew law in Smith, *Origin and History*, 245; Deuteronomy 15:12, 15:18; Sassoon, *Ancient Laws*, 31.

3   Plato, *Laws*, 783a; Smith, *Daughters*, 3–6, 353; Tannahill, *Sex in History*, 24, 41–46, 66; Roth, *Law Collections*, 200.

4   See Leviticus 15:19-30, 18:19; Ezekiel 18:6; Wenham, *Book of Leviticus*, 279; Epstein, *Tractate Niddah*, 5a–5b, 26–27, 174 (re: husband arrested for having sex with his wife during her menstruation); Epstein, *Tractate Keritoth*, 2b, 1 (re: death penalty); Ruggiero, *Boundaries of Eros*, 33–35; Tannahill, *Sex in History*, 352.

5   Tannahill, *Sex in History*, 27–29; Thornhill, *Natural History*; Van den Berghe, "Human Inbreeding Avoidance"; Lévi-Strauss, *Elementary Structure of Kinship*, 12; *Laws of Hammurabi (LH)*, in Roth, *Law Collections*, 154–58; Tetlow, *Women, Crime and Punishment*, 61. Babylonian men who had sex with their daughters were treated more mercifully, even though they were likely the aggressors. They were merely exiled. Scheidel, "Brother-Sister and Parent-Child Marriages,"; Pomeroy, *Goddesses*, 217–20; Middleton, "Brother-Sister and Father-Daughter Marriage," 604; Shaw, *Oxford History of Ancient Egypt*, 226–28; Hjerrild, *Studies in Zoroastrian Family Law*, 167, 183, 194–97, 203. Note that the blessings of Persian incest did not go so far as to wipe away the "sin" of sodomy, which was regarded with "revulsion" because it was not a procreative act. Persian men also had to do penance for their refusal to marry relatives. The period of atonement was calculated by totaling up the number of menstrual periods the brides experienced while waiting for the grooms to marry them: "[T]he number of [unproductive] menstruation periods and the length of time must be determined in order to decide on the magnitude of the sin." "Inbred Obscurity," 2464, 2469; Posner and Silbaugh, *Guide to America's Sex Laws*, ch. 10; see also "Inbred Obscurity," 2469–70.

6   Johnson, "The Legal Status of Women"; Cooper, "Virginity"; Tetlow, *Women,*
     Crime, and Punishment, 12; *LU* 6, 8, *MAL* 55, 56–59, *Laws of Lipit-Ishtar* 33,
     in Roth, *Law Collections;* Frymer-Kensky, "Virginity in the Bible," 81, 86–89;
     Genesis 34:25–31; Deuteronomy 22:13–21.

7   Tetlow, *Women, Crime, and Punishment,* 36, 69, 140, 144; *MAL* 22, Middle
     Assyrian Palace Decrees, *LH* 141–43, *Laws of Eshunna* 28, in Roth, *Law*
     Collections; Wenham, *Book of Leviticus,* 258; Roth, "Iron Dagger," 205–6;
     Roth, "Slave and the Scoundrel," 282; Greengus, "Textbook Case," 37–39;
     Jackson, *Essays,* 60–61. The laws of Hammurabi required that an adulterous
     wife and her lover be thrown into the water to drown, unless the cuckolded
     husband had a change of heart and decided to let her live—in which case the
     lover was also allowed to survive (see *LH* 129 in Roth, *Law Collections).*

8   *LH* 132–33, 141–43, *MAL* 13, 24, in Roth, *Law Collections;* Tetlow, *Women,*
     Crime, and Punishment, 66; Reynolds, "Sex Morals," 27–28; Heimpel, *Letters,*
     386; Tetlow, *Women, Crime, and Punishment,* 137; Roth, "Iron Dagger,"
     186–87; Herodotus, *Book II,* 111; Galpaz-Feller, "Private Lives and Public
     Censure," 155–56; VerSteeg, *Law,* 173–74.

9   Tetlow, *Women, Crime, and Punishment,* 140; *MAL* 2, *Hittite Laws (HL)*
     187–88, 199–200, *LU* 8, *LE* 51–52, *LH* 119, 127, 146, 171, 193–94, *MAL*
     12, *HL* 197, in Roth, *Law Collections;* Herodotus, *Book II,* 148–49; The belief
     that a man cannot rape his wife is actually quite modern. In 1957, the legal
     scholar Rollin M. Perkins accurately summarized U.S. law when he stated: "A
     man does not commit rape by having sexual intercourse with his lawful wife,
     even if he does so by force and against her will." The "marital rape exemption"
     was finally overturned in California in 1980. See Ryan, "Sex Right," 941–42;
     Finkelstein, "Sex Offenses," 359–60; see also Westbrook, "The Female Slave,"
     215, 222–23; Westbrook, *History of Ancient Near Eastern Law,* 1033.

10   *MAL* 14, *LH* 109, *MAL* 40–41 in Roth, *Law Collections;* Driver and Miles,
     Assyrian Laws, 44; Herodotus wrote that in Egyptian Thebes "a woman
     always passes the night in the temple of the Theban Zeus and it is forbidden
     to have intercourse with men," Herodotus, *Book I,* 82, 199; Herodotus, *Book*
     II, 126, 179; see also Westbrook, *History of Ancient Near Eastern Law,* 854
     (re: sex in temples as a violation of purity rules); Lise Manniche, *Sexual Life,*
     13–15; Johnson, "The Legal Status of Women," 175; Tannahill, *Sex in History,*
     61, 99; Graham-Murray, *History of Morals,* 12.

11   Graham-Murray, *History of Morals,* 21; Vern L. Bullough, *Sexual Variance,*
     53, 56. There were laws to guard the fertility of women, but those were
     intended to protect children, not mothers. Men who used violence on pregnant
     women and caused them to miscarry were fined (see *LH* 209–14 in Roth, *Law*
     Collections). In Babylon, if a pregnant woman from the upper classes died

during an assault, the assailant's daughter could be executed as punishment. Any woman who had an abortion in Assyria was impaled, and if she died during the abortion, her dead body was stuck through with a spike nevertheless (*MAL* 53 in Roth, *Law Collections*); Greengus, "Textbook Case," 37 (re: lack of evidence that male homosexuality was a crime in ancient Sumer or Babylon); *MAL* 19–20 in Roth, *Law Collections*; see also Olyan, "And with a Male," 194.

12 Scholars do not agree on when Leviticus was written. Some purists maintain that the book came from the time of Moses, but the majority hold that the book was actually composed approximately one thousand years later. See Wenham, *Book of Leviticus*, 8–13, 250, 252; Leviticus 11:42–44, 18:1, 18:25, 20:22.

13 DeMeo, "The Geography of Male and Female Genital Mutilations," 3–5, 18–20, 45–47, 73–74; see also Bullough, *Sexual Variance*, 59–60; Karass, *Sexuality*, 74–75; Hodges (citing Strabo), "Ideal Prepuce," 385–89.

14 Leviticus 18:23, 20:15–16. See also Olyan, "And with a Male," 21–29.

15 Leviticus 15:16–18; 18:6–18, 23–28; 20:11–12, 15–16; Leviticus 18:6–18, 20:11–12; see also Wenham, *Book of Leviticus*, 253–56; Mohrmann, "Making Sense," 68–70; Tannahill, *Sex in History*, 74; Stengers and van Neck, *Masturbation*, 21–22; Jackson, *Essays*, 60–61.

16 Brundage, *Law, Sex, and Christian Society*, 56; Deuteronomy 22:28–29; Exodus 22:16–17; Frymer-Kensky, "Virginity in the Bible," 91–93; Numbers 5:12–32.

17 Olyan, "And with a Male," 199–202.

18 Douglas, *Leviticus*, 236.

19 Leviticus 18:22; 20:13; Olyan, "And with a Male," 193–94, 199–202; Douglas, *Leviticus*, 236; Norton, "Destruction of Sodom and Gomorrah"; Tannahill, *Sex in History*, 154–55. Lot may have been saved from the fire and brimstone that wrecked his city, but the story still turns out badly for him and for his family. His wife, famously, turns into a pillar of salt when she looks back on the burning cities. Lot's daughters then follow him to a cave where they make their home, but soon decide that they have had enough of virginity. On two successive nights, they get their father drunk and have sex with him. See Genesis 19:30–38.

According to Philo of Alexandria, writing in the first century AD: "Not only in their mad lust for women did the Sodomites violate the marriages of their neighbours, but also men mounted males without respect for the sex nature which the active partner shares with the passive; and so when they tried to beget children they were discovered to be incapable of any but a sterile seed . . . little by little they accustomed those who were by nature men to submit to play the part of women." Later references to the story of Sodom and Gomorrah reinforce this canard, and expand the definition of sodomy. See Brundage, *Law, Sex, and Christian Society*, 122, 532–33; Jordan, *Invention of Sodomy*, 163 ("From the beginning, 'Sodomy' has meant whatever anyone wanted it to mean."); Ruggiero, *Boundaries of Eros*, 111, 140, 189; Hull, *Sexuality*, 67; Blackstone, *Commentaries*, 215–16; *Parris v. State*, 190 So.2d 564, at 565 (Ala. Ct. App., 1966); see also *People v. Santiago Vasquez*, 95 P.R.R. 581, at 584–85 (P.R. Sup. Ct., 1967); *State v. Stokes*, 163 S.E.2d 771, at 774 (N.C. Sup. Ct., 1968).

2

• • •

HONOR AMONG (MOSTLY) MEN: CASES FROM ANCIENT GREECE

1   See, generally, Antiphon, *Against the Stepmother*; Hamel, *Trying Neaira*, 5, 151–52; Demosthenes, *Against Neaera*, 21–22; Allen, "Punishment in Ancient Athens."

2   Kapparis, *Apollodoros*, 14; Aline Rousselle, *Porneia*, 30. Some religious practices tried to help men in the reproductive process by, for example, having women eat pastries shaped like genitalia, called *phalli* and *cunni*; see Kraemer, *Her Share*, 27. There is also some evidence that women did not always share the view that men were entirely responsible for conception. In a fascinating essay, historian John J. Winkler examines religious ceremonies in which Greek women jeered at wilted penile symbols. This laughter, in his view, was expressive of women's contempt of their men's mistaken sense of omnipotence in the reproductive process; see Winkler, *Constraints*, 205; Carson, "Putting Her in Her Place," 149–50, 156; Kapparis, *Apollodoros*, 16, outlines a number of outdoor duties for many Athenian wives; Plutarch, *Life of Alcibiades*; Pomeroy, *Goddesses*, 65, 90.

3   Hamel, *Trying Neaira*, 10. "Flute girls" were often auctioned off for sex at the end of symposia, when the accumulated drink and seductions of the evening guaranteed that the men would be ready to spend money. Lysias, *On a Wound by Premeditation*; see also Stephen Todd, *Commentary on Lysias*. Slaves were only permitted to give testimony in Athenian courts under torture. See Thür, "Role of the Witness," 151. See also Antiphon, *Against the Stepmother*, 10 (for the torture of slaves as the only way to "make even those prepared to lie confine their charges to the truth").

4   Cohen, *Law, Sexuality*, 80–81, 141; Thucydides, *Peloponnesian War*, 2.40;
     Carson, *Putting Her in Her Place*, 156; Thür, "Role of the Witness," 151;
     Demosthenes, *Apollodorus Against Stephanus* 2, 46.16; see also Isaeus, *On the
     Estate of Menecles*, 20; Pomeroy, *Goddesses*, 86.

5   MacDowell, *Law in Classical Athens*, 124–25; Lysias, *On the Murder of
     Eratosthenes*; Keuls, *Reign of the Phallus*, 5; Demosthenes, *Against Neaera*, 87:
     "When he has caught the adulterer, it shall not be lawful for the one who has
     caught him to continue living with his wife, and if he does so, he shall lose his
     civic rights and it shall not be lawful for the woman who is taken in adultery to
     attend public sacrifices; and if she does attend them, she may be made to suf-
     fer any punishment whatsoever, short of death, and that with impunity." Note
     that in Crete, women caught in adultery were far better off than their sisters in
     Athens; see Arnaoutoglou, *Ancient Greek Laws*, 24–25; Cantarella, "Gender,
     Sexuality and the Law," 240; Cohen, *Law, Sexuality*, 124.

6   Cary, "Return of the Radish"; see also Hamel, *Trying Neaira*, 68–70;
     Aristophanes, *Clouds*, 1079–85. Spartan law penalized those citizens who
     failed to produce children, and rewarded those who produced many. Men who
     did not marry were excluded from attending certain summer athletic games
     and, curiously, were paraded nude in winter around the agora and forced to
     chant a song saying they were being justly treated for disobeying the law. See
     Plutarch, *Life of Lycurgus*. Aristotle reported that men who produced three
     sons were exempted from military service; those with four sons were also
     exempted from taxation (Aristotle, *Politics*, 1270b 1–4). See also MacDowell,
     Spartan Law, 76; Pomeroy, *Goddesses*, 36.

7   *Lawrence v. Texas*, 539 U.S. 558 (2003); Plato, *Symposium*, 182(a), 189(c)–
     (e), 190(b), 191(b), 192; Mythologies merging male and female and providing
     a religious basis for multiple sexual inclinations are found in other Greek cults
     of bisexual divinities. Best known is the story of Hermaphroditus, the child of
     Hermes and Aphrodite. Hermes was, among other things, the god of boundar-
     ies and travelers. Boundaries throughout Athens were marked with herms-stat-
     ues whose most distinctive feature was a large, erect phallus. Aphrodite was the
     goddess most closely aligned with love, lust, and sex. Hermaphroditus was a
     handsome boy, raised by nymphs, who caught the fancy of Salmacis the naiad.
     He rejected her, but she refused to give up, and wrapped herself around him
     and called on the gods to merge their two bodies so they would never part. Her
     request was heard, and they became one intersex being. Ovid, *Metamorphoses*,
     IV, 317–88; Oscar Wilde trial transcript in Blasius and Phelan, *We Are
     Everywhere*, 111.

8   Cohen, *Law, Sexuality*, 193, citing Aristotle; Cantarella, *Bisexuality*, 4–7, 33;
     Jan Bremmer, "Greek Pederasty," 4; according to Plutarch, "The [adult] lovers
     shared the boys' reputations, both good and bad. It is said that on one occa-
     sion, when a boy in fighting let out an ignoble squeal, his lover was punished
     by the men in charge." Plutarch, *Life of Lycurgus*, 18.8; Brongersma, "Thera
     Inscriptions"; Aeschines, *Against Timarchus*, 12, 139; Cohen, *Law, Sexuality*,
     176. Approximately eighteen hundred years after the Athenian rules barring
     men from schools, Renaissance Venice also enacted a law that barred adult
     access to schoolboys, but that rule was intended to prevent all male-male sexual
     encounters, not merely to stop the wrong ones from taking place. See Ruggiero,
     Boundaries of Eros, 138.

9   Aeschines, *Against Timarchus*; *Winkler*, "Laying Down the Law," 225; Sissa,
     "Sexual Bodybuilding," 156.

10   Plato, Symposium, 183e–185c; Cohen, *Law, Sexuality*, 183–84, 197–200;
     the Greeks often viewed one man's gain of sexual honor as another's loss
     of same: "People do not find it pleasant to give honour to someone else, for
     they suppose that they themselves are being deprived of something." Winkler,
     "Laying Down the Law," 178, n.15 (quoting from anonymous Greek source);
     Cantarella, *Bisexuality*, 2, 213; Bremmer, *Greek Pederasty*, 9; Keuls, *Reign of
     the Phallus*, 291–92.

11   Aeschines, *Against Timarchus*, 133; Burg, *Gay Warriors*, 5; Plutarch, *Life of
     Pelopidas*.

12   Demosthenes, *Against Neaera*, 122; Exposure of unwanted infants, especially
     girls, was common throughout Greece. Abandoned babies automatically had
     slave status unless someone could prove they were freeborn. See Pomeroy,
     Goddesses, 140–41; Philentairos, *Huntress*, referenced in Hamel, *Trying
     Neaira*, 71–72; Keuls, *Reign of the Phallus*, 195–96; Kapparis, *Apollodoros*, 7;
     Isaeus, *On the Estate of Philoktemon*, 21.

13   Demosthenes, *Against Neaera*, 18, 21–22, 30–33, 54, 67–69. The historian
     Debra Hamel speculates that two men who bought Neaera from Nikarete got
     a better deal selling Neaera her own freedom rather than just turning her over
     to a brothel. A slightly past her prime prostitute would have had to service
     thousands of generous men to generate the kind of money they were demand-
     ing from Neaera, not counting her upkeep. A savvy brothel owner, therefore,
     would almost certainly have offered less than the two thousand drachmae.
     Hamel, *Trying Neaira*, 34.

14   There is some dispute as to whether Pericles met and fell in love with Aspasia
     before or after his divorce. See Pomeroy, *Goddesses*, 90; Kebric, Greek People,
     150; Henry, *Prisoner of History*, 60; Plutarch, *Life of Pericles*, 24, 32; Lysias,

Against Simon, 6; Waithe, *History of Women Philosophers*, 60, 75, 80; Aristophanes, *Acharnians*, 524–34; Bauman, *Political Trials*, 38.

15   Pomeroy, *Goddesses*, 66, 127–29 (quoting contract); Plutarch, *Life of Pericles*, 37.

<h1 style="text-align:center">3</h1>

• • •

<h2 style="text-align:center">IMPERIAL BEDROOMS:
SEX AND THE STATE IN ANCIENT ROME</h2>

1   Livy, *History of Rome*, bk. 39, sec. 8 (accessed at www.fordham.edu/halsall /ancient/romrelig2.asp). See also Gruen, *Studies*, 40–51, 72; Burkert, *Ancient Mystery Cults*, 52; Walsh, "Making a Drama," 191; Kraemer, *Her Share*, 42. Neither Dionysus nor his relations were strangers to the Romans. Anatomically ambitious depictions of Dionysus's son by Aphrodite, the permanently erect Priapus, stood everywhere in Roman lands. One statue of Priapus from Pompeii depicts him weighing his enormous member against a substantial quantity of gold. See also Robinson, *Penal Practice*, 29; Takács, *Vestal Virgins*, 97, 306.

2   Livy, *History of Rome*, bk. 39, sec. 6, 42–44 (accessed at http://mcadams .posc.mu.edu/txt/ah/Livy/Livy39.html); Kraemer, *Her Share*, 55–56; see also Pomeroy, *Goddesses*, 150–51, 177–79.

3   Valerius Maximus, "Women's Life"; see also Langlands, *Sexual Morality*, 11.

4   Juvenal, *Sixth Satire*; Ariadne Staples, *Good Goddess*, 59, 103; Valerius Maximus, "Women's Life;" Langlands, *Sexual Morality*, 97ff.; Livy, *History of Rome*, bk. 1, sec. 58 (accessed at www.perseus.tufts.edu/hopper/text?doc=Liv.+ 3+58&fromdoc=Perseus:text:1999.02.0153; Livy, *History of Rome*, bk. 3, sec. 48 (accessed at www.perseus.tufts.edu/hopper/text?doc=Liv.+3+48&fromdoc= Perseus:text:1999.02.0153); Tacitus, *Annals*, 3.34; Parker, "Vestals," 589.

5   Parker, "Vestals," 568; Pomeroy, *Goddesses*, 211; Plutarch, *Roman Questions*, 96; Plutarch, *Life of Numa*, 10. It seems that many vestals stayed longer than the required three decades, as many had bad luck in marriage after laying down their sacred offices. See also Wildfang, *Vestal Virgins*, 6–60. See also Dionysus of Halicarnassus, *Roman Antiquities*, bk. II, ch. 66: "And they regard the fire as consecrated to Vesta because that goddess, being the earth and occupying the central place in the universe, kindles the celestial fires from herself." The Vestals were involved in other rituals that seem incompatible with virginity, such as agricultural and fertility ceremonies. These included the Fordicidia rites, in which a Vestal burned a fetus torn from a pregnant cow; her chastity throughout their childbearing years gave them "stored up, potential procreative

power." See also Beard, "Sexual Status," 13; Robinson, *Ancient Rome*, 124; Livy, *History of Rome*, bk. 2, sec. 42 (accessed at www.perseus.tufts.edu /hopper/text?doc=liv.%202.42&lang=original); Cassius Dio, *Roman History*, bk. 26, sec. 87.

6   McGinn, *Prostitution*, 24–25; Staples, *Good Goddess*, 110; Pomeroy, *Goddesses*, 208–9; Lactantius, *Divine Institutes*, bk. 1, sec. 20.

7   Flavius Josephus, *Jewish Antiquities*, 18.65–80; Edwards, "Unspeakable Professions," 73; McGinn, *Prostitution*, 62–63, 168–69, 217–18; Cassius Dio, *Roman History*, 60.31.1; Seneca, *De Beneficiis*, 6.32.1; Edwards, *Politics of Immorality*, 61–62; Suetonius, *Lives, Tiberius*, 35; Habinek and Schiesaro, *Roman Cultural Revolution*, 29; Tacitus, *Annals*, 2.85.

8   Cassius Dio, *Roman History*, 56.25.7–8; Suetonius, *Lives, Nero*, 27, and *Caligula*, 40; Cantarella, *Bisexuality*, 174; Brundage, *Law, Sex, and Christian Society*, 105, 121; Robinson, *Penal Practice*, 165–66.

9   Tannahill, *Sex in History*, 125ff.; Dupont, *Daily Life*, 114–18; McGinn, *Prostitution*, 72–73, 146, 171, 192; Suetonius, *Lives, Augustus*, 65–69; Cassius Dio, *Roman History*, 54.16; Rousselle, *Porneia*, 85–88; Edwards, "Unspeakable Professions," 75; Parker, "Teratogenic Grid," 50–51; Blume, *Annotated Justinian Code*; Suetonius, *Lives, Tiberius*, 44–45; Brundage, *Law, Sex, and Christian Society*, 99–119.

10   Cantarella, *Bisexuality*, 180; Washburn, "Thessalonian Affair," 216–19; Williams and Friell, *Theodosius*, 67–68; Ambrose, "Letter to Theodosius"; Gibbon, *Decline and Fall*, 174–75.

11   Cantarella, *Bisexuality*, 150.

12   Parker, "Teratogenic Grid," 47ff.; Cantarella, *Bisexuality*, 104ff., 160–61, 175, 183–84; Walters, "Invading the Roman Body," 30; Crompton, *Homosexuality and Civilization*, 131, 144ff.; MacMullen, *Changes*, 182; *Bowers v. Hardwick*, 478 U.S. 186, 197 (1986) (*Burger, C. J., concurring*). Most U.S. sodomy laws would later be struck down by the Supreme Court in *Lawrence v. Texas*, 539 U.S. 558 (2003).

4
· · ·

THE MIDDLE AGES:
A CROWD CONDEMNED

1   See Brundage, *Law, Sex, and Christian Society*, 70–80; Boswell, *Christianity*, 114–27; Tannahill, *Sex in History*, 136–37.

2   Brundage, *Law, Sex, and Christian Society*, 59ff.; Boswell, *Christianity*, 114;
     Bullough, *Sexual Variance*, 175–76; I Corinthians: 6–7; Brundage, *Sex, Law,
     and Marriage*, 196.

3   Augustine, *City of God*, bk. IX, ch. 17, and bk. XIV, ch. 20, 24; Brundage,
     Law, Sex, and Christian Society, 80–84; Augustine, *Confessions*, 8.7.17.

4   Brundage, *Law, Sex, and Christian Society*, 64, 86–87; Bullough and Brundage,
     Sexual Practices, 2–8, 24; Karras, *Sexuality*, 37–42; Ranke-Heinemann,
     Eunuchs for Heaven, 118; Henriques, *Prostitution*, 20–21; Taylor, *Castration*,
     190–91; Coon, *Sacred Fictions*, 9.

5   On the subject of the penitentials, see, generally, Payer, *Sex and the
     Penitentials*; Brundage, *Law, Sex, and Christian Society*, 112, 150–77, 598–
     601; Tannahill, *Sex in History*, 144; Ranke-Heinemann, *Eunuchs for Heaven*,
     118–30, 139; Richards, *Sex, Dissidence*, 28–31; Brundage, *Law, Sex, and
     Christian Society*, 81–92, 204; Wemple, "Consent and Dissent," 240; Bullough,
     "Jus Primae Noctis," 164; Boswell, *Christianity, Social Tolerance*, 181.

6   Bullough and Brundage, *Sexual Practices*, 141–46; Gravdal, *Ravishing
     Maidens*, 7; Robinson, *Criminal Law*, 72–73; Ruggiero, *Boundaries of Eros*,
     156; Brundage, *Law, Sex, and Christian Society*, 119, 148, 164–65; Wemple,
     "Consent and Dissent," 230, 233, 240; Payer, *Sex and the Penitentials*, 42,
     117; Karras, *Sexuality*, 51; Carter, *Rape in Medieval England*, 155; Power, *Sex
     and Marriage*, 19, 46; Lacey and Danny Danziger, *Year 1000*, 172; Paul the
     Deacon, *History of the Langobards*, 182–83. For more on Henry Aldridge's
     comments on rape and pregnancy, see "In Wake of Aldridge's Comments,
     Group Works to Stop Reelection" in *The Virginian Pilot*, July 6, 1995.

7   Brundage, *Law, Sex, and Christian Society*, 241, 283, 312, 359, 505–6 (noting
     a fifteenth-century Italian town that adopted a law requiring men to treat their
     wives "with marital affection" or lose half of the women's dowries); Karras,
     Sexuality, 48, 75; Helmholz, *Litigation*, 67–68; Brundage, "Implied Consent,"
     248–52.

8   Karras, *Sexuality*, 86, 127; Bullough, "Jus Primae Noctis."

9   Carter, *Rape in Medieval England*, 36–38, 85, 105, 142–47, 155; Brundage,
     Sex, Law, and Marriage, 73–74; Ruggiero, *Boundaries of Eros*, 92–95. Note
     that rape was not criminalized throughout England. A fifteenth-century Italian
     traveler recorded that in Northumberland, men and children slept in fortified
     towers while leaving their women prey to Scottish bandits. The men reasoned
     that the worst that could happen to the women was rape, which they did not
     regard as wrong. See Stone, *Family, Sex and Marriage*, 604–5.

10 Brundage, *Law, Sex, and Christian Society*, 235–41, 457, 563–64; Karras, *Sexuality*, 71, 157; Ruggiero, *Boundaries of Eros*, 146–47; Rider, *Magic and Impotence in the Middle Ages*, 43–44, 79; Brundage, "Playing by the Rules," 23–41; Brundage, *Sex, Law, and Marriage*, 407–23.

11 Bullough and Bullough, *Sexual Attitudes*, 206–7; Henriques, *Prostitution*, 42–50; Richards, *Sex, Dissidence*, 126; Horne, *Seven Ages of Paris*, 39; Karras, *Sexuality*, 69, 105–6; Ruggiero, *Boundaries of Eros*, 185; Brundage, *Sex, Law, and Marriage*, 825–45; Brundage, *Law, Sex, and Christian Society*, 465–66, 524–25; Karras, *Common Women*, 19.

12 Brundage, *Sex, Law, and Marriage*, 827; Brundage, *Law, Sex, and Christian Society*, 465; Karras, *Sexuality in Medieval Europe*, 104; Ruggiero, *Boundaries of Eros*, 72–83; Henriques, *Prostitution*, 38; Wemple, "Consent and Dissent," 239. Note that medieval Naples had a special Court of Prostitutes, which resolved disputes in the whoring trade. The court was probably set up to guard prostitutes from abuse, but it soon degenerated into an official shakedown machine. Innocent girls were found on the streets by agents of the court and flung into jail, regardless of their offenses. They were held there until someone could come and pay for their release. Prominent citizens were also black-mailed by the court. See Sanger, *History of Prostitution*, 160–61; Henriques, *Prostitution*, 54–55.

13 Boswell, *Same-Sex Unions*, 253, 279–89; Boswell, *Christianity*, 169–70; Cantarella, *Bisexuality*, 184; Payer, *Sex and the Penitentials*, 135–39; Brundage, *Law, Sex, and Christian Society*, 121–22, 398–99, 473, 533; Hussey, *Paris*, 76–78; Burg, *Gay Warriors*, 68–69.

14 Trachtenberg, *Devil and the Jews*, 44, 48–52, 100–5, 175, 187, 213; Klaits, *Servants of Satan*, 20; Brundage, *Law, Sex, and Christian Society*, 399, 473, 534; Boswell, *Christianity*, 15–17, 277–93; Brundage, *Sex, Law, and Marriage*, 39.

15 Ruggiero, *Boundaries of Eros*, 111–13, 134.

16 Davidson, "Sodomy in Early Modern Venice," 67.

17 Karras, *Sexuality in Medieval Europe*, 132–38; Boes, "On Trial for Sodomy," 27–45; Davidson, "Sodomy in Early Modern Venice," 65–81, Ruggiero, *Boundaries of Eros*, 111–22; Monter, "Sodomy: The Fateful Accident," 192–216.

18 Brundage, *Law, Sex, and Christian Society*, 400; Crompton, "Myth," 11–25; Karras, *Sexuality in Medieval Europe*, 110–11, 143; Karras and Boyd, "Ut Cum Muliere," 101–16; Montaigne, *Complete Works*, 1059; Ruggiero, *Boundaries of Eros*, 136, 195; Crompton, *Homosexuality and Civilization*, 246–47.

19 Boswell, *Christianity*, 230–32, 298–300; Karras, *Sexuality in Medieval Europe*, 7–10; Foucault, *History of Sexuality*, 43.

20 See, generally, Tulchin, "Same-Sex Couples," 613–47; Boswell, *Same-Sex Unions*, 182–85, 190–91, 240–65; Eskridge, "History of Same-Sex Marriage," 1419–1513; Montaigne, *Complete Works*, 1165; Ladurie, *Peasants of Languedoc*, 35.

5
...
GROPING TOWARD MODERNITY:
THE EARLY MODERN PERIOD, 1500–1700

1 Stone, *Family, Sex and Marriage*, 530–31, 539, 559; see also Wilmot's "impromptus" on Charles II in John Wilmont, *Works*, 86.

2 Martin Luther, *Familiar Discourses*, 256; Hull, *Sexuality*, 20–25; Klaits, *Servants of Satan*, 79–81; Brundage, *Law, Sex, and Christian Society*, 207, 536, 554–57, 563–69, 587, 571; Roper, "Luther"; Karant-Nunn and Wiesner-Hanks, *Luther*, 157; Posner, *Sex and Reason*, 51; Tannahill, *Sex in History*, 334.

3 Stone, *Family, Sex, and Marriage*, 98–99, 144–45, 519, 631; Martin Ingram, *Church Courts, Sex and Marriage in England*, 69, 161, 212, 254–55, 294, 315; Wrightson and Levine, *Poverty and Piety*, 110ff.; Kermode and Walker, *Women, Crime and the Courts*, 33.

4 Stone, *Family, Sex, and Marriage*, 147, 520, 634–35; Ingram, *Church Courts*, 261–67; Wrightson and Levine, *Poverty and Piety*, 126ff.; Fissell, *Vernacular Bodies*, 191; Manzione, *Sex in Tudor London*, 96.

5 Ingram, *Church Courts*, 165, 295–96, 302, 313–15; Poos, "Sex, Lies," 602–4; Kermode and Walker, *Women, Crime and the Courts*, 32, 35, 57–58, 61–62; Stone, *Family, Sex and Marriage*, 93–94, 143–46, 623; Wrightston and Levine, *Poverty and Piety*, 110ff.; Ingram, *Church Courts*, 163–65.

6 Hull, *Sexuality*, 16–17, 25–28, 41–43, 66–71, 79, 81, 95–98, 104–5; see also the Bavarian decree of September, 20, 1635, against fornication, adultery, swearing, etc.: Bayerisches Hauptstaatsarchiv, München, General Registratur Faszikel 321 Nummer 7 in Hull, *Sexuality*, 96; Hunt, *Governing Morals*, 1; Ingram, *Church Courts*, 151; Stone, *Family, Sex and Marriage*, 631–33; Burg, *Boys at Sea*, 2–3.

7 DeJean, *Reinvention of Obscenity*, 4, 9, 124–25; see also Donald Thomas's introduction in Millot and L'Ange, *School of Venus*; "Sexy 'Venus' May Be Oldest Figurine Yet Discovered," Reuters, May 13, 2009; Bullough and

Bullough, *Sexual Attitudes*, 183–85. I thank Paula Findlen for the lovely turn of phrase "masturbating to the classics"; see Findlen, "Humanism, Politics," 52, 57, 81, 95–98; Talvacchia, *Taking Positions* (which delves into the provenance of the drawings in *Aretino's Postures*); Vignali, *La Cazzaria*.

8   DeJean, *Reinvention of Obscenity*, 39–41, 41–56, 62–63, 78; Rousseau, *Confessions*—interestingly, Rousseau was referring to women reading while masturbating, not men; Donald Thomas, introduction to Millot and L'Ange, *School of Venus*, 57; Hunt, *Governing Morals*, 113, 116–17; Millot and L'Ange, *School of Venus*, 11, 14, 22–23; 62–63; Pepys, *Diary*, entry for February 9, 1669.

9   Millot and L'Ange, *The School of Venus*, 16; Stone, *Family, Sex and Marriage*, 538; Hearne, Wood, and Leland, *Lives*, 187–88; Donald Thomas, introduction to Millot and L'Ange, *School of Venus*, 50–51.

10 Stone, *Family, Sex and Marriage*, 492–93, 559–60; Greenberg, *Construction of Homosexuality*, 327–28; Pepys, *Diary*, entry for July 1, 1663; Bingham, "Seventeenth-Century Attitudes"; Burg, "Ho Hum," 69–73. The term "buggery" originated in medieval Europe as an insult used to describe the rumored homosexual practices of heretics from the Buggre sect, which originated in Bulgaria. The sect's followers were called *bogomils*, which became *buggres* once its adherents spread abroad. See *New Oxford American Dictionary*, 2nd ed.; Cynthia Herrup, "Patriarch at Home." Despite the tendency of law enforcement to pursue the death penalty when same-gender sex also involved heresy, bestiality, or witchcraft, there were still quite a few straightforward homosexual-sodomy prosecutions in some areas of Europe. See Boes, "On Trial for Sodomy," 27; Monter, "Sodomy and Heresy," 41–55; Crompton, *Homosexuality and Civilization*.

11 Crompton, "Myth," 18; Boes, "On Trial for Sodomy," 33–35; Crompton, *Homosexuality and Civilization*, 324; Monter, "Sodomy and Heresy," 43–47; Masters, *Forbidden Sexual Behavior*, 37–39; Kadri, *The Trial*, 167–68; Maxwell-Stuart, "Wild, Filthie," 83–87, 92; Evans, *Criminal Prosecution*.

12 Klaits, *Servants of Satan*, 52–53, 57–59, 128, 138–39; Levack, *Witch-Hunt*; Midelfort, *Witch Hunting*, 22–24; Kadri, *The Trial*, 123; Robbins, *Encyclopedia of Witchcraft*, 289–90, 374, 464, 467; Levack, *Witchcraft Sourcebook*, 107–8, 199, 290; Stephens, *Demon Lovers*, 5, 101–2, 281; Roper, "Witchcraft," 136–37; Rémy and Summers, *Demonolatry*, ch. 6; Masters, *Forbidden Sexual Behavior*, 50.

13 Trachtenberg, *Devil and the Jews*, 45–47; Poliakov, *History of Anti-Semitism*, 142, 152–53. De Lancre's descriptions of sabbats have to be read to be believed. They go on for hundreds of nauseating pages, and involve thousands

of witches having sex with each other and with devils at the same time and the liberal enjoyment of monstrous satanic penises, incest, child cannibalism, homosexuality, and the preparation of poisons. See Klaits, *Servants of Satan*, 33, 52–53, 57, 72–73, Kramer and Sprenger, *Malleus*, Part 1, Question I, Part II, Question VII, Part III, Questions VII, XIII, XV; Robbins, *Encyclopedia of Witchcraft*, 492–94; see also Fudenberg and Levine, *Steady State Learning*, which applies game theory to water ordeals; James I, *Daemonologie*; Levack, *Witchcraft Sourcebook*, 82–83, 100.

14　Scott, *History of Torture*, 97; Deacon, *Matthew Hopkins*, 110; Maple, *Dark World of Witches,* 100; Kramer and Sprenger, *Malleus*, Part II, Questions XIII–XV, Part III, Section XV; Klaits, *Servants of Satan*, 134, 141; Stephens, *Demon Lovers*, 6; Rémy and Summers, *Demonolatry*, 161–65; Lea, *History of the Inquisition*, sec. 227; Ankarloo and Stuart Clark, *Athlone History of Witchcraft*, 2, 57; Gent, *Trial of the Bideford Witches*, 7.

6

...

THE NEW WORLD OF SEXUAL OPPORTUNITY

1　Rothman, *Notorious in the Neighborhood*, 149–63; Higginbotham and Kopytoff, "Racial Purity," 1967–2028; Bardaglio, "Rape and Law," 749–72; Block, *Rape and Sexual Power*, 183. In one Virginia case, a slave women named Sukie successfully resisted her master's advances by shoving him into a boiling cauldron, but her owner soon got rid of her:

"Ole Marsa was always tryin' to make Sukie his gal." One day when she was making lye soap and he approached her, she "gave him a shove an' push his hindparts down in de hot pot o' Soap. Soap was near to bilin', an' it burn him near to death . . . Marsa never did bother slave gals no mo'." But a few days later Sukie was sent to the auction block. (Rachel F. Moran, "Love with a Proper Stranger," 1665)

2　Wood, "Sexual Violation," 9; Sayre, "Native American Sexuality," 38–39; Burnard, "Sexual Life," 163–89.

3　Wood, "Sexual Violation," 11–19; Cave, *Lethal Encounters*, n.39; Sayre, "Native American Sexuality," 39.

4　Trexler, *Sex and Conquest*, 1, 40, 47, 65, 82, 146; Goldberg, *Sodometries*, 179–82, 193–202.

5　Brundage, *Law, Sex, and Christian Society*, 518; Elbl, "Men Without Wives."

6　Sayre, "Native American Sexuality," 40–41; Spear, "Colonial Intimacies," 75–98.

7   Spear, "Colonial Intimacies," 91–98; Donoghue, *Black Women/White Men*, 7; Lavrin, "Sexuality in Colonial Mexico," 47–95; Waldron, "Sinners and the Bishop," 157–77.

8   Brent Staples, "On Race and the Census: Struggling with Categories That No Longer Apply," *The New York Times*, February 5, 2007; Rowland Nethaway, "Government Census Methods Promote Enduring Racial Myths," *Los Angeles Daily Journal*, March 20, 2007; Woodson, "Beginnings of Miscegenation," 44.

9   Bardaglio, *Reconstructing the Household*, 51–53; Woodson, "Beginnings of Miscegenation," 45–48; Higginbotham and Kopytoff, "Racial Purity," 1989, 1991, 1996.

10   Higginbotham and Kopytoff, "Racial Purity," 1996, 2024; Woodson, "Beginnings of Miscegenation," 51–58; Zabel, "Interracial Marriage and the Law," 56–57 (noting that Florida declared people to be "Negroes" only if they had full "Negro" great-grandmothers).

11   Sweet, *Legal History*, 154–55. See also Rothman, *Notorious in the Neighborhood*, 38–46. The controversy as to whether or not Jefferson fathered children with Sally Hemmings has generated no small amount of debate and literature. Rothman takes the position that they indeed had children together, but of course there are reasonable arguments on both sides of the issue.

12   Ariela J. Gross, "Litigating Whiteness," 112, 126, 133, 138, 167, 170–75.

13   Bardaglio, *Reconstructing the Household*, 52; Higginbotham and Kopytoff, "Racial Purity," 1982–83.

14   Rothman, *Notorious in the Neighborhood*, 168–71, 177; Bardaglio, *Reconstructing the Household*, 63; Forret, *Race Relations at the Margins*, 209; Virginia Supreme Court quote comes from *Naim v. Naim*, 197 Va. 80, 84, 87 S.E.2d 749, 752 (1956). Naim involved a Chinese male and a white female who had a valid marriage ceremony in North Carolina and returned to Virginia to reside as husband and wife. For the 2009 quote from the Louisiana justice of the peace, see "Louisiana: Calls for Resignation," *The New York Times*, October 17, 2009.

15   Foucault, *Foucault Live*, 331; Wood, "Sexual Violation in the Conquest of the Americas," 16, 24, 33.

16   Elbl, "Men Without Wives," 68–69; Wood, "Sexual Violation," 23; Donoghue, *Black Women/White Men*, 13, 61–66, 69, 97–99; Burnard, "Sexual Life," 166–67, 177–78; Thomas, *Slave Trade*, 418.

17 Bardaglio, "Rape and the Law," 752–53, 769–70; Bardaglio, *Reconstructing the Household*, 64, 193–94; Block, *Rape and Sexual Power*, 163–64, 176–77, 194, 203; Higginbotham and Kopytoff, "Racial Purity," 2008–18.

18 Oaks, "Things Fearful to Name," 268–81; Crompton, "Homosexuals and the Death Penalty," 277–93.

19 See, generally, Burg, *Sodomy and the Pirate Tradition*.

20 Oaks, "Things Fearful to Name," 273–76; Burg, *Sodomy and the Pirate Tradition*, 107–78, 122–34, 144–46; Burg, *Gay Warriors*, 103–14; Dynes and Donaldson, *History of Homosexuality*, 134–42.

7
...
THE EIGHTEENTH CENTURY:
REVELATION AND REVOLUTION

1 Posner, *Sex and Reason*, 51–52; Peakman, *Lascivious Bodies*, 11ff.; Bullough and Bullough, *Women and Prostitution*, 175; Porter, "Mixed Feelings," 9. See also Hunt, *Politics, Culture, and Class*, 63–66 (describing the "Festival of Reason" held at Notre Dame).

2 Bullough, "Masturbation," 28–30; Stengers and van Neck, "Masturbation," 65–69, 75–77, 87–89; Hull, *Sexuality*, 258–80; Levins, *American Sex Machines*, 11–41. Note that antimasturbation campaigns also sometimes targeted girls, who were warned that they risked bladder infections, urinary incontinence, hysterical cravings for sexual intercourse, and loss of rosiness in the cheeks and lips.

3 Porter, "Secrets of Generation Display'd," 1–9; Clark, *Desire*, 102–7; Roodenburg, "Venus Minsieke Gasthuis," 84–107; Hitchcock, "Redefining Sex," 82.

4 The trial transcripts are collected in *Miss Marianne Woods and Miss Jane Pirie Against Dame Helen Cumming Gordon* (Arno Press, 1975). See also Lillian Faderman, *Surpassing the Love of Men*, 147–54.

5 The Hamilton case was reported both in the newspapers and in a pamphlet by the novelist Henry Fielding, titled *The Female Husband: or, The Surprising History of Mrs. Mary, alias Mr. George Hamilton Who Was Convicted of Having Married a Young Woman of Wells and Lived with Her as Her Husband, Taken from Her Own Mouth Since Her Confinement*. Fielding is generally believed to have embellished many of the facts for maximum sensational effect. See Norton, *Mother Clap's*, 407–9; Thomas, *Henry Fielding*, 253–57.

6   Peakman, *Lascivious Bodies*, 175ff.; McCormick, *Secret Sexualities*, 229ff.
      (Cleland text).

7   Crompton, "Myth," 18. The German law, Section 116 of the Constitution of
      the Holy Roman Emperor Charles V, held: "If anyone commits impurity with
      a beast, or a man with a man, or a woman with a woman, they have forfeited
      their lives and shall, after the common custom, be sentenced to death by burn-
      ing." See Ericksson, "Lesbian Execution," 27–40.

8   Clark, *Desire*, 134–35; Noordam, "Sodomy in the Dutch Republic," 207–28;
      Norton, *Mother Clap's*, 86–87; Bristow, *Vice and Vigilance*, 12–13; Bloch, *Sex
      Life in England*, 129.

9   Hunt, *Governing Morals*, 34–38, 48–51; Bristow, *Vice and Vigilance*, 17–21,
      30–31; Norton, *Mother Clap's*, 62–63, 68, 88, 98–99, 105.

10   Van der Meer, "Persecutions of Sodomites," 271–76; Noordam, "Sodomy in
      the Dutch Republic," 207–28; Steakley, "Sodomy in Enlightenment Prussia,"
      165–66.

11   Coward, "Attitudes to Homosexuality," 235–43; Copley, *Sexual Moralities
      in France*, 18–24; Merrick, *Order and Disorder*, 295–96, 307–8, 322; Rey,
      "Police and Sodomy," 134–35, 141–42.

12   Naphy, *Sex Crimes*, 66–67; Trumbach, *Heterosexuality*, 210–13; Simpson,
      "Vulnerability and the Age of Female Consent," 192–94; Hyde, *History of
      Pornography*, 148; Ulrich, *Midwife's Tale*, 118–27.

13   Stone, "Libertine Sexuality," 513–19; Peakman, *Lascivious Bodies*, 237, 246–
      50; Rousseau, *Confessions*, 10–11; Hyde, *History of Pornography*, 127.

14   Dekkers, *Dearest Pet*, 10–11; Parker, "Is a Duck an Animal?", 103–4; Evans,
      Criminal Prosecution, 150–51; Peakman, *Lascivious Bodies*, 255–61; Hayman,
      Marquis de Sade, 151; Copley, *Sexual Moralities in France*, 34, 55–56. Note
      that in 2009, an American man was sentenced to three years' jail time for a
      second sexual offense against the same horse. The animal's owner had become
      suspicious "because her horse was acting strange and getting infections, and
      she noticed things were moved around the barn and dirt was piled up near the
      horse's stall." The offender was caught on video. See "SC Man Gets 3 Years
      in Prison for Sex with Horse," Associated Press, November 4, 2009; see also
      Masters, *Forbidden Sexual Behavior*, 16, 130.

15   Hunt, "Pornography and the French Revolution"; Clark, *Desire*, 107;
      Hitchcock, *English Sexualities*, 14–15; Potts and Short, *Ever Since Adam and
      Eve*, 79; Wagner, "Pornographer in the Courtroom," 120–40; Pinkus, *Grub
      St.*, 54–55.

16 Wagner, "The Pornographer in the Courtroom," 129; Hunt, "Pornography and the French Revolution," 303; Hyde, *A History of Pornography*, 156–62; Paul Baines and Pat Rogers, *Edmund Curll*, 157–68; Norton, *Mother Clap's*, 92–99; Pinkus, *Grub St.*, 81.

17 See *Memoirs v. Massachusetts*, 383 U.S. 413 (1966). The first version of *Fanny Hill* contained a lengthy passage about the "odious" buggery of a young male "Ganymede" in Hampton Court, but that was soon deleted. See Norton, *Mother Clap's*, 177–78; see also McCord, "Charming and Wholesome Literature," 275–77; Bloch, *Sex Life in England*, 316–17; Hyde, *History of Pornography*, 97–100; Hitchcock, *English Sexualities*, 20; Kendrick, *Secret Museum*, 209–11; Grazia, *Girls Lean Back Everywhere*, 436–43.

18 Merrick, *Order and Disorder*, 21–33.

19 Guicciardi, "Between the Licit and the Illicit," 89–93; Merrick, *Order and Disorder*, 39; Bullough and Bullough, *Women and Prostitution*, 165–66; Merrick, "Sexual Politics," 77–79.

20 Burrows, *Blackmail, Scandal, and Revolution*, 3, 10–17, 27, 71, 90, 98–101, 219; Hunt, "Pornography and the French Revolution," 301, 312–15, 324–25; Merrick, *Order and Disorder*, 39; Merrick, "Sexual Politics," 81; Crawford, *European Sexualities*, 225–66.

21 Burrows, *Blackmail, Scandal, and Revolution*, 33–36, 152, 158–62; Hunt, "Pornography and the French Revolution," 324; Stengers and van Neck, *Masturbation*, 83–84. The necklace had originally been commissioned by Louis XV for Madame du Barry, but the king died before it was completed. By the time la Motte's scheme started, Louis XVI had already offered it to Marie Antoinette. The queen had refused it.

22 Hayman, *Marquis de Sade*, 150–51; Copley, *Sexual Moralities in France*, 31–34, 45.

23 Bullough and Bullough, *Women and Prostitution*, 166–75; Flaherty, "Law and the Enforcement of Morals in Early America," 63; Peakman, *Lascivious Bodies*, 14, 16, 19; Hitchcock, *English Sexualities*, 71, 93–94, 105–7; Jones, "Prostitution and the Ruling Class," 7–28.

8

. . .

THE NINETEENTH CENTURY:
HUMAN NATURE ON TRIAL

1   Robertson, "Age of Consent Laws"; Morone, *Hellfire Nation*, 247. By 1880, not one state had set the age of consent at older than thirteen. Odem, *Delinquent Daughters*, 9, 68–69.

2   Grand jury testimony of Samantha Jane Gailey in *People v. Polanski*, Case No. A-334,139, March 24, 1977.

3   Fisher, *Scandal*, 33–34, 53–57, 63; Weeks, *Sex, Politics and Society*, 88–89; Hunt, *Governing Morals*, 165–66; Morone, *Hellfire Nation*, 248; Roberts, *Making English Morals*, 267.

4   Roberts, *Making English Morals*, 267–68; Fisher, *Scandal*, 60–89; Hunt, *Governing Morals*, 167–68; Morone, *Hellfire Nation*, 247; Bullough and Bullough, *Sexual Attitudes*, 215–16; Hyde, *History of Pornography*, 148.

5   *Barton v. Bee Line*, 238 A.D. 501, 265 N.Y.S. 284 (1933).

6   *Braun v. Heidrich*, 62 N.D. 85, 241 N.W. 599 (1932). See also the non-bylined article in the *Fordham Law Review*, which expresses concern that aggressive protection against statutory rape "might conceivably be an incentive to [a girl's] active solicitation or voluntary acquiescence and might also develop into a very fertile field of 'legal extortion.'" *Fordham Law Review* 7 (1938): 275.

7   Arnot and Usborne, *Gender and Crime*, 233.

8   Burton, "Conjugality on Trial," 33–56; Van der Veer, *Imperial Encounter*, 96.

9   Morone, *Hellfire Nation*, 258ff.; Walkowitz, *Prostitution and Victorian Society*, 71–89; Clark, *Desire*, 132–33; Arnot and Usborne, *Gender and Crime*, 155–58; Bullough and Bullough, *Women and Prostitution*, 188–94; Jusek, "Sexual Morality," 123–42.

10   Walkowitz, *Prostitution and Victorian Society*, 71–89, 104–12; Fisher, *Scandal*, 15–26, 42, 55–58; Bullough, *Women and Prostitution*, 95–96; Arnot and Usborne, *Gender and Crime*, 160.

11   Bullough, *Women and Prostitution*, 217–24; Henriques, *Prostitution*, 268–70, 283–84; Horowitz, *Rereading Sex*, 125–27, 135, 147–49; Morone, *Hellfire Nation*, 258–59; *San Francisco Chronicle*, December 5, 1869.

12   Luibhéid, *Entry Denied*, 13, 35–38, 47–50; Abrams, "Polygamy, Prostitution"; Morone, *Hellfire Nation*, 261–67.

13   Largent, *Breeding Contempt*, 1–27, 31–32, 65; "Whipping and Castration and Punishments for Crime," *Yale Law Journal* 8 (1899): 371–86; Stengers and van Neck, *Masturbation*, 111–14; Block, *Rape and Sexual Power*, 143–52.

14   Roberts, "Society for the Suppression of Vice," 159–76; Hunt, *Governing Morals*, 70–73; Bristow, *Vice and Vigilance*, 42–48; Hyde, *History of Pornography*, 167–72; Thomas, *Long Time Burning*, 190; *R. v. Hicklin* (1868), LR 3 QB 360. (Hicklin was the magistrate who ordered the destruction of the pamphlets.)

15   See, generally, Elizabeth Ladenson, *Dirt for Art's Sake*, 11, 17–77.

16   The term "Comstockery" was coined by the playwright George Bernard Shaw after Comstock attacked his play *Mr. Warren's Profession*. See also Grazia, *Girls Lean Back Everywhere*, 4–6; Horowitz, *Rereading Sex*, 104–5, 317–18, 368–74; Comstock, *Traps for the Young*, 2, 28; Talese, *Thy Neighbor's Wife*, 43; Morone, *Hellfire Nation*, 230–31, 241; Meadow and Weiss, *Women's Conflicts*, 113–14; Abbott, *History of Celibacy*, 204.

17   Morone, *Hellfire Nation*, 228–40; Horowitz, *Rereading Sex*, 381–87, 405–18, 432–34; Grazia, *Girls Lean Back Everywhere*, 1–5.

18   See, generally, Albert, "Books on Trial," 119–39.

19   See the *London Times's* coverage of the Boulton and Park legal proceedings, gathered at www.victorianlondon.org; see also *Weeks, Sex, Politics and Society*, 101, discussing the fact that Dr. Tardieu in France had done considerable work identifying physical signs of homosexuality, but the lawyers for both the prosecution and the defense were wary of research originating in Britain's licentious neighbor across the channel; the attorney general observed that it was fortunate there was "very little learning or knowledge about this subject in this country," while the defense held that it was wrong to rely "on the new-found treasures of French literature on this subject—which thank God is still foreign to the libraries of British surgeons"; Fisher, *Scandal*, 141–42.

20   The word "homosexual" was coined in 1869 by the Hungarian Károly Mária Kertbeny in a pamphlet defending homosexual orientation. See Bullough and Bullough, *Sexual Attitudes*, 229–35; Weeks, *Sex, Politics and Society*, 101–5. In France, in 1857, Dr. Tardieu cautioned police to look for signs of masturbation in all men arrested for public indecency, as masturbation was tantamount to proof of a tendency toward "pederasty." Copley, *Sexual Moralities in France*, 106; Fisher, *Scandal*, 138–46; Wright, *Oscar's Books*, 218–20; Keeler and Meadley, *Sex Scandals*, 193–224.

21   See Arnot and Usborne, *Gender and Crime*, 233; Fisher, *Scandal*, 150; Wright, *Oscar's Books*, 223–39; Knappman, *Great World Trials*, 155.

22   On the subject of the Wilde trials, see also Hyde, *Trials of Oscar Wilde*.

23   Wright, *Oscar's Books*, 103; Krafft-Ebing, *Psychopathia Sexualis*, 255ff.; Wright, *Oscar's Books*, 238–39.

24   Clark, *Desire*, 137; Copley, *Sexual Moralities in France*, 102–3; William Peniston, "A Public Offense Against Decency," 12–32.

25   Nancy Erber, "Queer Follies," 186–208.

BIBLIOGRAPHY

Abbott, Elizabeth. *A History of Celibacy*. New York: Scribner, 2000.

Abrams, Kerry. "Polygamy, Prostitution, and the Federalization of Immigration Law." *Columbia Law Review* 105 (2005): 641–716.

Aeschines *Against Timarchus* Translated by Charles Darwin Adams. Cambridge: Harvard University Press; London: William Heinemann Ltd., 1919.

Albert, Nicole. "Books on Trial: Prosecutions for Representing Sapphism in Fin-de-Siècle France." In *Disorder in the Court: Trials and Sexual Conflict at the Turn of the Century*, edited by George Robb and Nancy Erber, 119–139. New York: New York University Press, 1999.

Allen, Danielle S. "Punishment in Ancient Athens." In *Athenian Law in Its Democratic Context* (Center for Hellenic Studies On-Line Discussion Series), edited by Adriaan Lanni. Republished in *Dēmos: Classical Athenian Democracy*, edited by C. W. Blackwell. Accessed January 5, 2012 at The Stoa: A Consortium for Electronic Publication in the Humanities (A. Mahoney and R. Scaife, eds.) at http://www.stoa.org/projects/demos/punishment.pdf.

Ambrose. "Ambrose to Theodosius I 390 [Letter 51]." *Medieval Sourcebook*. Internet History Sourcebooks Project, accessed August 29, 2011, www .fordham.edu/halsall/source/ambrose-let51.asp.

Ankarloo, Bengt, and Stuart Clark. *The Athlone History of Witchcraft and Magic in Europe*. London: Athlone Press, 1999.

Antiphon. *Against the Stepmother*. Edited by Gregory R. Crane and K. J. Maidmont. Perseus Digital Project, Tufts University, accessed September 3, 2011, www.perseus.tufts.edu/hopper/text?doc=Perseus%3Atext%3A1999.01 .0020&redirect=true.

Aristophanes. *Acharnians*. Edited by Gregory R. Crane. Perseus Digital Project, Tufts University, accessed September 3, 2011, www.perseus.tufts.edu/hopper/ text?doc=Perseus%3Atext%3A1999.01.0240%3Acard%3D1.

———. *Clouds*. Edited by Gregory R. Crane and William James Hickie. Perseus Digital Project, Tufts University, accessed September 3, 2011,

www.perseus.tufts.edu/hopper/text?doc= Perseus%3Atext%3A1999.01.0241
%3Acard%3D1.

Aristotle. *Politics*. Edited by Gregory R. Crane and K. J. Maidmont. Perseus Digital
Project, Tufts University, accessed September 3, 2011, www.perseus.tufts.edu
/hopper/text?doc=Perseus%3atext%3a1999.01.0058.

Arnaoutoglou, Ilias. *Ancient Greek Laws: A Sourcebook*. London: Routledge,
1998.

Arnot, Margaret L., and Cornelie Usborne. *Gender and Crime in Modern Europe*.
London: UCL Press, 1999.

Augustine. *The City of God*. Translated by Marcus Dods. Edinburgh: T&T Clark,
1871.

Baines, Paul, and Pat Rogers. *Edmund Curll, Bookseller*. Oxford: Clarendon Press,
2007.

Bardaglio, Peter W. "Rape and the Law in the Old South: 'Calculated to Excite
Indignation in Every Heart.'" *The Journal of Southern History* 60 (1994):
749–72.

———. *Reconstructing the Household: Families, Sex, and the Law in the
Nineteenth-Century South*. Chapel Hill: University of North Carolina Press,
1995.

Bauman, Richard A. *Political Trials in Ancient Greece*. London: Routledge, 1990.

Beard, Mary. "The Sexual Status of Vestal Virgins." *The Journal of Roman Studies*
70 (1980): 12–27.

Bingham, Caroline. "Seventeenth Century Attitudes Toward Deviant Sex." *Journal
of Interdisciplinary History* 1 (1971): 447–68.

Blackstone, William. *Commentaries on the Laws of England*. Book 4, Chapter 15:
"Of Offenses Against the Persons of Individuals." Accessed August 29, 2011,
http://ebooks.adelaide.edu.au/b/blackstone/william/comment/book4.15
.html#nr4.15.36.

Blasius, Mark, and Shane Phelan, eds. *We Are Everywhere: A Historical Sourcebook
of Gay and Lesbian Politics*. New York: Routledge, 1997.

Bloch, Iwan. *Sex Life in England*. New York: Panurge Press, 1934.

Block, Sharon. *Rape and Sexual Power in Early America*. Chapel Hill: University of
North Carolina Press, 2006.

Blume, Fred H. *Annotated Justinian Code*. Book IX, Title IX. University of Wyoming, accessed August 29, 2011, uwacadweb.uwyo.edu/blume&justinian /Book%209PDF/Book9-9.pdf.

Boes, Maria R. "On Trial for Sodomy in Early Modern Germany." In *Sodomy in Early Modern Europe*, edited by Tom Betteridge, 227–45. New York: Manchester University Press, 2002.

Boswell, John. *Christianity, Social Tolerance, and Homosexuality: Gay People in Western Europe from the Beginning of the Christian Era to the Fourteenth Century*. Chicago: University of Chicago Press, 1980.

———. *Same-Sex Unions in Premodern Europe*. New York: Vintage Books, 1995.

Bremmer, Jan N. "Greek Pederasty and Modern Homosexuality." In *From Sappho to de Sade: Moments in the History of Sexuality*, edited by Jan N. Bremmer, 1–14. London: Routledge, 1991.

Bristow, Edward J. *Vice and Vigilance: Purity Movements in Britain Since 1700*. Dublin: Gill and Macmillan, 1977.

Brongersma, Edward. "The Thera Inscriptions: Ritual or Slander?" *Journal of Homosexuality* 20 (1990): 31–40.

Brundage, James A. "Implied Consent to Intercourse." In *Consent and Coercion to Sex and Marriage in Ancient and Medieval Societies*, edited by Angeliki E. Laiou, 245–56. Washington, DC: Dumbarton Oaks Research Library and Collection, 1993.

———. *Law, Sex, and Christian Society in Medieval Europe*. Chicago: University of Chicago Press, 1987.

———. "Playing by the Rules: Sexual Behavior and Legal Norms in Medieval Europe." In *Desire and Discipline: Sex and Sexuality in the Premodern West*, edited by Jacqueline Murray and Konrad Eisenbichler, 25–41. Toronto: University of Toronto Press, 1996.

———. *Sex, Law, and Marriage in the Middle Ages*. Aldershot, UK: Variorum, 1993.

Bullough, Vern L. "*Jus Primae Noctis* or *Droit du Seigneur*." *The Journal of Sex Research* 28 (1991): 163–66.

———. "Masturbation: A Historical Overview." *Journal of Psychology & Human Sexuality* 14 (2002): 17–33.

———. *Sexual Variance in Society and History*. New York: Wiley, 1976.

Bullough, Vern L., and James A. Brundage. *Sexual Practices & the Medieval Church*. Buffalo, NY: Prometheus Books, 1982.

Bullough, Vern L., and Bonnie Bullough. *Sexual Attitudes: Myths & Realities*. Amherst, NY: Prometheus Books, 1995.

———. *Women and Prostitution: A Social History*. New York: Prometheus Books, 1987.

Burg, B. R. *Boys at Sea: Sodomy, Indecency, and Courts Martial in Nelson's Navy*. Basingstoke, UK: Palgrave Macmillan, 2007.

———. *Gay Warriors: A Documentary History from the Ancient World to the Present*. New York: New York University Press, 2002.

———. "Ho Hum, Another Work of the Devil." *Journal of Homosexuality* 6 (1981): 69–78.

———. *Sodomy and the Pirate Tradition: English Sea Rovers in the Seventeenth-Century Caribbean*. New York: New York University Press, 1995.

Burkert, Walter. *Ancient Mystery Cults*. Cambridge: Harvard University Press, 1987.

Burnard, Trevor. "Sexual Life of an Eighteenth-Century Jamaican Slave Overseer." In *Sex and Sexuality in Early America*, edited by Merril D. Smith, 163–189. New York: New York University Press, 1998.

Burrows, Simon. *Blackmail, Scandal, and Revolution: London's French Libellistes, 1758–92*. Manchester: Manchester University Press, 2006.

Burton, Antoinette. "Conjugality on Trial: The Rukhmabai Case and the Debate on Child-Marriage in Late-Victorian Britain." In *Disorder in the Court: Trials and Sexual Conflict at the Turn of the Century*, edited by George Robb and Nancy Erber, 33–56. New York: New York University Press, 1999.

Cantarella, Eva. *Bisexuality in the Ancient World*. New Haven: Yale University Press, 1992.

———. "Gender, Sexuality, and the Law." In *The Cambridge Companion to Ancient Greek Law*, edited by Michael Gagarin and David Cohen, 236–53. New York: Cambridge University Press, 2007.

Carey, C. "Return of the Radish, or Just When You Thought It Was Safe to Go Back into the Kitchen." *Liverpool Classical Monthly* 18 (1993): 53–55.

Carson, Anne. "Putting Her in Her Place: Woman, Dirt, and Desire." In *Before Sexuality: The Construction of Erotic Experience in the Ancient Greek World*, edited by David M. Halperin, John J. Winkler, and Froma I. Zeitlin, 135–69. Princeton: Princeton University Press, 1990.

Carter, John Marshall. *Rape in Medieval England: An Historical and Sociological Study.* Lanham, MD: University Press of America, 1985.

Cassius Dio. *Roman History.* Translation by Earnest Cary. Cambridge: Harvard University, 1927.

Cave, Alfred A. *Lethal Encounters: Englishmen and Indians in Colonial America.* Santa Barbara, CA: Praeger, 2011.

Clark, Anna. *Desire: A History of European Sexuality.* New York: Routledge, 2008.

Cohen, David. *Law, Sexuality, and Society: The Enforcement of Morals in Classical Athens.* Cambridge: Cambridge University Press, 1991.

Comstock, Anthony. *Traps for the Young.* New York: Funk & Wagnalls, 1883

Coon, Lynda L. *Sacred Fictions: Holy Women and Hagiography in Late Antiquity.* Philadelphia: University of Pennsylvania Press, 1997.

Cooper, Jerold S. "Virginity in Ancient Mesopotamia." In *Sex and Gender in the Ancient Near East: Proceedings of the 47th Rencontre Assyriologique Internationale,* Helsinki, July 2–6, 2001, edited by Simo Parpola and Robert M. Whiting, 94–112. Helsinki: Neo-Assyrian Text Corpus Project, 2002.

Copley, A.R.H. *Sexual Moralities in France, 1780–1980: New Ideas on the Family, Divorce, and Homosexuality: An Essay on Moral Change.* London: Routledge, 1989.

Coward, D. A. "Attitudes to Homosexuality in Eighteenth-Century France." *Journal of European Studies* 10 (1980): 231–55.

Crompton, Louis. *Homosexuality and Civilization.* Cambridge: Belknap Press of Harvard University Press, 2003.

———. "Homosexuals and the Death Penalty in Colonial America." *Journal of Homosexuality* 1 (1976): 277–93.

———. "The Myth of Lesbian Impunity: Capital Laws from 1270–1791." *Journal of Homosexuality* 6 (1981): 11–25.

Davidson, N. S. "Sodomy in Early Modern Venice." In *Sodomy in Early Modern Europe,* edited by Tom Betteridge, 65–81. New York: Manchester University Press, 2002.

Deacon, Richard. *Matthew Hopkins: Witch Finder General.* London: F. Muller, 1976.

DeJean, Joan E. *The Reinvention of Obscenity: Sex, Lies, and Tabloids in Early Modern France.* Chicago: University of Chicago Press, 2002.

Dekkers, Midas. *Dearest Pet: On Bestiality.* London: Verso, 1994.

DeMeo, James. "The Geography of Male and Female Genital Mutilations." In *Sexual Mutilations: A Human Tragedy,* edited by George C. Denniston and Marylin Fayre Milos, 1–16. New York: Plenum Press, 1997.

Demosthenes. *Against Neaera.* Edited by Gregory R. Crane. Perseus Digital Project, Tufts University, accessed September 3, 2011, www.perseus.tufts.edu/hopper /text?doc=Perseus%3Atext%3A1999.01.0080%3Aspeech%3D59.

———. *Apollodorus Against Stephanus* 2. Edited by Gregory R. Crane. Perseus Digital Project, Tufts University, accessed September 3, 2011, www.perseus .tufts.edu/hopper/text?doc=Perseus%3Atext%3A1999.01.0078%3Aspeech %3D46.

Dionysus of Haricarnassus. *Roman Antiquities.* Translated by Earnest Carey. Cambridge: Harvard University Press, 1937.

Donoghue, Eddie. *Black Women/White Men: The Sexual Exploitation of Female Slaves in the Danish West Indies.* Trenton, NJ: Africa World Press, 2002.

Douglas, Mary. *Leviticus as Literature.* Oxford: Oxford University Press, 2000.

Driver, Godfrey Rolles, and Sir John Charles Mills. *The Assyrian Laws.* Oxford: Clarendon Press, 1935.

Dupont, Florence. *Daily Life in Ancient Rome.* Oxford: Blackwell, 1993.

Dynes, Wayne R., and Stephen Donaldson. *History of Homosexuality in Europe and America.* New York: Garland Publishing, 1992.

Ebing, R. von. *Psychopathia Sexualis, with Especial Reference to Contrary Sexual Instinct: A Medico-Legal Study.* Translated by Charles Gilbert Chaddock. Philadelphia: F. A. Davis, 1892.

Edwards, Catharine. *The Politics of Immorality in Ancient Rome.* Cambridge: Cambridge University Press, 1993.

———. "Unspeakable Professions: Public Performance and Prostitution in Ancient Rome." In *Roman Sexualities,* edited by Judith P. Hallett and Marilyn B. Skinner, 66–95. Princeton: Princeton University Press, 1997.

Elbl, Ivana. "Men Without Wives: Sexual Arrangements in the Early Portuguese Expansion in West Africa." In *Desire and Discipline: Sex and Sexuality in the Premodern West*, edited by Jacqueline Murray and Konrad Eisenbichler, 61–86. Toronto: University of Toronto Press, 1996.

Epstein, A. L. *Urbanization and Kinship: The Domestic Domain of the Copperbelt of Zambia 1950–1956*. London: Academic Press, 1981.

Epstein, Isidore. *Babylonian Talmud*. Tractate Niddah and Tractate Keritoth. Brooklyn: Socino Press, 1961.

Erber, Nancy. "Queer Follies: Effeminacy and Aestheticism in Fin-de-Siècle France, the Case of Baron d'Adelsward Ferson and Count de Warren." In *Disorder in the Court: Trials and Sexual Conflict at the Turn of the Century*, edited by George Robb and Nancy Erber, 186–208. New York: New York University Press, 1999.

Ericksson, Brigitte. "A Lesbian Execution in Germany, 1721: The Trial Records." *Journal of Homosexuality* 6 (1981): 27–40.

Eskridge, William N. "A History of Same-Sex Marriage." *Virginia Law Review* 79 (1993): 1419–1513.

Evans, E. P. *The Criminal Prosecution and Capital Punishment of Animals*. London: Faber, 1906.

Faderman, Lillian. *Surpassing the Love of Men: Romantic Friendship and Love Between Women from the Renaissance to the Present*. New York: Morrow, 1981.

Findlen, Paula. "Humanism, Politics and Pornography in Renaissance Italy." In *The Invention of Pornography: Obscenity and the Origins of Modernity, 1500–1800*, edited by Lynn Hunt, 49–108. New York: Zone Books, 1993.

Finkelstein, J. J. "Sex Offenses in Sumerian Laws." *Journal of the American Oriental Society* 86 (1966): 355–72.

Fisher, Trevor. *Scandal: The Sexual Politics of Late Victorian Britain*. Stroud. Gloucestershire, UK: Alan Sutton, 1995.

Fissell, Mary Elizabeth. *Vernacular Bodies: The Politics of Reproduction in Early Modern England*. Oxford: Oxford University Press, 2004.

Flaherty, David. "Law and the Enforcement of Morals in Early America." In *American Law and the Constitutional Order: Historical Perspectives*, edited by Lawrence M. Friedman and Harry N. Scheiber, 53–66. Cambridge: Harvard University Press, 1988.

Flavius Josephus. *Antiquities of the Jews.* Edited by Gregory R. Crane and William Whiston. Perseus Digital Project, Tufts University, accessed September 3, 2011, www.perseus.tufts.edu/hopper/text?doc=J.+AJ+18&fromdoc=Perseus%3Atext %3A1999.01.014.

Forret, Jeff. *Race Relations at the Margins: Slaves and Poor Whites in the Antebellum Southern Countryside.* Baton Rouge: Louisiana State University Press, 2006.

Foucault, Michel. *Foucault Live (Interviews, 1961–1984).* Edited by Sylvère Lotringer. New York: Semiotext(e), 1996.

———. *The History of Sexuality,* Volume I: *An Introduction.* Translated by Robert Hurley. New York: Random House, 1990.

Frymer-Kensky, Tikva Simone. "Virginity in the Bible." In *Gender and Law in the Hebrew Bible and the Ancient Near East,* edited by Victor Harold Matthews, Bernard M. Levinson, and Tikva Simone Frymer-Kensky, 79–96. Sheffield, UK: Sheffield Academic Press, 1998.

Fudenberg, Drew, and David K. Levine. *Steady State Learning and the Code of Hammurabi.* Cambridge: Harvard University, Harvard Institute of Economic Research, 2004.

Galpaz-Feller, Pnina. "Private Lives and Public Censure: Adultery in Ancient Egypt and Biblical Israel." *Near Eastern Archaeology* 67 (2004): 152–61.

Gent, Frank J. *The Trial of the Bideford Witches.* Bideford, UK: Edward Gaskell Lazarus Press, 2002.

Gibbon, Edward. *The History of the Decline and Fall of the Roman Empire,* Volume II. New York: Harper & Brothers, 1840.

Gibson, McGuire. "Nippur—Sacred City to Enlil, Supreme God of Sumer and Akkad." *Al-Rafidan* 14 (1993), accessed August 29, 2011, http://oi.uchicago .edu/research/projects/nip/nsc.html.

Goldberg, Jonathan. *Sodometries: Renaissance Texts, Modern Sexualities.* Stanford: Stanford University Press, 1992.

Graham-Murray, James. *A History of Morals.* London: Library 33 Ltd., 1966.

Gravdal, Kathryn. *Ravishing Maidens: Writing Rape in Medieval French Literature and Law.* Philadelphia: University of Pennsylvania Press, 1991.

Grazia, Edward de. *Girls Lean Back Everywhere: The Law of Obscenity and the Assault on Genius.* New York: Vintage Books, 1993.

Greenberg, David F. *The Construction of Homosexuality*. Chicago: University of Chicago Press, 1988.

Greengus, Samuel. "A Textbook Case of Adultery in Ancient Mesopotamia." *Hebrew Union College Annual* 40 (1969): 37–39.

Gross, Ariela J. "Litigating Whiteness: Trials of Racial Determination in the Nineteenth-Century South." *Yale Law Journal* 108 (1998): 109–88.

Gruen, Erich Stephen. *Studies in Greek Culture and Roman Policy*. Berkeley: University of California Press, 1996.

Guicciardi, Jean-Pierre. "Between the Licit and the Illicit: The Sexuality of the King." Translated by Michael Murray. In *'Tis Nature's Fault: Unauthorized Sexuality During the Enlightenment*, edited by Robert Purks Maccubbin, 88–97. Cambridge: Cambridge University Press, 1987.

Habinek, Thomas N., and Alessandro Schiesaro. *The Roman Cultural Revolution*. Cambridge: Cambridge University Press, 1997.

Hamel, Debra. *Trying Neaira: The True Story of a Courtesan's Scandalous Life in Ancient Greece*. New Haven: Yale University Press, 2003.

Hayman, Ronald. *Marquis de Sade: The Genius of Passion*. London: Tauris Parke Paperbacks, 2003.

Hearne, Thomas, Anthony à Wood, and John Leland. *The Lives of Those Eminent Antiquaries John Leland, Thomas Hearne, and Anthony à Wood: With an Authentick Account of Their Respective Writings and Publications*. Translated by William Huddesford and Thomas Warton. Oxford: Clarendon Press, 1772.

Heimpel, Wolfgang. *Letters to the King of Mari: A New Translation*. Winona Lake, IN: Eisenbrauns, 2003.

Helmholz, R. H. *Marriage Litigation in Medieval England*. London: Cambridge University Press, 1974.

Henriques, Fernando. *Prostitution in Europe and the New World*. London: MacGibbon & Kee, 1963.

Henry, Madeleine Mary. *Prisoner of History: Aspasia of Miletus and Her Biographical Tradition*. New York: Oxford University Press, 1995.

Herdt, Gilbert. *Sambia Sexual Culture: Essays from the Field*. Chicago: University of Chicago Press, 1999.

Herodotus. *The Histories: Book I*. Translated by Aubrey de Sélincourt. London: Penguin, 1954.

———. *The Histories: Book II*. Translated by Aubrey de Sélincourt. London: Penguin, 1954.

Herrup, Cynthia B. "The Patriarch at Home: The Trial of the 2nd Earl of Castlehaven for Rape and Sodomy." *History Workshop Journal* 41 (1996): 1–18.

Higginbotham, A. Leon, and Barbara K. Kopytoff. "Racial Purity and Interracial Sex in the Law of Colonial and Antebellum Virginia." *Georgetown Law Journal* 77 (1989): 1967–2028.

Hitchcock, Tim. *English Sexualities, 1700–1800*. New York: St. Martin's Press, 1997.

———. "Redefining Sex in Eighteenth-Century England." *History Workshop Journal* 41 (1996): 72–90.

Hjerrild, Bodil. *Studies in Zoroastrian Family Law: A Comparative Analysis*. Copenhagen: Museum Tusculanum Press, 2003.

Hodges, Frederick M. "The Ideal Prepuce in Ancient Greece and Rome: Male Genital Aesthetics and Their Relation to Lipodermos, Circumcision, Foreskin Restoration, and Kynodesme." *The Bulletin of the History of Medicine* 75 (2001): 375–405.

Horne, Alistair. *Seven Ages of Paris*. New York: Knopf, 2002.

Horowitz, Helen Lefkowitz. *Rereading Sex: Battles over Sexual Knowledge and Suppression in Nineteenth-Century America*. New York: Knopf, 2002.

Hull, Isabel V. *Sexuality, State, and Civil Society in Germany, 1700–1815*. Ithaca, NY: Cornell University Press, 1996.

Hunt, Alan. *Governing Morals: A Social History of Moral Regulation*. Cambridge: Cambridge University Press, 1999.

Hunt, Lynn. *Politics, Culture, and Class in the French Revolution*. Berkeley: University of California Press, 1984.

———. "Pornography and the French Revolution." In *The Invention of Pornography: Obscenity and the Origins of Modernity, 1500–1800*, edited by Lynn Hunt, 301–39. New York: Zone Books, 1993.

Hussey, Andrew. *Paris: The Secret History*. New York: Bloomsbury, 2007.

Hyde, H. Montgomery. *A History of Pornography*. New York: Farrar, Straus and Giroux, 1965.

———, ed. *The Trials of Oscar Wilde*: Regina (Wilde) v. Queensberry, Regina v. Wilde and Taylor. London: Hodge, 1948.

"Inbred Obscurity: Improving Incest Laws in the Shadow of the 'Sexual Family.'" *Harvard Law Review* 119 (2006): 2464–85.

Ingram, Martin. *Church Courts, Sex, and Marriage in England, 1570–1640*. Cambridge: Cambridge University Press, 1987.

Isaeus. *On the Estate of Menecles*. Edited by Gregory R. Crane. Perseus Digital Project, Tufts University, accessed September 3, 2011, www.perseus.tufts.edu/hopper/text?doc=Perseus%3Atext%3A1999.01.0142%3Aspeech%3D2%3Asection%3Dhypothesis.

———. *On the Estate of Philoktemon*. Edited by Gregory R. Crane. Perseus Digital Project, Tufts University, accessed September 3, 2011, www.perseus.tufts.edu/hopper/text?doc=Perseus%3Atext%3A1999.01.0142%3Aspeech%3D6%3Asection%3D21.

Jackson, Bernard S., ed. *Essays in Jewish and Comparative Legal History*. Leiden, Netherlands: Brill, 1975.

Jacobson, Thorkild. *Toward the Image of Tammuz and Other Essays on Mesopotamian History and Culture*. Edited by W. L. Moran. Cambridge: Harvard University Press.

James I. *Daemonologie*. 1597. Accessed at www.gutenberg.org/catalog/world/readfile?fk_files=845529.

Johnson, Janet H. "The Legal Status of Women in Ancient Egypt." In *Mistress of the House, Mistress of Heaven: Women of Ancient Egypt*. Edited by Anne K. Capel and Glenn Markoe, 175–86. New York: Hudson Hills Press in association with the Cincinnati Art Museum, 1996.

Jones, Colin. "Prostitution and the Ruling Class in Eighteenth-Century Montpellier." *History Workshop* 6 (1978): 7–28.

Jordan, Mark D. *The Invention of Sodomy in Christian Theology*. Chicago: University of Chicago Press, 1997.

Jusek, Karin J. "Sexual Morality and the Meaning of Prostitution in Fin-de-Siècle Vienna." In *From Sappho to de Sade: Moments in the History of Sexuality*, edited by Jan Bremmer, 123–43. London: Routledge, 1991.

Juvenal. *Sixth Satire*. Translated by G. G. Ramsay. Internet Ancient History Sourcebook, accessed September 8, 2011, www.fordham.edu/halsall/ancient/juvenal-satvi.asp.

Kadri, Sadakat. *The Trial: A History, from Socrates to O.J. Simpson.* New York: Random House, 2005.

Kapparis, Konstantinos A. *Apollodoros "Against Neaira" (D. 59).* Berlin: W. de Gruyter, 1999.

Karant-Nunn, Susan C., and Merry E. Wiesner-Hanks, eds. *Luther on Women: A Sourcebook.* Cambridge: Cambridge University Press, 2003.

Karras, Ruth Mazo. *Common Women: Prostitution and Sexuality in Medieval England.* New York: Oxford University Press, 1996.

———. *Sexuality in Medieval Europe: Doing unto Others.* New York: Routledge, 2005.

Karras, Ruth Mazo, and David Lorenzo Boyd. "'Ut Cum Muliere': A Male Transvestite Prostitute in Fourteenth-Century London." In *Premodern Sexualities*, edited by Louise Olga Fradenburg and Carla Freccero, 99–116. New York: Routledge, 1996.

Kebric, Robert B. *Greek People.* Mountain View, CA: Mayfield Publishing, 1989.

Keeler, Christine, and Robert Meadley. *Sex Scandals.* London: Xanadu, 1985.

Kendrick, Walter M. *The Secret Museum: Pornography in Modern Culture.* Berkeley: University of California Press, 1996.

Kermode, Jennifer, and Garthine Walker, eds. *Women, Crime and the Courts in Early Modern England.* Chapel Hill: University of North Carolina Press, 1994.

Keuls, Eva C. *The Reign of the Phallus: Sexual Politics in Ancient Athens.* New York: Harper & Row, 1985.

Klaits, Joseph. *Servants of Satan: The Age of the Witch Hunts.* Bloomington: Indiana University Press, 1985.

Knappman, Edward W., ed. *Great World Trials.* Detroit: Gale Research, 1997.

Kraemer, Ross Shepard. *Her Share of the Blessings: Women's Religions Among Pagans, Jews, and Christians in the Greco-Roman World.* New York: Oxford University Press, 1992.

Krafft-Ebing, Richard. *Psychopathia Sexualis.* Translated by Charles Gilbert Chaddock. London: F. A. Davis Company, 1894.

Kramer, Heinrich, and James Sprenger. *Malleus Maleficarum.* Translated by Montague Summers, accessed September 8, 2011, www.malleusmaleficarum.org.

Lacey, Robert, and Danny Danziger. *The Year 1000: What Life Was Like at the Turn of the First Millennium: An Englishman's World*. Boston: Little, Brown, 1999.

Lactantius. *The Divine Institutes*. Translated by William Fletcher. Christian Bookshelf, accessed August 29, 2011, http://christianbookshelf.org/lactantius /the_divine_institutes/index.html.

Ladenson, Elisabeth. *Dirt for Art's Sake: Books on Trial from Madame Bovary to Lolita*. Ithaca: Cornell University Press, 2007.

Ladurie, Emmanuel. *The Peasants of Languedoc*. Translated by John Day. Urbana: University of Illinois Press, 1976.

Langlands, Rebecca. *Sexual Morality in Ancient Rome*. Cambridge: Cambridge University Press, 2006.

Largent, Mark A. *Breeding Contempt: The History of Coerced Sterilization in the United States*. New Brunswick, NJ: Rutgers University Press, 2008.

Lavrin, Asunción. "Sexuality in Colonial Mexico: A Church Dilemma." In *Sexuality and Marriage in Colonial Latin America*, edited by Asunción Lavrin, 47–95. Lincoln: University of Nebraska Press, 1989.

Lea, Henry Charles. *A History of the Inquisition in the Middle Ages*. New York: Harper & Brothers, 1888.

Lefkowitz, Mary R., and Maureen B. Fant. *Women's Life in Greece and Rome: A Source Book in Translation*. Baltimore: Johns Hopkins University Press, 2005.

Levack, Brian P. *Witchcraft Sourcebook*. London: Routledge, 2003.

———. *The Witch-Hunt in Early Modern Europe*. London: Longman, 1987.

Levins, Hoag. *American Sex Machines: The Hidden History of Sex at the U.S. Patent Office*. Holbrook, MA: Adams Media, 1996.

Lévi-Strauss, Claude. *The Elementary Structures of Kinship*. Boston: Beacon Press, 1969.

Livy. *The History of Rome*. Edited by Rev. Canon Roberts. New York: E. P. Dutton, 1912.

Luibhéid, Eithne. *Entry Denied: Controlling Sexuality at the Border*. Minneapolis: University of Minnesota Press, 2002.

Luther, Martin. *The Familiar Discourses of Dr. Martin Luther*. Translated by Henry Bell. London: Baldwin, Craddock and Joy, 1818.

Lysias. *Against Simon*. Edited by Gregory R. Crane. Perseus Digital Project, Tufts University, accessed September 3, 2011, www.perseus.tufts.edu/hopper /text?doc= Perseus%3Atext%3A1999.01.0154%3Aspeech%3D3.

————. *On the Murder of Eratosthenes*. Edited by Gregory R. Crane. Perseus Digital Project, Tufts University, accessed September 3, 2011, www.perseus .tufts.edu/hopper/text?doc=Perseus%3atext%3a1999.01.0154%3aspeech %3d1.

————. *On a Wound by Premeditation*. Edited by Gregory R. Crane. Perseus Digital Project, Tufts University, accessed September 3, 2011, www.perseus .tufts.edu/hopper/text?doc=Perseus%3Atext%3A1999.01.0154%3Aspeech %3D4.

MacDowell, Douglas M. *The Law in Classical Athens*. Ithaca, NY: Cornell University Press, 1978.

————. *Spartan Law*. Edinburgh: Scottish Academic Press, 1986.

MacMullen, Ramsay. *Changes in the Roman Empire: Essays in the Ordinary*. Princeton, NJ: Princeton University Press, 1990.

Manniche, Lise. *Sexual Life in Ancient Egypt*. London: KPI, 1987.

Manzione, Carol Kazmierczak. "Sex in Tudor London: Abusing Their Bodies with Each Other." In *Desire and Discipline: Sex and Sexuality in the Premodern West*, edited by Jacqueline Murray and Konrad Eisenbichler, 87–100. Toronto: University of Toronto Press, 1996.

Maple, Eric. *The Dark World of Witches*. New York: A. S. Barnes, 1964.

Masters, Robert E. L. *Forbidden Sexual Behavior and Morality: An Objective Re-examination of Perverse Sex Practices in Different Cultures*. New York: Julian Press, 1962.

Maxwell-Stewart, P. G. "'Wild, Filthie, Execrabill, Detestabill, and Unnatural Sin': Bestiality in Early Modern Scotland." In *Sodomy in Early Modern Europe*, edited by Tom Betteridge, 82–93. New York: Manchester University Press, 2002.

McCord, Brian. "'Charming and Wholesome Literature': Fanny Hill and the Legal 'Production of Production.'" In *Launching* Fanny Hill: *Essays on the Novel and Its Influences*, edited by Patsy S. Fowler and Alan Jackson, 267–83. New York: AMS Press, 2003.

McCormick, Ian. *Secret Sexualities: A Sourcebook of 17th and 18th Century Writing*. London: Routledge, 1997.

McGinn, Thomas A. J. *Prostitution, Sexuality, and the Law in Ancient Rome*. New York: Oxford University Press, 1998.

Meadow, Rosalyn M., and Lillie Weiss. *Women's Conflicts About Eating and Sexuality: The Relationship Between Food and Sex*. New York: Haworth Press, 1992.

Merrick, Jeffrey. *Order and Disorder Under the Ancien Régime*. Cambridge: Cambridge Scholars Press, 2007.

———. "Sexual Politics and Public Order in Late Eighteenth-Century France: The Mémoires secrets and the Correspondance secrète." *Journal of the History of Sexuality* 1 (1990): 68–84.

Middleton, Russell. "Brother-Sister and Father-Daughter Marriage in Ancient Egypt." *American Sociological Review* 27 (1962): 603–11.

Midelfort, H. C. Erik. *Witch Hunting in Southwestern Germany, 1562–1684: The Social and Intellectual Foundations*. Stanford: Stanford University Press, 1972.

Millot, Michel, and Jean L'Ange. *The School of Venus*. Translation and introduction by Donald Thomas. London: Granada Publishing Ltd., 1972.

Mohrmann, Doug C. "Making Sense of Sex: A Study of Leviticus 18." *Journal for the Study of the Old Testament* 29 (2004): 57–79.

Montaigne, Michel de. *Complete Works: Essays, Travel Journal, Letters*. Translated by Donald M. Frame. Stanford: Stanford University Press, 1957.

Monter, E. William. "Sodomy and Heresy in Early Modern Switzerland." *Journal of Homosexuality* 6 (1980): 41–55.

———. "Sodomy: The Fateful Accident." In *History of Homosexuality in Europe and America*, edited by Wayne R. Dynes and Stephen Donaldson, 192–216. New York: Garland Publishing, 1992.

Moran, Rachel. "Love with a Proper Stranger: What Anti-Miscegenation Laws Can Tell Us About the Meaning of Race, Sex, and Marriage." *Hofstra Law Review* 34 (2004): 1663–79.

Morone, James A. *Hellfire Nation: The Politics of Sin in American History*. New Haven: Yale University Press, 2003.

Naphy, William G. *Sex Crimes: From Renaissance to Enlightenment*. Stroud, Gloucestershire, UK: Tempus, 2004.

Nethaway, Rowland. "Government Census Methods Promote Enduring Racial Myths." *Los Angeles Daily Journal*, March 20, 2007.

Noordam, D. J. "Sodomy in the Dutch Republic, 1600–1725." *Journal of Homosexuality* 16 (1988): 207–28.

Norton, Rictor. "The Destruction of Sodom and Gomorrah." *A History of Homophobia*. April 15, 2002. Accessed August 29, 2011, http://rictornorton .co.uk/homopho2.htm.

———. *Mother Clap's Molly House: The Gay Subculture in England*. London: Chalfont Press, 2006.

Oaks, Robert F. "'Things Fearful to Name': Sodomy and Buggery in Seventeenth-Century New England." *Journal of Social History* 12 (1978): 268–81.

Odem, Mary E. *Delinquent Daughters: Protecting and Policing Adolescent Female Sexuality in the United States, 1885–1920*. Chapel Hill: University of North Carolina Press, 1995.

Olyan, Saul M. "'And with a Male You Shall Not Lie the Lying Down of a Woman': On the Meaning and Significance of Leviticus 18:22 and 20:13." *Journal of the History of Sexuality* 5 (1994): 179–206.

Ovid. *Metamorphoses*. Edited by Gregory R. Crane and Brooks More. Perseus Digital Project, Tufts University, accessed September 3, 2011, www.perseus .tufts.edu/hopper/text?doc=Perseus%3atext%3a1999.02.0028.

Parker, Graham. "Is a Duck an Animal? An Exploration of Bestiality as a Crime." In *Criminal Justice History*, edited by Louis Knafla, 95–109. Westport, CT: Meckler, 1987.

Parker, Holt N. "The Teratogenic Grid." In *Roman Sexualities*, edited by Judith P. Hallett and Marilyn B. Skinner, 47–65. Princeton: Princeton University Press, 1997.

———. "Why Were the Vestals Virgins? Or the Chastity of Women and the Safety of the Roman State." *American Journal of Philology* 25 (2004): 563–601.

Paul the Deacon. *History of the Langobards*, edited by William Dudley Foulke. Philadelphia: Department of History, University of Pennsylvania, 1907.

Payer, Pierre J. *Sex and the Penitentials: The Development of a Sexual Code, 550–1150*. Toronto: University of Toronto Press, 1984.

Peakman, Julie. *Lascivious Bodies: A Sexual History of the Eighteenth Century*. London: Atlantic Books, 2004.

Peniston, William. "A Public Offense Against Decency: The Trial of the Count de Germiny and the 'Moral Order' of the Third Republic." In *Disorder in the*

Court: Trials and Sexual Conflict at the Turn of the Century, edited by George Robb and Nancy Erber, 12–32. New York: New York University Press, 1999.

Pepys, Samuel. *The Diary of Samuel Pepys*. Google Books, accessed August 29, 2011, http://books.google.com/books?id=9Yyb5Hw2ILgC&pg=PA14&dq=samuel+pepys+lewd+book&ei=EQT8S9DrI47ezQTW4eilCg&cd=1#v=onepage&q=villainy&f=false.

———. Samuel Pepys *Diary* 1663 Extracts, accessed on August 29, 2011, www.pepys.info/1663/1663.html.

Perrin, Bernadotte, trans. *Plutarch's Lives*. London: W. Heinemann, 1914.

Pinkus, Philip. *Grub St. Stripped Bare: The Scandalous Lives & Pornographic Works of the Original Grub St. Writers* . . . Hamden, CT: Archon Books, 1968.

Plato. *Laws*. Edited by Gregory R. Crane. Perseus Digital Project, Tufts University, accessed September 3, 2011, www.perseus.tufts.edu/hopper/text?doc=Perseus%3Atext%3A1999.01.0166%3Abook%3D1%3Asection%3D624a.

———. *Symposium*. Edited Gregory R. Crane. Perseus Digital Project, Tufts University, accessed September 3, 2011, www.perseus.tufts.edu/hopper/text?doc=Perseus%3atext%3a1999.04.0090%3atext%3dintro.

Plutarch. *Life of Alcibiades*. Translated by Ian Scott-Kilvert. London: Penguin, 1960.

———. *Life of Lycurgus*. Translated by John Dryden. Internet Classics Archive, M.I.T., accessed September 3, 2011, http://classics.mit.edu/Plutarch/lycurgus.html.

———. *Life of Numa*. Translated by Bernadotte Perrin. Cambridge: Harvard University Press, 1914.

———. *Life of Pelopidas*. Translated by John Drydon. Internet Classics Archive, M.I.T., accessed September 3, 2011, http://classics.mit.edu/Plutarch/pelopida.html.

———. *Life of Pericles*. Translated by Ian Scott-Kilvert. London: Penguin, 1960.

———. *The Roman Questions*. Translated by Frank Cole Babbitt. Cambridge: Harvard University Press, 1936.

Poliakov, Leon. *The History of Anti-Semitism*, Volume I. New York: Vanguard Press, 1965.

Pomeroy, Sarah B. *Goddesses, Whores, Wives, and Slaves: Women in Classical Antiquity*. New York: Schocken Books, 1975.

Poos, L.R. "Sex, Lies and the Church Courts of Pre-Reformation England." *The Journal of Interdisciplinary History* 25 (1995): 585–607.

Porter, Roy. "Mixed Feelings: The Enlightenment and Sexuality in Eighteenth-Century England." In *Sexuality in Eighteenth-Century Britain*, edited by Paul-Gabriel Boucé, 1–27. Totowa, NJ: Manchester University Press, 1982.

———. "'The Secrets of Generation Display'd': Aristotle's Master-piece in Eighteenth-Century England." In *'Tis Nature's Fault: Unauthorized Sexuality During the Enlightenment*, edited by Robert Purks Maccubbin, 1–21. Cambridge: Cambridge University Press, 1987.

Posner, Richard A. *Sex and Reason*. Cambridge: Harvard University Press, 1992.

Posner, Richard A., and Katharine B. Silbaugh. *A Guide to America's Sex Laws*. Chicago: University of Chicago Press, 1996.

Potts, Malcolm, and Roger Valentine Short. *Ever Since Adam and Eve: The Evolution of Human Sexuality*. Cambridge: Cambridge University Press, 1999.

Power, Patrick C. *Sex and Marriage in Ancient Ireland*. Dublin: Mercier Press Ltd., 1976.

Ranke-Heinemann, Uta. *Eunuchs for Heaven: The Catholic Church and Sexuality*. London: A. Deutsch, 1990.

Rémy, Nicolas. *Demonolatry*. Translated by E. A. Ashwin and edited by Montague Summers. Whitefish, Montana: Kessinger Publishing, 1972.

Rey, Michael. "Police and Sodomy in Eighteenth-Century Paris: From Sin to Disorder." In *The Pursuit of Sodomy: Male Homosexuality in Renaissance and Enlightenment Europe*, edited by Kent Gerard and Gert Hekma, 129–46. New York: Harrington Park Press, 1989.

Reynolds, J. B. "Sex Morals and the Law in Ancient Egypt and Babylon." *Journal of the American Institute of Criminal Law and Criminology* 5 (1914): 20–31.

Richards, Jeffrey. *Sex, Dissidence, and Damnation: Minority Groups in the Middle Ages*. London: Routledge, 1994.

Rider, Catherine. *Magic and Impotence in the Middle Ages*. New York: Oxford University Press, 2006.

Robbins, Rossell Hope. *The Encyclopedia of Witchcraft and Demonology*. New York: Crown Publishers, 1959.

Roberts, M.J.D. *Making English Morals: Voluntary Association and Moral Reform in England, 1787–1886*. Cambridge: Cambridge University Press, 2004.

———. "The Society for the Suppression of Vice and Its Early Critics, 1802–1812." *The Historical Journal* 26 (1983): 159–76.

Robertson, Stephen. "Age of Consent Laws." In *Children and Youth in History*, Item #230, accessed August 29, 2011, www.chnm.gmu.edu/cyh /teaching-modules/230.

Robinson, O. F. *Ancient Rome: City Planning and Administration.* New York: Routledge, 1994.

———. *The Criminal Law of Ancient Rome.* Baltimore: Johns Hopkins University Press, 1995.

———. *Penal Practice and Penal Policy in Ancient Rome.* London: Routledge, 2007.

Roodenburg, Herman. "Venus Minsieke Gasthuis: Sexual Beliefs in Eighteen-Century Holland." In *From Sappho to de Sade: Moments in the History of Sexuality*, edited by Jan Bremmer, 84–107. London: Routledge, 1991.

Roper, Lyndal. "Luther: Sex, Marriage and Motherhood." *History Today* 33 (1983): 33–38.

———. "Witchcraft and the Western Imagination." *Transactions of the Royal Historical Society* 16 (2006): 117–41.

Roth, Martha T. "A Case Study from Mesopotamia." In *Gender and Law in the Hebrew Bible and the Ancient Near East*, edited by Victor Harold Matthews, Bernard M. Levinson, and Tikva Simone Frymer-Kensky, 173–85. Sheffield, UK: Sheffield Academic Press, 1998.

———. *Law Collections from Mesopotamia and Asia Minor.* Atlanta: Scholars Press, 1997.

———. "'She Will Die by the Iron Dagger': Adultery and Neo-Babylonian Marriage." *Journal of the Economic and Social History of the Orient* 31 (1988): 186–206.

———. "The Slave and the Scoundrel CBS 10467: A Sumerian Morality Tale?" *Journal of the American Oriental Society* 103 (1983): 275–82.

Rothman, Joshua D. *Notorious in the Neighborhood: Sex and Families Across the Color Line in Virginia, 1787–1861.* Chapel Hill: University of North Carolina Press, 2003.

Rousseau, Jean-Jacques. *Confessions.* London: Everyman, 1931.

Rousselle, Aline. *Porneia: On Desire and the Body in Antiquity.* Oxford: Blackwell, 1988.

Ruggiero, Guido. *The Boundaries of Eros: Sex Crime and Sexuality in Renaissance Venice*. New York: Oxford University Press, 1985.

Ryan, Rebecca M. "The Sex Right: A Legal History of the Marital Rape Exemption." *Law & Social Inquiry* 20 (1996): 941–99.

Saggs, H.W.F. *Civilization Before Greece and Rome*. New Haven: Yale University Press, 1989.

Sanger, William W. *The History of Prostitution*. New York: Arno Press, 1972.

Sassoon, John. *Ancient Laws and Modern Problems: The Balance Between Justice and a Legal System*. Bristol, UK: Intellect Books, 2005.

Sayre, Gordon. "Native American Sexuality in the Eyes of the Beholder 1535–1710." In *Sex and Sexuality in Early America*, edited by Merril D. Smith, 35–54. New York: New York University Press, 1998.

Scheidel, Walter. "Brother-Sister and Parent-Child Marriage in Pre-Modern Societies." Stanford University, accessed September 3, 2011, www.stanford .edu/~scheidel/incest.htm.

Scott, George Ryley. *The History of Torture Throughout the Ages*. London: Torchstream Books, 1951.

Shaw, Ian, ed. *The Oxford History of Ancient Egypt*. Oxford: Oxford University Press, 2000.

Simpson, Anthony E. "Vulnerability and the Age of Female Consent: Legal Innovation and Its Effect on Prosecution for Rape in Eighteenth-Century London." In *Sexual Underworlds of the Enlightenment*, edited by G. S. Rousseau and Roy Porter, 180–205. Manchester: Manchester University Press, 1987.

Sissa, Giulia. "Sexual Bodybuilding: Aeschines Against Timarchus." In *Constructions of the Classical Body*, edited by James I. Porter, 147–68. Ann Arbor: University of Michigan Press, 1999.

Smith, J. M. Powis. *The Origin and History of Hebrew Law*. Chicago: University of Chicago Press, 2005.

Smith, Page. *Daughters of the Promised Land: Women in American History*. Boston: Little, Brown, 1970.

Spear, Jennifer M. "Colonial Intimacies: Legislating Sex in French Louisiana." *The William and Mary Quarterly* 60 (2003): 75–98.

Staples, Ariadne. *From Good Goddess to Vestal Virgins: Sex and Category in Roman Religion*. London: Routledge, 1998.

Steakley, James D. "Sodomy in Enlightenment Prussia." *Journal of Homosexuality* 16 (1988): 163–75.

Stengers, Jean, and Anne van Neck. *Masturbation: The History of a Great Terror.* New York: Palgrave, 2001.

Stephens, Walter. *Demon Lovers: Witchcraft, Sex, and the Crisis of Belief.* Chicago: University of Chicago Press, 2003.

Stone, Lawrence. *The Family, Sex and Marriage in England, 1500–1800.* New York: Harper & Row, 1977.

———. "Libertine Sexuality in Post-Restoration England: Group Sex and Flagellation Among the Middling Sort in Norwich in 1706–1707." *Journal of the History of Sexuality* 2 (1992): 511–26.

Suetonius. *The Lives of the Twelve Caesars.* Accessed September 8, 2011, http://penelope.uchicago.edu/Thayer/E/Roman/Texts/Suetonius/12Caesars/home.html.

Sweet, Frank W. *Legal History of the Color Line: The Rise and Triumph of the One-Drop Rule.* Palm Coast, FL: Backintyme, 2005.

Tacitus. *The Annals.* Translated by Alfred John Church and William Jackson Brodribb. New York: Modern Library, 2003.

Takács, Sarolta A. *Vestal Virgins, Sibyls, and Matrons: Women in Roman Religion.* Austin: University of Texas Press, 2008.

Talese, Gay. *Thy Neighbor's Wife.* Garden City, NY: Doubleday, 1980.

Talvacchia, Bette. *Taking Positions: On the Erotic in Renaissance Culture.* Princeton: Princeton University Press, 1999.

Tannahill, Reay. *Sex in History.* New York: Stein and Day, 1980.

Taylor, Gary. *Castration: An Abbreviated History of Western Manhood.* New York: Routledge, 2000.

Taylor, Timothy. *The Prehistory of Sex: Four Million Years of Human Sexual Culture.* London: Fourth Estate, 1997.

Tetlow, Elisabeth Meier. *Women, Crime, and Punishment in Ancient Law and Society: The Ancient Near East.* New York: Continuum, 2004.

Thomas, Donald. *Henry Fielding.* New York: St. Martin's Press, 1991.

———. *A Long Time Burning: The History of Literary Censorship in England.* New York: Praeger, 1969.

Thomas, Hugh. *The Slave Trade: The Story of the Atlantic Slave Trade, 1440–1870*. New York: Simon & Schuster, 1997.

Thornhill, Nancy Wilmsen, ed. *The Natural History of Inbreeding and Outbreeding: Theoretical and Empirical Perspectives*. Chicago: University of Chicago Press, 1993.

Thucydides. *The Peloponnesian War*. Translated by Rex Warner. London: Penguin, 1972.

Thür, Gerhard. "The Role of the Witness in Athenian Law." In *The Cambridge Companion to Ancient Greek Law*, edited by Michael Gagarin and David Cohen, 146–69. Cambridge: Cambridge University Press, 2005.

Todd, S. C. *A Commentary on Lysias, Speeches 1–11*. Oxford: Oxford University Press, 2007.

Trachtenberg, Joshua. *The Devil and the Jews: The Medieval Conception of the Jew and Its Relation to Modern Anti-Semitism*. Philadelphia: Jewish Publication Society of America, 1943.

Trexler, Richard C. *Sex and Conquest: Gendered Violence, Political Order, and the European Conquest of the Americas*. Ithaca, NY: Cornell University Press, 1995.

Trumbach, Randolph. *Heterosexuality and the Third Gender in Enlightenment London*. Chicago: University of Chicago Press, 1998.

Tulchin, Allan A. "Same-Sex Couples Creating Households in Old Regime France: The Uses of the Affrèrement." *Journal of Modern History* 79 (2007): 613–47.

Ulrich, Laurel. *A Midwife's Tale: The Life of Martha Ballard, Based on Her Diary, 1785–1812*. New York: Vintage Books, 1991.

Valerius Maximus. "Husbands' Punishments of Wives in Early Rome." In *Women's Life in Greece and Rome: A Sourcebook in Translation*, edited by Mary R. Lefkowitz and Maureen B. Fant, 96. Baltimore: Johns Hopkins University Press, 2005.

Van den Berghe, Pierre L. "Human Inbreeding Avoidance: Culture in Nature." In *Behavioral and Brain Sciences* 6 (1983): 91–102.

Van der Meer, Theo. "The Persecutions of Sodomites in Eighteenth-Century Amsterdam: Changing Perceptions of Sodomy." *Journal of Homosexuality* 16 (1988): 271–76.

Van der Veer, Peter. *Imperial Encounters: Religion and Modernity in India and Britain*. Princeton, NJ: Princeton University Press, 2001.

VerSteeg, Russ. *Law in Ancient Egypt*. Durham, NC: Carolina Academic Press, 2002.

Vignali, Antonio. *La Cazzaria: The Book of the Prick*. Translated by Ian Frederick Moulton. New York: Routledge, 2003.

Wagner, Peter. "The Pornographer in the Courtroom: Trial Reports About Cases of Sexual Crimes and Delinquencies as a Genre of Eighteenth-Century Erotica." In *Sexuality in Eighteenth-Century Britain*, edited by Paul-Gabriel Boucé, 120–40. Totowa, NJ: Manchester University Press, 1982.

Waithe, Mary Ellen. *A History of Women Philosophers*, Volume I: *Ancient Women Philosophers, 600 BC–500 AD*. Dordrecht, Netherlands: M. Nijhoff, 1987.

Waldron, Kathy. "The Sinners and the Bishop in Colonial Venezuela: The Visita of Bishop Mariano Martí, 1771–1784." In *Sexuality and Marriage in Colonial Latin America*, edited by Asunción Lavrin, 156–77. Lincoln: University of Nebraska Press, 1989.

Walkowitz, Judith R. *Prostitution and Victorian Society: Women, Class, and the State*. Cambridge: Cambridge University Press, 1980.

Walsh, P. G. "Making a Drama out of a Crisis: Livy on the Bacchanalia." *Greece & Rome* 43 (1996): 188–203.

Walters, Jonathan. "Invading the Roman Body: Manliness and Impenetrability in Roman Thought." In *Roman Sexualities*, edited by Judith P. Hallett and Marilyn B. Skinner, 29–43. Princeton: Princeton University Press, 1997.

Washburn, Daniel. "The Thessalonian Affair in Fifth-Century Histories." In *Violence in Late Antiquity: Perceptions and Practices*, edited by H. A. Drake, 215–24. Aldershot, UK: Ashgate, 2006.

Weeks, Jeffrey. *Sex, Politics and Society: The Regulation of Sexuality Since 1800*. London: Longman, 1989.

Wemple, Suzanne F. "Consent and Dissent to Sexual Intercourse in Germanic Societies from the Fifth to the Tenth Century." In *Consent and Coercion to Sex and Marriage in Ancient and Medieval Societies*, edited by Angeliki E. Laiou, 227–43. Washington, DC: Dumbarton Oaks Research Library and Collection, 1993.

Wenham, Gordon J. *The Book of Leviticus*. Grand Rapids, MI: W. B. Eerdmans, 1979.

Westbrook, Raymond. "The Female Slave." In *Gender and Law in the Hebrew Bible and the Ancient Near East*, edited by Victor Harold Matthews, Bernard

M. Levinson, and Tikva Simone Kensky, 214–38. Sheffield, UK: Sheffield Academic Press, 1998.

———, ed. *A History of Ancient Near Eastern Law*, Volume II. Boston: Brill, 2003.

Wildfang, Robin Lorsch. *Rome's Vestal Virgins: A Study of Rome's Vestal Priestesses in the Late Republic and Early Empire*. London: Routledge, 2006.

Williams, Stephen, and Gerard Friell. *Theodosius: The Empire at Bay*. London: Batsford, 1994.

Wilmont, John. *The Works of John Wilmot, Earl of Rochester*. Edited by Harold Love. Oxford: Oxford University Press, 1999.

Winkler, John J. *The Constraints of Desire: The Anthropology of Sex and Gender in Ancient Greece*. New York: Routledge, 1990.

———. "Laying Down the Law: The Oversight of Men's Behavior in Classical Athens." In *The Construction of Erotic Experience in the Ancient Greek World*, edited by David M. Halperin, John J. Winkler, and Froma I. Zeitlin, 171–209. Princeton: Princeton University Press, 1990.

Wood, Stephanie. "Sexual Violation in the Conquest of the Americas." In *Sex and Sexuality in Early America*, edited by Merril D. Smith, 9–34. New York: New York University Press, 1998.

Woodson, Carter G. "The Beginnings of Miscegenation of the Whites and Blacks." In *Interracialism: Black-White Intermarriage in American History, Literature, and Law*, edited by Werner Sollers, 42–54. Oxford: Oxford University Press, 2000.

Wright, Thomas. *Oscar's Books*. London: Chatto and Windus, 2008.

Wrightson, Keith, and David Levine. *Poverty and Piety in an English Village: Terling, 1525–1700*. Oxford: Clarendon Press, 1995.

Zabel, William D. "Interracial Marriage and the Law." In *Interracialism: Black-White Intermarriage in American History, Literature, and Law*, edited by Werner Sollers, 54–61. Oxford: Oxford University Press, 2000.

PHOTO CREDITS

The Cully Flaug'd; Marcellus Laroon II; ©The Trustees of the British Museum

Marriage A-la-Mode, Plate III; William Hogarth; Bernard Baron ©The Trustees of the British Museum

Black, Brown & Fair; Thomas Tegg; Thomas Rowlandson; Henry William Bunbury ©The Trustees of the British Museum

Watercolour painting on paper of a Hindu wedding ceremony ©The Trustees of the British Museum

The monk in the cornfield; making love to a woman, c. 646; Etching and drypoint; Rembrandt ©The Trustees of the British Museum

Couple making love at the end of a four-poster bed, face at window, after Raimondi; corresponding to Aretino's Sonnet 11. Brush drawing in grey wash, over red chalk; Jean Frédéric Maximilien de Waldeck; Marcantonio; ©The Trustees of the British Museum

St. Ambrose & Theodosius. *Theodosius refused admission into the cathedral at Milan by St. Ambrose in 390 for the massacres recently carried out at his order at Thessalonica*: line engraving, late 19th century, after the painting by Anthony Van Dyck. ©TopFoto_Emperor

Censorship Seal, 1973. The seal of the Society for the Suppression of Vice, founded in 1873. On the left the purveyor of obscenity is being thrust into a cell, while on the right a Christian layman consigns infamous volumes to the flames. ©TopFoto

Christopher Columbus with Hernando Cortés receiving a native American girl as a gift (c. 1820–1839). Plate 5 from *Le Costume Ancien et Moderne*, Volume I, by Jules Ferrario. ©TopFoto

Jewish Mythology—Simon of Trent and Judensau. Top register shows the bound child, Simon of Trent, and the instruments of his torture and death. The bottom shows the infamous Judensau, with an attendant devil. The woman riding the goat hints at the connection believed to exist between the Jews and the Sabbat (or, to the transvection to the Sabbat). Copper engraving of the 17th century. Georg Liebe, *Das Judentum in der deutschen Vergangenheit*, 1903. ©TopFoto

Lot and His Daughters, Albrecht Altdorfer, 1537. ©TopFoto

Representing the last stage of mental & bodily exhaustion from Onanism or Self-pollution. From: *The Secret Companion*, a medical work on onanism or self-pollution, with the best mode of treatment in all cases of nervous and sexual debility, impotency, etc., by R. J. Brodie. Published by Brodie, R. J. & Co. Consulting Surgeons 27 Montague Street, Russell Squ., London 1845. ©Wellcome Library, London

A fish with spikes. Coloured etching. ©Wellcome Library, London

ACKNOWLEDGMENTS

WRITING AND PUBLISHING this book required a lot of help and I got it on all fronts. On the research side, I am grateful to the librarians at the UCLA research and law libraries, who were patient with my inquiries and generous with help. Online services can sift through millions of pages of material instantly, but nothing comes close to the creative thinking of a human being. The UCLA librarians are the best in the business.

In France, where this book was written, I found refuge at the American Library in Paris, a writer's dreamscape where everything one does feels significant. Thanks to generations of American donors, the ALP's collection is also surprisingly deep, and I made many useful discoveries there. The New York University libraries were another important source of research materials, and I thank my son Lawrence for keeping a steady stream of books flowing from NYU to me in Paris. Finally, the libraries at the Sorbonne and the Université Paris II—Panthéon-Assas were useful, even as they were manned by people bent on resisting efforts by non-French researchers to use their collections.

In the course of my research I formed intimate friendships with characters of all stripes. I grew close to many of the actors in the stories I uncovered, some of them gone for thousands of years but no less alive in my cloistered world. Key to my understanding of their lives was the work of the brilliant historians on whom I relied, and whose insights and superb writing both humbled and inspired me. Chief among these giants are Peter Bardaglio, John Boswell, James A. Brundage, Vern L. Bullough,

Eva Cantarella, David Cohen, Louis Crompton, Joan E. DeJean, Catharine Edwards, Brigitte Ericksson, Lynn Hunt, Paula Findlen, Debra Hamel, Helen Lefkowitz Horowitz. Isabel V. Hull, Ruth Mazo Karras, Rebecca Langlands, Thomas A.J. McGinn, Mary E. Odem, Holt N. Parker, Julie Peakman, Sarah B. Pomeroy, Martha T. Roth, Catherine Rider, Aline Rousselle, Guido Ruggiero, Ariadne Staples, Lawrence Stone, and John J. Winkler.

For the genesis of this book, I am indebted to Marc Cooper and Kenneth Starr, two outsized personalities at the University of Southern California who encouraged me to get busy writing books, and especially to Karl Fleming, the man who as much as instructed me to write a lively history of the law.

Once the writing of the book was underway, I depended on a number of people for feedback and suggestions. Tops on this list are Charles Fleming, Bill Groshelle, Adam Kaufman, Tony de Toro, and Rick Wirick, all of whom read my drafts and tolerated my ranting with grace, patience and intelligence. Charles and Rick—both accomplished writers—were also uncommonly generous in championing my work to publishers, agents, and the like. I hope that one day I can provide others with the kind of unselfish support they gave to me.

For editing of the text, I turned to Mitchell Albert, without whom this book would not exist. From that first drink-sodden evening in Frankfurt came Mitch's offer to publish some of my work in PEN International magazine, which he edited. His editing on that excerpt was so good, and my writing so much better for his efforts, that I asked him to edit the entire book. From that point forward, I trusted Mitch as the last word on questions of structure, style, tone, and focus. It is impossible to overstate my gratitude for his support. Mitch also introduced me to picture hunter extraordinaire Jennifer Jeffries.

The book was published with the intelligent and unwavering support of Laura Mazer, at Counterpoint, who became my advocate and friend.

Through Laura came the sage guidance of editors Jack Shoemaker and Charlie Winton, the help of maestro copy editor Matthew Grace, and the enthusiastic support of the rest of the Counterpoint staff.

No less important to my work have been my friends, whom I love dearly. In Europe, there are Glenn Burney, Valérie Latour-Burney, Laurence and François Brunet, Dominique Schneider, Sabine Haudepin, John Johnson and Francois Prieur, Florence Eclanchet, Marilyn Palik, Stephane Moisset, Maria Kassimova (who gave me Bulgaria), Christopher Forinash, Norma Jean and Frantisek Deak, Pierre Coret, Ingrid and Vincent Callies, and many others. In the United States, there are Jack Kaufman, Julie Singer, Paula and Phil Glosserman, Marion Solomon, JoEllen Brainin-Rodriguez, Josh Becker, Pam Becker, Curtis Kaufman, Helen Wu, Alan Zafran, Susan Utell, Amy Ziering, and Gil Kofman. This list goes on. Every one of these people gave me unwavering support. All of them are friends in the truest sense of the word.

Not one day could have been passed without the love of Lawrence, Claire and Gillian, my three children, and Jennifer, my wife, lover, and lifelong delight.

INDEX